Toward a Global Civilization?
The Contribution of Religions

PETER LANG
New York • Washington, D.C./Baltimore • Bern
Frankfurt am Main • Berlin • Brussels • Vienna • Oxford

Toward a Global Civilization?
The Contribution of Religions

Edited by
Patricia M. Mische
and Melissa Merkling

PETER LANG
New York • Washington, D.C./Baltimore • Bern
Frankfurt am Main • Berlin • Brussels • Vienna • Oxford

Library of Congress Cataloging-in-Publication Data

Toward a global civilization? the contribution of religions /
edited by Patricia M. Mische and Melissa Merkling.
p. cm.
Chiefly revised papers from a symposium held May 3–7, 1997 in Maryknoll,
N.Y.
Includes bibliographical references.
1. Religion and international affairs—Congresses. 2. Religion and civilization—
Congresses. I. Mische, Patricia M. II. Merkling, Melissa.
BL65.I55 T675   291.1'7—dc21   00-056753
ISBN 0-8204-5194-0

Die Deutsche Bibliothek-CIP-Einheitsaufnahme

Toward a global civilization? the contribution of religions /
ed. by: Patricia M. Mische and Melissa Merkling.
–New York; Washington, D.C./Baltimore; Bern;
Frankfurt am Main; Berlin; Brussels; Vienna; Oxford: Lang.
ISBN 0-8204-5194-0

Cover design by Dutton and Sherman Design

The paper in this book meets the guidelines for permanence and durability
of the Committee on Production Guidelines for Book Longevity
of the Council of Library Resources.

© 2001 Peter Lang Publishing, Inc., New York

Printed in the United States of America

This book is dedicated
in love and gratitude to the memory
of

Gerald F. Mische (1926–1995)
co-founder and first president of Global Education Associates
who initiated and for 25 years nurtured
GEA's Religion and World Order Project,
promoting multireligious initiatives and partnerships
for a more humane global order

and

Dr. M. Aram (1927–1997)
founder and president of Shanti Ashram,
President of the World Conference on Religion and Peace,
and Chair of the International Advisory Council of the
Religion and World Order Project

and in deep appreciation
to
Fr. Ted Hesburgh
and the Institute for International Peace Studies at
the University of Notre Dame
for their moral and material support
while this book was being prepared
during a sabbatical year.

We must overcome our fear of the future. But we will not be able to overcome it completely unless we do so together. The "answer" to that fear is neither coercion nor repression, nor the imposition of one social "model" on the entire world. The answer to the fear which darkens human existence at the end of the twentieth century is the common effort to build the civilization of love, founded on the universal values of peace, solidarity, justice, and liberty. And the "soul" of the civilization of love is the culture of freedom: the freedom of individuals and the freedom of nations, lived in self-giving solidarity and responsibility.

We must not be afraid of the future. We must not be afraid of [the human]. It is no accident that we are here. Each and every human person has been created in the "image and likeness" of the One who is the origin of all that is. We have within us the capacities for wisdom and virtue. We have these gifts, and with the help of God's grace, we can build in the next century and the next millennium a civilization worthy of the human person, a true culture of freedom. We can and must do so! And in doing so, we shall see that the tears of this century have prepared the ground for a new springtime of the human spirit.

— *Pope John Paul II*
Address to the Fiftieth Session of the General Assembly
of the United Nations, October 5, 1995

I do not believe that an individual may gain spiritually and those that surround him suffer. I believe in *advaita*. I believe in the essential unity of [humans] and for that matter of all that lives.

I would not like to live in this world if it is not to be one world.

I believe that true democracy can only be an outcome of nonviolence. The structure of a world federation can be raised only on a foundation of nonviolence, and violence will have to be totally given up in world affairs.

— *Mohandas Gandhi*
from Young India, *Dec. 4, 1924;*
Speech, March, 1947;
and Correspondence with the Government, 1942–1944

Table of Contents

INTRODUCTION

Toward a Civilization Worthy of the Human Person

Patricia M. Mische

In this book you are invited to join leading thinkers from diverse cultures, beliefs, and disciplines in exploring the role of religions in creating a more humane world order in the twenty-first century. It is hoped that the thinking in this volume, and the discussions that flow from it, will contribute to the *Dialogue Among Civilizations* being undertaken by the United Nations and related activities among religious and other networks.

The phrase "*dialogue* among civilizations" contrasts with, and seeks an antidote to, what Samuel Huntington calls the "*clash* of civilizations." In his now famous, if controversial, book *The Clash of Civilizations and the Remaking of World Order*, Huntington argued that the end of the cold war had not led, as many people had expected, to a more harmonious world order and an end to global conflict. Superpower conflicts may have declined, but in their place the world would increasingly be challenged by conflicts and wars between diverse cultural, ethnic, and religious groups in a "clash of civilizations."

Huntington repudiated the "end of history" thesis of Francis Fukuyama, who had written: "We may be witnessing the end of history as such: that is, the end point of [hu]mankind's ideological evolution and the universalization of Western liberal democracy as the final form of government." Huntington argued that rather than gaining power, the West was actually declining in relative influence in the world in the face of a new balance of power that was emerging in global politics. This new balance of power was not bipolar, nor unipolar under the remaining superpower, but multipolar and multicivilizational. The most important distinctions between peoples are now *not* ideological, political, or economic, he asserted, but *cultural*; and the most important groupings of states and conflict formation would no longer be the three blocs of the cold war, but rather the world's seven or eight major civilizations. Huntington predicted that the future would be riddled with conflict between these clashing civilizations. "Culture and cultural identities, which at the broadest level are civilization identities, are shaping the patterns of cohesion, disintegration, and conflict in the post-cold-war world." Huntington referred to the actors in this new world order as "the West and the rest," and urged Westerners to defend their own survival by reaffirming and preserving their Western identity against "challenges from non-Western societies." And, to avoid a global war of civilizations, he urged world leaders to accept, and cooperate to maintain, the multicivilizational character of global politics.

Religion as a Central Force in Culture and Civilizations

Religion will be "a central force—perhaps *the* central force"—that motivates and mobilizes people in this civilization-based world order, said Huntington. The importance of religion as a central force in culture and civilizations had been underscored four decades earlier by the eminent historian Arnold Toynbee, whose work Huntington sometimes cites. However, in contrast to Huntington, Toynbee was less concerned about the clashes *between* civilizations or religions, and more interested in the dynamic role religion and spirituality played in the *inner life* of civilizations, including their birth and death. Most civilizations died of suicide, he concluded, not from clashes with outside forces.

In his comprehensive study of the rise and fall of all the major civilizations in history, Toynbee found that religion and spirituality served as a chrysalis from which a civilization may grow. Between the death of one civilization and the rise of a new one were creative minorities who, with deep spiritual or religious motivation, served to birth a new civilization from the ashes of the old one. This spiritual core was vital to a civilization's ability to sustain itself. Civilizations that lost their spiritual core soon fell into decline. Thus, unlike many historians who saw the forces of religion as minor if interesting notes in history, or examined religious history as a subtopic of history, Toynbee became convinced that spiritual development and religion were the alpha and omega of history. Human history was "a vision of God's creation on the move, from God its source toward God its goal."[1] Religions were not the handmaids of civilization; rather, civilizations were the handmaids of religion, asserted Toynbee. We have civilizations in order that we may have higher religions.[2] The end or aim of human history is spiritual development—greater consciousness of and closeness to the sacred source.

Like Huntington, Toynbee prophesied a decline of Western civilization and influence in the face of counterforces, but unlike Huntington, Toynbee was not that concerned about the long-range preservation of Western civilization. He accepted that civilizations are finite, and that Western civilization, like others before it, would fade away, and another civilization would emerge in its place. Whereas Huntington rejected the notion that we were moving toward a *universal* civilization, Toynbee asserted that that is exactly where history is headed. Of course, in this, Toynbee was taking a longer-range view of history. In 1947 he projected a trajectory of the future over the next 100 to 3,000 years. To the question, "What will historians say in 2047?" he answered: "The great event of the twentieth century was the impact of Western civilization upon all the other living societies of that day." One thousand years later, however, in the year 3047, Western civilization would have been transformed "by a counter-radiation of influences from foreign worlds which we, in our day, are in the act of engulfing in ours." By 4047 historians would look back on developments leading up to the unification of humanity. By then, the parochial heritage will have been "battered to bits by the collision with other parochial heritages," and from this wreckage a new common life will emerge. Finally, in the year 5047 the historians will say that "the importance of this social unification of [hu]mankind was not to be found in the field of technics and economics, not in the field of war and politics, but in the field of religion."[3]

Religion and civilization are not synonymous, and distinctions between them should not be blurred. While religion influences and to a certain degree may affect the culture and shape of a civilization, it is not the same as a civilization. Toynbee advised Western Christians to sepa-

[1] *A Study of History*, X, 1954, 3.
[2] *Ibid.*, VII, 1954, 444.
[3] *Ibid.*, XII, 595–98.

rate their religious and spiritual heritage from Western civilization. Christianity did not originate in the West, but predated Western civilization. It became a midwife for the development of Western civilization, yet was never a monopoly of the West. From its early history, when it spread around the Mediterranean and to parts of Asia, Africa, and Europe, its members included people from many diverse cultures and civilizations. Moreover, it would outlive Western civilization, continuing to be a spiritual force thousands of years after Western civilization had passed away. Toynbee also cautioned that there are elements in Western civilization that are not Christian, and some that were de-Christianized over time. For example, the Western traditions of politics and war are not Christian in origin. Christianity grew up under Roman rule, and its adherents were marginalized within the Roman Empire. They had no political power, nor were they, by the tenets of their faith, to participate in military service.[4] In contrast, Western civilization had under the Greeks and Romans, and has today, a high commitment to political and military power.

Similarly, some other religions should not be made synonymous with, or over-identified with, one civilization. Today, the major world religions have adherents from many diverse cultures and civilizations and from diverse races and ethnic groups. These religions are global communities in microcosm. Their networks and activities bridge many cultures.

One of Toynbee's major concerns about Western civilization and modern ideologies such as nationalism, communism, and ungrounded faith in science and technology was that they replaced authentic religion with false ones. Instead of a higher spiritual power they "worshipped man" and "collective human power."[5] Toynbee warned against state idolatry and considered both nationalism and communism forms of worshipping collective human power.

Wars of religion did concern Toynbee, not only because of the senseless loss of life and displacement of people at the time, but also because they demeaned and undermined true religion, with profound and far-reaching consequences for future history. The Wars of Religion in the West, for example, were waged from the thirteenth century onward for some 400 years. This was a very militant chapter in the history of the Christian Church of the West, and although this period may now seem

---

[4] *Christianity Among the Religions of the World*, 1957, 62–67.
[5] *Ibid.*, 75–79.

remote, the forces it unleashed, and the reaction to them, are still active today. Not only did these wars fracture Western Christians into hostile groups and cause displaced Europeans of different Christian denominations to flow to the New World where they constructed a new political map around religious and anti-religious divisions, but it also filled many people with a horror or distrust of religion. There followed the secularization of the West, the "transfer of spiritual treasure" to the promotion of science and technology, and ultimately a misplaced faith in collective human power. In turn, this misplaced faith in, and competition over, collective human power fed dynamics that spiraled into the development of atomic weapons and the threat of mutual assured destruction.

Religious dialogue is key to overcoming these false gods and putting history on its true course, according to Toynbee. He called on religions not to drop their religious convictions, but to let go of their rivalries and hostilities and seek common ground. He suggested that the common ground they needed was already available in: (1) human nature (all religions are concerned with overcoming human self-centeredness—his definition of original sin); (2) the present state of the world (modern technology had unified the world to a certain extent by "annihilating distance"; problems that were previously local had now become global; all the world's religions are now confronted by a set of common problems; "We are all now one another's keepers," he wrote);[6] (3) the fact that all higher religions share a conviction that humans are "not the greatest spiritual presence in the Universe, but that there is a greater presence—God or absolute reality—and that the true end of [humans] is to place [themselves] in harmony with this"; and (4) the fact that all have a common adversary in the modern "worship of man" and "collective human power." "By comparison with this fundamental issue on which all the living higher religions find themselves on the same side, the issues that divide them seem secondary. In these grave circumstances, ought we not to consider whether the higher religions should not subordinate their differences with one another and stand together against their common adversary?"[7]

In advocating interreligious dialogue, Toynbee was not advocating syncretism—the construction of an artificial religion from elements from all the religions. Interreligious dialogue does not mean abandoning one's

---

[6] *Ibid.*, 87.
[7] *Ibid.*, 81.

beliefs or spiritual path; it may help to deepen them, said Toynbee. One can hold fast to one's own ideals and essential truths without succumbing to fanaticism, arrogance, or self-centeredness. By learning to respect, reverence, admire, and love each other's faiths, interreligious dialogue helps us make progress in our own. He saw interreligious dialogue as the antidote to religious suppression and a path to greater spiritual maturity in history. To suppress a rival religion is not an answer to the great problems of our day, said Toynbee; in the end it leads to spiritual impoverishment. He relates the lament of Quintus Aurelius Symmachus, the spokesman for the Roman Senate, when the Christian Roman imperial government forced the closure of pagan Roman temples: "It is impossible that so great a mystery should be approached by one road only."[8]

The mystery of which Symmachus spoke—the mystery of a greater spirit and power in the universe and in human life—is still alive and seeking expression in the world today. Interreligious dialogue may indeed be a key to opening the door to greater peace and a more humane world order in the twenty-first century.

Toynbee was much respected as a scholar and historian, but was also criticized by some fellow historians for what they considered his overemphasis on religion. Instead of relenting, he intensified his scholarship and asserted even stronger positions in this area. Huntington, too, has been criticized for this. Although one may question some of these authors' assumptions and assertions, it is hard to dismiss entirely the view that religion will be a significant factor in the world of the twenty-first century.

The Increase in Religious Identification and Interreligious Dialogue

Trends show that religious identification around the world has been growing and will continue to increase. Those identifying themselves as Christians were numbered at close to 2 billion in 1998 and are expected to reach 2.25 billion by 2025. Muslims, at close to 1.8 billion in 1998, will reach 1.96 billion by 2025. Hindus will increase from 767 million to more than 1 billion. Though with lesser numbers, Buddhists, Sikhs, Jews, and those identifying with tribal religions are also expected to increase steadily. In contrast, those identifying themselves as atheist numbered only 146 million in 1998, and are expected to increase only slightly to 152

---

[8] *Ibid.*, 112.

million.[9] While population growth (being born into a religious identification) will account for some of the increase, it does not account for all of
it. Interest in religion is growing in many world regions among people
who did not previously consider themselves religious.

There has also been a growing trend in interreligious dialogue. The
twentieth century may have been a century of terrible wars, including
genocides and ethnic cleansings committed or tolerated in the name of
religion; but it was also a century that, perhaps as a reaction to those wars
and an effort to prevent more conflict, saw unprecedented growth in interreligious dialogue. It also gave rise to many multireligious organizations
to facilitate such dialogue, including the International Association for
Religious Freedom, the Fellowship of Reconciliation, the World Conference on Religion and Peace, the Council for a Parliament of World Religions, the World Council of Churches, the Council of Christians and
Jews, the United Religions Initiative, the series of interreligious dialogues
on *The Contribution by Religions to the Culture of Peace* sponsored by the
UN Educational, Scientific and Cultural Organization (UNESCO), and
many more. This suggests growing interest in religion's potential not only
to be a force of clashes and conflicts, but also to prevent clashes, resolve
conflicts, and contribute to a more humane world order for the twenty-
first century.

The present volume benefits from this growing history of interreligious dialogue. Many of the authors in this book are not only leaders
within their own religious tradition, but also leaders or active participants
in networks for interreligious dialogue.

The Unique Contribution of This Book: A World-Order Focus for the Role of Religion

However, this volume also makes a unique contribution to ongoing interreligious dialogue. Up to now, interreligious dialogue has focused primarily on developing greater peace and understanding between people from
diverse religious traditions, and also, in some cases, on promoting values
of peace, social justice, human rights, and ecological integrity. There has
not been that much focus on the contribution of religions to the development of a *more humane world order* or *more effective global systems*. In a
period of increasing globalization, such a focus becomes ever more ur-

---

[9] *International Bulletin of Missionary Research*, January, 1998, Religion News Service.

gent.

Global Education Associates was founded, in part, to focus on the linkages between religion and world order, and since its founding in 1973 has sponsored a series of multireligious symposia on this theme, often with the co-sponsorship or partnership of religious and multireligious organizations around the world. The articles in this book were, for the most part, produced for a particular symposium in this series; however, they need to be understood in their proper context as part of an ongoing discourse. The present work is neither the first nor the last word in this dialogue. Rather, it represents a certain benchmark in the process, and a building block for future work. Some of the earlier symposia in this series were held in the 1970s and 1980s in India, Japan, Korea, the Philippines, Eastern Africa, and Europe, and important insights were contributed from the special cultural and religious experience of people in these world regions. The authors whose work is included in the present work are thus standing on the shoulders and building on the ideas of those who preceded them in more than 25 years of discourse.

Those involved in this discourse have not been mere armchair theorists or ivory-tower academicians. All have been actively engaged in seeking common ground and ways to cooperate across religious lines in the service of Earth and humanity. They have been seekers, doers, and path-pointers on the often uncertain, but nevertheless inexorable, human journey toward a global civilization—a civilization in which people of diverse cultures and belief systems will need to learn to live in true community.

Breakdown and Breakthrough in a Time of Global Transformation: Global Education Associates' Systems Analysis

The process explored in Global Education Associates' symposium series began in 1973 with the perception that we live in a time of profound, global-scale transformation. Earlier views on the nature and scope of this transformation, and the problems and opportunities emanating from it, were shared by Gerald Mische and me in our 1977 book, *Toward a Human World Order: Beyond the National Security Straitjacket*.[10] This work included an analysis of the constraints on full human development im-

---

[10] Gerald and Patricia Mische, *Toward a Human World Order: Beyond the National Security Straitjacket*, Paulist Press, 1977.

posed by existing world systems, and called for cross-cultural dialogue and cooperative initiatives to advance more humane global systems based on core human values and an ethic of global responsibility. It included a chapter on Religion and World Order that was the fruit of our inter-religious dialogues up to that time. The fruits of some of the subsequent dialogues in the series were shared in GEA publications, including *The Whole Earth Papers* and *Breakthrough,* and in the journals of some of GEA's partners in various symposia that were part of this process.

From our experience with local communities in Africa, Latin America, and Asia, Gerald Mische and I had seen firsthand how, by the early 1970s, rampant global economic forces were wreaking havoc on local communities and their goals for full human development. It was from a concern for local cultures and communities that we first founded Global Education Associates as a forum for multicultural dialogue on world order and alternative futures. With Margaret Mead, the first contributor to GEA, we believed that one should "never doubt that a small group of thoughtful, committed citizens can change the world. Indeed, it is the only thing that ever has." The number of GEA associates around the world soon grew to include men and women in 90 countries and more than 150 partner organizations, affiliates, and collaborating networks.

The signs of transformation we saw then, which became even more pronounced over the next decades, included symptoms of breakdown at every level of life—political, economic, cultural, ecological, and spiritual. Old systems that had been created to serve the needs of traditional civilizations of the past, and the state-centric system of the modern world, could no longer respond effectively to the new challenges presented by rapid globalization and increasing global interdependence. And new systems capable of meeting these challenges humanely and effectively had yet to be created.

We described this time/space as a certain *"between* times"—a parenthesis between one age that was dying (this was well before the end of the cold war and quite apart from it), and a new one trying to be born. Old systems and worldviews were breaking down under the pressure of global economic, technological, environmental, and other forces; new systems and worldviews capable of justly and peacefully managing the new economic, political, technological, and environmental problems had not yet been developed. There was a tremendous lag in human development—a lag both spiritual and systemic. Systems of the heart and mind, and systems of more humane governance, needed to be developed to cope with the depth and scale of these changes.

We believed that those of us living in these times were being challenged to new levels of creativity and cooperation to forge a path through the present confusion and uncertainties toward a more viable and humane future. We were challenged to become the creative minority of which Toynbee had written—the creative minority who, from deep spiritual commitment and motivation, would contribute to the development of a new civilization.

The Characteristics of Major Transformations in History

Historians suggest that in the whole span of human existence, humankind has previously experienced only two or three transformations comparable to the one we are now undergoing. These were:

1. the *biological evolution* from primate to hominid (pre-human) to *homo sapiens*, and the emergence of hunting and gathering societies and the *Tribal Age* over the last 5 million years. Within this longest period of human history came some of the greatest human developments, including the emergence of human consciousness (a spiritual/material evolution), human speech, and tool-making, symbol-making, artistic, rational, and teaching/learning skills. Humans learned to live in community and developed social, political, economic, and educational systems appropriate for life in small kinship or familial tribal structures, and ethical, spiritual, or religious systems that emanated from their sense of powerful, sacred forces operative in the Earth's processes. This period encompasses 99 percent of human history;

2. the *agricultural revolution* and rise of *traditional civilizations* over the last 10,000 years. The agricultural revolution made possible a planned and surplus food supply, and thus permanent settlements and cities. It also made possible role differentiation and specialization within societies, contributing to new developments in trade and economics, the arts, religion, education, and sociopolitical structures. This period gave birth to the rise of the great civilizations and world religions. Systems of governance shifted gradually from tribal structures to kingdoms and city-states and new ethical and normative systems appropriate for life in these traditional civilizations. In this

period, too, the war system, class system, system of slavery, and patri-archy arose as full-fledged systems;

3. the *scientific, industrial, humanistic* revolutions that marked the break-down of feudal structures and traditional civilizations and the rise of the *Modern Age* and *Age of Nation-States* over the last 500 years. The modern scientific revolution, which began in Europe and was then exported around the world, made possible unprecedented gains in human longevity, health, and wealth for those who benefited from it. It also had profound effects on worldviews and images of the Earth. Copernicus, Galileo, and Newton changed people's paradigms; the Earth was round, not flat, and not the center of the universe. Images of the primacy of God, gods, or a sense of the sacred were displaced and replaced by faith in man (masculine gender), machines, and na-tionalism—and later communism and other *isms*—to redeem and lib-erate humanity and produce happiness. The Earth was no longer sacred, but a place to be conquered and mastered by humans, and there transpired unprecedented human assaults and exploitation of the Earth. The war system was taken to new heights, with new mili-tary technologies threatening the destruction of all life on Earth.

All these past transformations were notable for the following char-acteristics:

1. *Crises of growth.* The Chinese use two characters to convey the con-cept of crisis. *Wei* means danger, breakdown; *chi* means new oppor-tunity, breakthrough. In any crisis both possibilities exist. In periods of transition, social upheaval and crises occur as old structures, sys-tems, and worldviews break down, and new worldviews and systems begin to emerge. Such crises can be characterized as crises of growth.

2. *Rate of change.* Each of the past transformations occurred more rap-idly than previous ones. The present crisis of transition is especially acute. Past transformations occurred over centuries, and people had centuries to develop new worldviews, identity systems, and patterns of relationship. In contrast, we must make the transition to a global community in only a few decades.

3. *Universality of change.* Each past transformation occurred in different regions of the world at different times, sometimes thousands of years apart. The present transformation is global and affects all peoples in

relatively the same time period.

4. *Increasing interdependence.* Each of these past transformations emerged out of widening circles of economic, environmental, social, and political interdependence. Each involved new formulations of systems of identity, community, and loyalty.

5. *Governance and political units.* From clans and tribes to city-states and kingdoms to nation-states, each of these transformations included changes in political structures, with the development of a public sector or polity at increasingly larger levels to manage the problems and opportunities resulting from increasing interdependence. The larger units did not necessarily eliminate smaller, local polities; more often they added a new layer to manage problems that could not be dealt with at the older, smaller levels. With new global-scale interdependencies and the problems of rapid globalization, effective global structures are needed to deal with problems that cannot be resolved locally or nationally. If global systems of governance are to be humane and not destructive, they must continually be informed by values and norms that uphold human dignity, justice, peace, and ecological integrity.

6. *New worldviews and relationships to the Earth.* Each of these transformations also brought changes in the way human beings perceived the world and their relationship to the Earth.

7. *Spirituality and images of the sacred.* Each also brought changes in images of the sacred, and new forms of spirituality.

Most historians agree that we are now in the midst of another major transformation, which is occurring more rapidly than any previous one and is global in scale. Some believe it will have more deep-reaching effects than any historical change since the emergence of human consciousness.

New communications, travel, and other technologies advanced over the last several decades are weaving a web in which previously isolated and sovereign nation-states, and even formerly remote tribal societies, are now interconnected in economic, military, resource, environmental, agricultural, technological, communications, and other interdependencies. All borders have become transparent and penetrable, and local and national self-interest is increasingly inseparable from global interest. The notion of national sovereignty is increasingly a fiction. Decisions made in one part of the world—whether over the price of oil, interest or currency-exchange rates, bank scandals and failures, trade barriers, or greenhouse gases that cause global warming—affect every other country, and missiles aimed from thousands of miles away can penetrate all national borders. Music, movies, sports, and other expressions of popular culture are shared across national lines. Professional development in virtually every field now involves or is affected by international communications. While some may seek to escape or retreat from the facts of increasing global inter-dependence, it is no longer practical to isolate ourselves within national boundaries.

The processes of globalization are accompanied by unprecedented problems that can no longer be resolved by employing old worldviews and/or only local or national systems of governance. Global forces are beyond the effective competence of individual nation-states. But the de-velopment of the necessary global vision, norms, policies, and structures to manage the problems and opportunities of a global age has not kept pace.

Three Views of the Current Transformation
Using Systems Analysis

In Gerald's and my work then, and in this volume today, the question has not been whether or not we live in a time of breakdown and transforma-tion, but rather how deep that breakdown goes, and what kind of break-throughs we should expect or strive to attain. For while many historians agree that we live in a time of major transformation, there is disagree-ment and uncertainty among them about the depth of the changes un-derway, and what values, worldviews, and social, economic, and political systems are likely to emerge in the new global period we are entering. There are at least three levels or time-frames of analyses. None is exclu-sive of the others, but each carries its own set of implications and chal-lenges for the future, including whether to expect the emergence of a global civilization and what, if any, forms of global governance are likely to emerge. Such differences in view are reflected among the authors in the present volume, and lead to different conclusions and recommenda-tions about the role religion can or should play in shaping a future world order.

Fifty-Year Time-Frame:
The Breakdown of the Postwar Order

The first view sees the current moment as the breakdown of a fifty-year time period. What is breaking down is the world order shaped by the victors of World War II. The international institutions created in 1944 and 1945 to deal with the monetary, trade, economic, and security problems of a postwar world are inadequate in the face of new global economic, environmental, and political realities of the twenty-first century. The two thirds of the world that had no voice in establishing these institutions is now pushing for democratization of, or a greater voice in, the UN Security Council, International Monetary Fund, World Bank, World Trade Organization, and other multilateral structures. Japan and Germany, crushed militarily and economically after the war, are now among the richest and most economically powerful countries and seek positions in multilateral institutions commensurate with their new position and related international responsibilities. The United Nations, which had been given a mandate to deal with threats to *inter*national peace and security (but was given insufficient power to deal effectively even with this mandate), is now faced by a new set of expectations for which it has no clear mandate or mechanisms: to deal with *intra*national threats to peace and security—e.g., interethnic or interreligious strife contained within national borders and presumably under national prerogatives.

This view also includes the breakdown of the bipolar system created in the cold war that followed World War II. In this system the rest of the world was dominated by two superpowers—the US and the USSR—and their allies, who maintained a perverse form of peace through the threat of mutual assured destruction. Under this system, the United Nations could play only a marginal role in the maintenance of peace and security—certainly much less than most of the world had hoped. For almost five decades, the UN Security Council was often blocked by the veto of one or the other major power. Moreover, the UN was not equipped to deal with the nuclear threat, which could always be used to trump UN peace initiatives.

When the UN Charter was drafted in 1945, none of the delegates from the 51 founding nations knew anything about top-secret efforts in the US to build atomic weapons; and so the UN was brought into existence without effective means to manage this new threat. In the resulting vacuum, the maintenance of international peace and security was primarily a prerogative of the superpowers under balance-of-power arrangements. With the end of the cold war, this bipolar system broke down, and in its place a unipolar system is emerging, dominated by the United States and its military allies in NATO. The peace dividends expected at the end of the cold war have not been realized; instead, militarism and rule by threat continues, in both old and new forms. Nuclear weapons continue to be stockpiled and the global arms trade is a thriving business. Ethnic conflicts and genocide formerly contained by superpower coercion have raised their ugly heads, leaving millions of bodies strewn across the killing fields of parts of Africa, the former Yugoslavia, and elsewhere.

For a while it had seemed that a trend toward regional security approaches would blossom into a new world order in which each world region maintained peace among its member states; but these arrangements, where they exist, are still too weak to assure world peace and security for the future. Even in Europe, where regional structures are stronger than elsewhere, the weak and underfunded Organization for Security and Cooperation in Europe (OSCE) was supplanted by NATO and the use of military force to resolve the crisis in the former Yugoslavia. Although NATO is also a regional organization, the fact that it was a military branch of one of the sides in the cold war suggests that (a) the cold war is not fully over and could rise again; and/or (b) the unipolar vision of world order carries more currency today than more benign visions of regional security.

This fifty-year view assumes that further shifts in world order will occur within the framework of the nation-state system and that the order that eventually emerges will remain essentially state-centric, with national governments being the main actors, and national sovereignty upheld as a core principle around which peace, security, and the well-being of peoples is assured. Within that frame a *de facto* form of global governance may evolve through default or design; this could be a continuation of a unipolar system, with the rest of the world continuing to be dominated by, and entrusting peace and security to, the remaining superpower, or it could be a further entrenchment and elaboration of a multipolar international system, such as *de facto* rule by the Group of Seven, in which a consortium of a few economically rich and powerful nations makes decisions that govern the rest, with little or no input from them—amounting to global governance by an international oligarchy. Or it could follow Huntington's scenario of a new world order that is both multipolar and multicivilizational, with a new balance of power emerging along cultural divisions.

A third alternative within the framework of the existing nation-state system has more democratic features. It involves (a) democratizing and strengthening the United Nations system to give the "two-thirds world" who were subordinated during the cold war an equal say in decisions affecting them; and/or (b) promoting and further developing regional arrangements for peace and security. In these alternatives global governance is not left to chance, but is approached as a matter of responsible choice and participation.

Five-Hundred-Year Time-Frame:
The Breakdown of the Nation-State System

A second view agrees with some of the above, but goes deeper. It sees the current transformation as the breakdown of a 500-year period characterized by the rise of the nation-state system, Enlightenment and secular-humanist ideals, Euro-American colonial and neocolonial domination, and the spread of capitalism culminating in its near-globalization.

Within this framework, some see shifts occurring *within* the existing nation-state system, including a redistribution of power and wealth away from Euro-American control and toward other states, such as the industrialized countries of Asia which have become powerful competitors in the global marketplace; others see a shift *away from* the nation-state system itself. The origin of the state-centric system, around which the present world order is constituted, is usually given as the 1648 Peace of Westphalia; this treaty ended both the Eighty Years' War between Spain and the United Provinces of the Netherlands, and the Thirty Years' War (really a 50-year struggle) in which the Austrian Hapsburgs and German princes battled for the European balance of power. The treaty gave full sovereignty to the member states of the Holy Roman Empire and launched the modern nation-state system, sometimes called the Westphalian system.

Although many people now take the nation-state system for granted and assume it is the final form in political evolution, when viewed within the long sweep of history it still seems very new, and its lasting capacity is unproven. Only in the twentieth century did it become a near-universal system as peoples from tribal societies, traditional civilizations, and former colonies were brought within its embrace. More than 100 new nation-states came into existence in the twentieth century, most of them in the second half.

The United Nations has wrongly been seen by some as a form of world government, or as a new form of world order superseding the state system. But the UN is not itself a state or government; it is an organization of states, governed by and for states, with a mandate to uphold the principle of state sovereignty. The UN cannot tell member states what to do; on the contrary, the member states tell the UN what to do and control the budget by which it is to do them. In short, the UN is, in essence, an extension of the state-centric system.

So future historians may well look back and name the twentieth century the Century of Nation-States. But on a closer look, they could just as well name it the Century That Began the Breakdown of the Nation-State System and the Rise of Global Systems. For, despite the apparent success and near-universality of the state-centric system by the end of the twentieth century, it had no sooner reached its zenith than its core principle—state sovereignty—began to be eroded by the forces of globalization.

This is not to say that the nation-state will soon go out of existence; as a form of political organization it has proven very resilient. However, it suffers from a certain "Goldilocks syndrome": while it is just right for addressing some problems, it is too large for resolving local problems and too small for resolving problems that are global. While the nation-state will remain an important unit of political organization and decision-making for national-level problems, it is an inadequate level of organization for dealing with global market forces and economic and ecological interdependencies, or for assuring peace and security in the twenty-first century. The power of the nation-state is also being eroded by the emergence of other actors and new power arrangements at global and regional levels, ranging from transnational corporations, cartels, and regional economic and trade regimes, to regional systems of governance such as the European Parliament.

The flow of economic power away from the nation-state is palpable. Of the world's hundred largest economies, only 49 accrue to nation-states; the majority—51—are internal to corporations. Two hundred corporations, with interlocking boards and strategic alliances, now control 29 percent of world economic activity.[11] And while some corporations now have more wealth and power than most nation-states, they are not subject to the same democratic accountability that binds most national governments, and can function outside the effective control of national laws simply by moving to another country. They suggest that a *de facto* new world order is already forming beyond the parameters of the nation-state system or democratic controls. There is as yet no effective form of global governance to assure that their behavior does not harm the global common good.

If aggregate economic growth is one's only—or primary—criterion of human well-being, this trend may not be a cause of alarm for some people. In the twentieth century the global economy grew seventeenfold, from an annual output of $2.3 trillion in 1900 to $39 trillion in 1998. The growth in economic output in just three years, from 1995 to 1998, exceeded that during the 10,000 years from the beginning of agriculture up to the year 1900.[12] Per capita income multiplied four times, from $1,500 to $6,600, with most of this increase in the second half of the century. Life expectancy increased from 35 years in 1900 to 66 in 1999. More food was produced in the twentieth century than ever before, and human products poured into an increasingly global marketplace at a record rate. Coupled with economic growth, advancements in science, medicine, industry, and technology made it possible for more people than ever before to live longer, healthier, and more productive lives.

From an aggregate view these trends seem to spell tremendous human success. But the benefits of this growth were not evenly distributed. While one fifth of the world population now lives better than ever before, another fifth struggles to survive, with no or little access to safe water, adequate nutrition, shelter, education, or employment. The stark contrasts are laid before us in a Bread for the World Report:

> Consider this: if trade were evenly spread around the land surface of the world, the inhabitants of each square mile, including Antarctic penguins and Saharan camels, would have more than $62,000 in products to trade each year. But it is not. The thousands of women who sew sneakers in Indonesia together make less than Michael Jordan gets for endorsing them.[13]

---

[11] United Nations Conference on Trade and Development, *World Investment Report 1996*, as quoted in *Hunger in a Global Economy*, Bread for the World's 1998 Report on Hunger.
[12] *Ibid.*, p. 10.
[13] *Ibid.*

This gap is compounded by the foreign debt of many of the poorest countries. Rich and poor countries alike are confronted by the need to survive growing global competition for favorable balances of trade and payments, and for access to scarce resources, markets, and new technologies. But the poorest countries that have borrowed heavily from international banks and agencies struggle under burdens of debilitating foreign debts, rising interest rates, adverse terms of trade, interrupted financial flows, and conditions imposed by lending agencies. Poor countries' debts not only cause hunger, disease, and illiteracy among people at home; their effects reach beyond borders to affect people in creditor countries as well, inciting violent conflict and refugee flows.

The power of the nation-state is being challenged from below as well as above. Even while governance is increasingly being ceded to global market forces, many national governments struggle with equally volatile domestic forces. A wave of interethnic, interreligious, and separatist conflicts has beset some countries, weakening—in some cases even obliterating—national governments and the state. The lack of constituted state or national governments has left some African populations in a perilous state, at the mercy of warlords, terrorists, or economic collapse.

The UN, as a state-centric system required to uphold the principle of state sovereignty, has neither the mandate nor means to respond quickly and effectively to protect the sovereignty of peoples within countries fractured by internal warfare, gross violations of human rights, or ethnic cleansings and genocides. The question of humanitarian intervention, although much discussed, still does not have clear criteria or mechanisms for superseding national sovereignty. The UN has also come up against the limits of state sovereignty in its efforts to deal with such international problems as disarmament and arms control, terrorism, trafficking in drugs, women, and children, the spread of AIDS and other diseases, environmental degradation, and other global concerns that cannot be resolved within the framework of unlimited state sovereignty. As we go further into an increasingly global age, the UN will either continue to erode along with the state system that created it, or must be greatly reformed and strengthened to meet both intranational and transnational challenges in the twenty-first century.

The need for a global polity or global structures of governance to deal with global problems becomes more and more manifest every day. On a positive note, the twentieth century saw a series of efforts to advance a more peaceful world order which led to the development of successively larger international organizations. A first attempt was made at the turn of the twentieth century, with two international peace meetings at the Hague aimed at arms control and disarmament and the development of a concert of nations. These negotiations were too slow to prevent World War I; a second attempt at an international polity was made after the war, producing the League of Nations. But, reluctant to surrender any sovereignty to the new international body, the founding states left it too weak to stop Hitler and prevent World War II.

A third attempt at a global order, initiated by the Allied forces before the end of World War II, resulted in the United Nations. The UN became a midwife to the historic process of decolonization and the entry into the international organization of many newly independent states. Through its specialized agencies it fostered international cooperation around a wide variety of issues, including economic development, education, environmental protection, food sufficiency, health care, housing, human rights, population, the advancement of women, and many others. The UN specialized agencies now constitute an important global infrastructure for cooperation and policy development; however, once more the founding states were reluctant to delegate sufficient sovereignty, leaving the UN system too weak to deal effectively with many of the military, economic, ecological, and other transboundary crises that now beset the world.

However, the UN system does not represent a final form of polity for dealing with transnational issues; it is an evolving structure. Over its first five decades the UN showed that it was a living organism with a capacity to learn, adapt, and respond to new problems within the limits and constraints imposed by its member states. Future historians may one day consider our present UN an embryonic form of a global polity, or a stepping-stone to it. With political will, the UN could be strengthened and developed into an effective global organization to serve the needs of people and the planet in the interdependent world of the twenty-first century.

Parallel with the development of intergovernmental organizations (IGOs), such as those that are part of the UN system, has been the development of thousands of international nongovernmental organizations (INGOs) and civil-society organizations. The first INGOs began emerging as early as the fourth century and were primarily religious communities with international membership. From the fourth to the nineteenth centuries the number of INGOs grew relatively slowly: the *Yearbook of International Organizations* needed only three pages to list all of those that existed in some 1,500 years.[14] But in the twentieth century their numbers skyrocketed. In contrast to 176 international nongovernmental organizations in 1909, by 1985 there were 18,000. These INGOs have international memberships and function across national borders in the pursuit of common goals ranging from athletic, artistic, educational, professional, scientific, and religious, to issue concerns such as human rights, development, environmental protection, and peace. They constitute an emerging global civic infrastructure that functions outside the traditional nation-state system. Today, thousands of nongovernmental and civil-society groups have representatives observing at the United Nations and trying to influence global-level policy development.

Where once states were the only legitimate actors in international affairs, now citizen groups and other sectors are claiming the right to a place at the global policy table. Local authorities, labor and trade unions, professional associations, business and industry, religious networks, and civil-society groups are all beginning to see themselves as global citizens—responsible members of a global, as well as a local and national, community.

In some cases local authorities and civil-society groups are doing more to implement global agreements than the national governments who negotiated them. An example is *Agenda 21*, the international plan of action for environment and development agreed to at the 1992 Earth Summit in Rio de Janeiro. While most national governments have lagged behind in implementing this international agreement, some 18,000 local communities around the world have adopted their own local versions of *Agenda 21*. These communities are no longer content to wait for national governments to do something about the destruction of the environment, nor do they believe it is enough to petition governments to act. Rather, with a new maturity, citizen groups are getting together among themselves and negotiating, developing, and promoting new policies to deal with global-scale problems beyond the competency of any one of their states. In many ways, these citizen groups are freer than national leaders to work across national lines in search of solutions to shared problems.

---

[14] Union of International Associations, *Yearbook of International Organizations, 1985–1986.* London: K.G. Saur.

In this view of transformation, then, the nation-state will continue to exist and play an important—but not the only—role in international and global affairs. New forms of governance will emerge at the global level, and new forms of global polity will bubble up from below.

However, it is not yet clear what these forms will be. We could continue to drift, as we are now, toward an order in which global governance continues to be ceded to market forces and more and more wealth and power flow into fewer and fewer hands; or we could decide to develop more democratic, participatory forms of global governance—either a greatly reformed UN or a new global organization that includes a stronger role for civil society. This would require reconceptualizing sovereignty as something residing less in the state and more in the people; it would also require that nation-states pool and delegate some of their sovereignty in a restructured UN or new global organization, to make it effective in addressing issues beyond the competence of single nation-states.

Ten-Thousand-Year Time-Frame:
The Breakdown of the Myth of Dominance

A third view agrees with the above analyses, but goes still deeper. It sees the breakdown of a ten-thousand-year time-frame dating from the agricultural revolution and the rise of traditional civilizations and the great world religions. In this period, the myth of dominance took root and grew in the human imagination and some belief structures. This myth was given expression in the war system and related systems of class and caste, slavery, racism, ageism, and patriarchy, and various other forms of hierarchical structure that pitted one human group against another. Together these systems of dominance comprised a total system governing human development and the direction of human history. Everything was affected—political, social, economic, cultural, and religious structures and relationships. The myth of dominance extended not only to interhuman relations, but also to human-Earth relations, in that some human groups began to see themselves as separate from and over the Earth, leading in the modern period to unprecedented human assaults on the natural world.

In this third view, what is now breaking down is the whole myth structure underlying systems of human dominance. These worldviews and systems are becoming dysfunctional to human survival and unacceptable to growing numbers of people in an increasingly interdependent world.

For evidence, those who espouse this view cite the growing waves of people struggling for democracy and liberation around the world over the last several hundred years, from the Enlightenment philosophers and the American and French revolutions in the 18th century, to movements for the abolition of slavery and for women's suffrage beginning in the 19th century, to the twentieth-century movements for racial justice, civil rights, women's rights, and an end to apartheid. They also point to anti-colonial and independence movements and human rights and peace movements, all pushing for greater realization of human dignity and participation; and to the environmental movements that in the latter part of the twentieth century began to appear everywhere around the world, challenging people to reassess their relationships with the Earth and to learn to reinhabit the Earth as responsible and functioning members of the larger community of life.

As the myth of dominance continues to be challenged, what is emerging in its place is a new vision of our common dependency on one Earth and our mutual interdependence with one another. The emphasis is on solidarity, mutuality, participation, and community, on horizontal rather than hierarchical relationships, and on the health and wholeness of persons and planet.

The old paradigm of dominance was given credence not only in some religious teachings, but also in modern scientific views that were atomistic and hierarchical. The Earth was depicted as a great machine with separately acting parts; humans were seen as the apex and masters of its life. Now a new paradigm is emerging from science; actually, it is not entirely new, for our tribal ancestors as well as spiritual visionaries through the ages intuitively understood what scientists are now discovering empirically: that the Earth is like a single cell in the universe, and humans are not over the cell, but part of it. We will live or die as this single cell lives or dies. The question of human survival and security is inseparable from the functioning integrity of the larger Earth community.

The spiritual, psychological, religious, political, economic, and environmental implications of this view are profound. The transformation envisioned is not a mere matter of tinkering with political policies or passing new laws. It involves turning upside down the way we think, and accepting a new, more mature and responsible role in the further evolution of the planet. It means taking responsibility for the state of our souls and for the state of the world.

For we have new powers never dreamed of by our ancestors: powers to destroy or build the Earth. In the twentieth century we stockpiled weapons beyond anything imagined in previous centuries; we buried millions of land mines which now kill and maim the world's children; we produced thousands of nuclear, chemical, and biological weapons and threatened one another with mutual assured destruction. The weapons created in the name of defending ourselves were so destructive they could not be used without killing those they were supposed to protect as well as those at whom they were aimed. Whatever purpose the war system might once have served, it has now become dysfunctional to future human survival; yet it has not been abolished.

In the twentieth century we also learned how to intervene in the DNA, the delicate genetic coding that had evolved through eons of natural selection, and how to create new species in test tubes and clone old ones, with as-yet unforeseen consequences. We caused hundreds of thousands of plant and animal species to go out of existence by overindustrialization, deforestation, and toxic and radioactive pollution; a part of creation, a part of the divine, is lost forever. We are, through our human choices and actions, altering the face of the Earth, changing its climate, depleting its ozone layer, and rendering the planet uninhabitable for future generations. We are shaping the next stages of planetary evolution.

No other generation has had such powers over life and death—powers that in the past some only ascribed to God. Yet we have not developed the moral maturity and wisdom to use these new powers in ways that will assure a healthy future for our planet, our children, or ourselves. There has been a tragic lag in our development. These new powers demand that we now overcome this spiritual and ethical lag, that we become more morally mature and wiser human beings than any previous generation. We must become spiritually attuned and conscious participants with the sacred processes at work on the planet, in the cosmos, and in ourselves.

In this view, we are moving toward a planetary civilization requiring new myths, a far deeper, more globally inclusive spirituality and ethic, and new understandings and relationships to one another and the Earth. A successful transition would be characterized by a greater sense of wholeness, interconnectedness, and mutuality in interhuman and human-Earth relations. It would be a shift away from competitiveness and toward more cooperative social models; away from the excessive individualism of Western capitalism and the excessive communalism of communism and toward a stronger embrace of unity and diversity within concentric circles of community at local, regional, and now global levels; away from "my nation (or racial or ethnic group) above all others" and toward an embrace of cultural and religious pluralism with mutual rights and responsibilities for all peoples; away from oppressor/oppressed and win/lose models and toward win/win and partnership models in mutual service to the larger human and Earth communities.

Is such a vision of transformation realistic? Those holding this view do not consider themselves dreamers; they point to many positive signs of such a transformation already underway. To the evidence already mentioned above they add the growing interest of people in a new cosmology and Earth-based spirituality; organic and community-based agriculture and holistic health movements that have worked their way from the fringes into mainstream journals, institutions, and businesses; and the engagement of scientists, community organizers, political leaders, and people from virtually every profession and religion in care of the Earth. They point also to growing movements to ban the proliferation and trade in weapons, from handguns and assault rifles to land mines and nuclear weapons. They point to gains in human rights in the twentieth century, including the Universal Declaration of Human Rights and the whole body of international human rights law that followed, defining the obligations of states toward citizens. They point to gains in rights for women around the world, including numerous international agreements and changes in the constitutions and laws of many countries against discrimination on the basis of gender. They also point to more than 150 international agreements for the protection of the environment, most of them in the latter part of the twentieth century; although still weak in implementation, many of these agreements show an increasing consciousness of the need for international standards and norms, and are laying the normative foundations for more responsible life in a global community.

Those holding this third view also point to the unprecedented level of cooperation across national lines in virtually every human pursuit. Never before in history has there been so much global cooperation; never before has there been such a vibrant global civil society working across national lines for our common global future.

But nothing is automatic. For this shift to succeed, current generations must still overcome a tremendous learning lag. We must learn more in the next few decades than our ancestors had to learn in the last 10,000. We have to rethink what it means to be human, and how to re-inhabit the Earth and live in community in new ways. We need to learn to live more intentionally, more consciously, and question our decisions hourly and daily, taking responsibility for their impact on the present and future life of the Earth and the human community. We need to learn to think in multigenerational terms, about the ways in which our decisions today will affect those yet to come—one, two, three, four, five, six, and seven generations into the future—because our choices today have such profound consequences on the world of tomorrow.

What Kind of World Order Will Emerge from the Breakdown?

If any of the above analyses are correct, the period of history ahead of us will evolve in ways significantly different from that of the twentieth century. This is not merely the residue of millennial thinking; the above changes were underway well before the turn of the millennium, and will continue evolving in one way or another as the new millennium progresses.

We live in an axial period of history, with major changes underway in political, economic, and social systems, and possibly also psychospiritual systems and structures of thought. Despite differences in the above analyses, they all assume that we are entering an age where local and national realities are increasingly penetrated by global forces, and that some re-ordering of structures at the global level is inevitable and essential. The question before us, then, is not *whether* a new world order will emerge in response to new global imperatives, but rather *what kind* of world order? Based on what worldview? What values? What ethic and ethos? What kind of leadership will guide and shape it? What kind of structures and systems will evolve to govern it? Who will benefit and who will pay? Will it be a world order that oppresses and represses some for the sake of the many, or many for the sake of the few? One in which two thirds of the people remain poor, hungry, and fearful, or a more equitable, humane, and less violent one for all peoples? One that opens the way to truer freedom, with shared responsibility for the common good in a global community? Will it be a future where the life of the Earth is degraded, squandered, sold in the marketplace, and lost to future generations—or will it be built on new understandings of the integral relatedness we and our great-grandchildren have with one living Earth?

We do not know the answers with certainty. A new world order does not necessarily mean a better one. Converging and colliding trends portend that unless we change our direction, the world order that emerges in the twenty-first century could be a very nasty one, especially for those who are on the underside of existing systems of dominance.

A new world order may emerge in one of three ways: crisis, drift, or the conscious, democratic choice of a preferred alternative. Each path is likely to generate a different outcome.

If a new world order comes through *crisis*—or multiple, interactive crises such as the collapse of global economic, financial, communications, or ecological systems—the outcome is not likely to be more humane or democratic. A collapse of the international banking system, for example, could cause global panic, leading to severe measures to maintain order. Major ecological changes, such as global climate change, loss of biodiversity, or continuing loss of clean water and other vital resources, could intensify global competition for remaining resources, leading to resource wars or major civil unrest. In the potentially chaotic climate of fear and uncertainty generated by the collapse of major systems, a despotic form of global governance, backed by military power, might be imposed on the world's peoples to prevent global anarchy.

The path of *drift* is no more promising. If we continue to cede questions of global governance to the market system, we will beget an undemocratic world order in which increasing wealth flows into fewer and fewer corporate hands and critical decision-making is the prerogative not of citizens or their elected representatives, but of corporate boards and stockholders. Burying our heads in the sand and abdicating responsibility for the outcome, or merely railing against the forces of economic globalization, will not change this undemocratic drift.

Positive alternatives need to be consciously envisioned and sought. Informed citizens in all cultures and world regions need to dialogue, negotiate, and work together to shape a more humane, participatory, and environmentally responsible world order. In contrast to the top-down models of world order that are likely to result from the crisis or drift scenarios, this third path would build a new world order from the bottom up, with the participation of strong, vibrant, and informed global citizens. If global governance in some form is inevitable and essential to coordinate decisions affecting our shared future in an interdependent world, then should it not be a form of global governance that is *of* the people, *by* the people, and *for* the people and planet?

This we know: the vision and path that ultimately prevail, and the form of global governance that ultimately evolves, will depend greatly on who is willing to participate now in shaping global systems, and what worldviews and values they bring to the process. Those who do not participate also affect the outcome, by abdicating their choices to others.

This we know, too: the inner and outer dimensions of a new world order must advance simultaneously. If a future global civilization is to be more humane, we must expand our hearts, minds, souls, and consciousness as well as our political, economic, and social structures. The systems we develop must be able to assure for present and future generations greater peace, economic well-being, ecological integrity, and human dignity than were realized on the blood-soaked killing fields of the twentieth century. This is no small challenge.

This is, therefore, a defining and deciding moment in the life of world. The vision and understandings we have and don't have, the decisions we make and don't make, the values and ethical standards we set or don't set, the actions we take and don't take now will make a major difference in shaping the world order of the twenty-first century.

This is also a time of uncertainty. Like Dr. Dolittle's two-headed Pushmi-Pullyu, we feel pulled in seemingly opposite directions at the same time. Centrifugal forces that impel us toward global integration activate countervailing centripetal forces that seek more familiar identity systems at family, ethnic, or local community levels. With this tension tugging at the seams of our political, economic, cultural, and psychospiritual systems, we must rise to new levels of creativity and cooperation. For better or worse, we now live in one global neighborhood with interlocked destinies. All our separate past histories are now converging toward one shared future history. Decisions and activities in one part of the world affect everyone else in the neighborhood. Our common security, peace, and mutual well-being require that we work together to shape norms, standards, and systems that work for the benefit of not only some of us, but all of us.

Religions Matter

In this defining moment, religions matter. Religion and spirituality have mattered for millions of years in helping to shape and maintain past civilizations, and they will matter in shaping a future global civilization.

History shows that the true shapers of past cultures and civilizations have not been political leaders so much as spiritual leaders: Lao-tzu, Confucius, Buddha, Abraham, Moses, Jesus, Paul, Mohammed, Bahá'u'lláh. Their teachings have shaped values and ethics, informed social systems, legitimized and delegitimized political regimes, evaluated the justice and injustice of economic systems. In short, religions have provided norms of behavior that, while not constituting government, constitute a powerful moral force—a governing force, a form of governance—in human affairs.

We also know that the role of religion (or more correctly, of people professing to act in the name of religion) has not always been positive. Religions have sometimes been powerful rivers separating us from one another. At times these rivers have seemed impossible to cross in order to reach each other, hear and see each other, be with each other, and stand inside each other's stories and histories. People professing religion have sometimes closed their eyes and ears to the hungry, the homeless, the imprisoned who were not of their ways and beliefs; they have sometimes been the cause of hunger and homelessness, and have themselves been the jailers and executioners. Organized religion has sometimes been a tool of the state, used to manipulate people toward blind obedience to state power; at times it has been indistinguishable from the state, wielding political power for its own gain. Religion has sometimes been a factor in genocide and war, used to justify killing all those who are "other."

Yet all this needs to be distinguished from the authentically spiritual, the truly religious, which, if pursued to its core, leads to an experience of oneness.

The psychiatrist Carl Jung suggested that there is an important difference between *authentic religion* and *religious creed*. Creedal religion or collective belief runs the risk of becoming oppressive when, like a totalitarian state, it is imposed on people as an absolute, and the individual is submerged in the mass authority. This is the opposite of authentic religion, which in Jungian terms is a living, "incontrovertible experience of an intensely personal relationship between [humans] and an extramundane authority." The religious impulse—called by some the search for God, by others ultimate concern, by others an awareness of our relatedness to a Ground of All Being, and by still others the path of liberation or salvation—is not something that can be superimposed. It is, says Jung, "an instinctive attitude peculiar in [humans]" and will seek its own course. Nor can it be separated from the so-called secular aspects of our existence without resulting in feelings of alienation or incompleteness.

The Latin word *religare*, from which the word *religion* in many Western languages is derived, means "*to bind together again.*" In Sanskrit, one of the original meanings of *dharma* (eternal religion) is the same: "*to bind together as one the whole universe.*" Religion has also been defined as the experience of harmony, of the holy or whole or ultimate, of the sacred, of the unknowable. Religion has evolved out of a human sense of a reality greater than self, greater than the sum total of quantifiable physical, economic, political, or social facts and phenomena. For some, religion is an effort to discover order (cosmos) in disorder (chaos).

Religion is also a means by which societies interpret life, and develop and reinforce codes of morality and conduct in keeping with these interpretations and the requirements of community life. Religion also includes those beliefs and practices by means of which a group designates its deepest problems of meaning, suffering, and injustice, and specifies its most fundamental ways of trying to reduce those problems. Moreover, religion, through its sacred stories and scriptures, often carries the symbols and archetypes by which a people coalesce and define their identity as a community, culture, or civilization.

Religion as Source and Resource

No wonder Toynbee, Huntington, and other historians and social analysts have persisted in claiming that religions will play a central role in shaping a future world order. All the above definitions and understandings of religion suggest that religion is of immense significance for questions of world order. The converse is also true—world order is not peripheral to the world's religious and spiritual traditions; it is at the deepest core of religious meaning, experience, and interest. As you will see when reading other articles in this volume, religious and spiritual traditions are a valuable source of wisdom for a world struggling to find direction in a time of global transformation.

In addition to the spiritual meaning and content religions bring as sources for world-order thinking, the major world religions also have networks of organizations, educational and health-care institutions, alumni, research institutes, spiritual communities, social and civic-action groups and programs. People of religion can and often do operate across national lines with greater ease than government officials, and have contributed important scholarship and professional expertise to help resolve some of the grave issues confronting humanity.

If Toynbee's analysis is right, our spiritual journeys now will be vitally important to the development of an emerging global civilization. Spiritual growth and transformation are as important as, and possibly more important than, political changes in global systems, for these inner transformations of soul and mind prefigure, inform, inspire, and sustain the outer work. The inner and outer world order—spiritual growth and the development of more humane global systems—are inseparable parts of a holistic world order. They develop in conformity to one another and are mutually reinforcing. We need to draw from our deepest spiritual waters in nurturing a more humane world order.

About the Authors and Articles in This Book

The authors in this volume are aware that their respective religions have sometimes failed to live up to their promises or deepest purposes, or, like wide rivers, have divided people from one another. Some of them refer in their articles to these past failures. But these authors did not come together to blame or belabor failed pasts: they came together to ride with one another the currents of transformation rushing through the world, knowing that the rivers of their respective religious traditions would be swept into these currents, and hoping to create together a rudder with which to move toward a safe passage. They came together to share from the deepest insights of their diverse traditions, beliefs, spirituality, and scholarship. They came together, too, to chart a vision and explore cooperative ways to advance more just and humane global systems.

For at their deepest level, the rivers of authentic religions and spirituality all spring from and tap into the same underground sea. If followed to their deepest source, the rivers of diverse religious traditions are one water, water that unites.

Most of the authors in this volume were participants at the May 3–7, 1997, symposium on Religion and World Order sponsored by Global Education Associates and co-sponsored by the Center for Mission Research and Study at Maryknoll and Fordham University's Institute on Religion and Culture. After sharing their initial views in papers presented at the symposium (held at Maryknoll, New York), and with the benefit of feedback from three days of intense discussion, they then revised their papers for publication in this book. A few of the authors could not be at the symposium in person but sent their papers for inclusion in the discussion and book.

Most of these papers were prepared specifically for the symposium and have not been previously published; one, by John Mbiti on African traditional religions, was previously published by GEA and is reprinted here with the author's permission because of the importance attached by the editors to this viewpoint. We regret the absence of articles by Native Americans; although Native American invitees were scheduled to participate, at the last minute they were unable to do so. For reasons of space, not all papers presented at the symposium could be included in the present volume; some of those that are included have been shortened.

In preparing papers for the symposium and this volume, most authors were asked to respond from the perspective of their own tradition to a set of Guideline Questions prepared for GEA's ongoing Religion and World Order Project. These Questions, which can be found in Appendix A, were developed in 1991 and have guided the Religion and World Order Project's areas of inquiry since that time. They were the basis for earlier GEA-sponsored symposia and dialogues on religion and world order in Istanbul (1996) and Washington, DC (1994). Summaries of presentations made at the Washington symposium are available from GEA as a bound volume, and can also be found on the GEA website at www.globaleduc.org.

A few authors were invited to give overview observations or perspectives about multireligious and ecumenical movements as they affect or are related to world order, or to concentrate on the contribution of religions to special issues, such as peace, human rights, care of the environment, or economic development. And one, Richard Falk, whose academic expertise is in international law and world order, was asked to offer a secular view of the role of religion from the perspective of world order concerns. But most were invited to respond to the Guideline Questions from the viewpoint of their spiritual or religious tradition.

The Guideline Questions cover four broad areas of project inquiry, outlined below.

Working Toward a Shared Global Ethic

In an interdependent global community, there is a need for a shared ethic which, while respecting national, cultural, and religious differences, provides a common framework for responding to global challenges and developing global public policy. Presenters and authors in this volume were asked to consider the values and principles in their sacred texts, ethical systems, teachings, traditions, and lived experience that could contribute to the development of a shared global ethic, with special emphasis on values and principles that would advance (a) peace and security, (b) economic and social justice, (c) human rights, (d) cultural identity and integrity, and (e) ecological well-being.

This project's focus on a global ethic should not be confused with the initiative of Hans Küng and the Council for a Parliament of World Religions, which was first published in 1993. While the editors and authors in this volume appreciate and support this parallel effort, as well as those of other groups, the GEA focus on a global ethic precedes them as part of the Religion and World Order Project dating from the 1970s. The Religion and World Order Project includes but goes beyond an ethic, both in seeking to develop and apply such an ethic to global structures and systems, and in focusing on the development of a global public sector and polity that can codify an ethic in global policy and law. Moreover, the dialogue on a global ethic within the Religion and World Order Project does not assume that a global ethic can be divorced or separated very easily from the spiritual and religious traditions in which meanings are defined, social consciences are shaped, and moral commitments are made by a people. A global ethic might be constructed on the force of reason alone and therefore engage those who are not adherents of any particular religion, but for many people around the world, an ethic or ethos flows from their spiritual and religious roots and is given credence and commitment in the context of their sacred stories, archetypes, and meanings. From this perspective, it would make more sense to build a global ethic from the spiritual roots up, helping people find and ground it from within their tradition, rather than apart from it.

Working Toward Just World Systems

In this second set of questions, authors were invited to build on the values and principles of their religious or spiritual tradition which they had identified in responding to the above question, and to make recommendations relative to the development of (a) criteria for a true global civilization, a global civic society, and global citizenship; (b) global policies, systems, and structures for a preferred world order; (c) local initiatives and "bottom up" participatory processes that, along with transnational processes, would provide effective transitions to a desired world order; (d) balancing tensions between the individual and common good, between rights and responsibilities, between the role of private and public sectors, between local, national, and global sovereignties, etc.; and (e) resources within their religious tradition and institutions that could be used to help advance a more just world order.

Collaborating with the United Nations and Its Specialized Agencies

This third set of questions assumes that a more just and humane world order will be built not in a vacuum, but on existing foundations, some of which could be provided by the UN system. The UN system has shown a capacity to adapt and grow in response to new challenges over its first five decades, and could be further adapted to meet new challenges in the next few decades. Although still largely a state-centric system, it has been responding to initiatives and pressures from non-state actors, such as scientific, educational, and civil-society groups.

Moreover, some UN agencies have been experimenting with partnerships with civil-society groups in areas such as humanitarian aid, refugee and human rights work, child welfare, and educational and economic development programs. Since the end of the cold war, many UN-related agencies have also shown an interest in the role and contribution of religious and spiritual communities. Religious institutions working with local peoples can reach these people more effectively than many government programs.

For their part, some religious groups are also interested in collaborative work with the United Nations. In the late 1980s, GEA began initiating partnerships between nongovernmental organizations and UN agencies, and in 1990 formally launched Project Global 2000, involving a partnership between four UN agencies and 16 nongovernmental organizations. UNESCO, as one of the UN-related partners, endorsed and became a partner with Project Global 2000's Religion and World Order Project in connection with its series on the Contributions by Religions to the Culture of Peace. The United Nations Children's Fund (UNICEF), the United Nations Environment Program (UNEP), the United Nations Development Program (UNDP), and the World Bank are a few of the other UN-related agencies and programs that have been exploring collaboration with religious and multireligious networks.

With this set of questions, authors were invited to propose ways the existing UN system could be made more effective as an instrument for a more just world order, and ways that religious networks and institutions could effectively collaborate or work in partnership with the UN on global issues of common concern. Some current and past UN officials participated in the symposium as respondents to these proposals.

Developing Multireligious Initiatives

In this fourth area of inquiry, participants and authors explored ways their religious networks could incorporate and respond to world-order questions in their educational and advocacy programs, and the kind of multireligious initiatives they recommended for advancing more just world systems.

A Rainbow-Hued Mosaic

I will not attempt here to summarize the authors' views and responses to these areas of inquiry. They do not paint one unified, harmonious picture. If they did, it would be far less interesting, and perhaps disappointing, to read their views. Instead, they present a beautiful, intricate, rainbow-hued mosaic of human experience on Earth. In tackling a very big problem, they offer a composite picture of the Human Being, as seen from diverse perspectives and a great variety of traditions. Collectively, the papers build a magnificent edifice, but their ranges, focuses, and viewpoints are extremely diverse: some give a simple or vague outline of the finished building; others concentrate on constructing a sturdy foundation, or one beautiful door or window, or an elaborate tower with flags flying. What is really interesting in the end is not only what the authors say, but who they are—the personal identity that comes through their writing; how (and whether) they answer the questions; and which ones they choose.

To the question "What is religion?" some authors seem to answer "That which underlies the human worldview," while others would answer, "One of the building blocks of society." The religious beliefs of some include belief in God; for some there is not a God as understood by the others, but a sacred presence greater than human beings.

To the question "What is world order?" there are also different perceptions. Some authors focus on world order as signifying a pattern of relationships between political, especially *inter*national, entities. But others have a multilayered understanding of the term: within their religious frame of reference and at the deepest level, world order refers to ultimate reality, the spiritual as well as physical ordering of the universe. Some have a more static view of world order as hard to change, others the more dynamic view that world order is a process of ordering or re-patterning and is constantly in motion, from macroscopic to microscopic levels.

Some essays are very general, others extremely specific; some theoretical, others practical and narrowly focused. Authors interpreted the Guideline Questions differently: some at the personal level, some at the societal level. Some answered all the questions; some answered some; and some answered none, but offered new questions and insights.

It should be stressed here that the aim of this book, and of GEA's whole 25-year series of symposia on Religion and World Order, was not to create a new religion, and not to unify existing religions into one world religion. Like Toynbee, we do not advocate syncretism, or the invention of some artificial religion combining what *somebody* thinks is "the best" of each. Instead, an aim of this project was to involve members from each major religion in a self-evaluation and a process of discovering elements of truth from each other, making each stronger, and thus more compassionate and more empowered to contribute to the development of a more humane world order.

After 25 years of dialogue and work with people from diverse religious beliefs, including authors whose work appears in this book, it is my conviction that religion does indeed hold a key for creating a more human world order. Religion, after all, tells people what is worth doing and what is not worth doing—what will give them true inner peace and fulfillment, and what will not. If everybody truly lived by the spirit of his or her religion—whichever religion it might be—we could not help but achieve our goals, because we would all have reached that underground sea of compassion, non-materialistic values, and devotion to the sacred in the world and one another.

However, it should not be assumed that no one can contribute effectively to a more humane world order until they themselves have reached spiritual perfection or are fully developed human beings. Years ago, the psychologist of human potential, Abraham Maslow, in his book *The Farther Reaches of Human Nature*, refused to speculate on the question of which comes first, the good person or the good society. "There is a kind of feedback between the Good Society and the Good Person," he wrote. "They need each other. They are *sine qua non* to each other....It is quite clear that they develop simultaneously and in tandem. It would in any case be impossible to achieve either one without the other. By good society I mean ultimately one species, one world."[15] For Maslow, the far goal was world peace through world law. For Sri Aurobindo, the Indian mystic who was a spiritual force in India's struggle for independence, a world political order—global governance—was a necessary step in the larger spiritual journey of the human community. The far goal was spiritual union, a spiritual order. Aurobindo saw political unification as an essential middle step that could not be separated from, or skipped over in, the spiritual journey.[16]

Whether or not the different authors in this volume would identify with Maslow or Aurobindo, none advocate a privatized spirituality that walls off individual human development from questions of world community or world order. All enter the dialogue with a spirituality that is engaged in the world—i.e., which sees integral relationships between the individual and collective human journey, the journey toward full development of the human person and the full development of the human community.

The Religion and World Order Symposium Statement

Finally, attention should be drawn to the statement prepared by participants at the Religion and World Order symposium, which appears in Appendix C. It crystallizes the authors' views and recommendations relative to the Guideline Questions, as well as to other questions and concerns that surfaced at the symposium. Participants prepared a first draft at the symposium; they then consulted fellow members of their various religious networks, and with the benefit of this input, the statement went through

---

[15] Viking Press, 1971, 19.
[16] *The Future Evolution of Man*, Theosophical Publishing House, 1974; and *Human Cycle, Ideal of Human Unity*, International Publishing Service, 1971.

several revisions before being finalized and signed in its present form for inclusion in this volume, and for sharing in various international and interreligious fora. We encourage readers to duplicate and share it with colleagues and friends, and to sign it yourself if so moved.

Also included in the Appendices, for your reference, are some interreligious statements that were produced at other meetings and either cited or shared by presenters at the symposium on Religion and World Order. These include the *Declaration of Principles on Tolerance* adopted by the General Conference of UNESCO, November 1995; the *Declaration on the Role of Religion in the Promotion of a Culture of Peace* adopted at the December 1994 meeting in Barcelona on "The Contributions by Religions to the Culture of Peace," also sponsored by UNESCO; and *Toward a Global Ethic*, adopted at the 1993 Parliament of World Religions in Chicago. While not a comprehensive collection of the many multireligious statements relevant to the present discussion—including them all would require a huge volume—these provide a small indication of some of the important areas of multireligious dialogue and initiative in the final decade of the twentieth century, and point at directions for the twenty-first.

SOME GENERAL PERSPECTIVES

The Religious Foundations of Humane Global Governance
by Richard Falk

The Multireligious Engagement of Civil Society:
The Need for Bilingualism
by William Vendley

Religion and ...
by Robert Traer

The Religious Foundations
of Humane
Global Governance

Richard Falk

Locating the Inquiry

The religious dimension of human experience has generally been excluded from the serious study and practice of governance for several centuries, especially in the West. The exclusion is definitely a consequence of the European Enlightenment and its endorsement of autonomous reason as the only reliable guide for human affairs, as well as its general tendency to ground politics upon a secular ethos, a principal feature of which is the separation of church and state. Of course, as with many questionable moves in history, this development had positive aspects, and was rooted in a particular set of historical circumstances in Europe at the time of the formation of the modern state system, a process whose origin is difficult to locate with precision but is often (although somewhat arbitrarily) dated to coincide with the Peace of Westphalia in 1648.

Without entering into this complex story in any detail, the justification for the exclusion of religion had to do with the perception that religious institutions were inimical to the rise of science and material progress in human affairs, and the undeniable reality that the split in Christendom had contributed to a series of terrible wars. The exclusion of religion always had certain normative costs, including the realization that religious attachments are so strong in society that religion excluded from entering the front door of political life will tend to enter other entrances, including concealed trapdoors. The effects of this reassertion of religious relevance may be to obstruct an understanding of how public policies are actually being shaped.

So in an important sense, historically, it is necessary to understand that the exclusion of religion from political life was seen as a vital step in the direction of humane governance: that is, basing governance on reason, religious tolerance, and the primacy of the individual human being. In many respects Hugo Grotius, a typical Renaissance figure, was generally regarded as the founder of modern international law, and an intellectual figure who sensitively embodied the passing of medieval Europe to the new Europe of independent, sovereign, territorial states. Grotius was a witness to the Thirty Years' War that ravaged Europe and represented a struggle fought along the geographical and ideological fault line that separated Catholicism from Protestantism. Grotius was, in a sense, seeking to restore the religious possibility to human life by removing it from the political realm. In his vivid words, "Throughout the Christian world I observed a lack of restraint in relation to war, such as even barbarous races should be ashamed of; I observed that men rush to arms for slight causes, or no cause at all, and that when arms have once been taken up there is no longer any respect for law, divine or human; it is as if, in accordance with a general decree, frenzy had openly been let loose for the committing of all crimes."[1]

In adopting this critical stance, Grotius combined two of the defining characteristics of modernity whose lineage has deep roots in the Enlightenment: a claim of moral superiority associated with the specific identity of "the Christian world" that should inform political life to the extent possible, and the implicit deprecation of non-Christian societies as the vast domain of "barbarous races." The first impulse led to the idea that the relations among states are to some extent governed by law, while the second gave a sort of underpinning to the Eurocentric conceptions of world order and relations between Western and non-Western peoples that came to flourish in the colonial age. Such liberal rationalizations for the politics and structures of domination were issued by the most admired Enlightenment figures: Hegel, Kant, John Stuart Mill, and Grotius among others. Neither led to humane governance for the peoples of the world:

---

[1] Para. 28, Prolegomena, On the Law of War and Peace, 20 (New York: Bobbs-Merrill, 1925).

international law was too weak to contain the passions of nationalism or dreams of empire; and the validation of colonial rule amounted to little more than a rationalization for the exploitation and domination of non-Western peoples, and seems to have generated in many instances deep patterns of resentment that surfaced in the form of intense intrasocietal violence after independence.

There have been attempts in the recent past to associate this normative orientation toward political reality with an emergent and evolving world order that had within it the potentiality to achieve humane governance for the entire world. Hedley Bull depicted an international society of states that sustained a balance between sovereign rule within territorial limits and a kind of prudent moderation, safeguarded by the benevolence of leading military powers in the relations among states—a type of world order described as an "anarchic society."[2] Myres McDougal and a group of collaborators depicted the spread of Enlightenment values, through the commitment to democratic types of public order systems, as an evolving foundation for a humane intercivilizational pattern of governance that had the capacity eventually to produce a peaceful and equitable world order of benefit to the entire world.[3]

Both these approaches to the future of world order were premised on the persistence of the states system as the basis of world order, and in that sense were in some way rooted in anti-utopian traditions of political realism. Additionally, building on the heritage of Woodrow Wilson and the experiments in world organization represented by the League of Nations and the United Nations, there emerged a more utopian strain of secular thought that fundamentally believed that the only secure and legitimate form of world order depended upon the establishment of world government—a body of thought that came to be associated with world federalism, and is probably still best represented by the work of Grenville Clark and Louis B. Sohn in the form of World Peace Through World Law.[4]

Even the World Order Models Project, with its explicit undertaking to consider the diverse world order perspectives representative of the

---

[2] Bull, The Anarchic Society: A Study of Order in World Politics (New York: Columbia University Press, 1977).
[3] See McDougal and Associates, Studies in World Public Order (New Haven, Connecticut: Yale University Press, 1960); McDougal and Harold D. Lasswell, Jurisprudence for a Free Society (New Haven, Connecticut: New Haven Publishers, 1992), see esp. Vol. II.
[4] Cambridge, Massachusetts: Harvard University Press, 3rd ed., 1966.

leading regions and ideologies active in the world, failed to include in any serious or systematic manner the relevance of religion, although it did acknowledge that world order values, widely shared on an intercivilizational basis, provided the normative framing of any successful project to establish, or even to envisage, humane global governance.[5]

Although the perspectives arising from the work of Bull and McDougal remain useful as moderating guides, with normative foundations, for operations within the existing framework of world order, their regulative capabilities and potentialities seem far too modest to address the deficiencies of international political life that arise from the persistence of war and militarism, the pervasiveness of poverty and economic deprivation, the circumstances of political oppression and religious extremism, the disregard of environmental decay and danger, and the neglect of the spiritual sides of human nature and aspiration. The advocacy of world government as a normative project seems strangely discordant with the current weakening of support for even feeble efforts to sustain existing world political organizations, as epitomized by the recent travails of the United Nations, and although there is an increasingly frequent framing of political life in relation to the metaphor of a "global village," it is seen primarily as an expression of the potency of economic globalization or as expressive of the new borderless cyberworld of the Internet.[6] In effect, the best of secular thinking falls short of providing either a plausible path to travel in pursuit of humane global governance or a sufficiently inspiring vision of its elements to mobilize a popular grassroots movement for drastic global reform.

The position of this paper is that this failure is partially due to the exclusion of religious and spiritual dimensions of human experience from the shaping of the vision and practices associated with the quest for global humane governance. The paper is organized as follows: first, a section on dominant world order trends and tendencies with respect to

---

[5] For representative works from WOMP over the period of its existence see Saul H. Mendlovitz, ed., *On the Creation of a Just World Order* (New York: Free Press, 1975); R.B.J. Walker, *One World/Many Worlds: Struggles for a Just World Peace* (Boulder, Colorado: Lynne Rienner, 1988); Richard Falk, *On Humane Governance: Toward a New Global Politics* (University Park, Pennsylvania: Penn State University Press, 1995).

[6] But see articulate argument in favor of world government by David Ray Griffin in "Global Governance: Objections Considered" in Errol E. Harris and James A. Yunker, eds., *Toward Genuine Global Governance: World Federalist Reactions to "Our Global Neighborhood"* (Westport, Connecticut: Greenwood, 1999).

global governance; then some consideration of the extent to which these recent trends that are shaping the historical situation at the beginning of the third millennium are also creating a new, unexpected opening for religious and spiritual energies—a development that, as with the secularist era of exclusion, has problematic as well as encouraging aspects; then a discussion of this religious resurgence as part of the double-edged relevance of religion to global governance; and a final section which argues in support of the inclusion of emancipatory religious and spiritual perspectives in world order thinking and practice, along with an enumeration of potential contributions.

Current World Order Trends, or Pathways to Inhumane Governance

Without entering into a detailed inquiry, it seems evident that several dominant world order trends are converging in such a way as to generate a more integrated form of governance at the global level, but in a form that significantly undermines world order values and thus qualifies the emergent world order as a variant of "inhumane governance."

Such an indictment is not meant to be a total condemnation. There are aspects of these globalizing developments that represent normative improvements on prior conditions (for instance, a reduction in the prospect for large-scale nuclear war, a diminishing likelihood of international warfare in general, and the alleviation of poverty and economic deprivation for hundreds of millions of people, particularly those living in several of the most populous—and previously some of the most severely and hopelessly impoverished—Pacific Rim countries), but the overall impact is to fracture the peoples of the world, to neglect the plight of those who are most deprived and vulnerable, to place nonsustainable burdens on the environment that seem likely to diminish the life quality of future generations, and to engender an ethos of consumerism that forecloses the most fulfilling forms of individual and social self-realization. As such, despite this mixed picture, it seems appropriate to describe the resultant arrangements of global governance as cumulatively contributing to "global inhumane governance."

The Dynamics of Economic Globalization. There is no doubt that the greater mobility of capital is facilitating a more materially efficient use of resources, if the benchmarks are the return on capital (profitability), economic growth, and the expansion of world trade. This pattern of global economic development is fostered as well by a "global media" that is one aspect of globalization, but is also pushing a consumerist conception of human happiness and fulfillment. The interdependence of economic activity and the growing complexity arising from technological capabilities are creating a growing need for regional and global governance in the form of policy coordination and institutionalized regimes of control. The strength of global market forces is such that existing governance structures at the level of the sovereign state are losing their political independence and autonomy; the discipline of global capital is becoming an iron cage defining policy choice. This pattern is most evident in relation to the heavily indebted countries of the Global South, a reality made actual generally by way of the intrusion of the World Bank and IMF into the policymaking spheres of government. But the process is almost as evident in the affluent countries of the Global North that make seemingly spontaneous adjustments in their policy options to reflect the priorities of global capital, encouraging fiscal austerity and subordinating societal claims on resources.

The governance consequences are twofold: the creation of formal and informal arenas for the coordination of global economic policy according to the priorities of capital, and the creation of institutional arrangements that can give behavioral effect to such priorities. In the first category one can mention the Annual Economic Summit of Industrial Countries, the so-called G-7, in which the heads of state of these leading countries gather each year in one of their member countries for several days of discussion and photo opportunity; these G-7 meetings are far less significant in relation to their substantive achievements than in signaling to the world the ascendancy of economistic forces within the global setting. The attention given to these economic summits far outweighs the participation of these leaders in the activities of the United Nations, where it is rare indeed for any leader to remain in attendance for more than a few hours, if at all.

An informal arena along the same lines, although operating in a more obscure fashion, is the annual World Economic Forum in Davos, Switzerland, in which the main participants are business leaders. Eligibility depends on representing a company or financial institution that has sales of more than $700 million per year. It is at Davos, and less-publicized similar occasions, that the priorities of global capital are articulated in relation to changing market conditions.

With respect to institutionalization, the main effort has been to liberalize global trade, reducing the significance of national frontiers and national economic policy. The GATT negotiations have tried to establish a liberalizing dynamic, negotiating away protectionist policies and prerogatives and pushing toward an integrated single market for the world. A big step in the process of carrying this vision forward involved the establishment in Geneva of the World Trade Organization, which has an expanding mandate to override national efforts to place burdens on most internationally traded goods and services.

The emerging global governance framework is seeking to implement a conception of the future that is responsive to the logic of market forces. Territorial states are contributing to this process to the extent that their political elites have been globalized to view their role as primarily one of carrying out the policies decreed by adherents of the economistic world picture.[7] Such a cumulative trend is not without resistance in leadership circles. The more geopolitically oriented elites, often associated with the more militarized sections of government bureaucracies and the armaments industry, continue to favor a conception of world order that emphasizes rivalry among leading states (and their allies) and the importance of such traditional ideas as containment, deterrence, and balance of power, as well as the closely related academic fixation, especially in the United States, on "grand strategy."[8]

This tension between the economistic and geopolitical world pictures is currently being worked out primarily with respect to the relationship with China, and to a lesser extent with reference to the NATO enlargement issue in Europe. In both settings, there is a renewed sense that despite globalization, territorially oriented bases of political and military power remain decisive in working out the future of world order.

The effects of this rising economistic view of global governance can briefly be set forth:

1. *heavy investments* in situations where conditions are such that rapid and large returns on capital can be expected, which has favored eco-

---

[7] For helpful discussions see *Millennium* Special Issue on "Liberalism in an Age of Globalization" (Vol. 24, Winter 1995), pp. 377–576; also Yoshikazu Sakamoto, ed., *Global Transformation* (Tokyo: UNU Press, 1994).

[8] See Barry R. Posen and Andrew L. Ross, "Competing Visions for US Grand Strategy," *International Security* 21:5–53 (1996/97).

nomic situations in which skilled labor exists but does not have high expectations in terms of wages or unionized operations;

2. *very impressive economic growth rates* for an expanding number of countries in the Asia/Pacific area, leading to massive alleviations of poverty, but also to predatory forms of labor abuse and a promiscuous disregard of environmental harm and disruptive social effects;

3. *a refusal to invest* in those settings where returns on capital were not positive, either because of political instability, unskilled labor force, or high degrees of regulatory interference—factors that on balance have led to the disregard of most of sub-Saharan Africa and the Caribbean, as well as to selective deindustrialization in parts of the Global North;

4. as a consequence of the "marketization" of government policy, a *steady downward pressure* on the provision of public goods (welfare, higher education, the arts, environmental protection) outside the area of military defense, which means that even when a national economy and its leading companies are doing very well, as exhibited by record highs on stock exchanges, there are few benefits for ordinary citizens, even those in the middle classes. Economic growth continues impressively, but the quality of life declines as people are increasingly squeezed in the struggle to sustain living standards;

5. this atmosphere of diminished support for public goods is accentuated by *a shift in fiscal orientation*, away from Keynesian ideas about deficit financing and demand creation and toward balanced budgets, deficit reduction, and monetarist approaches to economic policy;

6. in this atmosphere, *political support* for public goods (protection of the global commons, United Nations) *falls away* with adverse consequences, given the absence of either a supportive constituency or any significant perceived contribution to the short-term prospects of economic globalization.

The Ideological Climate. These various tendencies associated with the imprecise, slippery, yet indispensable term "globalization" have been accentuated by certain developments associated with the historical circumstances existing in the closing years of the second millennium. The ending of the cold war provided a convenient occasion to discredit socialist and so-called "socialistic" ideological alternatives to capitalism.

Indeed, the virtual disappearance of any serious socialist challenge has encouraged the architects of economic policy to believe that it is no longer politically necessary to make concessions to the "dangerous classes."[9] This ideological circumstance is reinforced by two additional factors: the decline in the political leverage exerted by organized labor on government policy and the national electoral strategies of mainstream political parties; and the widespread disillusionment of publics in the democracies of the Global North with an activist state, as well as criticisms of the excesses of the welfare state and a growing skepticism about the problem-solving capabilities of political leaders of states.

In the background, as well, are the convergent attitudes associated with "netizens," the new militant political identities arising out of close affiliation with the Internet, political sensibilities that gravitate toward the ethos of self-adjusting systems and a libertarian resistance to governmental regulation in any form. In relation to governance, the prevalence of such attitudes works against exhibitions of compassion for victims of globalization. Such exhibitions of social concern are resisted because they would seem to validate activist interventions by government to protect those who are being painfully marginalized by globalization.

The resistance to alternative world pictures was temporarily suspended by the global economic crisis of 1997–1998. Even mainstream advocates of an economistic approach to global policy revealed welcome signs of self-doubt, and there was, for the first time since the end of the cold war, political space within which to propose alternative standpoints and far-reaching innovations. Ideas of capital controls, a global reserve system, a central bank, and a single global currency have been put forward and taken seriously. This receptivity, hopefully, extends to a questioning of the social harm resulting from unregulated global market forces.

Normative Results from the Perspective of Global Governance, or Why "Inhumane"? To some extent the preceding paragraphs explain why economic globalization, while clearly improving the material conditions of life for many millions, is still properly viewed as responsible for a dangerous momentum that is leading in the direction of "inhumane global governance." Three adverse normative effects will be stressed, although there are others.

---

[9] See Immanuel Wallerstein, *After Liberalism* (New York: New Press, 1995).

1. *Polarization and global apartheid:* It is undeniable that globalization has fostered widening income gaps, whether these are measured by class, region, or race.[10] The contrast between the economic conditions and political supremacy of whites in the Global North and blacks in the Global South as situated at the two ends of the poles gives plausibility to the allegation that world order as now constituted bears a significant resemblance to apartheid as it functioned in South Africa during its period of racist governance, although there are some important differences, as well. This inflammatory contention of global apartheid also pertains to the flows of refugees, drugs, nuclear and other ultrahazardous wastes, and weapons, with the white Global North being ever more vigilant gatekeepers while the black portions of the Global South become more and more looked upon as dumping grounds for whatever is unwanted by those who are prospering.

2. *Neglect of human suffering:* This dynamic of polarization, even if separated from its racial and civilizational implications, is also destructive of an ethos of human solidarity and community, as it rationalizes the distinction between winners and losers, treating the range of outcomes as justifiable results of market operations, and not occasions for remedial action. To the extent that the state becomes implicated in this outlook, there is a shift by stages from the compassionate to the cruel state, a social circumstance that recalls the earliest phases of the industrial revolution when market logic reigned supreme and worker abuse was rampant—conditions influentially depicted in Marx's critique of capitalism but also in the novelistic portrayals of such writers as Charles Dickens and Emile Zola. By neglecting vulnerable sectors of national, regional, and global society, globalization has the unintended side effect of creating forms of governance that are minimally motivated to act for the relief of human suffering.

3. *Decline of the global public good:* Globalization, as accompanied by neoliberal economic outlooks, relies on private-sector initiatives to uphold the claims of the public good. Such an orientation operates in various ways, including through disempowerment of the state by constraining its capacity to mobilize resources and undermining public confidence in the willingness of political leaders to engage in disin-

---

[10] For documentation see annual Human Development Reports of the 1990s of the United Nations Development Program.

terested action for the public good of their own citizenry.

One expression of this disposition is the current effort to "downsize" the United Nations, while making sure that the organization does not challenge the priorities of global capital. In this regard, to the extent that portions of the UN system earlier became oriented in favor of an overall ethos of global equalization and democratization, the organization was widely perceived in the North as an antagonist of globalization. Such a perception seemed confirmed by the tenor of UN-sponsored conferences on large global issues during the 1990s, when transnational social forces (women's groups, human rights and environmental NGOs, people's coalitions against Third World debt) challenged the market/statist coalition with ideas about governance that were premised on human solidarity, empathy with the marginalized, and a commitment to upholding the public good of all peoples in the world. The 1995 UN Social Summit in Copenhagen tried in its way to place the social claims of people on the global agenda, thereby seeming to reject the economistic world picture as the wave of the future.

Such events engendered a backlash within the UN, led by its dominant members and giving rise to reforms that would remove or drastically downgrade UN activities regarded as hostile to market forces. "Downsizing" was less about money than about this restructuring of the organization to satisfy the demands of the guardians of globalization, and to ensure that the United Nations operates primarily as a vehicle for neoliberal ideas and relies mainly on the market-oriented Bretton Woods institutions when it comes to economic matters. Beyond this, the UN is seen as potentially useful to implement global security in situations of the sort vividly prefigured in the Gulf War.

What has been said about the UN also applies to efforts to protect the global commons. Already at the 1992 Earth Summit in Rio, there was an effort to subordinate the environmental movement to the guiding role of the market, with a thinly disguised move to give business effective control over the way in which environmental standards were to be implemented and articulated, even nurturing the grand illusion that business could be trusted to heed market signals in a sufficiently timely fashion to provide adequate environmental protection with only minimal reliance on institutional governance.[11]

---

[11] Stephan Schmidheiny and The Business Council for Sustainable Development, *Chang-*

In effect, the social forces aligned to globalization were acting to ensure that governance structures responsive to the public good were contained, if not rolled back. This required challenging certain democratizing
tendencies that were moving the United Nations in an opposite direction
and giving the UN and other governance structures a stronger identity as
agents of the global public good, as delimited primarily by transnational
activist initiatives on behalf of the peoples of the world.[12] This confron-
tation can also be schematically simplified as an encounter between globalization-from-above (transnational corporations/banks/states) and globalization-from-below (transnational civic initiatives/women/indigenous
peoples/human rights/environmental activists).

A Summary Assessment. These negative developments confront us with
the likelihood that the third millennium will witness the fashioning of a
durable form of inhumane governance that poses severe risks of ecological and social catastrophe. Such an outcome is the latest, purest, and
most ambitious phase of the fundamental application of the Enlightenment Project to human affairs: the continuous stream of technological
innovations adapted to secularized political space to achieve the greatest
material advantage for the owners of capital goods. To be sure, important
contradictory tendencies are evident, as are progressive varieties of resistance, described here beneath the label of globalization-from-below, but
the political leverage of such forces is likely to remain limited to local
battlegrounds and the nuisance value of "global gadfly," unless such dis-
positions are strengthened by religious commitments and by support from
important sectors of the organized religious community. It is, in the end,
this possibility of a religiously grounded transnational movement for a just
world order that alone gives hope that humane global governance can
become a reality sometime early in the twenty-first century.

Why Religion? Openings and Regressions

Among the surprises of the last several decades has been a multifaceted

---

ing Course: A Global Business Perspective on Development and the Environment (1992); also
Richard Falk, "Environmental Protection in an Era of Globalization," Yearbook of International Environmental Law (New York: Oxford University Press, 1996), 3–25.
[12] See Daniel Archibugi, David Held, and others, Cosmopolitan Democracy (Cambridge,
UK: Polity, 1995); Held, Democracy and Global Governance (Stanford, California: Stanford University Press, 1995).

worldwide resurgence of religion as a potent force in human affairs, suggesting a relevance to the concerns of the public sphere as well as the private sphere. From the perspective of humane governance, this religious resurgence has a double-coded message: portending the hopeful possibility and necessity of transcending the constraints of economistic secularism, which has become the signature of a disturbing interface between late modernity and a nihilistic postmodernity, but also simultaneously disclosing a range of regressions in the form of extreme variants of inhumane governance that arguably, in certain instances, make the repudiation of secularism a terrifying descent into repression and violence.

On the negative side, I have in mind what religion has brought to such countries as Iran, Afghanistan, Algeria, and to some extent, India and Sudan in recent years, but also religious cults such as Heaven's Gate and Aum, which have seemingly been incubated in the midst of secularized contemporary modernity. Historically, then, it would appear that the outer limits of secularism are giving rise both to transformative possibilities that lead in the direction of humane governance, and to regressive potentialities that mix in various ways the most severe deficiencies of premodernity with the most frightening sequels to modernity.

It is, of course, difficult to give an account of this religious resurgence that adequately situates it within the framework of the present, but it seems closely related to an exhaustion of the creative capacity of the secular sensibility, especially as it is embodied in the political domain. It is within this domain, of course, that modernity has been so closely associated with the preeminence of the territorial sovereign state.[13] Such a preeminence has been virtually unchallenged in this century with respect to the organization of governance in international society. Even the innovations associated with the establishment of the League of Nations and the United Nations were deeply rooted in a statist system of world order, and mainly represented extensions of statism that perpetuated the allocation of governance capabilities to territorial sovereigns, with the management of the whole entrusted to geopolitical arrangements reflecting the special governance role of leading states—what political scientists have called "hegemonic actors." In other words, a statist world order,

---

[13] See Stephen Toulmin, *Cosmopolis* (New York: Free Press, 1990); R.B.J. Walker, *Inside/Outside: International Relations as Political Theory* (Cambridge University Press, 1993); Hendrick Spruyt, *The Sovereign State and Its Competitors* (Princeton, New Jersey: Princeton University Press, 1994).

although claiming to respect sovereign equality, was always based on a series of hierarchies, especially strong against weak, center versus periphery, Western or Eurocentric versus non-Western.[14] It also presupposed the availability of war as a geopolitical instrument, despite a certain lip service to restraints on the use of force.

But although this statist world order validated many patterns of abuse, either by way of immunizing domestic political order from scrutiny or through the interventionary and exploitative behavior of dominant states, it also gave rise to important normative ideas: limitations on the legitimate use of force, human rights, humanitarian intervention, criminal accountability of leaders. These normative ideas were often subordinated to geopolitical manipulations of various sorts, but they provided some encouragement for liberal perspectives that were imbued with the idea of progress in human affairs, and anticipated a gradual evolution of this statist world in the direction of peace and harmony. This approach to humane global governance was associated with the "democratic peace" hypothesis, which asserted that the spread of constitutional democracy brings an assurance of peaceful relations among democratic states, and thus if the whole world could be made to consist of nothing but democracies, then it would be a peaceful world, and if buttressed by an effective international law of human rights, it would fulfill the requirements of humane governance for the planet without requiring either disarmament or the centralization of political authority in international institutions.[15]

The world order difficulty with this approach to humane governance is that it neglects the social impact of economic globalization as enacted in an ideological climate shaped by neoliberalism. As earlier discussed, the overall cumulative impact of economic globalization, despite its positive aspects, is to predispose world order toward third-millennium forms of inhumane global governance. And what is more, the influence of the economistic world picture upon governing political elites and the mainstream media is such as to condition and constrain the action of states. States, as now oriented, lack the will and capacity to safeguard their own

---

[14] See Immanuel Wallerstein, *The Modern World-System* (New York: Academic Press, 3 vols., 1974, 1980, 1989); Samir Amin, *Eurocentrism* (New York: Monthly Review, 1989) and *Rereading the Postwar Period: An Intellectual Itinerary* (New York: Monthly Review, 1994).

[15] E.g., see Bruce Russett, *Controlling the Sword: The Democratic Governance of National Security* (Cambridge, Massachusetts: Harvard University Press, 1990), esp. pp. 119–145.

autonomy, much less to fashion the ingredients of a just and peaceful world order. In this regard, it is notable that it is political elites that are most enthusiastic about institutionalizing the economistic worldview at regional and global levels as seen, for instance, in the political controversies associated with the World Trade Organization, NAFTA, and Maastricht, despite the fact that such advocacy means that governance responsibilities are transferred from the level of the state to incipient supranational actors.

Expressing this interpretation in the context of this paper, then, it is a matter of understanding that the secular imagination is dependent upon the problem-solving capacities of the state, and that these have relinquished their initiative to the main arenas of economistic authority (that is, Davos, G-7, WTO, etc.). One possible development with relevance is the degree of territorial backlash that might conceivably reverse this political energy and restore the role of the state as an autonomous source of authority, becoming potentially capable of creating a new social equilibrium between human needs/public goods and the logic of the market.[16] In the nineteenth century a kind of social equilibrium emerged out of the backlash against market-led industrialization, partly as an effort to coopt or at least moderate working-class discontent. It was essentially a secular reaction that had its revolutionary expression in the Communist movement spearheaded by Marxism/Leninism/Maoism, which was avowedly atheistic and aggressively antireligious, partly attributing acquiescence to an unjust social order to the otherworldliness of religious teaching and doctrine.

Of course, there was an important insight in the assault on the role of religion, as religious institutions were generally aligned with ruling elites, and even otherwise radical religious leaders (e.g., Luther, Calvin) were at the same time hostile to the claims of the poor and of underclasses generally. But beneath this social line of criticism was the more fundamental spirit of modernity, with its search for truth in the realms of secular knowledge, illustrated here by the Marxist insistence that its interpretations were based exclusively on social laws and that the resulting normative outlook was one of "*scientific* socialism," as contrasted with "utopian socialism," which was scorned. That is, the acute social tensions of the early industrial revolution were addressed within the frame of modernity

---

[16] This argument is developed in Richard Falk, "Siege of State: Will Globalization Win Out?" *International Affairs* (Vol. 73, No. I, January 1997), pp. 123–136.

and secularism, relegating religion to positions of either irrelevance or antagonist.

In the present setting, revisioning of governance is by way of the market, and is to some extent reinforced by the self-organizing, globalist ethos of the digitized sensibility that shapes the Internet world picture; it is generally opposed to the social functions of government, to public goods, and to any deliberate effort to achieve humane governance. In opposition is the transnational array of networks, coalitions, associations, and initiatives that has been earlier labeled as "globalization-from-below."[17] It is my contention that this early effort to construct a democratic global civil society is informed by religious inspiration, and if it is to move from the margins of political reality to challenge entrenched constellations of power in a more serious way, it will have to acquire some of the characteristics and identity of a religious movement, including building connections with the emancipatory aspects of the great world religions.[18] Without religious identity, prospects for global humane governance are without any social or political foundation; and more importantly, they are without the spiritual character that can mobilize and motivate on a basis that is far more powerful than what the market, secular reason, and varieties of nationalism have to offer.

What is meant by religion here requires considerable clarification in the course of constructing a global civil society and recasting the meaning of citizenship and democratic practice.[19] It is evident that religion cannot be reduced to any single religious tradition, although it can draw strength from the collaborative support of the various traditions, and that some aspects of certain religious traditions are antithetical, especially claims of being "the chosen people" or the exclusive or superior instruments of a divine or sacred design for human affairs, or the enactment of some apocalyptic scenario for ascent to a higher form of existence than what is

---

[17] For further clarification see Paul Wapner, *Environmental Activism and World Civic Politics* (Albany, New York: SUNY Press, 1996); Ronnie D. Lipschutz, *Global Civil Society & Global Environmental Governance* (Albany, New York: SUNY Press, 1996); Richard Falk, *Explorations at the Edge of Time: The Prospects for World Order* (Philadelphia, Pennsylvania: Temple University Press, 1992).

[18] The work of Hans Küng has moved in this direction in recent years. See *Global Responsibility: In Search of a New World Ethic* (New York: Crossroads, 1991).

[19] For a closely comparable revisioning of religious consciousness, see the important book by Charlene Spretnak, *The Resurgence of the Real: Body, Nature, and Place in a Hypermodern World* (Reading, Pennsylvania: Addison-Wesley, 1997).

offered on earth. Such aspects of the overall religious heritage may authentically engage the lives and sensibilities of persons of genuine faith, but they offer nothing constructive in relation to the struggle to create patterns of humane global governance for all the peoples on earth.

From Religion—What?

Having identified forms of religious expression inimical to the quest for humane governance, let us now consider the potentially helpful contributions of religion. In setting forth these contributions, it is necessary that we allow considerable cultural space for a wide spectrum of interpretations of specific implications, and that we acknowledge that humanist styles of thought are also capable of reaching parallel points of reference but lack the foundations of religion in the collective memories and experiences of peoples of varied backgrounds to arouse widespread adherence. The relevance of religion cannot be separated from its persistence in human consciousness and its role throughout history in the social construction of human nature. Religion is understood here as encompassing both the teachings and beliefs of organized religion and all spiritual outlooks that interpret the meaning of life by reference to faith in and commitment to that which cannot be explained by empirical science or sensory observation, and is usually associated with an acceptance of the reality of the divine, the sacred, the transcendent, the ultimate.

It is also necessary to admit that the account of religious relevance offered here is intended only to be suggestive, and is designed mainly to stimulate discussion, reflection, and dialogue on the positive roles of religion in the context of a global democratic movement for humane governance. To avoid any possible confusion about the meaning of this disclaimer, a series of contributions by religion will be identified and listed, without elaboration, and absent any consideration of intercivilizational variations:

- *Taking suffering seriously:* the religious impulse is strongly associated with an acknowledgment of "the last man (or woman)," the lowliest class, caste, and race, and a central commitment to lift up those who suffer acutely.

- *Civilizational resonance:* whereas secular transformative thought tends to appeal mainly to alienated intellectuals, religious revolutionary language and aspirations have deep roots in popular culture, and possesses great mobilizing potential.

- *An ethos of solidarity*: closely related is the unitive feature of religious consciousness, the oneness of the human family, giving rise to an ethos of human solidarity, and with it the sense of both the wholeness of human experience and the dignity of the individual.

- *Normative horizons*: responding to suffering and affirming human solidarity imply a belief in normative horizons that define human potentialities in a manner that contradicts present conditions, with their neglect of many forms of acute human suffering and their tendency to elevate the claims of the part or fragment over those of the whole.

- *Faith and power*: a belief in the transformative capacities of an idea that is sustained by spiritual energy, and hence is receptive to nonviolent forms of struggle and sacrifice, thereby challenging more materialist views of human history as shaped primarily by warfare and command over military technology.

- *Limits*: a profound humility in relation to human thought and action that is sensitive to human fallibility, if not sin and evil, and appreciates the limited capacity of the inquiring mind to grasp the fullness of reality or to claim the truthfulness and correctness of any particular interpretation of what needs to be done in the world, thereby remaining open at all stages to dialogue with strangers and apparent adversaries that can serve to correct mistakes.

- *Identity*: a realization that identity can emerge from many sources, and that it is existentially being reshaped by overlapping appeals to aspects of human nature and experience, but that the era of exclusive subjection to the expectations of loyalty to the state is being surpassed both by various modes of reexperiencing the deepening reality of the whole and by the increasing sense of the yet unfulfilled future—an emphasis that can be highlighted by replacing the idea of "citizen" with that of "citizen pilgrim," a distinctly religious understanding of essential political identity by reference to a spiritual journey that is unseen and unlikely to be completed with the span of this lifetime, but whose value is an object of intense faith.

- *Reconciliation*: the realization that diverse ways of knowing are alternative means of coping with the effects of human finitude and the impingement of limits, thereby clearing away obstacles to a needed reconciliation of science, reason, and spirituality.

Religion and Humane Global Governance:
A Concluding Observation

The perspective that has been developed here is that a religious/spiritual orientation needs to inform the energies of globalization-from-below if it is to have any serious prospect of launching a political project that offers an alternative to that being foreshadowed and actualized by the largely economistic forces associated with globalization-from-above. It is not a matter of repudiating state or market, but of insisting that these organizing arenas of authority and influence be spiritualized in accordance with the generalized attributes of religion. But it is also not expecting a miraculous rescue from above (*deus ex machina*), whether in the form of a sudden embrace of world government or the emergence of regional institutions and the United Nations as political actors no longer constrained by geopolitics and the reigning neoliberal world picture.

Humane global governance will only occur as the outcome of political struggle, and in this sense is similar to past efforts to overcome slavery, colonialism, apartheid. Each of these struggles was substantially inspired by direct and indirect religious thought of the sort proposed here. Each undertaking seemed "impossible" at its point of origin, given the array of social forces and the fixed beliefs affirmed by the conventional wisdom of the day to validate support for inhumane practices. In the recent past we have experienced the struggles against oppression carried on by the peoples of Eastern Europe and the Soviet Union, of many countries in Asia, of the victims of apartheid in South Africa. They have enjoyed limited or overall success against the historical odds.

We do not know enough to conclude pessimistically that humane global governance is an impossibility. We do know enough to understand that such an outcome, if it occurs, will not come about spontaneously or without anguishing struggles, and that given the historical ascendancy of market forces and the widespread acceptance of the economistic world picture, an alternative orientation can only hope to emerge if nurtured by religious energies creatively adapted to the specific problems and concerns that exist at all levels of social reality.

The Multireligious Engagement of Civil Society: The Need for Bilingualism

William Vendley

Introduction

Three sets of sweeping tasks face the global community at the close of the twentieth century. First, there is the challenge of *human survival*: the issues of population, hunger and health, energy and environment. Second, there is the fundamental task of *building a global community* that truly functions as such and that, while embracing pluralism, provides sufficient shared meanings and values to enable its members to arrive at consensus on matters of common concern. Third, there is the need to *end wars* and reduce the threat of increasingly dangerous rivalries in a post-cold-war world destabilized by arms proliferation and economic pressures. Armed conflicts and wars are not only cruelly destructive, but they sap desperately needed human and financial resources from the challenges of human survival and global cooperation for the common weal. Meeting these challenges will require cooperation among highly diverse communities and moral leadership on a level unprecedented in human history. Yet the inescapable need for cooperation comes at a time of increasingly militant manifestations of ethnic and religious nationalism and of social fragmentation around the world.

These three sets of tasks raise the question of political order. While issues within each of the sets can and indeed must at times be addressed piecemeal, each set in its own way points to the need for a form of political order that can serve the common good by being responsive both to the major challenges of our time and the deepest memories of what it means to be a human being in community. Religious visions are typically "utopian" in character; they proffer normative notions of personal and communal fulfillment. If the fact of religious pluralism bars the adoption of one community's utopian vision as the basis for political order, what are the possibilities for discerning shared normative moral commitments among the world's religions and relating these shared commitments to questions of political order?

What, then, is the role that religious cooperation can serve in bringing forth a new form of political order? The question is large and perhaps best clarified with a series of questions dealing with political theory, the history and current practice of religion, and international instruments related to political order.

Questions of Political Theory

- In what ways did the Enlightenment solution(s) privatize ranges of human experience relevant to the establishment of political order? Or more positively, how can religious meanings be mediated in non-sectarian ways toward the building up of "non-reductive," "just" political order in pluralistic society?

- How does the tension between (1) a resurgent religious nationalism and (2) the forces which serve to de-center the nation-state impact on the emergence of political order?

- What are the heuristic features of a political order open to (1) the questions of the Enlightenment, (2) being informed by the levels of meaning foundational to religious communities, and alert to (3) the transnational forces which are de-centering the nation-state?

Questions to Religious Traditions

- How have religions *de facto* related their foundational meanings to notions of political order? What are the forms/models by which religious meanings have been related to political order?

- How can central meanings foundational to specific religious traditions be re-imagined in their relevance to the building up of political order in ways which are both faithful to historical traditions and public in manner, but nonsectarian?

- Can a convergence be discerned among the central meanings of the major religious traditions in their relevance to creating nonsectarian moral political order? How can these shared meanings be mediated as a constructive force in the development of political order?

Questions of International Instruments

- What is the at least implicit "horizon of meaning" of existing international instruments of political order, e.g., the United Nations and agencies such as the World Bank? What "reductive" features of existing instruments can be disclosed by relating them to the desired heuristic model of political order?

- What new kinds of international instruments need to be envisaged to serve the development of non-reductive notions of political order, alert to the convergence of the foundational meanings among religious communities and the pressures that are de-centering the nation-state?

Answering these types of questions necessarily goes far beyond the scope of this small essay. We limit ourselves to proposing the modest thesis that religious communities will increasingly need to speak two distinct forms of language if they are going to cooperate on matters of common concern, including those that pertain to political order. Indeed, even prosecuting the above types of questions can be shown to require the ability to differentiate between two distinct modes of religious discourse.

How, then, can an attention to language assist people with different religious histories and convictions to cooperate on matters of ultimate concern such as the concern for political order, precisely as religiously committed persons?

This essay is based on two convictions. The first is that the world's many religions differ in important ways in their histories, teachings, and practices. A careful and searching examination of religions reveals their distinctive characteristics. Even apparent similarities among religions often turn out, upon close examination, to mask major differences which remain highly important to their respective believers and thus need to be frankly admitted. In this essay I want to acknowledge the differences of the world's religions by suggesting that each particular religion can usefully be described as having its own "primary language." Each primary language can be understood to be related to a particular religion's "originating experience" and to be constituted by a central set of "stories" which together make up an overarching "narrative."[1] This narrative grounds a dynamic set of religiously ordered meanings and values that function within a horizon of ultimate concern or care. Understanding each religion in terms of its primary language can help us appreciate each religion's distinctive character and the roots of its moral sensitivities.

The second conviction upon which this essay is based is that multireligious cooperation on issues of shared concern can be facilitated by the use of what I will call a "secondary language."[2] By this I intend a form of secular discourse which, though not religiously sectarian in character, can nevertheless be employed by diverse religious communities to express with at least some degree of adequacy the moral concerns which are rooted in their respective primary languages.

My thesis is that distinguishing primary and secondary language can facilitate multireligious cooperation on issues of shared concern and simultaneously avoid syncretistic[3] tendencies that do not respect the real differences of religions and their respective primary languages. If my thesis is correct, the distinction between primary and secondary languages should assist different religious communities to cooperate with one another when they attempt to face the moral dilemmas, including the need for change in political order, that define our present time in history.

The Narrative Structure of Religion Understood as Primary Language

"We tell ourselves stories in order to live," writes Joan Didion.[4] Human life is somehow given its most elemental identity by story or narrative. "For we dream in narrative, daydream in narrative, remember, anticipate, hope, despair, believe, doubt, plan, revise, criticize, construct, gossip,

---

[1] Our use of the words "story" and "narrative" in this essay in no way suggests that religious stories or narratives are not true. As noted above, however, we are prescinding from the truth claims of religions and of their founding stories or narratives.

[2] It should be noted that what we are describing as a secondary language for religious believers can be for nonreligious secular persons a form of primary language.

[3] From the nineteenth century on, the term "syncretism" has chiefly been used in comparative religion to mean the fusion or blending of different conceptions of the divine.

[4] Joan Didion, *The White Album* (New York: Simon & Schuster, 1979), p. 11.

learn, hate, and love by narrative," says Barbara Hady.[5] It is a story or narrative structure which provides overarching coherence to the diversity of experience and which grounds the set of meanings and values by which people can coherently live. All things human refer to a narrative story of some kind.[6] Both individuals and—one must especially stress—the communities that form them are shaped in a most foundational and elemental way by narrative.

What is true of human groups generally is also the case with religious communities. Religious communities are organized around central stories and narratives. These narratives can be mediated or transmitted in a variety of ways. They can be passed on orally, by means of sacred texts, through learned commentaries or elaborate and penetrating systems of thought based upon sacred texts, through rituals or forms of prayer and meditation, and by a variety of other carriers of meaning such as music, song, and dance. For example, for the Christian the central narratives are the biblical texts. There are many different stories in the Bible, but they combine into an overarching narrative of God's redemption of history. But in Christianity this overarching narrative is "filled out" by the myriad expressions of its meaning which, collectively and across time, have attempted to offer an expression of the meaning of God's relationship with history consistent with the vision of the Scriptures. Like Christianity, each religion has its own set of stories which combine into an overarching narrative that provides the deepest base and fertile foundation of the particular religion's interpretations of reality. Importantly, religious narratives can be recognized as founding a particular religious tradition's understanding of ethical responsibility and providing its followers with norms and principles for a requisite moral stance in life.

---

[5] Barbara Hady, quoted in Wicker, The Story-Shaped World: Fiction and Metaphysics: Some Variations on a Theme (Notre Dame, Indiana: University of Notre Dame Press, 1975), p. 4. The writer first encountered this quote in Charles V. Gerkin, Widening the Horizons: Pastoral Responses to a Fragmented Society (Philadelphia: Westminster Press, 1986), p. 29. Gerkin's book explores the importance of narrative for Pastoral Theology. I wish to acknowledge the positive impact of Gerkin's work on my attempt to reflect on the influence of narrative on multireligious cooperation.

[6] This is true, in its own way, even for "apophatic" or image-less religious experience, which is often described as being beyond language. For as soon as one attempts to interpret this experience—even, for example, to say that it was an image-less experience of God—one has "fallen back" into the story or narratives which give meaning to the word "God."

The deep stories which combine into an organizing or overarching narrative of a given religion, however they are understood by a particular religious tradition, I wish to designate as *primary language*—the language which defines a religious community. Thus each religious community has its own primary language or interpretations of primary language. The stories or narratives which make up a given primary language may be understood to be the actual Word of God or some other manifestation or mediation of religious meaning. In any case, primary religious language constitutes the core of the living memory of a religious community; it offers the grammar of identity; it provides for the possibility of shared experience and a shared interpretation of experience; it installs a community of believers in a shared moral space; and it provides a fertile foundation for the community's passage through time, orienting it to the past, present, and future.[7]

The primary languages of the world's religions are different. Two brief examples can make this quite evident. First, in orienting their believers in time, a given religious primary language typically asks "whence" a people have come and "whither" they are going. For example, Christians understand the "whence" as being "created" by God *ex nihilo*, and the "whither" as a passage through death, prefigured in baptism, to a resurrected life in God. Very different answers to these questions would be offered by a Hindu, Buddhist, Zoroastrian, or believer in any indigenous religion.

Second, religious primary languages virtually always employ some variation of two related concepts: pathology and soteriology. I am not suggesting that these terms are used in every primary religious language; indeed, the word "soteriology," which refers to the mystery of salvation, is a Christian theological term. However, I am suggesting that virtually all primary religious languages engage in some sort of questioning about what is (or went) wrong with the present state of affairs (pathology) and by what religious means the currently disordered state of affairs shall be remedied (soteriology).

Questions of pathology and soteriology go to the heart of primary religious languages. Hindu, Buddhist, Zoroastrian, indigenous and other religions' stories and narratives which raise questions of pathology and soteriology are remarkable for their profundity, fecundity, and differences.

---

[7] Paul Ricoeur notes that our experience of time has a narrative structure. We experience time as a story with a past, a present, and a future. See Paul Ricoeur, *Time and Narrative*, Vol. 1 (Chicago: University of Chicago Press, 1984), p. 52.

If I am at pains to underline the differences of religious primary language, it is because primary language founds a given religion's moral framework and ethical codes. Underlining the differences of primary languages brings a sharper focus to our central question: how can different religions really collaborate when their primary languages and corresponding moral frameworks and ethical codes vary so greatly? As another step toward an answer, let us look at the way religious communities respond to new ethical problems or crises, particularly in today's situation of religious and secular pluralism.

Religions' Responses to New Moral Crises: Speaking Out in Primary and Secondary Language

What goes on within a religious community, within its collective memory, to prepare it to respond to a new crisis in a way that is consistent with the deepest meanings and values of its tradition? What really happens, for example, when a religious community allows itself to confront the fact that 14 million children die needlessly every year, or that our present models of development imperil the natural world and therefore ourselves with incalculable harm? What happens when morally committed religious people try to confront the prospect of nuclear conflict, or the more foundational task of constructing a new political order?

I would like to suggest that religious communities respond by engaging in two highly creative types of activities.[8] On the one hand, they are driven back into the roots of their own histories, back to their central religious stories. The new experience, if it is to be grasped by a given religious community, needs to be interpreted in relationship to that community's primary language. Perhaps not all stories in the primary language appear immediately helpful in the sense that they can be readily connected with the new problem at hand. The community is driven back in search of a "usable past." What story, what chapter of a story, what teachings or practices embodied in at least some episode of the overarching narrative of a particular tradition can help orient contemporary believers before the new situation they face? This task of "turning back"

---

[8] These two types of activities are not necessarily distinguished by all religious communities in accord with our analysis. However, attention to the actual performances of religious communities indicates that they engage in two such activities, however interpreted, to at least a limited degree, if they are functioning in relationship to contemporary problems in any fashion at all.

to listen to or "hear" the narratives of a religious tradition from the perspective of a new problem or situation is itself a highly creative activity. The religious community has to work out a connection, to discover a correlation, between the religious narrative and a new situation.[9]

On the other hand, when confronted with a new challenge, each religious community must also move forward. It has to try to "say anew" what it has "heard" of the tradition in relationship to the new crisis being faced. This hearing of tradition and saying anew what one has heard are not at all the same thing. To really say anew what it means to be a Buddhist, Hindu, Jew, Christian, Muslim, or member of another religion in relationship to a new challenge requires a dynamically creative set of acts which orient believers affectively, cognitively, morally, and spiritually before the new crisis. By "saying anew" we mean not just words, but the total religious response in words and actions which addresses the many dimensions of the problem being faced.

How, then, does a religious community say anew what it means to be faithfully religious when confronting a new and grave crisis? I would suggest that there are two fundamental ways. The two ways correspond to two types of language: primary language and secondary language.

Speaking in Primary Language

Members of religious communities speak among themselves. Religious primary language is employed again and again to say anew what it means to be a religious believer within one's own circle of believers. For example, Christians regularly speak among themselves with the rich symbolic language of their faith about the meaning and moral demands of contemporary events. Using the primary speech of Christianity, they enjoy a shared access to all the stories which make up the complex narrative of the Christian religion. Symbols of pathology and soteriology are creatively employed to interpret the significance of contemporary challenges. This conversation takes place in the minds and hearts of individual Christians whenever they reflect on what their faith means to them in a given situa-

---

[9] The fact that religious communities are challenged to search for a usable past—something within their collective store of narrative which connects with a current challenge—offers a clue as to how religions can subtly change their major foci over time. What may previously have been a comparatively minor story in a tradition can, due to its relevance to a major historical challenge, begin to assume an ever-greater relative importance within the tradition.

tion; it is given a particular focus every Sunday in churches in various forms of reflection and worship; it is also extended in seminaries and special schools, and further still by means of an ever-expanding literature of theology and spirituality. In turn, this extended Christian conversation bears fruit by clarifying Christians' moral sensibilities and guiding them into responsible forms of action precisely as Christians. Analogous activities occur within other religious traditions insofar as they say anew what it means to be believers with their own unique primary languages in relationship to contemporary issues.

On the one hand, the great strength of saying anew one's identity in one's primary language is the wealth of primary language. The extraordinary fecundity of primary language can be seen in its ability to secure continually the religious identities of believers and reorient them morally in the constantly changing vicissitudes of history. On the other hand, speaking in primary speech, for all of its richness, limits one for the most part to the circle of believers who share the same language. Primary language is not a language for multireligious cooperation.

Speaking in Secondary Language

Today religious communities do not restrict the expressions of their ultimate concern to their own members. Under the pressures of religious and secular forms of pluralism, and through the engagement of urgent issues involving more than a single community, representatives of religious communities are now learning to speak a secondary language of moral care beyond their particular circle of believers. Religions now feel compelled by their own sense of the truth and universal relevance of their central stories to "speak their concerns" in the public square by translating, or better transposing, the ethical sensibilities which are rooted in their respective primary languages into a secondary language. This secondary language is the language increasingly shared by today's modern pluralistic societies. It is the language currently used by modern governmental institutions, public schools, and nightly news programs. It varies, no doubt, from country to country, but is becoming increasingly universal. It serves, for example, as the language of international organizations such as the United Nations, the Red Cross, or Amnesty International. It can be banal or express such elevated notions as universal human rights. In a word, it is "secular" language.

There has been a long tradition in some societies and religious communities of notions of natural law, which attempt to give expression to an intelligible moral sphere available to human intelligence without the direct assistance of religion. This intelligible moral sphere has been recognized as a basis for the organization of a nonsectarian understanding of political order. Today, however, there is no widely shared consensus about natural law. In its stead, the notion of human rights as set forth in international declarations and covenants provides a slender but essential area of public social/moral consensus expressed in secular language. And increasingly the world's religions are learning to root the notions of human rights in their own rich primary languages.

These advances in correlating the tradition(s) of human rights with religious traditions suggest the need for analogous creative advances around questions of political order. More specifically, each religious community is challenged to re-imagine its central meanings in their relevance to the building up of political order, and to re-express these meanings in public terms. Using secondary language as a medium, the search for convergence among the central meanings of religious traditions in their relevance to nonsectarian political order can go forward.

Religions, however, cannot simply "adopt" existing secular language as an automatically adequate carrier of their deepest meanings. Religions must be creative in their use of secular language. Secular language must always be challenged by religions to become ever more morally adequate, without at the same time becoming sectarian. Even the word "secular" has its dangers: all too often it is understood to intend a social sphere bereft of religious meaning. In that derelict reading of the term, the public square can easily be interpreted as having nothing to do with religious meanings and values. In turn, religious convictions will easily be misunderstood as a private, individual affair having nothing to do with public life and its attendant moral issues. The speeches of Martin Luther King, Jr., offer an instructive example of the religious employment of secular language. King successfully transposed his Christian convictions regarding the dignity of all persons into a form of nonsectarian public speech addressed to all Americans by utilizing the secular concept of civil rights.

There is an enormous advantage for religious communities in being able to speak a secondary secular language. First, when different religious communities express their ultimate senses of caring through the employment of secondary secular language, they can often discern important areas of convergence of moral concern. Indeed, a shared secondary language artfully employed by different religious communities can provide a medium to clarify agreements on matters of moral concern and a basis for cooperative action. Of equal importance, a shared secondary language also allows different religious communities to clarify where they disagree on moral issues. With a shared secondary language, religious communities are given the freedom to agree on some issues and disagree on others without violating the religiously normative character of their respective primary languages.[10] Secondary language provides a medium for multi-religious cooperation which avoids the dangers of conflating different primary religious languages.

The Perdurable Importance of Both Religious Languages

Both primary and secondary languages will remain of major importance for religious communities. Neither can be collapsed into the other without impoverishing a religious community's ability to know and act upon its deepest possibilities for care in today's pluralistic world.

What are the limits of secondary language? From the religious point of view, why does secondary language remain perpetually in need of the more primordial primary language? Why are both primary and secondary forms of religious language necessary today?

Contemporary secondary secular language is a composite language. It has been composed by highly diverse and often competing narratives.[11] Importantly, there is no one overarching narrative to secular language except perhaps the intentional disestablishment of any particular primary religious language as a privileged, state-sanctioned public language. Secular language has no central narrative, no single organizing plot. For example, Robert N. Bellah has discerned major competing secular narratives operative in the United States.[12] People in American society, Bellah

---

[10] More generally, the religious employment of secondary language provides the key to understanding how communal beliefs, be they religious or nonreligious, should be related to public life in secular societies. The use of secondary public language allows religious or other ideological communities to express their concerns in the public square side by side with other men and women of goodwill, regardless of their particular religious or ideological convictions.

[11] Primary languages are also typically composed of many sub-narratives. However, in primary languages these sub-narratives, even when they are seen as "competing" with one another in some way, are either components of, or at least subsist in the presence of, an overarching narrative.

[12] See, for example, Bellah et al., Habits of the Heart: Individualism and Commitment in

suggests, are often quite unaware of the fact that they are trying to live by diverse and often competing secular narratives. As a result, people continuously switch back and forth through the course of a day between the strands of the different narratives underlying what we have, in this essay, all too innocently named secular secondary language. This "makes for not only a fragmentation of language worlds among members of a social context but also for fragmentation within the day-to-day experience of the individual."[13] This particular liability of secular language shows up with particular force when the "plotless" secular language becomes a person's form of primary language.

Again, Joan Didion is instructive. She writes:

> We interpret what we see, select the most workable of the multiple choices. We live entirely...by the imposition of a narrative line upon disparate images, by the "ideas" with which we have learned to freeze the shifting phantasmagoria which is our actual experience.[14]

Didion's perceptive lines affirm the importance of narrative in the perception and interpretation of experience and even in the construction of our lives. But when read more deeply with respect to the way narrative contributes to the formation of a coherent self, Didion's lines can be profoundly disturbing. Attend to her words with care: is reality really a matter of multiple, seemingly arbitrary choices as secular language would suggest? Do we really just arbitrarily "impose" a narrative line on an otherwise shifting and incoherent phantasmagoria of experience? Or, alternatively, do the religious depths of reality perhaps make a claim upon us; do they summon us to an ultimate caring and moral responsibility through primary religious language? For example, are the injunctions "Thou shalt not kill" and "Love your neighbor as yourself" merely arbitrary? Religious primary language is not a matter of multiple choice, nor a matter of the arbitrary imposition of a narrative line; rather it is the of-

---

American Life (Berkeley: University of California Press, 1985), where Republicanism and three different forms of Individualism (Expressive, Utilitarian, and Radical) are discerned as competing narratives in American society. One would also have to add to Bellah's analysis the enormous impact of scientific positivism as a seedbed for additional forms of competing narratives in American life.

[13] Gerkin, *Widening the Horizons*, p. 15.

[14] Didion, *The White Album*, p. 11. The writer wishes to acknowledge gratefully David Toolin's brilliant, if somewhat eccentric, *Facing West from California's Shores* (New York: Crossroad Press, 1987) for both this and the following quotation from Joan Didion and for his insight into their significance in relationship to secularity.

fering of a particularly powerful form of narrative line, one that gives speech to different communities' understandings of the "call" of the divine on the human, however differently the divine and the call may be experienced and interpreted. Didion continues:

> I was supposed to have a script, and I had mislaid it. I was supposed to hear cues, and no longer did. I was meant to know the plot, but all I knew was what I saw: flash pictures in variable sequence, images with no "meaning" beyond their temporary arrangement, not a movie but a cutting-room experience....I wanted still to believe in the narrative's intelligibility, but to know that one could change the sense with every cut was to begin to perceive the experience as rather more electrical than ethical.[15]

Didion's remarkable lines illustrate the dangerously frail character of secondary secular language. First, the self is described in a haunting image as "a cutting-room experience." It is not coherently formed because secondary secular language taken as a primary language cannot offer the self a coherent and overarching narrative. Second, and correlative to the fragmented self, reality is experienced as "rather more electrical than ethical." Secular language is dangerously weak in both its capacity to form a coherent community of selves and assisting them to sustain an ethical stance through the vicissitudes of history. These possibilities are, of course, precisely the strengths of primary religious language. Discourse with both forms of language will, I suggest, be required if we are to have diverse religious communities composed of well-formed and coherent members with durable moral sensibilities and, at the same time, find a medium for their collaboration in facing the global problems of our day.

---

[15] Didion, *The White Album*, p. 13.

Religion and...

Robert Traer

R eligion and..."—you name it, there is probably a program or conference being held this year about it. Religion and world order,
religion and human rights, religion and peace, religion and....
Perhaps this is a way of recognizing the importance of religion in achieving world order, human rights, peace, and so forth; on the other hand, it
might also be a way of suggesting that religion is a barrier to the great
causes of our time. In most cases, it seems both attitudes are present.
"Religion and..." implies a need to separate the nourishing wheat from
the useless chaff of religion.

"Religion and..." programs and titles reflect the perception that religion will either help or hinder us in achieving a better world (order,
human rights, peace, etc.). Religion obviously contributes to conflict in
the world in many contexts; moreover, the truth claims of religious traditions have long divided the world's peoples. But might religion also offer
ways of overcoming these divisions? Usually "religion and..." programs
assume so.

It would seem, therefore, that "religion and..." programs think of
religion as a potential resource for achieving whatever human goal is to
be pursued. This is such an obvious observation that one may wonder
what is to be achieved by making it. But I wish to suggest that thinking
about religion in this way may make it more difficult to achieve the desired outcomes for which religion is identified as a resource. That is, understanding religion as a resource, for the attainment of world order,
human rights, and peace, may undermine the real contribution which
religious life can make in the creation of a more humane world.

Religion as Resource

If we think of religion as a resource, then we believe that religious teachings and institutional programs are important insofar as they help in creating a better world. It may seem that religious life has no value in itself. In this way of seeing the world, religion is not so much a part of who we are, but is only of value to us to the extent that it contributes to achieving our chosen world.

Those who see religion as a resource for a better world also see that religion can make the world worse. Thus they seek to extract from religious teachings the insights they find useful and even inspiring, leaving the rest behind. Publications that collect religious statements from the world's scriptures about one good idea or another are commonplace. We know from these books that religious traditions contain teachings in support of peace, justice, ecology, etc. Of course, we also know (from our experience) that many of those who claim to follow these religious teachings do not live up to them. Religious communities fall far short of the summaries of their religious teachings that we make in order to show the world (particularly its religious members) how they should live. (We may also know that not all religious teachings are so generous and helpful as those quoted in "religion and…" anthologies.)

Religious leaders who advocate religious teachings in support of a better world are an additional resource. Enlisting them in our "religion and…" programs is also a form of resource utilization. We add their names to our statements in order to show others that our position has authority behind it. Furthermore, we organize cooperative activities for religious organizations in order to demonstrate that there is institutional support for building a better world, although in many places religious conflicts continue to prevent peace and the realization of human rights.

This is all so commonplace that it may seem silly to summarize it and churlish to question it. Yet, in this way of thinking and acting, there is a view of religion that is basically exploitative. "Religion and…" programs are based on the premise that religion may be useful. Such a view of religion reflects the utilitarian view of all reality, which identifies the earth and its cultures as means of attaining the good life. As this attitude has proven to be devastating for the earth and many of its peoples, we might wonder about adopting it in our quest for a better world.

Religion as Source

Is there any alternative? We are so accustomed to thinking in utilitarian categories that we can hardly suppose there is any other way of understanding religion. May we not, however, conceive of religion as a source rather than a resource? What if we saw religious experience as shaping who we are, as already ordering the world, and not merely as a possible resource for a better world? What if we understood our traditions and communities of faith as defining a world in which there is divine purpose as well as human problems and promise?

In this perspective, a world community that includes religious communities cannot be "ordered" apart from the meanings that these communities give to the "world." And if by religion we mean the teachings and activities of religious communities, then surely world order is not only a way of utilizing these communities to preserve peace and promote justice, but is also a means of protecting the fundamental rights of these communities to their way of life. To see religion in this way is at least to empathize with those for whom religious faith and life are one.

Of course, those who see the world as religious use different ideas, like God or karma or *dharma*, to describe the world in which they live. Such differences are why we refer to the religious traditions of the world, when we are forced to explain what we really mean by religion. Moreover, the fact that there are many different religious traditions seems to justify the notion of religion as a resource, because obviously no one religion can provide the vision of order required by a world with many religious traditions. It would seem then that to obtain the support of religious people and institutions for a better world, we would be inclined to embrace only ideas and practical assistance from each religion that are acceptable to the others.

Such an approach to a more peaceful world order that protects human rights may seek to distill the essentials from each religious tradition and express these as the common wisdom of humanity and the basis for a better world. But distillation tends to leave a residue, the waste of the refining process. As the exploitation of natural resources has had a devastating impact on the nature from which they have been extracted, we should expect that extracting wisdom from religious traditions may harm the religious communities that have cherished this wisdom.

Consider what it may mean for a Christian when the teachings of Jesus about loving one's neighbor are lifted from the tradition, but the commandment to love God is left behind and thus rejected. For the Christian, these two commandments are inseparable because God and humanity are joined in Jesus the Christ. To accept the one command-ment and not the other is to misunderstand and fall prey to the illusion that, with good intentions, one can simply extend goodwill to all others.

Similarly, what might it mean for a Muslim to hear that others, who want to incorporate into their universal wisdom the Islamic notion that God is merciful, reject the teaching of God's judgment? For the Muslim, the teachings of divine mercy and judgment cannot be separated, for each informs and shapes the understanding of the other, and both ex-press the divine will. To affirm mercy without judgment is to reject the call to submission that God requires and that is necessary not only for personal salvation, but for justice in the world.

It should not be surprising, therefore, that some Christians and Mus-lims have become defensive about attempts to extract from their teach-ings nuggets of wisdom that are then amalgamated with other meanings to support certain notions of a better world.

Native Americans have helped us see the exploitation of nature as a form of spiritual death. Can we also see that our use of religious traditions may lead people of faith to resist our well-intentioned efforts, in a desper-ate effort to preserve their way of life? Surely, if we are honest, we must admit that the use of religion as a resource is an attack on religious com-munities that embrace their religious faith as their source of life and not as a resource to be used for some other purpose.

I use the word "religion" here reluctantly, because those for whom religious experience is the source of their life and world do not speak about their experience and their faith in such an abstract and general way. For Christians, it is God in Jesus the Christ who saves. For Muslims, it is the one God, Allah, who demands obedience from those who would be saved. For Jews, it is keeping the covenant with the one God, whose name is so sacred that it cannot be spoken, that is saving. For Buddhists, it is being awake to the Buddha nature within each person that offers liberation from the world of suffering.

For none of these is "religion" saving. For all, salvation comes through faith, but faith that takes a variety of forms. And these forms of faith cannot be expressed apart from specific beliefs and practices that form the life of religious communities in different places and times. For religious persons, their experience within their community of faith is saving and a source both of who they are and the world in which they are. In this sense, very generally and abstractly, we may conclude that their "religion" is more a source for their lives than a resource for a better world. But we need to be reminded that our way of talking about "their religion" may not engender trust among those we wish to encourage to join us in creating a better world.

Sharing Our Stories

If we see religion as a resource, we inevitably begin to look for ways to minimize or divert our attention from the differences among religious peoples. We begin to employ other abstract nouns to express the "unity within the diversity" among the religions of the world. We may speak of what is "absolute" or "fundamental" or "universal," as though we know what we mean by these words. In fact, these words merely point to what we can only express cogently within the particular religious vocabularies of our various communities. We may avoid words like God and *dharma* in an effort to remain neutral, but clearly the "neutral" language of philosophy or psychology or social science is not at all neutral.

Language about religion that isn't religious is largely antagonistic to religious faith. Can we admit that, we who talk about religion because it is useful for us to do so? Can we see that we are using religion for our own ends? Perhaps our intentions are good but, nonetheless, we are engaged in the exploitation of what is precious to other people in order to attain a world that we believe will be better for them (and for us!) than the present world. But what if, to create our better world, we are sacrificing the religious worlds of others?

Are we so sure that harvesting the fruits of religious life will provide us with more than a sumptuous meal? Who will cultivate the seeds of faith for the future? Who will tend our religious communities once we have stripped the meanings relevant for our purposes from their teachings and rituals? For most people, this call to self-criticism falls on deaf ears. The dangers we face are so horrendous, so obvious, so pressing, that no cost to religious life is too high a price to pay. Don't we have to extract from the religious traditions the wisdom and experience that will help us survive together in a better world? How can we afford not to use the religions as resources for the new world we seek? Is there any alternative?

I believe there is. If we can see how important it is to nurture the religious experiences that are a source of life and meaning for hundreds of millions of people, so that these experiences may continue in ways that these people find compelling, then perhaps we can open ourselves to the real wisdom to be found within these traditions of faith. That is, if we can stop thinking about "religion" or "religions" and begin to think about people and their communities of faith and practice, perhaps we will learn how to understand one another and work together for a better world.

The first step in this approach to understanding is to invite others to tell us about their religious life. They will share with us not only their ideas, but also their stories by which they order the world. We will then be talking not about religion but about life, not about religions but about our world, not simply about our beliefs but about our faith. In this sharing we may discover ways to add to our stories in order to incorporate in them more of the human experience and insight we find reflected in the stories of others.

Such an approach puts the emphasis on the particular rather than the universal, but affirms our common humanity by fostering communication between members of different religious communities and cultures. It also moves us out of "resource" language, which involves "us" in talking about "them." Once we are talking about the ways we all see and shape the world, we are using "source" language. We are talking about the life we know and the world we cherish; we are talking about our faith.

Those who share their stories derive meaning from the sharing, may become friends and allies through the sharing, and will discover that they have much in common despite their obvious differences. But what they share will be affirmed most meaningfully for their own people through changes in their own stories and in the teachings and practices derived from them. That is, our goal is not to achieve one story for everyone, nor one "religion." Our goal is to learn from the stories of others so our stories may reflect more accurately the world that we share.

Within our story, within the narrative framework that defines our community of faith and those who are within it, we may come to see the need for change. And as others from different communities of faith enter our story, our story will inevitably change. We will be tempted to defend our past against the demand in the present to make room for other people of faith in our self-understanding. But if we can make room for them, if we can take them into our story, then our story *and* their story will change. And the possibilities for living together in peace in a better world will increase.

When we experience people of other religious communities as part of our story of faith, and not merely as "others," then we may be able to work with them to identify and utilize the resources of the world we share. For our religious insights *are* resources when we identify them from within a common story of faith, which is the source of our life together. This is vastly different from the present tendency of looking at the religion of others as a resource for us and our world.

The crux of the matter is in the shift in pronouns. To avoid looking at *their* religion as a resource, we look at the world through *our* stories of faith, which include various religious experiences and communities, to see how best to strengthen *our* life together. We are not discussing how religion—meaning someone else's way of experiencing the world—may be useful for our world; rather we are seeking to discern together how our stories of faith and communities of religious experience may help us conceive of a world that will not only realize the wisdom of our traditions but nurture the many communities of faith that have preserved this wisdom.

This is the purpose of interfaith dialogue. The goal is to share the way we see the world through our religious traditions in order to find points of agreement and opportunities for cooperation. The sharing of *my* faith is a story, as is the sharing of *your* faith. The telling of our stories to each other creates a new story, a story of *our* dialogue. The interfaith movement is an example of how the religious faith of persons from different traditions may be woven together as strands in a rope, each with its own integrity, but strengthened by being intertwined.

Our Faith Communities

I have suggested that the "religion and..." approach is flawed because it sees religion abstractly, whereas our challenge is to understand and engage communities of faith that shape the lives of religious people. A language that has "us," as observers, looking at the religions of "others" to discover "resources" for solving the world's problems will not bring people together to create a better world. Only a dialogue that encourages the sharing of stories and teachings of faith, with all their particularities, will enable us to conceive a common story that may embrace a more humane future for the peoples of the world.

In this sharing we all come to the dialogue with stories of faith, whether we are religious or not. We may put our faith in reason rather than religion, but then our story has its roots in the writings of the ancient Greeks and all those who have tried to apply their insights to the history of the West. In fact, it is bringing together the Western story of faith in reason with other stories, which we call religious, that may yield the next step forward, as it is the separation of the world into secular and sacred categories that so divides it. Only a story allowing both, which may come from a dialogue between those for whom reason and those for whom revelation are the source of their world, will heal the conflicts which now tear at our global community.

Does this challenge the notion that today, in order to solve our problems, we need a global ethic that represents the religious wisdom of the world? Yes, it does. If by a global ethic we mean a synthesis of the wisdom of the religious traditions, then I believe such a quest will rightly be perceived as undermining the peoples it claims to represent. Such an ethic will not value the communities of faith by which the wisdom of a religious tradition is sustained and adapted to everyday life. It will seek to transcend these communities, thus making them irrelevant.

If, however, by a global ethic we mean the telling of a new compelling story through the old stories of our religious and cultural communities, then I believe there may be real hope. What might this mean? It is happening today, for instance, as human rights affirmations are being taken into every culture and religious tradition, and as concern for nature and the earth becomes for all peoples a matter of life and death.

For example, when Vatican II affirmed human rights, the story of the Catholic Church changed. Even more important than the Vatican's support for international law was the development in Catholic teaching of the concept of human rights as the social conditions necessary for human dignity. This development required new interpretations of the Bible and the role of the Bible in the life of the church, and it meant wrestling with new ethical questions in the light of ancient teachings. It has also led to Catholic priests, sisters, and lay leaders being martyred for human rights. Their deaths have not only helped to bring pressure on governments to enforce human rights law, but have given new meaning to the death of Jesus and new life to the Christian story of sacrificial love that is saving.

To see all this as essentially a matter of using the resources of the Catholic Church in the struggle to support international human rights law is to misunderstand how, in fact, these international legal standards may be realized in a new world order. It is more important for Catholics to learn to embrace human rights through the teachings of their church than to be schooled in international law. Catholics may well see the latter as simply global politics, whereas the teachings of the church about human rights and human dignity describe the life for which God calls them to be responsible.

Therefore, religious cooperation for a better world must be concerned less with religion and religions and more with religious communities and the people whose lives are ordered by these communities. We must come to appreciate that, for religious people, religion is the source of life. But this source is not abstract and general; it is personal and particular. It concerns faith. Only the pursuit of a world order which recognizes this fact can help us discern, through our cultural and religious stories, the faith which lies behind them and unites us all.

The World We Choose

The problem with the "religion and..." approach to our problems is the world it creates. This world is defined objectively. In this "world" there are problems, there are resources, and the solutions involve using the resources to resolve the problems. In this "world" religions are often part of the problem, but religions also have resources for solving problems. In this "world," religions, to the extent they have not effectively used their resources, become part of the problem. The logic of this "world" leads to attempts to extract these resources from the religions as a way of making good use of them in constructing a better world. If, in the extracting, the religions are gutted and left in ruins, that's too bad for those who cared for them in the past, but no great loss for the rest of us. After all, the religions were part of the problem; we are probably better off without them.

In this "world," religious communities and traditions are perceived negatively as institutionalized forms of wisdom and practice that have little relevance to today's needs. Certain teachings are understood more positively, as fostering the values and behaviors needed for a more peaceful world. The task, therefore, is to free these useful (true) teachings and practices from the religions, so they might be more effectively utilized.

In the world of "religion and..." there is much talk about common values, as though simply affirming these will sustain the humane behaviors that have not been achieved by religious life. There is also a tendency to speak of spirituality, as though this recent abstract noun referring to the spiritual dimension of life is somehow capable of calling forth in human beings the qualities of peace and compassionate concern that religious traditions have manifestly failed to instill.

Those who speak of values and spirituality seek to foster a more humane world. But such talk may easily become a ploy to free the resources of religion from the religious institutions and organizations that have preserved these ideals but failed to realize them. Often those using these terms are participants in new religious movements; most of these movements define themselves over against "the religions" as spiritual practices that have overcome the limitations of the historic religious traditions.

This is, however, largely "resource" language. Values and spirituality are presented as what works. We are told that these values or this spirituality, whether gleaned from the teachings of the past or forged in New Age movements, will save our world. The assertion is less that these values and spiritual practices are true and, therefore, will work, but that they are true because they will work. At least, this is how they are marketed. And only a moment's glance in a contemporary bookstore will verify how effectively such resources are being marketed today.

Yet, the claims are hardly credible once one suggests a different world perspective. The more historical view of the world, which the "religion and…" mentality aggressively resists, reminds us that the abstract, well-intended notion of "resource" has been used to rape the earth of its natural bounty (much of it irreplaceable) and to take food and the fruits of labor from the great majority of the earth's peoples for the benefit of a small minority. History reveals that this was done for the good of all the world's people, for the cause of civilization, and for the saving of souls. Even the recent concept of development, which was proclaimed as the answer to the problem of a world divided into "haves" and "have-nots," has proven in its emphasis on productivity, rather than on the lives of people, to be primarily a form of continued exploitation.

A view of religious history that sees clearly the stories of communities of faith and the worlds created by these stories and the rituals and practices derived from them will help us focus on people rather than problems. It is only when people and their choices are clearly emphasized that the problems caused by people may be resolved. (It is, after all, people who make problems.) The religious experience of people, expressed with so much diversity and such intensity, tells us a great deal about our world, as through our religious experience, or lack of it, we are all making the world we understand and embrace.

This way forward involves a look back. There is no returning, of course, to a world in which what are called the religions are distinct and separate ways of living. (This might be described as the "museum" approach to religion.) But neither is the way forward to be found simply in exploiting the historic religious traditions for their spiritual and moral resources. We must look back to understand more profoundly the legacy of all those who have preceded us in this great earth adventure, in order to see clearly the way forward. We must come to appreciate as well as understand their diverse religious experience and the ways they sought in the past to respond with faith, in order to find for ourselves how to live more faithfully in the present.

History suggests that we will not succeed by merely being more clever than our ancestors. We cannot simply craft a better future, patching together statements about values and pieces of religious teaching. Even as material technology is not by itself an answer, neither is "spiritual technology." Instead, we have to enter into the religious and spiritual experience of our time and place in history, when the communities of faith are coming together in new and challenging ways, with an openness to how the meanings of the past may call forth from us new ways of living together in the present.

Our choices will come with the way we tell our stories and describe one another. If we concentrate on our problems, then we will look at one another—and our different ways of conceiving the world by being religious—only as potential resources. We will cooperate when it seems useful but compete for resources whenever that seems better for "us." If, however, we focus on peoples, and on their histories and understandings and ways of living, then we may find new ways to add to and modify our stories. Moreover, we may come to experience and know our world, with its rich religious diversity, as a wondrous gift that we are all called to cherish.

EASTERN TRADITIONS

Hinduism

Hinduism and Global Society
by K.R. Sundararajan

Gandhian Values, a Global Ethic, and Global Governance
by M. Aram

Jainism

Toward a Culture of Nonviolence: The Jain Way of Life
by P.N. (Bawa) Jain

Buddhism

Religion and World Order from a Buddhist Perspective
by Sulak Sivaraksa

Buddhism and Global Governance
by Pataraporn Sirikanchana

Confucianism

Confucianism and a New World Order
by Julia Ching

Working Toward a Shared Global Ethic:
Confucian Perspectives
by Mary Evelyn Tucker

Hinduism
and Global Society

K.R. Sundararajan

The question of what a religious tradition can contribute toward the establishment of world order is an interesting and challenging one. This important issue in the contemporary world has not been dealt with seriously or meaningfully in the past: religious traditions have either remained largely ethnic, with outsiders marginalized, or have sought to convert the whole of humankind to one brand of belief—and consequently one kind of worldview and lifestyle. In the past, religious and cultural diversity have never been a serious question for the different traditions; today it has become one, as we increasingly accept the concept of a global village where diversity and cooperation are watchwords.

In elaborating the theme of Hinduism's possible contributions to world order, I will call on the actual and potential resources of the Hindu tradition.

To begin with the situation of the "global village," we must focus on the cultural and religious distinctions historically drawn between "insiders" and "outsiders." All religious traditions, including Hinduism, have drawn such distinctions. On one hand, the Hindu tradition has historically remained somewhat insulated from outsiders, since it has not sought to convert outsiders into its fold; to that extent, we could say that it has not developed a theology to deal with non-Hindu outsiders. On the other hand, the Hindu culture has remained tolerant of outsiders. India has had a religiously pluralistic society for a long time. The settlement of the Zoroastrians in India, according to some historians, dates to pre-Christian times. Christian missionaries seem to have arrived early in the Christian

Era, and there is a strong popular tradition in South India that the apostle Thomas, one of the direct disciples of Jesus, lived and died in India. India also had one of the earliest Jewish settlements, predating the Christian Era, although many of its descendants left after the modern state of Israel was formed.

As long as all religions have to contend with the fact that their creator God must be creator of everything, they contain an element of universalism. However, outsiders may be considered non-human or even demonic, hence not falling within the purview of the human beings on whom a religion is focused. I like to argue that this is not the case with regard to the Hindu tradition, though one could say that Hindu geography glorifies *Bharatavarsha*—the land of *Bharata*, the traditional name for India—as the most sacred land in the whole of creation. This pride in the holiness of their land made Hindus unwilling to communicate freely with outsiders and exchange ideas, complains Al-Biruni, an Islamic scholar who visited India in the eleventh century CE. He writes:

> We can only say that folly is an illness for which there is no medicine, and the Hindus believe that there is no country like theirs, no nation like theirs, no kings like theirs, no religion like theirs, no science like theirs. They are haughty, foolishly vain, self-conceited and stolid. They are by nature niggardly in communicating that which they know, and they take the greatest possible care to withhold it from men of other caste among their own people; still much more, of course, from any foreigner.[1]

Traditionally, the Hindu response to outside groups such as the Buddhists and Jainas, whose religions are of Indian origin, has been mixed. While there are descriptions of these communities living peacefully side by side, there are also episodes of attempted conversions, often resulting in violence.

Manimekalai, one of the Tamil classics of the early Christian Era, describes life in South India as peaceful, with Hindus, Buddhists, and Jains living side by side. Possibly to highlight this peaceful life, we are told that when the heroine Manimekalai wanted to pursue her studies, she was told to go to Kanchipuram, one of the traditional South Indian centers of learning, to study in academies that taught the Brahmanical Hindu philosophical systems as well as philosophies of the Buddhists and Jainas.[2]

---

[1] Cited in S.K. Ikram, *Muslim Civilization in India* (New York: Columbia University Press, 1964), p. 28.

[2] See Nilakanta Sastri, *A History of South India from Prehistoric Times to the Fall of Vijyana-*

The famous Chinese pilgrim Yuan Chaung, who visited India in the seventh century CE, reported that Hindus and Buddhists lived in harmony, and noted only some conflict among the Buddhists themselves.[3] However, historians tell us that in the seventh and eighth centuries CE there were conflicts within certain Hindu denominations, such as between the Vaisnava (worshippers of Visnu) and Saiva (worshippers of Siva), and also between these and the Jainas and Buddhists.

Tirunavukarasar, one of the Nayanmar saints of South India, is said to have converted a South Indian ruler by the name of Mahendravarman to the Saiva faith.[4] It is said that as the result of this conversion Mahendravarman put to death about 3,000 Jainas.[5] Among the devotees of Visnu, Tirumangai Alvar, one of the Alvar saints of South India, is said to have been a Jaina, a Buddhist, and a worshipper of Siva (Saiva) before he became a worshipper of Visnu (Vaisnava), renouncing his Saiva faith.

The hostility between the various denominations within the Hindu tradition and with outside non-Hindu groups has also been carried out intellectually, especially in philosophical writings. The Hindu philosophical writings are required to state their viewpoints (*siddhanta*) only after establishing the absurdity of opponents' viewpoints (*purvapaksa*). The Buddhist and Jaina philosophical formulations have been the primary targets for traditional Hindu philosophers. In this connection it is interesting to see that a great philosopher like Sankara has been labeled a "Buddhist in disguise" (*praccana bauddha*) by his opponents, suggesting that he has betrayed the tradition by incorporating Buddhist philosophical formulations into his (Hindu) philosophical system, known as Advaita Vedanta. Yet in spite of the negative connotation of *praccana bauddha*, such descriptions also indicate a degree of openness, in the sense that it is possible for a Hindu theologian to be, intellectually at least, influenced by the viewpoints of other schools of philosophy.

There are indications that lively discussions between Hindu, Buddhist, and Jaina theologians went on for a long time—though the purpose was not "dialoguing," but rather "defeating" and eventually "converting" the opponent. Hence we do not find an explicit openness to outside tra-

---

gar (Madras: Oxford University Press, 1955), pp. 41–44.

[3] See Heinrich Zimmer, *Philosophies of India* (New York: Pantheon Books, Bollingen Series XXVI, 1951), pp. 510–511.

[4] Nilakanta Sastri, *A History of India* (Madras: S. Viswanathan, 1950), p. 423.

[5] *Ibid.*

ditions, though it could be said with justification that one of the ways the Hindu tradition has handled the challenges of Buddhism and other religions is by slowly absorbing some of the best of their teachings into its own fold, and validating them from within its own teachings.

A Global Theology

With these comments, I would like to move on to the task of constructing a global theology on the basis of Hindu theology. At the outset, we should remember that this is essentially a "construction" whose purpose is to make Hinduism meaningful by having the resources to deal with some of the conditions of the modern world, in which religious diversity and pluralism is an issue.

From the Hindu point of view (*Weltanschauung*), the notion of individuality or "individual existence" is not spiritually meaningful. Individuality is considered part of human experience in the "fallen" state, described as *samsara* (literally, "bondage"). In this state, our personal preferences become the prime focus of our lives, and everything is judged and valued in terms of our self-interest. The state of freedom (*moksa*), on the other hand, is a rising above the restrictive and limited awareness "individuality" imposes on us, to a level of consciousness where we are aware of unity more than differences, and our private preferences are no longer central. The point is that the ultimate goal of Hindu spirituality is to gain a vision of unity which is nondiscriminatory, where every kind of life form is important. If this is seen as the very dynamic of Hindu spirituality, it could be said that the goal of Hindu religious life is to gain a global vision, a vision of interconnectedness rather than separateness. Such a vision, then, should foster a sense of equality and a deep respect for one another.

In the *Veda*, which is the collective name for the Hindu scripture, many prayers highlight the spirit of religious tolerance. The most inspiring passage, often cited by modern Hindus, is one from the *Rgveda* which reads: "The seers call in many ways that which is One…" This has often been cited as the Hindu approach to religious pluralism and diversity, affirming the validity of all religions as engaged in pursuit of a common goal, namely the seeking and experiencing of the One Reality. Here, the paths that the various religions pursue are parallel, not hierarchical. So also in the *Bhagavad-Gita*, Krsna tells Arjuna:

In whatever way any come to Me,
In that same way I grant them favor.
My path follow
Men altogether, son of Partha. (IV.11)

One of the modern saints of Hinduism, Ramakrishna Paramahamsa, expresses the theme of the essential unity of all religions based on the common goal they are seeking, using a different kind of analogy:

> So many religions, so many paths to reach the same goal. I have practiced Hinduism, Islam, Christianity, and in Hinduism again, the ways of different sects. I have found that it is the same God toward whom all are directing their steps, though along different paths.
>
> The tank has several *ghats*. At one Hindus draw water and call it *jal*. At another Mohammedans draw water and call it *pani*; at a third Christians draw the same liquid and call it water. The substance is one though the names differ, and everyone is seeking the same thing. Every religion of the world is one such *ghat*. Go with a sincere and earnest heart by any of these *ghats* and you will reach the water of eternal bliss. But do not say that your religion is better than that of another.[6]

Swami Prabhavananda comments on the passage from the *Rgveda* cited above, thus:

> Casual visitors to this ancient land carry with them the impression of an elaborate polytheism. True it is that India has always had many gods—but in appearance only. In reality she has had but one god, though with prodigal inventiveness she has called him "by various names." Indra, Varuna, Hiranyagarbha, Rama, Krsna, Siva: what does it matter? Whichever of these or many others the Hindu chooses for his adoration, that one becomes for him God himself, in whom exist all things, including, for the time being, all other gods. It is because India has been so much permeated with the spirit of *Ekam sat vipra bahuddha vadanti* (The seers call in many ways that which is one) that she has known relatively little of religious fanaticism, of religious persecution, of religious wars. Characteristically she has sought the truth in every faith—even in faiths not her own.[7]

Another passage from the *Rgveda* describes God as the common Lord of all. The theme of humanity consisting of people speaking different languages and residing in different places is expressed in the following verse from *Atharvaveda*:

---

[6] Cited in Prabhavananda, *The Spiritual Heritage of India* (Hollywood, California: Vedanta Press, 1979 edition), p. 341.

[7] *Ibid.*, pp. 34–35.

May the Earth that bears people speaking in varied language
With various rites according to the places of abode,
Enrich me with wealth in a thousand streams
Like milch-cow that never fails.[8]
If, Varuna, we have sinned against the man who loves us, or against a friend
or a comrade forever, or a brother,
or against a neighbor who is always with us, or against a stranger,
From that sin may thou release us.[9]

A prayer in *Yajurveda* expresses the theme of friendship among every being in the world:

May all human beings look on me with the eye of a friend;
May I look upon all beings with the eye of a friend;
May we look on one another with the eye of a friend.

The notion of one humankind is often stressed in the Hindu creation stories. Those in the early Vedic writings suggest that all created human beings belonged to the four social classes (*varna*) of Hindu society. This is stated in a famous verse from the *Rgveda* called "Hymns to the Primordial Person (*Purusasukta*)." Here the creation of the four classes (*varna*) is a primordial phenomenon; it happens alongside the creation of human beings themselves. Human beings are not created as such; they are created as *brahmins, ksatriyas, vaisyas,* and *sudras,* the members of the Hindu *varna.* According to the *Visnu Purana,* a later work, the seven created regions (continents) were populated with a fourfold division of social classes, descendants of the same "first family," Manu Svayambhuva.

In the beginning and in the *treta yuga* the entire earth, the seven continents with their mountains, oceans, and mines were inhabited, land by land, by the sons of Priyavrata, the grandsons of Svayambhuva.[10]

According to these stories, the continent called *Jambhudvipa* is the place where *Bharatavarsha,* the traditional name for India, is located. Though the Hindu sacred geography considers *Bharatavarsha* as superior to other lands, it could be argued that other regions (continents also) are superior to *Bharatavarsha* since they are not subject to the cycle of four ages, a cycle that affects only *Bharatavarsha,* according to *Visnu Purana!*

---

[8] XII.1.45. Cited in A.C. Bose, *Call of the Vedas* (Bombay: Bharatiya Vidya Bhavan, 1960), p. 283.

[9] 26.2 (cited A.C. Bose).

[10] C. Dimmitt & J.A.B. van Buitenen, eds. & trans., *Classical Hindu Mythology* (Philadelphia: Temple University, 1978), pp. 56–57.

There are four *yugas* or ages in the *Bharatavarsha*, O Great Muni, namely the *krita*, the *treta*, the *dwapara*, and *kali*—there is no such cycle of ages in any other land.

The cycle of ages is the movement of time from the time of perfection to the time of most imperfection. These are represented by various metals. Time moves from the perfect *krta* (golden) age to the most imperfect *kali* (iron) age. The *krta* age is followed by *treta* (silver) and then by *dvapara* (copper) and *kali* (iron) in a declining manner.

Bharata is the most excellent division of *Jambhudvipa*; for this is the land of works, while others are places of enjoyment. Perhaps in a thousand births, a living being obtains here that most excellent condition, humanity, the receptacle of virtue. The gods sing, "Happy are those beings, who when the rewards of their merits have been exhausted in heaven, are, after being gods, again born as men in *Bharatavarsha*."[11]

The philosophy of identity based on the notion of an all-pervasive reality, *Brahman*, is the core of the Upanisadic teachings, which represent the final phase of the *Veda* and are fully developed in the Hindu philosophical schools known as *darsanas*. It is also the basis for the Hindu worldview I mentioned earlier. From the theological perspective of the Upanisads, the notion of the oneness or unity of all life forms is the ultimate and final truth. "Verily the whole world is *Brahman*,"[12] says the *Chandogya Upanisad*. The first verse of *Isavasya Upanisad* says:

The whole world is to be dwelt in by the Lord,
whatever living being there is in the world.
So should you eat what has been abandoned;
and do not covet anyone's wealth.[13]

The famous Upanisadic statement in *Chandogya Upanisad,* "That Thou art" (*tattvam asi*), not only establishes the identity between the individual self (*atman*) and the Supreme Being (*Brahman*) but also indicates that everything that exists is an aspect or expression of *Brahman*. Hence any sense of discrimination among the created beings is reflective of the state of ignorance. From the point of view of Advaita Vedanta, a Hindu philosophical system based on the teachings of the Upanisads, "the ideal person" (*jivanmukta*) is one who looks at all things as equal, since that person transcends the state of duality (the "I and thou" or "I and they"

---

[11] John Muir, *Original Sanskrit Texts* (Amsterdam: Oriental Press, 1967), pp. 495–496.
[12] 3.14.1.
[13] Patrick Olivelle, trans., *Upanisads* (Oxford: Oxford University Press, 1996), p. 249.

perspective). One of the modern commentators of Advaita Vedanta suggests that the theological basis of Advaita (and derivatively the Upanisads) provides justification for the fellowship of all humankind.

> It is the realization of the *fundamental oneness* of Reality that makes us feel effectively the truth of fellowship of men. To the Advaitin the concept of brotherhood of man is not a social exhortation nor a mere doctrine. It is proved on his pulse. It is only men who have this experience, that can be real humanists.[14]

Another modern commentator states that *sarvamukti*, the liberation of all, is the very goal of religious life in the Upanisads.

> Individuals cannot be transformed in separation from each other. The word *sarvamukti* means the liberation of all. In a deeply spiritual sense there can be no other salvation. *Brahma-loka* or the Kingdom of God implies corporate salvation. We are all wayfarers toward the Divine Kingdom and so cannot rest until the goal is achieved.[15]

Social Relationships in Hinduism

We could now consider the social dimensions of Hinduism and look into the implications of the concept of *dharma*, since it is *dharma* that regulates the individual, family, and social lives of Hindus. There is an interesting contrast between the vision of unity that one gets from the Upanisads and the hierarchical structuring of social classes based on the principles of *dharma*. This is the *varna dharma,* by which, based on the principle of ritual purity and impurity, the social class of *brahmins* is considered superior, followed by the *ksatriyas*, the *vaisyas*, and the least-pure *sudras*. This structure is certainly not conducive to the "equality" vision we could construct from the Upanisads.

In order to understand this somewhat paradoxical situation, we must realize that the hierarchy is representative only of the "fallen state" of human existence, caused as it is by ignorance (*avidya*) of our "true" nature, where we are essentially linked to *Brahman*, the all-pervasive reality. Hence we are in *samsara*, experiencing an unsatisfactory life from which we should gain freedom (*moksa*). As long as we emphasize our "individual identity," based on our "mistaken" identification with our physical body

---

[14] P. Nagaraja Rao, *Introduction to Vedanta* (Bombay: Bharatiya Vidya Bhavan, 1966), p. 226.

[15] S. Radhakrishnan, *The Brahma Sutra: The Philosophy of Spiritual Life* (New York: Greenwood Press, 1960), p. 218.

and its experiences, we are firmly grounded in *samsara*. We have to over-come this narrow identification of our self, and rise to a unitive vision where we are related to every other creature in the world.

From the perspective of *dharma*, a *brahmin* is indeed the model person. According to Manu, "Of created beings the most excellent are said to be those which are animated; of the animated, those which subsist by intelligence; of the intelligent, mankind; and of men, the *Brahmanas*."[16] The *Apastamba Dharma Sutra* gives the following as the qualities of *brahmin*: "Freedom from anger, from exultation, from covetousness, from perplexity, from hypocrisy and hurtfulness; truthfulness, silencing slander, freedom from envy, self-denying liberality, extinction of passions, subjugation of senses, peace with all created beings, peacefulness and contentment."[17] We could, therefore, say that from the perspective of Hindu *dharma*, the goal is to create a society of *brahmins*. Looking at the list of qualities needed for *brahmins*, we could claim that the ideal *brahmin* is indeed a world citizen, and in the creation of a society peopled by *brahmins*, who are exemplars of "wisdom, tolerance, forbearance and humility,"[18] Hinduism is devoted to the creation of a global order where people can live in harmony and with respect for one another.

The debate as to whether a person is *brahmin* by birth or by the possession of certain noble qualities alone, irrespective of one's social or caste status in society, has continued throughout the history of Hinduism. Here we could cite two stories from the Hindu epic of *Mahabharata*.

> There is an interesting dialogue in the *Mahabharata* between Yuddhishtra and a serpent in which Yuddhishtra emphasizes that character alone should form the basis for caste distinctions. When asked by the serpent as to who is a *brahmin*, Yuddhishtra replies: "Know him to be *Brahmin* who is truthful, charitable, forgiving, gentle, soft, merciful, and who behaves according to *dharma*." The serpent asked whether a *sudra* with these qualities could be called a *brahmin*. Yuddhishtra replied: "If a *Sudra* shows these qualities and a *Brahmin* does not show them, then that *Sudra* is not a *Sudra*, neither that *Brahmin*, a *Brahmin*. Know him only to be a *Brahmin* who reveals these characteristics and him to be *Sudra* who does not reveal them."[19]

---

[16] K.R. Sundararajan, "Hindu Ethics," in *Hinduism*, K.R. Sundararajan *et al.*, eds. (Patiala: Punjabi University, 1969), p. 25.

[17] Cited in Sundararajan, *op. cit.*, p. 45.

[18] Satguru Sivaya Subramuniyaswami, *Dancing with Siva Hinduism's Contemporary Catechism* (India: Himalayan Academy, 1993), p. 697.

[19] Sundararajan, *op. cit.*, pp. 49–50.

This story is to be contrasted with the story of Matanga given in the *Mahabharata*. Matanga was trying his best to elevate his caste status.

> To Matanga, who tries through utmost religious austerities to become a *brahmin*, Indra says that it is impossible for a man of low caste to attain *brahminhood* by any amount of austerities. Finally, Matanga cries in sheer desperation: I am a person who has concentrated on becoming a *brahmin*, who has attained release from happiness and misery, who has no family. I am always nonviolent and controlled in respect of my senses. Even then how is it that I am not fit to obtain *brahminhood*? What bad luck for me that even though I am the knower of *dharma*, I am doomed to this position due to fault of my father. I am sure a man may strive and strive, but fate is still powerful.[20]

In spite of one's lower status in the caste hierarchy, it is still possible to strive to perfect one's condition. This is due to the fact that *dharma* is also expressed in the form of *asrama dharma*: duties and obligations related to the "stages of life." In the scheme of *dharma* one passes through four stages of life. These stages are: student; married householder; forest-dweller—in which, having fulfilled one's family household obligations, one is ready for retirement and shifts one's focus to the pursuit of religious disciplines with the increasingly meaningful and relevant goal of freedom or *moksa*; and the final stage, "renouncer" or *sannyasi*—one who has renounced all ties to the outside world, including social or family responsibilities, and focuses exclusively on the pursuit of *moksa*.

In this fourfold scheme of Hinduism, the stages of householder and renouncer are central. Interestingly enough, the householder carries the burden of family and social responsibilities, whereas in principle the renouncer has no family or social responsibilities.

The Life of the Householder. The householder's responsibility is, in the first place, the support of the family. In traditional society, it is the husband's responsibility to seek financial resources, thus the first aim of life (*artha* or "wealth") is fulfilled by the husband. The second aim of life—*kama*, "seeking pleasure," includes both husband and wife, resulting in a family with children. The third aim of life, *dharma*, meaning social and ritual responsibilities, also requires both wife and husband, although the male is the direct agent performing actions—but without the active involvement of the female these responsibilities cannot be discharged properly. Therefore, Manu, the chief exponent of householder *dharma*,

---

[20] *Ibid.*, pp. 50–51.

says, "Where women are honored, there the gods are pleased; but where they are not honored, no sacred rite yields rewards."[21]

Each householder carries fivefold obligations in accordance with the principles of *dharma*. These are obligations to ancestors, other living creatures, fellow human beings, the gods, and the sages. Of these, the obligations to the sages are fulfilled by learning; this is done in the first stage, that of a student. One fulfills one's obligations to the gods by worship and sacrificial offerings. Obligations to the ancestors are fulfilled by having children, especially a male child who could assume family responsibilities when the parents are ready move into the third stage of life. Obligations to fellow human beings are fulfilled by acts of charity, especially by offering food to travelers and to the *sannyasis* (renouncers) who come and beg for food. According to Manu, "He who prepares food for himself (alone) eats nothing but sin; for it is ordained that the food which remains after (the performance of sacrifice) shall be the meal of virtuous men."[22] The obligation to the living creatures is also done by offering food. According to Manu, one who honors all being, human and non-human, "goes, endowed with resplendent body, by a straight road to the highest dwelling place (Heaven)."[23]

The Life of the Renouncer. The fourth and highest stage of life according to *asrama dharma* is that of the *sannyasi* or renouncer, another model of ideal person in the Hindu tradition besides that of the *brahmin*. Manu's description of a *sannyasi* runs as follows:

> He must show no anger
> to one who is angry.
> He must bless the man who curses him....
> He must not utter false speech.
> Rejoicing in things of the spirit, calm,
> caring for nothing, abstaining from sexual pleasure, himself his only helper,
> he may live in the world, in the hope of eternal bliss.

Though Manu's *sannyasi* is a solitary wanderer focused on his own salvation, having renounced social responsibilities by giving up the life of a householder, we also find in the tradition *sannyasis* with some degree of social responsibility. This could be seen in the order of *matas* (monastic orders) that Sankara established in the eighth century CE, followed by

---

[21] Georg Buhler, trans., *The Laws of Manu* (Delhi: Motilal Banasidass, 1964), III.56, p. 85.
[22] *Ibid.*, III.118, p. 97.
[23] *Ibid.*, III.93.

matas in other religious orders, such as the Vaisnavas. In the setup of religious *matas*, the head of the *mata* becomes an *acarya*, responsible for a
large section of lay members of the community. It is interesting that
whereas teachers and spiritual guides in the Upanisads and epics were
mostly householders or at best forest-dwellers (the third stage of life),
subsequently the *sannyasis* (the fourth stage, supposedly having renounced all social responsibilities) came to assume such tasks. It is as if by
renouncing particular social identities, *sannyasis* come to have broader
identities as religious leaders. Some *sannyasis* in modern times have broken ethnic and national barriers and assumed responsibilities for global
society, so to speak. We see this in one of the letters of Swami Vivekananda:

> I want to preach my ideas for the good of the world....I have a message to give;
> let me give it to the people who appreciate it and who will work for it and who
> will work it out. What care I who takes it? "He who doeth the will of my father"
> is my own.

It is appropriate here to refer to the very last verse of the *Rgveda*,
which calls for human unity and harmony:

> United your resolve, united your hearts,
> May your spirit be at one,
> that you may long together dwell
> in unity and concord.

Commenting on the above verse, Raimundo Panikkar writes:

> The last mantra knows only Man's ordinary language and Man's own cherished
> ideas; it comes back to the simplicity of the fact of being human; a union of
> hearts and a oneness of spirit, the overcoming of isolating individualisms by
> harmonious living together....[24]

Conclusion

To sum up, Hinduism has the potential to address the needs of world order and global society. Global society will be marked by religious and
cultural diversity. Human life will be governed by *dharma*, understood
here in a very general sense as a system of duties and obligations. The
well-being of an individual will be linked with the well-being of others.

---

[24] Raimundo Panikkar, *The Vedic Experience: An Anthology of the Vedas for Modern Man
and Contemporary Celebration* (Berkeley: University of California Press, 1977), pp. 682-
683.

Human beings will enjoy a healthy and positive relationship with the natural world. The fivefold obligations spoken of by Hinduism strongly reinforce the indebtedness of the individual to other human beings, to other forms of life, and even to the dead (ancestors), for the quality of life one enjoys.

For the Hindus, "love" is within the framework of duties and responsibilities, and is expressed in one's eagerness to fulfill one's *dharmic* obligations. Hence, from the Hindu perspective, the basis for global ethics is a system of duties and obligations extending beyond one's own personal well-being to concern for all others. It would include concern for the natural world, since for the Hindu tradition, nature is "spiritual," comprised of divine forces to be reckoned with while leading a fully human life. The early Vedic religion is marked by such recognition, and by a distinctly respectful attitude toward nature and spirit forces associated with natural phenomena.

Though there is some ambiguity within the Hindu tradition about the "reality" of the world (whether it is *ultimately* real or illusory), and whether *dharmic* obligations are ultimately meaningful in terms of salvation (*moksa*), it should be remembered that *dharma* is as important for a Hindu as *moksa*. It appears that even those who have renounced their "worldly life," namely the *sannyasis*, are not free from *dharmic* obligations. This is found in the *mata* tradition, where the *sannyasis* assume responsibilities as pontiffs or spiritual heads of a community. In this sense, Hinduism is very much "world-affirming," stressing the interdependence and interconnectedness of all creatures, and the responsibility of humans toward maintaining a proper relationship with the natural world.

Gandhian Values, a Global Ethic, and Global Governance

M. Aram

Introduction

We live today at a rare moment in human history, during which we have a unique opportunity to play a creative role in shaping the future of the world. We live in a small, interdependent world—a global village, as it is popularly called. Robert Muller aptly says, "The world is becoming so interdependent, it is like one body. We have a nervous system which is very advanced. We have a global brain. Now we need a global heart and a global soul." I would add that we also need a global conscience, based on a global ethic.

About 2,000 to 2,500 years ago, we passed through a similar "transformative" period. That was the first "axis period," in the words of Arnold Toynbee, with the extraordinary emergence of moral and spiritual geniuses in different parts of the world. Buddha and Mahavir arose in India, Lao-Tzu and Confucius in China, Christ in Israel. Earlier, Moses arose in Israel, and Zoroaster in Persia; later, the prophet Mohammed in Arabia. Thus various religions came into existence: Buddhism, Jainism, Taoism, Confucianism, Christianity, Judaism, Zoroastrianism, and Islam. These religions proclaimed moral and ethical values.

In India, the *Vedas* and Upanisads, *Bhagavad-Gita* and *Thirukkural* proclaimed new values and principles. Hinduism, the major religion, is unlike other religions in the sense that it was not founded by a particular prophet. Rather it was a galaxy of saints and sages who proclaimed the supremacy of the Spirit. They discovered the Ultimate Reality and said, "*Ekam sat*" (truth is one); "*Vipra bahuddha vadanti*" (sages call it by several names).

Later, India saw the emergence of another religion, Sikhism, and also welcomed the religions that originated outside. Zoroastrianism came to India when a group of Parsis who were persecuted in Persia landed on the Gujarat coast in western India. The leader of the group met the king of the region and sought asylum. The king gave them permission and granted land to settle down. The Parsi leader thanked the king. Then he brought a large vessel full of milk and put some sugar in it. He said "Sir, we will be like the sugar in the milk." Even to this day the Parsi community, small in size, is a precious part of Indian society. Thus, India became a hospitable home for all the religions of the world, twelve in number, including the Bahá'í faith.

International visitors to India are always struck by the pervasive role that religion plays in personal, family, and social life. Vincent Sheean, a student of human societies, has remarked that in no other society has the "transcendental" permeated social life as it has in India. Swami Vivekananda, a well-known modern Hindu saint, said that every nation had a special genius, and in the case of India it is religion. Indeed, religion is India's life-breath.

Gandhian Values

Therefore, it is not surprising that in the twentieth century India produced a personality like Mahatma Gandhi (1869–1948). He was a profoundly religious person who appealed to the spiritual susceptibilities of the Indian people and mobilized them for the freedom struggle which was a unique event in human history. India won political independence through nonviolent methods and processes.

To understand Mahatma Gandhi, we must go to his religious roots. In his autobiography he describes the beginnings of his religious consciousness. He learned religion from his nurse, Ramba; from his sixth to his sixteenth year, at school, he was taught "all sorts of things except religion." Gandhiji also tells how the reading of the *Ramayana*, India's famous epic, made a deep impression on him. A significant aspect of his early religious experience was the fact that his father was visited by many friends from other religions. Jain monks, Muslims, and Parsi friends came to his home, and Gandhiji developed, even in childhood, "a toleration of all faiths."

Gandhiji says, "One thing took deep root in me: the conviction that morality is the basis of things, and that truth is the substance of all morality; and truth became my sole objective." He also says that a Gujarati poem made a powerful impression on his mind and heart:

> For a bowl of water give a goodly meal;
> For a kindly greeting bow thou down with zeal;
> For a simple penny pay thou back with gold;
> If thy life be rescued, life do not withhold.
> Thus the words and actions of the wise regard;
> Every little service tenfold they reward.
> But the truly noble know all men as one,
> And return with gladness good for evil done.

This poem contains the precept "return good for evil." It is, in other words, *ahimsa*, nonviolence at its best. We see how truth and nonviolence, *satya* and *ahimsa*, thus became the two guiding principles or values for Mahatma Gandhi, even from his childhood.

In the chapter in his autobiography entitled "Religious Ferment," Gandhiji refers to his intimate interactions with Christian friends. He also says that he had already started following his "inner voice." Later, he mentions how Tolstoy's book *The Kingdom of God is Within You* overwhelmed him and left an indelible impression on him; when he started an *asram* in South Africa, he named it Tolstoy Farm. Gandhiji further says that he had accepted "the religion of service." He felt that "God could be realized only through service." He also made introspection a habit.

Gandhiji made a historic contribution to the evolution of human society when he applied nonviolence to social issues. He says, "We have to make truth and nonviolence not matters for mere individual practice, but for practice by groups and communities and nations. That, at any rate, is my dream. I shall live and die in trying to realize it."

The Gandhian Movement in South Africa thus developed a new methodology of social action which Gandhiji called *satyagraha*. This word was coined by him to distinguish it from "civil disobedience" and "passive resistance." This methodology of nonviolent action was different and new, a creative and original contribution, causing perceptive people around the world to take note. When *satyagraha* became successful in South Africa, word spread around the world. On his return to India, Gandhiji used the same method of *satyagraha* in successfully resolving regional and local issues. Eventually the entire country became his laboratory and the method of nonviolent action was experimented with on a truly large scale. India won independence in an unprecedented manner, and the practicality of nonviolence was demonstrated.

Gandhiji listed seven social sins: politics without principles, commerce without morality, wealth without work, education without character, science without humanity, pleasure without conscience, worship without sacrifice. Thus he emphasized the place of ethics in every sector of social life. Further, Gandhiji envisioned a world where national interest would be subordinate to global interest: "Just as the cult of patriotism teaches us today that the individual has to die for the family, the family has to die for the village, the village for the district, the district for the province and the province for the country, even so, a country has to be free in order that it may die, if necessary, for the benefit of the world."

The contribution of the Gandhian movement to the twentieth century was the value of "active nonviolence" to solve political and social issues. Martin Luther King, Jr., in the United States stated that while he got his basic principles from Jesus Christ, he obtained the operational methods from Mahatma Gandhi. His nonviolent movement for civil rights produced positive results. The methods followed by Nelson Mandela in South Africa were not entirely nonviolent, but his preference was always for nonviolence. His long tenure in prison and his positive outlook, "free from bitterness," made him a universally respected leader. He, too, was successful when apartheid finally ended—another demonstration of the power of nonviolence. Thus Mahatma Gandhi, Martin Luther King, Jr., and Nelson Mandela have made creative contributions toward the formulation of a global ethic. Nonviolence, as a moral value and practical method of problem-solving, can be a constituent part of the emerging global ethic.

A Global Ethic

A common core of ethical values is found in all religious traditions. This is an important requirement for building a new global order. There can be no global order without a global ethic.

When the centenary of the Parliament of Religions was held in Chicago in 1993, the focus was on developing a global ethic. One hundred years before, in 1893, leaders of various religious traditions had met on a common platform for the first time in human history. Speaking on that historic occasion, Swami Vivekananda declared, "The bell tolling to open the Congress will be the death-knell of all fanaticisms." The Chairman of the 1893 Parliament of Religions, Dr. Barrows, said, "Oh wise men of the East and the West, this Congress may be the morning star of the 20th century." At the end of the Congress, he said, "Henceforth the religions of the world will make war, not on one another, but on the giant evils that afflict mankind."

At the Centenary Assembly, which I had the privilege to attend on behalf of the World Conference on Religion and Peace, a nucleus of about 200 religious and spiritual leaders held a special meeting to consider the declaration of a global ethic. While there was a broad consensus on the contents of the declaration, we had the feeling that there was room for further refinement. So the conference decided to add the word "towards." At the final open session of the Assembly, the declaration was issued with the title "Towards a Declaration of a Global Ethic."

The main elements of the newly declared global ethic are interdependence and respect for all life; mutual respect and tolerance; a culture of solidarity; humankind as one family; a culture of nonviolence; peace with justice; equal partnership between men and women; a just social and economic order; self-discipline and positive thinking. Social peace must be built on the foundation of inner peace—what Patricia Mische has called "inner governance"—which is emphasized by all religions.

The Chicago Declaration describes the present scenario and spells out the principles underlying the global ethic:

> Our world is experiencing a fundamental crisis: a crisis in global economy, global ecology and global politics. The lack of a grand vision, the tangle of unresolved problems, political paralysis, mediocre political leadership with little insight or foresight, and in general too little sense for the common weal are seen everywhere.
>
> Hundreds of millions of human beings on our planet increasingly suffer from unemployment, poverty, hunger and destruction of their families. Hope for a lasting peace among nations slips away from us. There are tensions between the sexes and generations. Children die, kill and are killed. More and more countries are shaken by corruption in politics and business.
>
> It is increasingly difficult to live together peacefully in our cities because of social, racial and ethnic conflicts, the abuse of drugs, organized crime, and even anarchy.
>
> Our planet continues to be ruthlessly plundered. A collapse of the ecosystem threatens us.

We condemn these blights and declare that they need not be. An ethic already exists within the religious teachings of the world which counters the global distress. Of course, this ethic provides no direct solution for all the immense problems of the world; but it does supply the moral foundation for a better individual and global order—a vision which can lead women and men away from despair, and society away from chaos.

We confirm that there is already a consensus among the religions which can be the basis for a global ethic—a minimal fundamental consensus concerning binding values, irrevocable standards and fundamental moral attitudes.

The Chicago Declaration further states that there can be no new global order without a new global ethic. It demands that every human being must be treated humanely. Later it lists four basic commitments.

1. *Commitment to a culture of nonviolence and respect for life.* In the great ancient religious and ethical traditions of humankind we find the directive: You shall not kill. Or in positive terms: Have respect for life!

2. *Commitment to a culture of solidarity and a just economic order.* In the great ancient religious and ethical traditions of humankind we find the directive: You hall not steal. Or in positive terms: Deal honestly and fairly!

3. *Commitment to a culture of tolerance and a life of truthfulness.* In the great ancient religious and ethical traditions of humankind we find the directive: You shall not lie. Or in positive terms: Speak and act truthfully!

4. *Commitment to a culture of equal rights and partnership between men and women.* In the great ancient religious and ethical traditions of humankind we find the directive: You shall not commit sexual immorality. Or in positive terms: Respect and love one another!

Finally, the Chicago Declaration stresses the importance of a transformation of human consciousness. What is required is that human beings around the world change their mental attitudes. There should be a radical change in the collective consciousness of humankind, and this can be done by all working together. Particularly the vast networks of religious institutions, which have pervasive influence upon millions of people, could change their mindset. The Chicago Declaration calls all the religious communities around the world to do this.

The Declaration ends thus:

We pledge to work for such transformation in individual and collective consciousness, for the awakening of our spiritual powers through reflection, prayer, meditation, or positive thinking, for a conversion of the heart.

Together we can move mountains. We commit ourselves to a common global ethic, to better mutual understanding, as well as to socially beneficial, peace-fostering, and Earth-friendly ways of life.

We invite all men and women, whether religious or not, to do the same.

One of the useful suggestions made at Chicago for follow-up action was that the various professions, such as physicians, scientists, business-people, journalists, and politicians, could formulate "up-to-date codes of ethics which would provide specific guidelines for the vexing problems of these particular professions."

From March 22 to 24, 1996, the InterAction Council convened a seminar of a high-level Expert Group on the theme "In Search of Global Ethical Standards." The consultation was chaired by the former chancellor of Germany, Helmut Schmidt. I was one of the participants. After three days of intensive and in-depth deliberations, the Expert Group came out with the following important recommendations:

- the compiling of a common code of ethics which could then be put into booklet form and disseminated across the globe;

- in addition to this general code, specific codes of ethics for the professions, business, political parties, mass media, and other critical interests, which would contribute to self-regulation;

- suggestions to the world's leaders that in 1998, the fiftieth anniversary of the Universal Declaration of Human Rights, the United Nations convene a conference to consider a Declaration of Human Obligations to complement the earlier crucial work on rights;

- development of a global educational curriculum that would include the best contributions of the world's religions and philosophies, to be made available to every educational institution and accessible through current communication technologies—radio, educational television, videos, the Internet, etc.;

- to broaden understanding and combine the intellectual resources necessary for the development of such a curriculum, the United Nations should consider establishing as part of the UN University system a World Interfaith Academy that would bring together scholars, students, and leaders of the world's faiths.

Further, the Vienna Expert Group said:

There have been landmark advances to strengthen human rights in international law and justice, beginning with the United Nations' adopting the Universal Declaration of Human Rights and Social, Cultural and Economic Rights, and the Covenants of Civil and Political Rights and Social, Cultural and Economic Rights, elaborated by the Vienna Declaration on Human Rights and

Program for Action. What the UN proclaimed on the level of rights, the Chicago Declaration confirmed and deepened from the perspective of obligations.

The Expert Group also said:

We note the ongoing participatory process, initiated by the Earth Council and Green Cross International, to develop an Earth Charter. We welcome this initiative as an example of an effort to involve the world's religions and other groups in defining the basic change in values, behavior, and attitudes of government, private sector, and civil society, needed for a shift to sustainable development.

Global Governance

What kind of global governance system do we visualize? I for one do not visualize a centralized world government. In the past there have been references to "world government," vaguely meaning a world authority. But we have to be clear as to what exactly we mean.

When we talk about world government, we have the image of a national government in our minds. National governments as they are constituted today are powerful institutions, armed with military power, police force, and bureaucratic machines. But the nation-state has to change. In the new world order that we visualize, nation-states should become softer, more responsive, less powerful, and less oppressive. As a matter of fact, there should be a two-way movement of the powers of the nation-state, to be transferred to local governments on the one hand, and to the global governance system on the other.

A global governance system will include multilateral and multilevel structures of decision-making bodies. The new world will consist of vast networks of local communities in which participatory democracy flourishes. So the first principle I would advocate is the principle of *decentralized polity*. Around the world today, local communities are in varying stages of empowerment; in some societies they are strong and vital. In tribal and hill societies, the "village council" is still a powerful body. In modern democracies like the United States, local bodies are strong.

In countries like India, historically speaking, the village councils and local bodies lost their original strength during colonial rule. Even after the advent of independence, in 1947, as per its new Constitution India had only two tiers of governance: national government and state government. There was a list of subjects for the national government, a concurrent list of subjects shared by the central government and the state

governments, and a third list of subjects which were the exclusive jurisdiction of the state governments.

But this was not what Gandhiji visualized for independent India. He
visualized a vast commonwealth of powerful local communities and even
went to the extent of saying that each village should be a "republic." Now
India has amended its Constitution; the 73rd Constitutional Amendment
on Panchayati Raj is a mighty step toward a decentralized polity where
power resides with the people. We have now a participatory democracy.

The grand vision of Mahatma Gandhi is given below:

> In this structure composed of innumerable villages, there will be ever-widening,
> never-ascending circles. Life will not be a pyramid with the apex sustained by
> the bottom. It will be an oceanic circle whose center will be the individual al-
> ways ready to perish for the village, the village ready to perish for the circle of
> villages, till at last the whole becomes one life composed of individuals, never
> aggressive in their arrogance but ever humble, sharing the majesty of the oce-
> anic circle of which they are an integral part.

Today we have hundreds of thousands of locally elected leaders participating in the governance process. What is more, under the new system of Panchayats, women have come to the forefront and are members
and presidents in one third of the local bodies. Similarly, there is a constitutional provision for Indian society's weaker sections to be represented
in the governance system, according to their proportion of the population. Thus social and gender justice have been incorporated constitution-
ally into the decentralized governance system now prevailing in India.

Democratic Decentralization. I would suggest that all over the world
the movement should be toward democratic decentralization and participatory democracy. People at the grass roots must have the power to shape
their own destiny. It is becoming increasingly clear that the basic problems of humankind such as population, primary health, primary education, and food security can be solved only by the constructive efforts of
people in local communities; national governments can play an important enabling role. Thus, in the future world order, we visualize at the
basic tier a powerful local democracy. Then we move on to national democracy, and then to global democracy.

Global Democracy. I agree with Johan Galtung that the future global
system should be based upon global democracy. The present situation in
the world is far from democratic. In some countries, democracy does not
prevail; in some it is limited. How to democratize the future world system

is the challenge before us. One basic reform that we shall demand of the United Nations is that it should become more democratic; how to democratize the UN system is a matter requiring serious thought.

UN as Basis of Global System. This brings me to a second basic proposition, namely that the future global governance system should grow out of the present United Nations system. With all its strengths and weaknesses, the UN system has come to stay, growing from strength to strength. It is true that during the cold-war decades the United Nations could not play its due role; but after the cold war's end, it can play a new role. The two basic documents brought about by the former Secretary-General, Mr. Bhoutros Bhoutros-Ghali, namely the *Agenda for Peace* and the *Agenda for Development*, give guidelines for the UN's future role. The Commission on Global Governance has come out with good suggestions for the restructuring of the United Nations: for instance, the Security Council should be made more broad-based, and its veto power should be abolished. Further, the UN General Assembly alone is not enough; it is only an assembly of official delegates of the national governments.

People's Assembly or World Parliament. We should have a People's Assembly where representatives of the world's peoples will gather and voice their views about the future of the world. In a way this parliament of the world will be similar to the legislative bodies of various nations.

Restructuring the UN. The Commission on Global Governance has made several suggestions regarding UN restructuring, including these:

- the Trusteeship Council should be given a new mandate to exercise trusteeship over the global commons;

- the UN specialized agencies should develop as centers of authority in their fields;

- the International Court of Justice must be made stronger and all members of the UN should accept its compulsory jurisdiction;

- an International Criminal Court should be established in order to enforce international law;

- an appropriate body should be asked to explore new ways in which international lawmaking can be accepted.

Economic Governance. Some of the Commission's suggestions follow:

- an Economic Security Council should be established within the United Nations;

- all governments should enact legislation to implement the Uruguay Round agreement to set up the World Trade Organization;

- the role of the International Monetary Fund should be further enhanced;

- governments should renew their efforts to meet the target of 0.7 percent of Gross Domestic Product for official development assistance.

In the course of several recent years, the United Nations has succeeded in developing a system of global law regarding Antarctica and the Law of the Sea. Taking advantage of these past successes, the UN should be encouraged to move into other areas of global law.

Common Security System. Since the world is moving toward a common global security system, radical changes could be brought about to improve the present position. The Charter of the United Nations should be revised to allow the Security Council to act in situations within countries; and the UN should continue to work for a nuclear weapon-free world and to ban nuclear testing and weapons production.

Demilitarization. Demilitarization should be given increased priority in the new global order. National governments should be encouraged to adopt lower levels of global defense spending. States should undertake to bring about a convention on the curtailment of the arms trade. There should be a worldwide ban on the manufacture and export of land mines. A demilitarization fund should be established to help developing countries reduce their military expenditure. Indeed, taking a long-term view of the future of the world, the enormous resources now spent on armaments and standing armies should be diverted to peaceful purposes through mutual understanding between nations, and there should be reciprocally accepted decisions of low spending on defense.

Free and Open National Borders. A free and open border between India and Nepal, for instance, and between the United States and Canada, are examples of how national borders can be free and friendly without armies facing one another. The example of Costa Rica, where a country (albeit a small one) has no armed forces at all and depends only on the goodwill and friendship of its neighbors, is a principle that should be accepted more and more around the world.

Conclusion

This paper is in the nature of an exploration and must be taken as a tentative document. Along with other papers by friends and colleagues from around the world and from different religious and national backgrounds, it will constitute a joint quest.

Toward a Culture of Nonviolence: The Jain Way of Life

P.N. (Bawa) Jain

Ahimsa parmo dharma (nonviolence is the greatest religion). (Mahavira)

Nonviolence is a weapon of the strong. (Mahatma Gandhi)

The dawn of nonviolence shall usher in an era of peaceful coexistence, where the oneness of all religions becomes the foundation stone of the oneness of humanity. (H.H. Acharya Sushil Kumarji Maharaj)

I believe that the Jain way of life is universal and the teachings are pertinent in today's context. I shall attempt to express my interpretation and understanding of the Jain religion and philosophy. My approach to answering the Guideline Questions will not be specific, but I believe the questions are answered to some extent by discussing the cardinal principles of the Jain way of life. The views expressed in this paper are mine personally and are derived from my own experiences and learning of the teachings of the Jain way of life, as preached by my spiritual father and teacher H.H. Acharya Sushil Kumarji Maharaj, to whose memory I dedicate this paper.

Background

The present form of Jainism was inspired by the teachings of Tirthankar Mahavira, who lived about 2,500 years ago and brought about a synthesis between religion and philosophy. Historians have not been able to trace the origin of Jainism, but have established that it is undoubtedly an ancient religion and that Mahavira was not its founder, but merely reiterated and rejuvenated it.

Jaina history contains references to the 63 Salaka-Purusas (the Supreme Personages), who lived during the ancient periods of the two great recurring cycles of the ages, the *avasarpini-kala* and *utsarpini-kala*. These Salaka-Purusas inspired the people to follow religion and ethics during the course of the advancement of human civilization. The Tirthankaras occupy the highest position among the Salaka-Purusas. During the fourth part of the present cycle of *avasarpini-kala*, 24 Tirthankaras were born. The last of the Tirthankaras was Mahavira, who lived about 2,500 years ago; Buddha Tathagata was his contemporary. The Buddhist scriptures mention Mahavira as Niganthanaputta. The tradition is without a beginning or an end; who knows how many 24 Tirthankaras have gone by, and how many will come in the future?

The Principle of *Aparigraha*: The Oneness of All Beings

Paraspar upagraha jivanam (all souls are rendering service to one another).

Today we are living in a world that is growing consciously interdependent. This reality emanates from the Jain principle of *aparigraha*, which for centuries has taught that we are all one, all interdependent. For humanity to survive, we have to ensure the preservation and nurturing of an environment for all forms of life to coexist peacefully and harmoniously. We must remind ourselves that local actions have global consequences, and our actions have repercussions for ourselves. In fact, what distinguishes the Jain theology from its praxis is the emphasis on the immediate repercussions of one's thoughts and actions.

Humanity is going through a spiritual renaissance. As we lay to rest perhaps the bloodiest century in human history, there is greater recognition of and emphasis on the principles of *ahimsa* (nonviolence—perhaps the greatest gift of the Jain way of life) as the key to global survival. The twentieth century witnessed the exemplary lives of Mahatma Gandhi, Martin Luther King, Jr., and others who lived by the principles of *ahimsa* and emerged victorious in wars, not by weapons of mass destruction and violence, but by their firm conviction in the power of nonviolence. These people have also demonstrated to us the responsibility and the power of every individual. This is the Jain way of life.

The Tradition of the Nonexistence of God

Appa so parmappa (soul is God).

The basic foundation of all religions in the world is the *atma* and the *parmatma*, the soul and the Supreme Soul. The grand edifice of religion stands on the pillars of these two principles. Some religions believe in the existence of God along with the existence of the soul; some are atheistic. Those who believe in the doctrine of the existence of God regard him as the Creator, Protector, and Regulator of the Universe, the all-powerful Supreme Soul. He is called the Brahma, the Supreme Father, and so on.

The second tradition believes in the existence of the soul but not of God; as a creator of the universe, it believes in the independent progress of the soul. The soul reaches the highest position after attainment of supreme purification by the destruction of attachment, indulgence, and hatred, and the acquisition of complete detachment. It is an eternal, self-regulated existence: the human being is his or her own friend and foe. Jainism follows this philosophy, which has an independent and scientific outlook. This tradition is known, in brief, by the name of Sramana culture. The other Indian tradition, of believers in the existence of God, is known as the Brahman culture. Buddhism is another Indian religion which follows the philosophy of non-creation of the universe by God, but believes in the cycle of birth and death.

Viewed from the point of cultural evolution, it would be apparent that there is not much spiritual difference between the Vedic (Brahmanic) and Sramanic cultures; but the difference from the popular viewpoint, with respect to principles, conduct, and faith, is quite clear. The two cultures have influenced each other to a considerable extent, as amply evidenced by the rich ancient literature of India. Even in one family, people with different traditions used to follow their respective modes of religious worship.

A Scientific Philosophy

To know how the whole mechanism of the universe works, to apprehend the cosmic spell and break through the outward layers of the tangible and visible forces of the cosmos, is the final goal of human life and the pursuit of Jainism. Most of the basic principles on which Jaina philosophy is constructed are now corroborated by modern science and psychological analysis. Scientific theory postulates that every substance is made of atoms, and every atom, when analyzed, reveals the energetic interplay of electrons, protons, and neutrons.

Jainism maintains that the whole universe can be broadly divided into two categories, *jiva* (spirit) and *ajiva* (matter). On the basis of this finding, about 2,500 years ago, Jaina seers saw the life-force not only in plants and vegetables but also in so-called inanimate matter such as earth, water, and air. They went further in their analysis and subcategorized the two categories, examining their characteristics. They concluded that *jiva* and *ajiva* are eternal, uncreated, unending, and perpetual. There is a constant interplay between the two, resulting in the bewildering cosmic manifestations in material, psychic, and emotional spheres around us. This led them to the theories of transmigration and rebirth. Change, not the total annihilation of spirit and matter, is the basic postulate of Jaina philosophy; it is the same thing science teaches us when it says that matter is indestructible.

The theory of *karma* (action) came as a natural deduction from the theory of causation, just as science recognizes the fact that every effect is the result of some cause. Jainism considers the whole universe as a great cosmic mechanism with its own self-propelling force, uncreated and uncontrolled by any superimposed outside force. Its unitary character can be properly identified only by recognizing and giving proper place to each of its parts. This leads a logical mind to the theory of total nonviolence, *ahimsa*. For if you believe the universe to be a unitary whole, a self-propelling mechanism, wherein every part, from the smallest to the largest, has a role to play, you cannot destroy even a nut or bolt of that machine without damaging it, as well as your own self.

To know this mechanism, to understand and explain its working, is the task of a philosopher; but to live according to its rules, to play one's own role as a part of it so that it can work properly, is the task of a religious person. This philosophy and this religion cannot be carried out successfully without accepting the doctrine of total nonviolence in thought, speech, and action. A weak person cannot practice nonviolence, for the simple reason that *the concept of total nonviolence is not a negative one*—it is not just doing nothing. True nonviolence is not the product of a merely intellectual understanding, but a product of both head and heart. One cannot be nonviolent unless one understands the real nature of irritating causes; but for this, two interdependent things are required, namely love and the capacity to appreciate the totality of the causes. Without love, the capacity for total comprehension is not developed; and without the capacity for total comprehension, the element of love is not developed.

This has led Jaina thinkers to emphasize the development of a broader outlook—the open-mindedness to understand things as they are. Cultivation of mind was found to be the key to the Halls of Heaven, but the thinkers realized that mind cannot be cultivated and disciplined by force, only through reason. Logic is the only feature which distinguishes human beings from the rest of the animal world.

The Theories of *Syadvada* and *Karma*: Relativity and Action

To develop this reason and logic, Jaina thinkers provided the theory of *syadvada*, or relativity—Jainism's greatest contribution to the thinking process of humankind, unfortunately little-known to Occidentals. This theory propounds that every judgment is relatively true, because its truth value depends on its relation to other objects: known and unknown circumstances, modes of expression and reception, and many other facts. After a period of 2,500 years, this theory has been recognized by Einstein and others on the plane of physics.

How to comprehend reality? Can any outside agency be of help? No, says the Jaina tradition; your salvation is in your own hands. You are your own master, the architect of your own destiny. If your pleasure and pain are the result of your own action (*karma*), the way of salvation is also in your hands, because what you have done can be undone only by you.

The theory of *karma* teaches us how to attain freedom from the bondage of likes, dislikes, and desires. It teaches us not to surrender meekly to human weaknesses, described as our real enemies. It further tells us that, just as your savior is not outside you, neither are your enemies; you have to seek them within. Once you identify them within you, it is not very difficult to overcome them. One who has succeeded in such annihilation is called *arihanta* (in Sanskrit *ari* means "enemy," and the root *han* means "to kill"). An *arihanta* is free from bondage and becomes *siddha*, one who has achieved final salvation—the real freedom.

Many in this universe have achieved the positions of *arihantasin and siddhas*, and many will achieve the same in the future. Since they have achieved that which ought to be achieved, they are entitled to our respect and homage. We, therefore, bow to them. There are learned sages, the path-seekers who show us the path; they are called *acharyas*; we bow to them. There are those who preach and interpret the gospels of truth. They are called *upadhyayas*; we bow to them. There are those who are still seriously striving to achieve the above goal. They are called *sadhus* (saints); we bow to them also. Thus the Jains bow down to those who have attained, to those who are on the path of attainment, and to those who are path-seekers, irrespective of their religious levels. We pay homage to them not because we want favor, but because they are the source of inspiration for our own actions.

Jainism admonishes us: *Appa katta vikatta ya, duhanna ya suhana ya. Appa mittamamittam ca, dupatthiya supatthio.* (It is your own self which is the doer as well as enjoyer of your pleasure and pains. Your friend and foe is also your own self, engaged in good and bad activities, respectively.)

The Importance of Bheda-Jnana

The Jaina approach to the constitution of the world is altogether scientific and logical. The concept of *bheda-jnana* (*bheda* means respecting distinctions and differences; *jnana* means knowledge) involves the firm belief in the existence of soul and non-soul as the constituents of the world. A logical approach to the constitution of the universe can easily convince us of the existence and efficacy of both. There is nothing religious or sectarian in the proposition that there are two basic constituents of this phenomenal world—*jiva* and *ajiva*, sentient and non-sentient things. If this conviction is heeded by a discerning human mind, there is little difficulty in concluding that our true self is purely a knower, the permanent conscious element which knows and motivates all our activities in life, and that the rest is only an object of our knowledge and thus foreign to us.

If this is so, should I not concentrate on that which is permanent, that which is my own self? For to devote our attention to the things which are foreign to "self" is to seek satisfaction from objects which do not belong to us. This is bound to result in despair, dejection, and tension. Jaina seers, therefore, emphasize that *the realization of the distinction between self and non-self is the first essential condition for a blissful life.* This, however, does not mean that as householders we should shun all activities of material life. In fact, all the Tirthankaras and leading Jaina *sravakas* (householders) were successfully engrossed in activities of life, but the key to their attainment of spiritual bliss was their awareness that real happiness resides in one's own self and can never be obtained through the enjoyment of worldly objects.

Once such a firm conviction is developed, worldly activities and their results do not touch us; then all our doubts, dejections, and despairs vanish and one begins to get a taste of real happiness and bliss. Without such an awareness or conviction, one easily identifies oneself with worldly objects of enjoyment which are transitory and foreign to the self. The fickle character of these objects, when identified with our self, brings in its train all the tensions and turmoils of our day-to-day existence.

So the first postulate of a blissful life is the discrimination of self and non-self, and the conviction that the self's indulgences in non-self are bound to result in suffering. Such a realization would greatly reduce our usual tensions and enable us to face the realities of life with unprecedented calm and fortitude. We would then be no more pulled and pushed by outside factors, because the exigencies generated by these forces are not able to touch our "self." We, and not the outside forces, become masters of ourselves.

The Jaina masters have prescribed practical and workable methods to train our psyche in this direction. They have asked us to bear constantly in mind the twelve *bhavanas* (reflections), i.e., the reflection of *anityatva* (transitoriness), *asaranatva* (helplessness), etc. These reflections are logical conclusions derived from the behavioral pattern of the human mind in its interaction with material objects of the universe. The Jaina insistence on austerities, daily repentance, and meditations greatly helps in shaping our personality, leading to a life of peace, tranquillity, and contentment.

The Doctrine of *Ahimsa*: Nonviolence in Thought, Action, and Deed

Nonviolence is the foundation of Jain ethics. However, the observance of nonviolence is not possible without an attitude of "many points of view" or relativity, because from the Jaina point of view, *a person can be nonviolent even when committing violence.* The commission of violence or nonviolence is dependent upon the mental condition of the doer, not on the act. He who conducts himself with the utmost caution is nonviolent in his thought, hence he is nonviolent; and he who does not observe caution in his active daily life has violence in his mental state, so even if he actually commits no violence, he is ethically violent.

All this analysis is not possible unless one possesses the "many points of view." Hence a person who possesses an attitude of "many points of view" is regarded as being possessed of right faith, and the person possessed of right faith can acquire right knowledge and right conduct. Righteousness or right faith has special significance in the Jaina faith; it is the foundation stone to the path of liberation.

Mundane life is bondage. The soul is involved in this bondage from time immemorial; we have forgotten our real nature on this account, and it is this forgetfulness that is responsible for our bondage. We will realize this mistake only when we discover that our nature is endowed with infinite consciousness, that our strength is greater than what is seen in mundane life, that we are the treasure-house of infinite knowledge, faith, bliss, and power. It is only when we become alive to this faith that we try to achieve firmness of conviction about our real nature through our right conduct. Hence the pathway of Jaina ethics is the royal road that leads to the state of conquest of attachment in accordance with right knowledge.

The doctrine of *ahimsa* to be practiced in mind, speech, and action is yet another factor of practical utility in soothing, softening, and harmonizing the international, national, and individual relationship. Jaina thinkers touched new heights of philosophical refinement by introducing the doctrine of *ahimsa* even in the process of thinking. Their evolution of the theories of *naya* (the analytical process of ontological inquiry) and *syadvada* (relativity) is an attempt to recognize even the partial truth, whenever evident, so that reality can be comprehended to the fullest possible extent. Adoption of this method of establishing truth positively leads to the development of tolerance of every viewpoint, however contrary it may be to the current and traditional view. If the theories of *naya* and *syadvada* were extended to every sphere of human activity, individual and social life on this planet would be completely revolutionized. Softness and love are qualities developed by the practice of *ahimsa*; all hatred and cruelty automatically stop once these qualities are developed and applied.

Ahimsa has been an important principle in the history of human civilization. As a moral injunction it was universally applicable in the religious sphere: Jesus asked us to love our neighbor as ourselves. It has been accepted as moral principle in Indian thought and religion. Gandhiji extended the principle of nonviolence to the social and political fields. For him nonviolence was a creed. He developed a method and a technique of nonviolence for attaining social and political justice. *Ahimsa* is the first principle in the *dharma* (religious practice) of saints or sages by which they lift themselves out of the normal human range of action.

In the history of Indian thought, *ahimsa* arose out of the need to re-sist the excesses of violence performed in the name of religion, for the sake of salvation. Animal sacrifice was prevalent in the Vedic, and to some extent Upanisadic, periods. However, a gradual awareness of the undesirability of animal sacrifice was being felt at the time of the Upani-sads, in whose texts one finds passages upholding the virtues of nonvio-lence. In the *Chandogya Upanisad*, life is described as a great festival in which qualities like *tapas* (self-renunciation) and *ahimsa* are expressed.

Consequences of *Karma* Theory

1. Once you believe that universal phenomena are governed by the law of causation, you rule out the existence of any outside agency to gov-ern our fate.

2. The theory is based on the premise that karmic forces, which set in motion the law of causation, are eternal; their motivating force, *jiva*, is also eternal; there is no need to import the idea of a creator, sus-tainer, and destroyer.

3. The theory of *karma* rules out the propitiation of gods to seek their favor and save yourself from calamities.

4. On the contrary, the theory insists on self-reliance and asks us to de-velop our own moral character and increase our spiritual power to save ourselves from the evil effects of our own past *karma*.

5. You have to own your ethical responsibility for the things of life, and it is possible to discharge this responsibility with equanimity and un-derstanding.

The Doctrine of *Anekantavada*: Multiplicity of Truth

The importance of *anekantavada*, a comprehensive synthesis of *syadvada* (relativity) and *anekanta-naya* (multiplicity of truth and the analytical process of ontological inquiry) in day-to-day life, is immense, inasmuch as these doctrines supply a rational unification and synthesis of the mani-fold, and reject the assertion of bare absolutes.

Mahatma Gandhi wrote in 1926,

It has been my experience that I am always true (correct) from my point of view, and often wrong from the point of view of my critics. I know that we are both (myself and my critics) right from our respective points of view....

I very much like this doctrine....It is this doctrine that has taught me to judge a Muslim from his standpoint and a Christian from his.... From the platform of the Jainas, I prove the non-creative aspect of God, and from that of Ramanuja the creative aspect. As a matter of fact, we are all thinking of the unthinkable, describing the indescribable, seeking to know the unknown, and that is why our speech falters, is inadequate, and has been often contradictory.

The history of all conflicts and confrontations in the world is the history of intolerance born of ignorance and egocentrism. If only we could become conscious of our own limitations. *Anekanta* or *syadvada* tries to make us conscious of our limitations by pointing to our narrow vision and limited knowledge of the manifold aspects of things, and asks us not to be hasty in forming absolute judgments before examining various other aspects—both positive and negative. Obviously, much of the bloodshed and tribulations of humankind could be saved if we showed the wisdom of understanding contrary viewpoints.

In reality, even the highest knowledge acquired by an embodied soul in this vast world is limited, imperfect, and one-sided. It is not possible for persons to comprehend simultaneously the infinite qualities of an object, let alone express them, which is far more difficult. The inadequacy of language creates conflicts and disputes; the human ego further accentuates the matter. The doctrine of *anekanta* paves the way for harmony and removal of conflicts. *There is an element of truth in every statement, and it is possible to dissolve the conflict in a straightforward manner by understanding that element of truth.*

If we are not obstinate or persistent in our point of view, we can easily solve almost every problem. So long as the sight is obscured by the veil of persistence, it is not possible to get a proper perspective of an object. The doctrine of *anekanta* proclaims the independent existence of an object. In the world of thought, *anekanta* is the tangible form of *ahimsa*. Whoever is nonviolent possesses the *anekanta* view of life; whoever possesses the *anekanta* view of life shall be nonviolent in thought and action. The harmony between knowledge, faith, and conduct can lead human beings toward liberation from misery. Action without knowledge or knowledge without action are both futile; only when the practice of truth that is known, and the knowledge of truth that is practiced, are combined, can there be a fruitful result.

The moment one begins to consider the angle from which a contrary viewpoint is put forward, one begins to develop tolerance, which is the basic requirement of the practice of *ahimsa*. *Syadvada* makes all absolutes in the field of thought quite irrelevant and naive, imparts maturity to the thought process, and supplies flexibility and originality to the human mind. If humankind will properly understand and adopt this doctrine of *syadvada*, it will realize that the real revolution was not the French or the Russian one, but the one which taught humanity to develop the power of understanding from all possible aspects.

The Doctrine of *Aparigraha*: Restrictions in Possession

Aparigraha is more relevant today than it was in the time of Mahavira. Those who try to accumulate possessions are entangled in a web of materialism. We become slaves of our possessions and like our slavery because we are accustomed to it. We forget that all objects in the world are constantly changing in form and qualities, and are also changing hands. This is the reality of life; the idea of possession is in fact illusory. But we like to remain in illusion and when our possessions change hands, we become sad. The process of living in illusion causes grief and tormentations. If one hankers after worldly things, it is a sure sign of uncontrolled desires, resulting in uncontrolled activities on the material plane.

And desires have no end: the German philosopher Schopenhauer pointed out that for every wish that is satisfied there remain ten that are denied; desire is infinite, fulfillment is limited, and so long as we give in to desires we can never have true and lasting happiness and peace. Lord Buddha, therefore, rightly emphasized the necessity to curtail our desires. The principle of *aparigraha* teaches us to restrict our possessions to the minimum. This can be done only if we discipline our wants. Even earning more than necessary offends the principle of *aparigraha*. Good Jainas take a vow to fix their possessions of material things, including wealth.

The economy of Indian society was, till recently, dominated by this principle of *aparigraha*. However, the more we have come under the influence of Western materialism, the more our attitude toward life has become superficial. India's history is replete with examples of multi-millionaires leading the life of a poor person and donating all their wealth for a public cause. There was no marked difference between the lifestyle and standards of persons belonging to different financial strata of society. A rich man did not desire more luxury simply because he could afford to spend. Now standards, outlook, and lifestyle have changed: earn more and spend more, increase your standard of living, "simple thinking and higher living" (in contrast to what the English poet Wordsworth said) are the mottoes of modern life. The result is licentiousness, absence of moral discipline, unnecessary and fruitless spending, lack of equilibrium in the prices of consumer goods, diversion of essential raw materials for the production of luxury goods, exploitation of labor and consumers, unequal distribution of wealth, and the resultant unrest and class war.

It is unfortunate that even socialist ideology, led by thinkers like Marx, who revolted against social injustices resulting from economic imbalances, failed to get to the root of the problem and could not go beyond materialistic conceptions of history and economics. These thinkers forgot to take into account that a human being is the unit of society, hence no social structure can be improved effectively without improving its units.

Indian seers, on the other hand, have always kept this aspect in mind, emphasizing the advancement of the individual character of each person. What they taught by *aparigraha* was not a mere religion; it was sociology in its truest sense. To create class conflict and then fight it was, to them, an absurd process: better to prevent the generation of conflict.

The lack of inherent restraint from within, the lack of awareness of life's realities, the lack of the knowledge that real enjoyment of life is not in material pursuits—these are responsible for our present unrest and sense of insecurity. The problem can never be solved by mere economic reforms. All economic theories have to be worked out among human beings with psychological, emotional, and sentimental needs. Economists and political theorists are great ignoramuses in such treatment.

Among modern political leaders, Mahatma Gandhi may be credited with practicing what he preached. He himself had no *parigraha* (possessions). He taught the Indians, and the whole world, that limitation of desires and restraint of possessions, "simple living and high thinking," are the only realistic way to live a happy, contented, and peaceful life, without conflicts and constraints.

The Conquest of Attachment: Self-Realization

The aim of the Jaina religion is the attainment of complete conquest of attachment, and realization. This victory over attachment becomes possible by a harmonious accomplishment of the Three Jewels: right faith (*samyag darshana*), right knowledge (*samyag gyana*), and right conduct (*samyag charitra*). By following the path of the happy combination of faith, knowledge, and conduct, one can attain salvation or perfection. The basic teaching of Jainism is that right knowledge should be acquired by looking at mundane things with an eye of right faith, and that the same should be translated into conduct. However, the pivotal point is the attainment of conquest over attachment. Even the greatest riches of the world are futile in the face of conquest of attachment; but this path cannot be reached without the aid of an attitude of "many points of view."

The ethical ideal of a Jaina is not pleasure of the senses, nor gratification of the body. These are insatiable: the more we get them, the more we want and the more pained we are. There is a glue, as it were, in pleasure: those who are not given to pleasure are not soiled by it and will be liberated; those who love pleasure must wander about in *samsara* (the world). Like two clods of clay, one wet and one dry, flung at the wall, those who love pleasure stick to the influx of *karma*, but the passionless are free. Not the pleasures of the moment, nor even the greatest happiness of the greatest number, are attractions to the truly pious, for their ultimate end is to attain perfection and lead others to the path of righteousness. Yet the Jaina does not say that pleasures of the senses are to be avoided completely, especially for the lay disciple. Mortification of the body is equally one-sided: rigorous asceticism for a monk is a means to an end, not an end in itself. A lay follower may continue an occupation, earn money, live a family life, and enjoy the normal pleasures of life in a good spirit according to the needs and status of an individual in society.

Jainism aims at self-realization, and the self to be realized is the transcendental and pure self. The empirical self is to be cared for and its energy is to be channeled in the direction of the attainment of the highest ideal of *moksa*, freedom from the wheel of *samsara*, the world. The soul gets entangled in the wheel of *samsara* and is embodied through the operation of *karma*. It is embodied in various forms due to materially caused conditions (*upadhs*), and is involved in the cycle of birth and death. But the Jainas believe in the soul's inherent capacity for self-realization. Deliverance from the wheel of *samsara* is possible by way of voluntary efforts on the part of individuals.

When all obstacles are removed, the soul becomes pure and perfect and attains liberation or *moksa*. However, the soul's journey to freedom is long and arduous, because the removal of *karma* involves a long moral and spiritual discipline through fourteen stages of self-realization called *gunasthana.* The soul has gradually to remove the five conditions of bondage—*mithydiva* (perversity), *aviran* (lack of control), *pramada* (spiritual inertia), *kasaya* (passion), and *triyoga* (threefold activity of body, speech, and mind). In the highest stage of spiritual realization, the soul reaches the stages of perfection and omniscience. This is the consummation of the struggle.

It is not possible to give a true description of the liberated soul. The state of perfection is described as freedom from action and desire, utter and absolute quiescence, and unaffected peace, since the energy of past *karma* is extinguished. It is the perfect liberation. After its pilgrimage of innumerable existences in various inferior stratifications, nothing can happen to the soul anymore; it has put aside the traits of ignorance, those heavy veils of individuality that are the precipitating causes of biographical events. In the higher stage of perfection, the individuality, masks, and formal personal features are distilled away. This is the *siddha* state. The freed soul has a beginning but no end, while the soul in *samsara* has no beginning, but an end in the attainment of freedom.

A New Orientation of Values

We are in the midst of a life where hatred, injustice, and tolerance reign supreme. A new orientation of values would be necessary for us to destroy the inverted values and then "rebuild to our heart's desire." What we need today is not prejudice and pomp but love and sympathy, understanding, and a sense of fellowship between the peoples of the world. And *anekanta* would give us a *Weltanschauung* and a scientific interpretation of things. We would then learn to "love our neighbors as ourselves."

The Jaina doctrines are helpful to anyone in living a vibrant and purposeful life, conducive to the development of social, ethical, national, and international harmony. As they are based on scientific analysis of universal components and human psychology, their appeal is universal and confined only to logic and reasoning, containing nothing sectarian. It is a process of thinking and a way of life which are as relevant today as they were 2,500 years ago in the times of Mahavira.

International Cooperation

In the international context, in 1991 International Mahavir Jain Mission was the first Jain organization to be accorded affiliated status at the

United Nations. In North America alone there are over 70 Jain centers. In fact, the first Jain *Tirth* (pilgrimage center), where for the first time the different sects of Jainism are represented on one platform, was established in Blairstown, New Jersey, in 1991 by H.H. Acharya Sushil Kumarji Maharaj, who revolutionized Jain history in 1975 when he became the first Jain monk to travel overseas (Jain ascetics do not use any form of transportation and travel only on foot). Ever since his historic journey, many monks and nuns have adapted to the needs of society and are traveling to new lands to preach the Jain way of life. Today Jain temples are being established all over.

The Jains are taking an active part in addressing problems and challenges not only within their communities, but in the global arena. My approach has been to create an awareness of the Jain way of life in the United Nations community, and to participate actively, alongside the world's other major religions, on key issues the UN addresses. In my opinion, the UN's ability to create a widespread awareness of global issues is among its greatest successes. This has been demonstrated by the series of global conferences, on some of the most pressing issues of our times, convened by the UN in this decade; the Jains have actively participated.

For the UN to remain relevant and meaningful, it must restructure and reform itself so that it is more capable of addressing the reality of modernity. There are numerous areas of reform upon which the UN is currently embarked, but in the context of our discussion I would like to focus on the following.

- The UN's greatest challenge is the growing differences among the religions of the world. The Trusteeship Council has served its purpose; create a Spiritual Council in place of the Trusteeship Council, on the lines of the Security Council, to address conflicts among the world's religions and work closely with the Security Council in seeking to make our world more peaceful.

- Create an Economic and Social Security Council, as there are growing differences and enormous tensions on economic and social issues. In this era of globalization the UN must be equipped to deal with new realities and meet the challenges of the future.

- Create Nonviolent Conflict Resolution centers all over the world, within the present structures of the UN system, to engage in nonviolent and peaceful resolution of conflict, impart nonviolence education, and impart training in conflict resolution, especially at the community level.

- The UN must set up mechanisms to foster collaborations and part-nerships with nongovernmental and civic society organizations to empower them to deal with humanity's challenges, especially in local initiatives within national borders, because present structures do not allow the UN to be reactive or proactive in an internal matter. NGOs are the UN's biggest resource and are dealing with the most pressing problems of our times; there needs to be a threefold partner-ship: the UN, member nations, and civil society.

The above are some suggestions within the UN system. The religions of the world in today's context must also be more practical and engage in active initiatives to address humanity's problems at local, national, and international levels. Some specific initiatives follow.

- The religions of the world must develop curricula to work with edu-cational institutions in (a) interreligious understanding, to create a knowledge base of the various religions, their practices and customs (this will help engender tolerance, thereby laying the foundations for creating harmony in our societies); (b) nonviolence education, starting at the primary level; (c) conflict resolution education and training, especially to the clergy, to enable them to better deal with conflict situations at all levels.

- Work toward a Universal Declaration of Animals' Rights. If we are to survive, then we must ensure the survival of all forms of life.

- Actively participate in the creation of interfaith centers to foster in-terreligious dialogue, for a better understanding of the diversity within our communities. This is a very important dimension because of the reality of ever-growing interreligious dwellings. We are con-fronted with new dynamics in our global village; this demands that we devise systems to better understand each other's cultures and re-ligions. With the emergence of interfaith and intercultural centers, space would be created to interact, address problems, resolve con-flicts, and foster a human community.

There exist fundamental values in every society, in every culture, in every heritage. Let us consciously choose the values we want to live by, for there needs to be a core set of values around which we can unite.

BUDDHISM

Religion and World Order from a Buddhist Perspective

Sulak Sivaraksa

Working Toward a Shared Global Ethic

I do not believe that a world ethic can be imposed as a product of philosophical ratiocination. It will not be deduced from universal moral principles or derived from the postulation of a common human nature. The search for some underlying metaphysical truth as a ground for morality entails a subject-object dualism that is rejected in Buddhist teachings. Moreover, an axiology that serves the cause of civilization does not exist as some abstract conceptual doctrine but is formulated by the attitudes and beliefs that serve to condition the behavior of individuals.

The moral principles that are meaningful for a given society are those that are embedded in the culture and traditions of that society. They are historically conditioned and contingent. They do, however, represent the principles that evolved from the villages and communities to govern social organization before new values were superimposed through violence or propaganda.

A cultural dialogue that involves comparing and contrasting the values of various societies should not be undertaken as a means of establishing the inherent validity of any particular set of values. Nor should it be assumed that all conflicts can be resolved and that one consistent ethic will emerge from the process. The dialectical process can reveal the common elements of the moral view of different cultures and the manner in which those elements are contravened by incompatible strictures. In this process Buddhism can provide an evaluative standard, rooted in human experience, by which the efficacy of a given tenet may be assessed.

The elimination of suffering is the ultimate concern of Buddhist teachings. All conduct can be evaluated in terms of its capacity to promote or delimit suffering. In some respect all values which can be defined as ethical values must address suffering. No moral system can be oblivious to this factor, although the concepts may be expressed in various vocabularies.

For Buddhism it is the practice of individualizing experience which is the essential cause of suffering. Characterizing experience dualistically in terms of objects existing in relationship to a transcendental subject generates the greed, anger, and delusion which forms the substratum of discontentment. The path to personal liberation entails the renunciation of this worldview in favor of a recognition of the interdependence of all beings. This transformation requires that the maxim of every action reflect interrelationship with others and responsibility for their well-being.

An ethical system must define the relationship of the individual to the community. A moral decision by our general understanding of the term requires that some consideration be given to something beyond parochial self-interest. Somehow the needs and interests of others must be taken into account. Compassion, the core concept of Buddhist morality, entails the appreciation of these needs and interests.

Every community has, by virtue of its existence as a community, been required to confront the antinomy between self-interest and the social conception of justice. For Buddhists no contradiction exists, because compassion simultaneously serves both the community and the individual. Compassion is an instrumentality of liberation and a means by which an individual frees himself or herself from suffering. All great ethical systems suggest a higher stage of self-attainment through unselfish conduct. Ethical behavior must diminish suffering if there is to be some purpose or justification for moral conduct.

Throughout history, currents of nationalism and racism have attempted to circumscribe the scope of ethical concerns. These efforts to limit compassion to national boundaries or specific ethnic groups are incongruent with the essential character of compassion as understood in the Buddhist tradition. The dialectical method can reveal that these exclusionary doctrines negate the moral significance of compassion and create what is in effect an expanded version of self-interest.

We ourselves are subject to our own historiography. We cannot emerge from it to evaluate another culture objectively. The intercultural dialogue should not be expected to produce agreement on a uniform set of ethical standards. I have not attempted to suggest that Buddhism represent any such universal system. Buddhism can, however, provide insight into the manner in which we can evaluate any canons of behavior which, from our current perspective, we would acknowledge as constituting an ethical system.

Peace and Security

Desirous attachment sees the other as essentially desirable and seeks to draw him or her into one's possession or sphere of influence. Aversion, on the other hand, sees the other as essentially undesirable or even repulsive and attempts to remove the person from one's field of contact. Indifference is an attitude in which the other simply does not matter, and his suffering and joys are of absolutely no consequence. In this way our relationships with others are limited to the manipulation of a few individuals who impinge on the domain of our personal concern, and the ignoring of all the many others who fall outside of that domain.

The dominion of the ego in the emotional sphere appears most conspicuously in the weight of the unwholesome roots—greed, hatred, and delusion—as determinants of conduct. Because the ego is essentially a vacuum, the illusion of egohood generates a nagging sense of insufficiency. We feel oppressed by an aching incompleteness, an inner lack requiring constantly to be filled. The result is greed, a relentless drive to reach out and devour whatever we can—of pleasure, wealth, power, and fame—in a never-successful attempt to bring satisfaction. When we meet with frustration we react with hatred, the urge to destroy the obstacle preventing our satisfaction. If the obstructions to our satisfaction prove too powerful for the tactics of aggression, a third strategy will be used: dullness or delusion, an attitude of deliberate unawareness adopted as a shell to hide our vulnerability to pain. (Bhikkhu Bodhi's *Nourishing the Roots,* Kandy, 1978: *Wheel* No. 259/260)

When we approach the issue of security from a spiritual perspective, we are directed to a consideration of the nature and quality of personal being. From a Buddhist perspective, security or the harmony between people and nations is conditioned by the internal harmony and tranquility attained by the individuals who comprise society. An individual in conflict and distress will often act toward others in a hostile and aggressive manner. Peace reigns in the society when each individual in the society is at peace.

Buddhists recognize greed, hatred, and delusion as defilements which corrupt human consciousness. The path to enlightenment entails overcoming these forces through spiritual practice.

It is apparent that greed, hatred, and delusion in their various mani-festations are also the factors which generate insecurity among people. Greed leads to exploitation and subjugation; hatred promotes aggressive conduct directed against others. These are fueled by the delusion of the independent and individualized self, constantly striving for self-definition through acquisition and the rejection of the other.

Real security, pursued from the spiritual perspective, means that we must seek to improve our society by improving ourselves as individuals. This course of achieving social transformation as a product of personal transformation might at first appear an exercise in impracticable senti-mentality, but I suggest that it is far more quixotic and utopian to assume that a radical reformation of social conditions can occur without a fun-damental change in the attitudes of people. One of the great lessons of recent history has been that the restructuring of political and economic institutions will not in itself serve the cause of personal liberation. Until greed, hatred, and delusion cease to govern human affairs, they will find voice in any institutional structure and quell spiritual development.

I do not intend to suggest that the spiritual dimension of security would ignore the role of social, economic, and political institutions within society. The injustices occasioned by these institutions should, however, be confronted as an aspect of spiritual practice. If I allow certain conduct, I implicitly affirm that conduct's maxim. If I accept a system that serves to exploit or repress others, I reaffirm the exaltation of self-interest. This practice will clearly conflict with the path to liberation, which is grounded on the doctrine of *anatta* or no-self. For the Buddhist, personal and social liberation are merely different aspects of the same practice.

Human Rights

Nonviolent strategies ultimately depend upon the moral authority of the position to predominate. If the enunciation of human rights abuses meets with indifference, then the oppressed will remain powerless. Accordingly, a correlate role for the human rights defender is to address the deficiency of values that allows for indifference in the face of the suffering of others. This introduces the spiritual dimension to human rights endeavors which has been present in every great human rights movement. If we look to some contemporary champions of human rights in Asia from the Bud-dhist tradition—His Holiness the Dalai Lama, Maha Ghosananda, Aung

San Suu Kyi, Thich Nhat Hanh—we can see the effect of the spiritual component of human rights advocacy.

Indifference to the violation of human rights can occur only when individuals fail to recognize the interdependence and interrelationship of all beings. The lack of compassion with the plight of others can exist only when people maintain the delusion of the independence and self-sufficiency of individual existence. All communities have confronted the tension between the individual and common interest, and all communities have developed an ethic that addresses that conflict. In Buddhism, compassion is a path to personal liberation. The commitment to the well-being of others is deeply embedded in traditional Buddhist thought.

The human rights defender in Asia must cause societies to examine the values that inhere in the culture and to reclaim the underlying authentic principles of social organization that have in the present become obscured by consumerism and other forms of forgetfulness. The human rights advocate must work to reinstate the conditions of the moral order so that subjugation of others will not be tolerated.

Working Toward Global Governance

The effects of globalization are often assessed purely in economic terms. Advocates of the globalization of the economy often do not concern themselves with the effects of these policies on the distribution of resources within the country. Marginal consideration is given to an analysis of which segments of the society prosper and which find themselves further disadvantaged. The result has often been the creation of greater disparities of wealth. Furthermore, the extent to which this economic activity promotes satisfaction or despair is not deemed relevant.

As a Buddhist, I cannot consider economic efficiency as the ultimate value for a social order. I am constrained to evaluate a system of social organization in terms of its capacity to address human suffering, promote distributive justice, and allow for individuals within the society to realize their full potential.

I have seen the effects of the commitment to international trade in my country, where rural farmers have been convinced to abandon their lives of simple self-sufficiency and pursue the development of crops for export. They have often been unable to compete with larger and more efficient operations. Many have lost their land while the male members of the family have been forced to seek employment in construction or manufacturing in the city, earning about five dollars a day. Many of the daughters have been induced to venture into prostitution. The family unit and the community have been decimated in pursuit of international trade. This unfortunate set of circumstances represents a success story, to the economist who measures social trends in terms of enhancement of the gross national product. This social derangement and the concomitant destruction of the environment has been characterized as an aspect of the East Asian Miracle by the World Bank.

The globalization of financial markets has been devised in furtherance of these trends. In this structure it is the transnational corporation which becomes the fundamental economic unit. It comes to replace the village or the community as the matrix for human interaction. With the development of economic control comes a further transmigration of political power. The ethical values which are dependent upon an appreciation of oneself as a member of a community, with a responsibility for the welfare of others in the community, cannot be sustained when the institutions which govern our lives are centralized and remote and preclude meaningful participation in the decision-making process.

Rather than the global economy projected for the second decade of the twenty-first century, we should seek the reinstatement of the community as the most significant social, political, and economic entity. With the globalization of the economy in Asia has come the incursion of consumerism, which is a by-product of Western capitalism. Greed and waste have replaced compassion and sharing. Instead of focusing on creating an international economic and social order, we should look to our culture and the traditions manifested in our public life as a source of value. We should be aiming for small-scale, interdependent economies and decentralized institutions.

The centralization of power that has developed has deprived the individual of any significant control of his destiny. And while it may be true that power corrupts, so does powerlessness. It is only through the establishment of a public sphere, where one becomes engaged in the process of making decisions which will affect oneself and other members of the community, that one comes to recognize one's social responsibilities and the nature of human interdependence. The individual is not afforded any such role in the international economic order which emerges from APEC (Asia-Pacific Economic Cooperation) meetings.

The increased dependency of the Asian economies on international trade has created certain dilemmas which can best be confronted through an international strategy. Currently, the transnational corporation is capable of favoring the country that allows for the greatest exploitation of its workers and the most unrestrained degradation of the environment. Suppression of wages and of workers' rights has become an aspect of national economic policy for countries which perceive their comparative advantage to be the availability of cheap labor. The protection of workers' rights on a national level may prove self-defeating if it merely serves to cause the employer to relocate to a less conscientious country. International standards can be established and enforced to prevent corporations from forcing Asian countries to compete by offering the worst working conditions.

Similarly, environmental protection is a matter that can best be regulated by an international organization. The unilateral imposition of regulatory measures designed to protect the environment will probably result in business migrating to less restrictive places. An enforceable agenda to restrict environmentally destructive enterprise would prevent a country from having to sacrifice the environment in order to prevent businesses from seeking a less responsible neighbor. Given the current dependence of the Asian economies on international trade, a transition to alternative economic structures must be pursued carefully. Surely an economic system that truly promotes human values, that seeks to limit suffering and is committed to true democratic principles, will require more thought than a blind commitment to neoliberal policies. But let that be our aspiration for the next century: one that we will pursue mindfully and with skillful means.

Local Initiatives

Bookchin, Illich, and Schumacher have reasserted the primacy of small communities taking responsibility for their own condition of life. Across a range of disciplines thinking has turned to biology, the nature of living systems, and to principles of self-organization as the only viable way to cope with change and complexity....At the core of the idea of community...are three basic principles which are not only important, but also helpful in thinking about a more sustainable politics for the next century.

The *first* is the simple recognition of people's social nature, and one might add, of the sociability, sense of fairness, sympathy, and duty that evolutionary psychologists now see as hardwired into our genetic makeup. Two hundred years of history have done much to nurture institutions for freedom and equality, but very little for the fraternity and solidarity that hold societies together.

Yet this softer value—a social capital that enables people to work together, to trust each other, to commit to common causes—has proved absolutely critical to societal success, whether in narrow economic terms or in terms of well-being.

The *second* principle is about scale. Community is deliberately a different word for society. It may refer to neighborhoods or workplace, but to be meaningful it must imply membership in a human-scale collective: a scale at which it is possible to encounter people face-to-face...[and] to nurture human-scale structures within which people can feel at home. Social science is ill-at-ease with such ideas. Strangely there is very little theory about the importance of scale and form in economics and sociology (unlike in biology, where thinkers like D'Arcy Thompson long ago made the connection).

The *third* principle is a reassertion of ethics—the recognition that any viable politics needs to be prepared to make judgments about behavior, and about what types of behavior work against the common interest and against the interest of future generations. Without a strong sense of personal ethics, societies require an unacceptable level of policing and contracts; and without a strong sense of personal responsibility it is inevitable that costs will be shunted out onto the natural environment and onto future generations. (Geoff Mulgan, "A Sense of Community," in *Resurgence* No. 172)

In Southeast Asia many of the significant efforts at social and economic reform have been initiated by religious leaders from the Buddhist tradition. This provides a unique character to these initiatives as a consequence of the Buddhist recognition that social transformation and personal transformation are interrelated. One cannot meaningfully commit himself or herself to the common good if one is personally overwhelmed by the forces of greed, anger, or delusion. Likewise, one cannot find personal liberation if he or she is prepared to ignore the suffering of others. Thailand has provided exemplars of socially engaged Buddhism.

In Surin province in the impoverished Northeast, an abbot recalled that when he was young the people seemed happier: they got along with each other, and there was the Thai zest for life. The villages were surrounded by jungles and elephants roamed freely. The people were poor, but they managed to produce enough food for their families, as well as the monks. They had the four essentials of food, clothing, shelter, and medicine. Over the last 30 years, the abbot had witnessed constant development and construction. Today, the jungle and the elephants had disappeared, and the people were suffering.

The abbot knew that something was wrong. Local products were going to Bangkok to multinational corporations, and then to the superpowers. He told the people, "Meditation must not be only for personal salvation, but for the collective welfare as well. There needs to be collective mindfulness. We need to look to the old traditions that sustained us for many centuries." When he started to speak this way, people did not believe him, but they listened out of respect. He said, "Let us try alternative ways." He used controversial words, like "communal farming." In Siam, anti-communism is very strong, and if you use words like "communalism" you can be accused of being a communist. But when a monk who was pure in conduct spoke this way, he aroused the interest of the people.

He encouraged people to farm together and to share their labor with each other. He explained that ambition and competitiveness had only brought them more suffering. The abbot suggested starting rice banks to overcome the shortage of rice, and the temples cooperated. Whatever was cultivated that was left over was offered to the temple, where the grain was kept for anyone in need to receive free of charge. In this way, the traditional concept of giving alms to the temple was translated to address the social reality of today.

The next project he started was a buffalo bank. Being Buddhists, we do not like to kill buffaloes. So the temple kept the buffaloes and offered the offspring to those who could not afford to buy one. The only conditions were that the buffalo had to be treated kindly and that 50 percent of all future offspring would be returned to the buffalo bank.

Another local initiative was pursued by a Thai monk in Samut Sakorn province, one province away from Bangkok. Most people who live there are impoverished, illiterate farmers. The province is usually flooded with seawater, which perennially destroys the paddies, leaving the people with little or no means of subsistence.

Many of the people had been driven to gambling and drinking. Aware of the situation, the monk decided to help the people before making any improvements in his own temple or spending a lot of time preaching Buddhist morals. He organized the people to work together to build canals and some roads. He realized that poverty could not be eliminated unless new crops were introduced, since salt water was ruining the rice fields. He suggested planting coconut trees, based on the example of a nearby province.

Once the people of Samut Sakorn started growing coconuts, the monk advised them not to sell the harvest because middlemen kept the price of coconuts very low. He encouraged them to make coconut sugar using traditional techniques. With assistance from three nearby universities that were interested in the development and promotion of community projects, the people of Samut Sakorn began selling their coconut sugar all over the country. The monk has since encouraged the growing of palm trees for building material and the planting of herbs to be used for traditional medicine.

Balancing Tensions

The binary opposition of forces suggested by this section heading is not endorsed in the Buddhist worldview. The bifurcation of human experience into individual good versus common good, rights versus responsibilities, entails a kind of dualism incongruent with Buddhist logic. Most significant, however, is the recognition that by enhancing the common good, one serves to diminish suffering, including one's own.

Religious Resources for Global Governance

Any form of meaningful change must have a spiritual dimension. I have helped to establish various organizations which have confronted social problems from a spiritual perspective.

One of these is *Alternatives to Consumerism*, which recognizes the spiritual vacuum that engenders many destructive behaviors in the contemporary cultural setting. People are driven to accumulate goods as a means of self-definition. Discontentment is a systematic feature of the consumer economy. Individuals continuously strive to reach the next highest level of consumption and spending. A concomitant factor is the disintegration of the community and the values that the community propagated.

The purpose of establishing Alternatives to Consumerism was to explicate the manner in which the failure of spiritual values has produced the new demonic religion of consumerism. In international fora, the organization has sought to identify various manifestations of consumerism and to propose alternatives that are more conducive to true self-fulfillment.

The International Network of Engaged Buddhists allows individuals interested in Buddhist teachings to explore the social responsibilities that inhere in the practice. Through a journal and annual meetings, the organization coordinates campaigns to eliminate land mines, promote human rights, preserve the environment, and address other issues that reflect the Buddhist commitment to compassion and interrelatedness.

The Spirit in Education Movement reflects the commitment to the propagation of spiritual values in education. Educational systems that purport to be value-neutral in actuality propagate a distinct set of economic values. People are thought to pursue certain ends without consideration for their most important spiritual needs. SEM is an effort to reintroduce subjects that are truly significant to the well-being of the individual. Through regularly held seminars, these ideas have been propagated in Siam and elsewhere.

Kalyanametta is an overarching organization of various groups opposing the natural-gas pipeline which is proposed to run from Burma through Siam. Kalyanametta means "good friends," and the purpose of organizing was to demonstrate the underlying unity of the diverse efforts. Some organizations are principally concerned with the environmental consequences of the pipeline, while other groups focus on the human rights questions involved. The Buddhist ethic, however, provides a bridge and unveils the commonality of the undertaking.

It is this factor, the fundamental commonality provided by Buddhist thought, which informs all of these endeavors. It is what makes Buddhism a compelling resource for global governance.

The United Nations

The United Nations has proven inadequate as a means to promoting a just world order, for reasons endemic to its structure and purpose. Its members are nation-states which pursue their political and economic self-interest. The power of the organization is highly centralized and inherently unresponsive to the needs of the people. Individual morality is a product of the participation of the individual in the community and the concomitant recognition of the interdependence of beings. No institution comparable to the community exists to establish ethical standards for nations. No social order has evolved from which states can derive a notion of moral responsibility.

The members of the United Nations fervently preserve national sovereignty, which essentially places them beyond the control of moral imperatives. The UN seeks to enforce universally recognized values. It has operated on the assumption that moral standards have already been developed which only require enforcement through various offices. This neglects the constitutive function of the social order. A true community of nations must exist before a global ethic can emerge and a sense of international moral obligation serve to control the affairs of states.

Broader standing must be afforded to NGOs in order to transcend the nationalism of the organization and allow for a more democratic level of participation in the decision-making process. Alternatives to the UN, like UNPO (Unrepresented Nations and Peoples' Organizations) should be considered, where people who are unrepresented in the current scheme, such as Tibetans and those of East Timor, would be provided membership.

Developing Multireligious Initiatives

Above I discussed some of the multireligious initiatives that I believe can be effective. I am committed to the proposition that human well-being is ultimately a matter that entails spiritual values, and that any movement which will fundamentally improve the human situation must address spiritual needs.

Buddhism
and Global Governance

Pataraporn Sirikanchana

Buddhism has been the Thai people's religion since the beginning of the Thai kingdom. It has cultivated and encouraged prominent Thai values such as hospitality, kindness, and friendliness, leading to the identity of Thai characteristics and culture. Through Buddhism, Thais learn to realize the Law of Karma, which reveals the truth of cause and effect: those who do good will have good in return, and vice versa. In addition, they are trained to purify their minds and be aware of the danger of materialistic lives. Some Thai Buddhists who are not good followers of the Buddha are still selfish and cause trouble to themselves and others; they need to know more of the teachings and improve themselves so that they can live in peaceful happiness with others.

Working Toward a Shared Global Ethic

Buddhism is a religion among many which guide their followers to a universal mind of love and purity. Its teachings and practices contribute much to a shared global ethic for the good of this interdependent world. Fundamentally, Buddhism promotes ethical practices toward the end of physical and spiritual suffering, in both the mundane and supramundane sense. In the supramundane or ultimate sense, Buddhist teachings promote spiritual purification by means of the eradication of defilements until one attains *nirvana*, the final emancipation from suffering which is the end of one's cycles of birth and death. In the mundane or worldly sense, Buddhism provides guidelines, principles, and values for Buddhists to cope with problems in daily life.

The Buddhist doctrine asserts that the cause of war, conflict, crime, abuse, and suffering is mental defilement. As soon as this cause is removed, suffering is gone. For Buddhists, the fact that the world is full of suffering needs to be overcome by the practice of self-discipline, wisdom, meditation, and enlightenment. It is primarily important for a person to cultivate himself or herself before attempting to cultivate others.

The practice of self-discipline encourages a person to avoid evil and do good. The Buddhist Scriptures show the Buddha's approval of a person who avoids killing:

> Him I call indeed a Brahman who withholds the rod of punishment from other creatures, whether feeble or strong, and does not kill nor cause slaughter. Him I call indeed a Brahman who is tolerant with the intolerant, mild among the violent, and free from greed among the greedy. (The *Dhammapada*)

Nevertheless, it is not enough to avoid killing; we also need to protect life and promote the peace and security of all life forms. Through the Buddhist teachings of compassion, loving kindness, and karma (the volitional act), all life forms are viewed as interrelated. Thus, human beings are not the masters of the universe and have no right to destroy nature. Because the Buddha heard complaints that monks on their wanderings were crushing the green grass and injuring and destroying many small animals, he prescribed the monastic rule, requiring monks to stay in their places during three months of the Buddhist Lent.

Through self-discipline one learns the meaning of human rights, which always intertwines with duty and responsibility. Buddhist teachings do not differentiate rights from responsibilities. Rights based on self-attachment and personal benefits are not promoted by Buddhist teachings since they cannot yield peace and happiness to anyone. For example, the teachings forbid killing both oneself and others and promote loving kindness toward all living beings: thus they deny the right to kill, abuse, commit suicide, have an abortion, and so on. However, certain actions which are both good and evil in themselves, such as mercy killing or the death sentence for a murderer, are considered both merit and demerit to the doers—because while they release someone from suffering or secure a society, they are also harmful to life. A public poll in Thailand recently showed that most Thai people favor the death sentence for those who commit capital crime, indicating that most Thai Buddhists do not take Buddhist precepts literally but would rather have them fit social contexts.

While good intentions, loving kindness, and compassion toward one-self and others are valued, wisdom (*pañña*) is crucial to the quest for enlightenment or the attainment of Arahatship (for Theravada Buddhists) and the fulfillment of Buddhahood (for Mahayana Buddhists). Wisdom alone can solve dilemmas in Buddhist logic and practices, e.g., the problem of the sense of self, which can be both the inspiration for a good work and an obstruction to emancipation from suffering.

According to one Buddhist text, the *Visuddhi-Magga*, wisdom is "knowledge consisting in insight and conjoined with meritorious thoughts." Wisdom helps Buddhists to act and to judge their actions. A wise Buddhist, therefore, is neither a fundamentalist, a conservative, nor a dogmatist. He or she is broad-minded, can live a moderate life, and can live happily with others who are different. If he is a monk, he knows how to work for other beings and be socially engaged without transgressing his monastic discipline.

In Buddhism, wisdom can be attained through meditation. The principle of meditation is the training of mindfulness. Whenever we pay attention to our own thoughts, words, and deeds, we are conscious of ourselves and aware of our movements; we feel ashamed of doing evil, and thus do not let ourselves go wrong. Meditation is the universal way of peace. Since the object of meditation can be anything suitable for each meditator, meditation is beneficial to all, including non-Buddhists. Christians may meditate on Jesus; Hindus on Shiva or Vishnu; Muslims on Allah. Since meditation is a means to calm one's mind, those who meditate every day will stay away from war. In short, meditation can keep the world at peace, preserve and protect forest and wildlife, and promote global understanding among all peoples.

In today's world of free trade and materialism, those with greater opportunity who are clever in business learn to take advantage of others and become wealthy. Without moral restraint and self-discipline, the economic gap between rich and poor widens. Buddhism reveals that materialistic enslavement, prodigality, selfishness, and greed are the sources of all injustice. If we want to establish economic and social justice in society and the world, we should learn to give more, take less, live a simple life, and free ourselves from the clingings and attachments which are sources of suffering. In order to avoid suffering, both personally and socially, one should get rid of one's selfishness and learn to live for others. Knowing that all material objects are impermanent and not worth craving, one can free oneself from selfishness and contribute more to others.

Buddhist doctrine is intended to cultivate rich and poor, ruler and ruled. It encourages all Buddhists to be conscious and aware of their duties and responsibilities. For example, the poor are inculcated to work hard and persevere in their lives, the rich to be more charitable and just. Similarly, leaders are taught to be merciful and benevolent, and followers obedient. A Buddhist text, the *Jataka*, illustrates the king's virtues as follows: charity (*dana*), morality (*sila*), self-sacrifice (*pariccaga*), honesty (*ajjava*), kindness and gentleness (*maddava*), self-control (*tapa*), non-anger (*akkodha*), nonviolence (*avihimsa*), patience (*khanti*), and conformity to the law (*avirodhana*); on the other hand, according to the *Digha-Nikaya* in the Buddhist Canon, servants and workmen should get up before and go to rest after their masters, take only what is given, do their best at their work, and proclaim the honor and prestige of their masters. Problems arise because most people expect others to follow such teachings and forget to improve themselves.

Essentially, Buddhism considers all beings subject to the Law of Karma (the Law of Cause and Effect, or of Nature), which mandates that all volitional acts have their own retribution—i.e., good deeds yield good effects, and vice versa. It also asserts the holistic view that all things in the universe relate to one another. Human beings and animals, according to their karma, have to go through endless cycle of birth and death and may be reborn in the form of one another. Their actions, good or bad, sooner or later have an effect on themselves and others. For example, an act of mercy can save someone's life and bring joy to the heart of the actor; by contrast, war can destroy many lives and damage physically and spiritually those who wage it. Karma is our responsibility and destiny, as shown in the following Buddhist passage:

> But every deed a man performs,
> With body, or with voice, or mind,
> 'Tis this that he can call his own,
> This with him take as he goes hence.
> This is what follows after him,
> And, like a shadow, ne'er departs. (*Samyutta-Nikaya*)

Thus, the Buddhist doctrine of Karma makes us aware of the value of human rights, the danger of materialism, and the necessity of ecological sustainability. In the light of Buddhism, an act for human rights is neither an expression of self-assertion nor a sociopolitical demand, nor is it the outcome of a Western philosophy promoting humans as the center of the universe. It is rather a human consciousness of those who share the same fate on earth.

The Buddhist respect for human rights can be seen in the Thai constitution, which states that the king must be a Buddhist and the Great Upholder of all faiths. Though approximately 95 percent of Thailand's population professes Buddhism, Buddhism is not its national religion. All religions are equally protected and supported. Some Thai cabinet members are Muslims, some Christians; the head of Parliament is a Muslim. Since according to the Scriptures the Buddha allows his disciples to join all ceremonies of other faiths which neither harm life nor promote violence, a Buddhist can freely participate with others in building a global civic society and contributing to public affairs. With this spirit, all Buddhists can live an ideal life of unity in diversity.

In addition, the Buddhist doctrine is against the danger of materialism, a way of life dominated by material preference and attachment which brings about consumerism and economism and encourages prodigality and indulgence. Human life nowadays is trapped in materialism; the more we are materialists, the less we can find spiritual happiness and peaceful lives. Buddhism also advocates the necessity of ecological sustainability. Monks are forbidden to cut down trees; they should keep themselves and their places clean. All lay Buddhists are taught to be thrifty and responsible for their living and environments.

In sum, the Buddhist teachings of loving kindness and altruism enable peace and security. The teachings of duty and responsibility of all social members, of moderation, and of the effects of good and bad actions promote economic and social justice, human rights, and ecological sustainability. In addition, the assertion in the Buddhist doctrine of goodwill toward all beings, tolerance, and an unprejudiced attitude toward other religions can balance the tension between different cultures and thus be beneficial to cultural identity and integrity in a global civic society. Religion can equip us with the spiritual inspiration to work for a peaceful world, but as members of a global civic society, we cannot confine ourselves to literal meanings in our own religious doctrines. We need to enhance the spirit of mutual understanding and cooperation.

Working Toward Global Governance

In this age of globalization and interdependence, one cannot wait for one's government to solve problems. One needs to work with others, by means of one's own religious guidance, to provide essential services and leadership at local, national, and global levels.

Global Civic Society

Nongovernmental organizations and individual members of society need to help governments solve the problems of the people. When national and cultural boundaries are transcended in this process, it becomes much more efficient. From the Buddhist perspective, the criteria for citizenship in a global civic society would be the cultivation of loving kindness, non-violence, altruism, and wisdom. With loving kindness, one can transcend racial prejudice and egoism and work nationally and internationally. By means of nonviolence, one does not wage war and is able to keep the world at peace. Good Buddhists are trained to be altruists, having learned of the ill effects of selfishness and greed: for example, loneliness and helplessness. Through wisdom, the true knowledge of oneself and the world, one can penetrate the causes and effects of all things and find solutions to all problems.

In order to strengthen a global civic society, members from each country should work together, communicate regularly, and share and solve problems jointly. For example, an ecological problem in a member country will be a problem for all and should be taken care of by all.

Global Structures and Systems

In order to cultivate a global civic mind and a global civic society, each member of society should clearly understand the essence of his or her own religious teachings. All world religions similarly aim to improve human life externally and internally, and teach their followers to work for all world beings, not only for their own community. For example, Buddhist values and principles differentiate human beings according to their deeds, not their origins, races, or families, and show that all human beings can be improved by means of education. Thus, the preferred world order should be established by virtuous, well-trained interreligious leaders who can cooperate efficiently with one another and the members of society; and global citizens should be educated to an awareness of issues of peace and security, economic and social justice, human rights, and so on.

It is necessary to establish a global committee of interreligious leaders who represent (and constitute) unity in diversity and a world culture of nonviolence. This committee would serve as a coordinator and work for public relations among people at different levels—community leaders, villagers, academicians, church members, and government. Especially, the committee would initiate and maintain dialogue among diverse religious traditions on global morality and ethics, for example, the protection of local communities, environments, and cultures.

Local Initiatives

Many social problems such as juvenile delinquency and drug addiction arise from the lack of moral training and moral cultivation in children. If children are acquainted with Buddhist teachings and follow Buddhist precepts properly, they will be able to attain peaceful happiness and live a successful life. In Thailand, governmental and nongovernmental organizations are aware of their responsibility to educate Thais morally from the beginning of their lives.

To prepare children for school and provide the socially disadvantaged with an opportunity for literacy, the Ministry of Education initiated the Temple Preschool Center in 1963. The project gained the support of the Buddhist *Sangha* (Church), which allowed temples to establish schools in which monks taught preschool children. In addition to the 2,554 preschool centers around the country, the government and the *Sangha* support Buddhist Sunday Schools, which inculcate both moral discipline and general knowledge. This type of school originated in Sri Lanka; Thailand's first Buddhist Sunday School was established in 1958 by Phra Pimaladharma of Bangkok's Mahachulalongkorn Buddhist College.

Balancing Tensions

According to Buddhist teachings, an individual can avoid suffering and attain true happiness through knowledge of the middle path. If one learns to live properly, without harm to oneself and others, one can survive in all areas of tension.

Individual Good and Common Good

Generally, human beings tend to live primarily for their own good and are selfish rather than altruistic. Through Buddhism, they are trained to overcome their primitive instincts and encouraged to help others. For example, though a monk's primary concern is to follow the path toward *nirvana* (the final goal of ultimate peace), he is willing to engage in some activities for the sake of others. Worth mentioning are the cases of Phra Khamkhian Suvañño and Phra Vidya Cittadhammo.

Phra Khamkhian Suvañño of Sukhato Forest Hermitage in northeastern Thailand founded the Center for Child Development in 1978 to care for small children whose parents had to work in the fields all day. Most northeastern villagers were poor farmers who brought their children to the fields because nobody was home to look after them; waiting for their parents, the children played in the rain or were exposed to the sun the whole day, and some became severely ill and died. The center began with 20 children, who were taught to read and write and fed with food donated to monks. Phra Khamkhian brought these children up himself. Some years later, a few volunteer assistants came to teach. The center provides this free service to the community from March to November.

Phra Vidya Cittadhammo of Mount Sarb Temple School in the province of Rayong also works for disadvantaged children. He is a developer monk who provides boys with an opportunity to complete their education through ordination. Mount Sarb Temple School emphasizes the moral cultivation of students' minds and accepts underprivileged boys who are ordained in the temple and study in its secondary school, free of charge, for three years. The Temple School helps young people fulfill their human qualities and survive happily in this suffering world.

Rights and Responsibilities

Buddhist teachings do not differentiate rights from responsibilities. The awareness of rights based on self-attachment and personal benefits is not promoted since it cannot yield peace and happiness, and nobody can possess rights without responsibilities to himself or herself and to others.

Private Sector and Public Sector

Buddhists are taught to live both for themselves and for others. According to the Buddha, monks should live in solitude in order to meditate and train themselves spiritually for their enlightenment, but their duties include teaching others to attain *nirvana* as well. Thus, they should live not too close and not too far from a village so that they have their private lives and are able to serve the community at the same time.

In order to fulfill one's ethical conduct, a Buddhist needs to help himself or herself before helping others in order not to become a burden. Similarly, although a Buddhist has belongings, he or she is taught to understand the truth that nothing really belongs to anyone. Thus, in certain cases, one may choose to detach from one's belongings for the public good.

Long-Term and Short-Term Objectives

Buddhist tradition values both the long-term and short-term objectives of a desirable society. The Buddhist teachings of wisdom, tolerance, and perseverance are helpful in deciding on objectives; however, the values of the objectives are more important than the time period for their fulfillment. For example, spiritual and transcendental objectives are more valuable than material and worldly objectives, though more time-consuming to fulfill. Moreover, the method used in proceeding toward the objectives needs careful consideration, since Buddhism advocates peace as both a means and an end.

Economic and Environmental Needs

Thailand today faces a conflict between economic growth and environmental disaster. While we enjoy tall buildings, excessive numbers of cars, and wildlife products, we are participating in the destruction of nature through logging, habitat destruction, urban dust and soot, and so on.

Humankind's selfishness and materialism will lead to doomsday and the end of nature. According to Buddhism, one should live in accordance with nature and free oneself from the materialistic life. One needs only life's four necessities to survive: clothing, food, lodging, and medicine. Even if one wants excessive quantities of these, acquiring them should cause no trouble to oneself or others. Buddhism thus balances human economic and environmental needs through its teachings of the middle path of moderation and contentment, leading to a disciplined way of life.

Local, National, and Global Sovereignties

Local, national, and global sovereignties will not be in conflict if one follows the supremacy of righteousness. The Buddhist teachings differentiate the dominant influence of human life into three categories: self-dependence, world-dependence, and *dhammic*-dependence.

Those who are self-dependent are interested only in their own benefit. They think only for the sake of themselves, their family, their community, and their country. They care nothing about humanity and trade others' property for their own good.

Those who are world-dependent follow all values of the world. If the world's beings today are materialistic and take wars as solutions to all problems, they will agree with that. They are victims of the world.

By contrast, those who are *dhammic*-dependent follow the way of righteousness. They work for the sake of all beings and can differentiate right from wrong. They consider local, national, and global benefits interrelated and equally important, and can thus balance and justify local, national, and global sovereignties.

Religious Resources for Global Governance

The Buddhist teachings advocate solving a problem by addressing its cause rather than suppressing its outcome. In light of the teaching that a good mind yields good speech and actions, Buddhist courses are prepared for Thai children from the beginning of their school years.

Since the educational reformation of King Rama V (1868–1910), Thailand has had two Buddhist colleges for monks, Mahamakuta and Mahachula. After graduating with a proper knowledge of Buddhism, monks work in temple schools throughout the country, seek higher academic degrees abroad, or leave monastic life. Whether monks or laymen, they have been trained during monastic life to value a just world order. In addition, many Thai universities offer a master's degree in Buddhist Studies, Ethics, and Comparative Religions. Monks, nuns, and lay students who pass an entrance examination are welcome to these programs. The Buddhist Studies Center at Chulalongkorn University also promotes academic research on Buddhism and Buddhist philosophy.

In order to regain morality for our frail society, monks, government offices, and nongovernmental organizations are working hard to awaken in the public mind a sense of duty and responsibility for the whole world. Through media and communication networks, they disseminate standard patterns of Thai Buddhist culture based on love of peace, modesty, and honesty, as well as images of ecological preservation, wildlife protection, poor children of the world, and so on.

In addition, some universities, nongovernmental organizations, and Buddhist monasteries have also initiated community-based networks and programs leading to mutual understanding and cooperation within and

between communities. For example, the work of Phra Khamkhian Suvañño among villagers in northeastern Thailand provides the community
with both spiritual and economic development. He teaches the villagers
meditation and introduces them to proper methods of earning their living, for example, forming trade unions and growing herbs. They learn to
be self-sufficient and friendly to others, both Thais and foreigners.

Some nongovernmental organizations, such as the World Fellowship
of Buddhists, headquartered in Thailand, are working for mutual understanding and cooperation with Buddhists around the world. The Fellowship's regional centers in 30 countries are situated amid other religious
communities and get along very well with them; they most certainly
know how to participate in building a just world order.

Collaborating with the United Nations
and Its Specialized Agencies

In order to establish a just world order, the UN system and some of its
specialized agencies need to be reformed to improve functions and regulations. For example, the Security Council should be restructured and its
veto power abolished. Also, the UN Economic and Social Council
(ECOSOC), which aims for the well-being and spiritual growth of all
peoples, should be improved functionally. In practice, ECOSOC's functions are limited since each specialized agency, e.g., UNESCO or FAO, is
organized separately, is governed by its own constitution and elected
bodies, and submits only annual reports to ECOSOC.

Buddhists and Buddhist organizations cooperate with UN organizations and programs through community work and report regularly to the
UN. For example, the World Fellowship of Buddhists is a member of
ECOSOC and works for peace and the spiritual growth of all Buddhists.
In order to become more active partners with the UN, Thailand's Buddhist community and its programs and institutions need more financial
assistance and global training.

Developing Multireligious Initiatives

The essential teachings of all world religions aim at the same goal: spiritual growth and the attainment of the Highest Good. All religions teach
human beings to conduct themselves morally and do good to others; thus
they support a just world order. Religious members should learn to attain

the core teachings of their own religions and transcend verbal languages and excessive practices. Having gone beyond the barriers of one's official religion, one learns the value of universal love and global community.

In this age of globalization, we need to develop a holistic perspective in which values are initiated by diverse religions. Multireligious initiatives are needed, and religious institutions should be more active in inculcating constructive values in their members and encouraging them to get rid of fundamentalist attitudes so they are ready to work on a global level. Today the world's religions can no longer retain narrow-minded dogmas and transcendental aspects: they need to be socially engaged and globally supportive. As sources of moral inspiration and resources for global governance, religions can shape world history and establish the world order.

Confucianism and a New World Order

Julia Ching

Introduction

> Just as the government of…a household is modeled on the government of one's self…on account of similitude, [the Chinese] came to equate the notion of a state to that of a house or family, with the ruler representing the head of the family, thus arguing by virtue of an analogy from a family to a civil society.[1]

The eighteenth-century German philosopher Christian Wolff is correct in his interpretation of Chinese political theory. To regard a state as a family is in many respects to promote a patriarchy of enlightened despotism. However, to regard a world of nations as a family, a family of nations, is a different matter, especially if the notion of the patriarchal ruler is replaced by an international organization like the United Nations and its general secretariat, with its moderating rather than domineering role in international conflicts.[2]

I mention this as an example of how Confucian ethics, especially its political ethics, is to serve a modern and postmodern world order. I think that it retains its usefulness, provided we are aware both of its insights

---

[1] Christian Wolff, "On the Philosopher King and the Ruling Philosopher," section 6. See Julia Ching and Willard G. Oxtoby, *Moral Enlightenment: Leibniz and Wolff on China*, Monumenta Serica Monograph Series, no. 26 (Nettetal: Steyler Verlag, 1992), p. 195. Wolff's works were read with admiration by Frederick II of Prussia—the European Enlightenment's model despot, a patron (for some time) of France's Voltaire, and like Wolff a friend of Chinese civilization.

[2] I wish to draw attention to a recent book: *United Nations Reform: Looking Ahead After Fifty Years*, Eric Fawcett & Hanna Newcombe, eds. (Toronto: Science for Peace, 1997).

and of its limitations. The Confucian text, the *Great Learning*, says: "...when the personal life is cultivated, the family will be in order; when the family is in order, the state will be well-governed; when the state is well-governed, there will be peace in the world."

The basic insight is contained in the exhortation to personal self-cultivation. For the family of nations to be well-governed today, there is need on the part of our global leaders to unite action and intention, and to make sure that the intention arises out of a well-cultivated personal life and a well-grounded altruism.

East and West: Cultural Identity and Integrity

East and West both need to recognize in themselves a history of self-centeredness, based on a rightful sense of self-consciousness together with an ignorance that each had of the other.

There are parallels as well as differences between the Chinese and Western European civilization. We find in China a uniquely coherent and integrated civilization, ancient yet enduring, which developed more or less independently of other civilizations. With this came the consciousness of uniqueness and even superiority, a consciousness strengthened by the fact that the Chinese civilization extended its benefits to the whole of East Asia. And, as the center of its world, China had a low regard for all that is called "foreign" (also called "barbarian"). This recalls the custom in ancient Greece to call "barbarian" what is not Greek. But Chinese culture has enjoyed a more continuous and less interrupted history over a larger continental land mass, and spread over to Japan, Korea, and what is now Vietnam. Greek culture, by contrast, served as an impetus for, more than the actual content of, what today we call Western civilization.[3]

And then there is the figure of Confucius, who lived in the sixth century BC. In the West, people are accustomed to an image of Confucius as a wise man or sage, teaching how to live a virtuous life, much as did Socrates in ancient Greece. Socrates is regarded as a humanist; in fact, he was condemned by the state for misleading youth, turning them away from the gods of their fathers. Confucius had his own struggles with the state, but died a natural death. In a world where military valor was

---

[3] Consult Julia Ching, *Chinese Religions* (London: Macmillan; New York: Orbis, 1993), Introduction.

highly esteemed, he instructed the youths instead in the ideal of a humane person, who valued moral relationships above all else. Confucius
seldom discussed religious matters and has always been known as a humanist. Indeed, he transformed the particular virtue of ren, the kindness
that characterized the man of high birth, into the universal virtue of humaneness, which made every person who practiced it a gentleman or junzi
(literally "the prince's scion"). Understandably, he distanced himself from
the religion of antiquity, with its emphasis on divination and sacrifice—including human sacrifice, which he is reported to have condemned in strong terms. And Confucius' teaching of ren was extended to
the political order, where it is defined as benevolent or humane government, as government of moral suasion, in which the leader gives the example of personal integrity and selfless devotion to the people.

The Confucian teaching of moral relationships, defined as those between ruler and subject, parent and child, husband and wife, elder and
younger siblings, and friends, appears to uphold a vertical hierarchy in
society while urging for responsibility and reciprocity. In many ways it did
have this effect socially. Besides, the Chinese view of the human being
tends to see the person in the context of a social network rather than as
an individual. But the fourth- to third-century Mencius (372–289 BC)
further developed Confucius' thought to articulate his conviction that
every human being could become a sage. Implicit in this doctrine of the
universal accessibility of sagehood is a teaching of human equality, of
what we may call "moral equal opportunity." And we should remember
that becoming a sage was tantamount to gaining the rights to kingship,
since the most revered sages were the sage-kings of ages past.[4]

The teachings of Confucius and Mencius have been revered in China
and East Asia for several thousand years. There are timeless elements in
these teachings, even if there are also time-bound elements, and even if
the feudal and patriarchal society in which they developed also tended to
stifle the moral creativity which gave such a vital form. Confucianism did
not give rise to political despotism or polygamy, although it accepted the
system in which it found itself, seeking to exercise an influence that was
at times moderating and at other times almost revolutionary, by pointing
to the source of moral inspiration in the human mind and heart, which it
regarded as reflecting a higher moral force. If Confucius and Mencius

[4] Consult Julia Ching, Chinese Religions, ch. 3–4.

were alive today, we have no reason to think that they—especially Mencius—would approve of any unjust war or inhumane government or social system, since they had condemned such in their own times.

Mencius gave voice to a doctrine justifying tyrannicide, declaring that killing a "tyrant" is not killing a "king" (*Mencius* 1B:8). In fact, the Chinese word for king (*wang*) connoted philosophically the meaning of a *good* king, even an ideal king. In an age when the altars of the earth and grain signified political authority, Mencius' words were: "The people come first; the altars of the earth and grain come afterwards; the ruler comes last" (7B:14).

Mencius also affirmed that everyone could be a *Yao* and a *Shun*. In so doing, he extended the possibility of sagehood to everyone. Presumably, having seen that actual kings were usually not sages, Mencius and others implicitly redefined both kingship and sagehood by extending accessibility to everyone.

The United Nations Universal Declaration on Human Rights says that human rights should be protected by the rule of law "[if] man is not to be compelled to have recourse, as a last resort, to rebellion against tyranny and oppression."[5] In the case of China, the age-old doctrine regarding the legitimization of power is that the ruler rules only by a divine mandate, called the Mandate of Heaven (*tianming*), which he could lose by misgovernment. Indeed, the Chinese word for revolution is literally "to remove the Mandate" (*geming*).

In ancient China, Heaven was regarded as a personal deity. With philosophical evolution, Heaven became a symbol for a transcendent moral force. The mandate was still associated with it, and rulers were still responsible to this Heaven for their manner of governing.

And so Confucian China shares with Christian Europe the idea of vicarious authority in kingship. But the doctrine of tyrannicide, which developed so early in China, emerged only much later in Europe. The late sixteenth-century treatises by an anonymous Huguenot author and by the Spanish Jesuit Luis Mariana were either publicly burned or condemned, although they were to wield enormous influence.[6] In China, too, some of Mencius' teachings were considered inflammatory. This was the

---

[5] Walter Laqueur and Barry Rubin, *The Human Rights Reader* (New York: New American Library, 1989), p. 197.

[6] I am referring to the *Vindicae contra Tyrannos* (1579) and to Mariana's *De rege et regis institutione* (1598–99).

opinion of the fourteenth-century founder of the Ming dynasty, who sought to delete from the *Book of Mencius* those passages that approved of tyrannicide.[7]

Implicit in the political teachings cited above is that government rests on popular consent. More explicitly, the third-century BC Confucian thinker Xunzi (Hsün-tzu) speaks of human beings coming together in society to achieve the strength and harmony without which they cannot conquer other beings—presumably the birds and beasts.[8] Before him, the fifth-century BC thinker Mozi (Mo-tzu) already discussed the origin of social authority through a form of consent on the part of human beings who gather together to prevent disorder and injury by the election of wise leaders.[9]

The Universe and Us: Ecological Sustainability

From the East Asian viewpoint, the traditional belief has been expressed in a familiar adage describing the harmony underlying Chinese thought and civilization: that Heaven and humanity are one—*tianren heyi* (literally, Heaven and the human being join as one). It is an adage that has frequently been misunderstood by those who claim that the Chinese cannot distinguish between the two orders, the divine and the human. But it is an adage that I believe to have originated in the very mystic and ecstatic union between the human being and a possessing deity or spirit. This was the primeval experience, the experience of a shaman. It was never forgotten. It has been celebrated in songs, myths, and rituals. It was formulated philosophically as an expression of the continuum between the human being as microcosm and the universe as macrocosm. And this microcosm-macrocosm correspondence has been basic to most philosophizing in China. It was also the profound experience of many mystics, whether Confucian, Taoist, or Buddhist. In later ages, with increasing Buddhist influence, it was also transformed into the philosophical adage that all things are one (*wan-wu yi-t'i/wanwu yiti*), representing more pantheism than personal theism. And this articulation of human har-

---

[7] Julia Ching, *Confucianism and Christianity* (Tokyo: Kodansha International, 1977), p. 193.

[8] "The Regulations of a King," in *Hsün Tzu: Basic Writings*, Burton Watson, trans. (New York: Columbia University Press, 1963), p. 46.

[9] "Identifying with One's Superiors," in Burton Watson, *Mo Tzu: Basic Writings* (New York: Columbia University Press, 1963), pp. 34–35.

mony with the cosmos is what I believe to lie at the very heart of Chinese wisdom.

The Confucian or Taoist view of nature is different from that of the West. It does not refer to what is "other" to the self, but to that which includes the human self. Nature is not a foe to be conquered, a resource to be harnessed. Nature is mother, and we are its children. Return to nature is, in a sense, return to the eternal womb. In this nondualist context, both Confucians and Taoists regard the human being as the microcosm of the universe, which is the macrocosm.

This reference to nonduality suggests as well a certain experiential dimension of awareness, transcending the subject-object division. We read about the similarity of what I call nature mysticism to the discovery of the Tao, which is made in an *apophatic* (abstract or non-imaging) meditative processes, emptying the mind of all concepts, images, and affections. We understand this better when we reflect upon the effort of concentration in meditation, beginning with concentration on a certain object, for example, the act of breathing, but concluding possibly with a state of consciousness where the inner faculties of mind and heart are all gathered at a point of stillness, beyond the subject-object division. This contrasts with *kataphatic* meditation, which fills the mind with concepts or images, such as in Christian discursive meditation or in visualization exercises such as of a Buddha image, or of the inner viscera of the body and the "Taoist" deities that rule them. In the case of visualization, an experience transcending the subject-object division may also occur as the meditator identifies himself or herself increasingly with the object of meditation, for example, the Buddha image.

To speak of meditation and spirituality may seem a diversion from the subject of earth ethics, except that nature draws us to both quiet contemplation and, at times, fear of its awesome power. Even though we seek to do what we can, we are not always competent to deter the forces of nature when these become fearsome, whether in earthquake or volcanic eruptions. But we can learn to respect these forces, not to provoke them, and to appreciate all the more the consolations of nature in harmony with itself and with us.

"Oneness between Heaven and humanity" usually refers to the correspondence and harmony between two realms: the human, and the natural or cosmic. We search in vain in the *Analects* and classics for an explicit articulation of these four Chinese words. However, the meaning is implicit as a philosophical presupposition for several of these texts, in particular the Appendix to the *Book of Changes*—actually a commentary added in the early Han dynasty. And we find in Mencius a philosophical development that we may well associate with these words, especially if we remember that with Mencius, the term *tian* or Heaven came to represent much more of a transcendent moral force, rather than the supreme personal deity it appeared to have been with Confucius.

> For a man to give full realization to his mind or heart is for him to understand his own nature, and a man who knows his own nature will know Heaven. By retaining his mind or heart and nurturing his nature he is serving Heaven. (*Mencius* 7A:1)[10]

The Chinese word *xin* may be translated as either mind or heart, or both, since it is the seat of both intelligence and will. In the above passage, Mencius talks about "realizing" or "fulfilling" the mind or heart, bringing out its full potential, and asserts that such will lead to "knowing Heaven." In other words, he is proposing a certain continuum between the mind or heart, which is within us, and Heaven, which we tend to think of as outside of us, above us, and transcending us. As he has also said,

> The myriad things are all within me. There is no greater joy for me than to find, on self-examination, that I am true to myself. This is the shortest way to humaneness [*ren*]. (*Mencius* 7A:4)

"The myriad things" is another term for the exterior universe. But for Mencius, the universe is also interior to human beings. It is both inside and outside, both transcending our human limitations and yet immanent in us. The insight expressed has puzzled many Western scholars and philosophers, who have argued that what transcends cannot also be what is immanent. But it has also served as the principal foundation for much of Chinese thought, both for later followers of Mencius and for philosophical Taoism.

The "oneness between Heaven and humanity" has been a troubling idea for Western philosophers. It seems to deny the separation between object and subject, the natural and human orders, the other and the self, transcendence and immanence. And that would indeed be so, if the statement were taken in its literal sense. Even Chinese philosophy has

---

[10] English translation adapted from D.C. Lau, *Mencius* (Harmondsworth: Penguin Books, 1970), p. 182.

witnessed an entire spectrum of positions regarding this issue, with certain thinkers within Confucianism and Taoism (and, later, Chan Buddhism) favoring "oneness" to the point of almost denying "otherness," and other thinkers preferring more distinction, or even complete separation between the natural and the human. And there are others who understand the "oneness" in an analogical manner, as maintaining a distinction between the two realms while pointing out a relationship of the human as microcosm to the natural as macrocosm. I shall be dwelling especially on this third interpretation.

That the transcendent is also immanent does not necessarily destroy the meaning of transcendence. What is being described is not perfect identity, but the discovery of the transcendent on one level—that of human consciousness, in the depth of the mind or heart. I am referring to an insight associated with mystical consciousness: what a fourteenth-century Western thinker, Nicolas of Cusa, has called the "coincidence of opposites," holding that the divine may be discovered in the human heart. We are not necessarily also saying that the divine is present *only* in human consciousness. This is an insight also developed by the seventeenth-century German philosopher G.W. Leibniz, who sensed a personal affinity with Chinese thought, and whose own philosophy of monads has affirmed a similar insight.[11]

Mencius spoke in mystical terms about the oneness of Heaven and humanity. For him, human beings participate in the moral force that is Heaven. This is existentially so on account of the *qi* (air, breath, energy) that is in the universe and in all living beings. And this *qi* takes on a special moral character in the case of human beings, moral judgment being the distinguishing mark between humans and animals.

This is not to say that the Confucian philosophers had nothing more specific to say about ecological sustainability. Mencius told a king that

> If the mulberry is planted in every homestead of five *mu* of land, then those who are fifty can wear silk; if chickens, pigs and dogs do not miss their breeding season, then those who are seventy can eat meat; if each lot of a hundred *mu* is not deprived of labor during the busy seasons, then families with several mouths to feed will not go hungry.[12]

Elsewhere, he complains about the over-logging of trees and the

---

[11] Consult Julia Ching and Willard G. Oxtoby (eds.), *Moral Enlightenment: Leibniz and Wolff on China.*

[12] *Mencius* 1A:3; in D.C. Lau's translation, p. 51.

over-pasturing of the mountain:

> There was a time when the trees were luxuriant on the Ox Mountain. As it is
> on the outskirts of a great metropolis, the trees are constantly lopped by axes. Is
> it any wonder that they are no longer fine? With the respite they get in the day
> and in the night, and the moistening by the rain and the dew, there is certainly
> no lack of new shoots coming out. But then the cattle and sheep come to graze
> upon the mountain. That is why it is as bald as it is.[13]

And so we may find a source for universal harmony and global ethics
in the original, mystical insight found in the Chinese tradition, but with
its parallel in Western neo-Platonist philosophy and in the traditions of
spirituality that it helped to nourish. I am speaking of the unity between
the human and the heavenly, be that called divinity, nature, or the Tao. I
am speaking of the oneness of all things, that unity in which the whole
universe finds itself, in which all human beings are related and interrelated, as children of heaven and earth, as stewards of nature and of one
another, without being separated from nature itself.

Applying Righteousness (yi): Economic and Social Justice

Mencius taught ren together with yi (righteousness or justice). In doing
so, he focused often on issues regarding economic and social justice. In
his conversations with various rulers of small states, Mencius often appears to put the kings on the defensive regarding their luxurious lifestyles.
As King Hui of Liang, for example, stood over a pond, he asked Mencius:
"Are such things enjoyed even by a good and wise man?" The answer
was: "Only if a man is good and wise is he able to enjoy them…. It was by
sharing their enjoyments with the people that men of antiquity were able
to enjoy themselves."[14]

He went on to say:

> There is fat meat in your kitchen and there are well-fed horses in your stables,
> yet the people look hungry and in the outskirts of cities men drop dead from
> starvation. This is to show animals the way to devour men…. If then, one who
> is father and mother to the people cannot…avoid showing animals the way to
> devour men, wherein is he father and mother to the people?[15]

Throughout Chinese history, enlightened Confucian officials sought

---

[13] *Mencius* 6A:8; Lau, p. 165.
[14] *Mencius* 1A:2; see D.C. Lau's translation, p. 50.
[15] *Mencius* 1A:4; Lau, *op. cit.*, p. 52.

to bring about more equity among the people by land reform, frequently justifying their measures with ancient precedents. The Chinese Communist government also attempted land reform on a large scale, only to end up during the Cultural Revolution (1966–1976) by making communes out of land previously redistributed; in recent years, it has reversed the process. It is interesting to note that Taiwan's present-day prosperity can also be partly attributed to successful land reform, undertaken in the 1960s.

Such reform measures usually have their roots in a concern for economic and social justice, which in turn is based on a concern for human welfare grounded in the Confucian tradition. As a former expert from China explained, human rights encompass the right to life, economic rights, political rights, and cultural rights.[16] We all know that *talk* of human rights, or even of economic rights, will not fill any stomach. But the enforcement of respect for human beings, their welfare and their needs, and, if we wish to add, their rights, will go a long way to enhancing economic rights. And indeed, the enhancement of economic rights is in no way a contradiction to the acceptance of more basic human rights.

That collective rights are more important than individual rights has also been the argument of the Communist government, who claims to have liberated the country from colonialism and imperialism, as well as what it calls the "feudalism" of past oppressions. However, what is often implied is that individuals should be sacrificed for the collectivity when necessary, and that those in power should decide what is good for that collectivity.

Another area in which Confucian humanism shows its limitations regards the role of women. The process for subjugating women to men began before Confucius, with the development of the patriarchal kinship system associated to the ancestral cult in the Chou period, together with confirmation of the hereditary male principle in successions to the throne. The ritual texts speak about the "three obediences," subjecting women to their fathers, then to husbands, and then to sons during widowhood.[17] Doubtless, Confucius supported the patriarchal character of society in general. He has said: "Women and people of low birth are very

---

[16] Yu Haocheng, "On Human Rights and Their Guarantee by Law," in Michael C. Davis, ed., *Human Rights and Chinese Values: Legal, Philosophical and Political Perspectives* (Hong Kong: Oxford University Press, 1995), p. 99.

[17] Li-chi Cheng-chu, 8:9b.

hard to deal with. If you are familiar with them, they get out of hand. If you keep your distance, they resent it" (*Analects* 17:25). We might note that women and people of low birth were both excluded from education. And while Confucius sought to be more inclusive in his teaching of disciples, he did not extend that privilege to women.

A story tells how Master Kong once paid a visit to a lady infamous for her incestuous relationships: Nanzi, the wife of Duke Ling of Wei. This action makes us think he was not above some politicking with a ruler's inner court. That it happened shows that noblewomen in his times were still able to maintain their status while enjoying their notoriety, even receiving unrelated male guests on their own, and also wielding enough power over their spouses regarding the possible employment of these male guests. But this act greatly displeased the disciple Zilu, which led the Master to swear (literally "with an arrow"), "If I have done anything improper, may Heaven's curse be on me, may Heaven's curse be on me!" (6:28).[18]

What did the oath mean? In my opinion, it was only a social visit, as the Master was above ingratiating himself sexually with a ruler's spouse, which, after all, would be a punishable crime. But the question was of propriety, and Kong defended himself on that ground, which demonstrates a rather broad view of permissible social interaction between men and women.

Within the framework of Confucian thinking, the individual was regarded always as a member of a much more important, larger group, be that family or society. The gender question therefore constituted part and parcel of a larger complex of questions involving the Five Relationships.

If we examine Confucian texts, we actually find little treatment of the position of women and their obligations. But it is the little we do find that makes an important difference. For example, the *Book of Changes* was for ages past an important text for philosophical reflection. There, the hexagrams *qian* (Heaven) and *kun* (earth) represent, respectively, the *yang* and *yin* forces, which in turn represent male and female. Thus woman is to man as earth is to Heaven: lowly and inferior, weak and receptive.

Mencius emphasized that human nature is originally good, and

---

[18] The translation is from D.C. Lau, trans., *Confucius: The Analects* (Harmondsworth: Penguin Books, 1979), p. 85. On the point of the oath-taking, consult Arthur Waley, trans., *The Analects of Confucius* (London: Allen & Unwin, 1938), pp. 240–241.

therefore perfectible. He taught that every person could become a sage (*Mencius* 6B:2). Logically, the teaching has served to strengthen a basic belief in human equality, regardless of class or even gender distinctions. Mencius also emphasized that the taboo between the sexes should not prevent a man from helping to rescue a drowning woman, such as his sister-in-law. Let us quote the conversation (*Mencius* 4A:17):

> "Is it the rule that males and females are not to touch each other in giving or receiving anything?"
>
> "It is the rule."
>
> "If a man's sister-in-law is drowning, should he stretch his hand to rescue her?"
>
> "He who would not rescue such a drowning woman is a beast. While it is the *general* rule that males and females not touch each other in giving or receiving, it is a *particular* exigency to stretch one's hand to rescue a drowning sister-in-law."

In this way, human life and dignity—a woman's life and dignity—was placed before ritual law. On balance, however, the position of women continued to weaken as Confucianism gained ascendancy. And it would further deteriorate in later ages, with the emergence of the neo-Confucian philosophers. The Confucian tradition, for example, has always emphasized the importance of keeping the body in good form, as a filial response to the gift of one's parents and ancestors. But few Confucian philosophers before the twentieth century protested the custom of foot-binding which so deformed women, affecting not only their personal health but also that of their children. While women were never formally excluded from the teachings of Confucian humanism, they were nonetheless excluded from many of its benefits, including those of a formal education.[19]

With the passage of time, and as the established school of thought, Confucianism took on more and more the rigidity of ideology. The position of women continued to decline whenever this ideology was in force. The eleventh-century philosopher Cheng Yi is especially remembered for having said that it is better to starve than to remarry, which Zhu Xi (Chu Hsi) reiterated in the twelfth century. After all, "To starve to death is a

---

[19] In this respect, we accept the fact that despite Confucius' personal efforts and those of many of his followers, education remained mainly elitist in traditional China, and appears still to be such in mainland China, on account of there being few schools and small enrollments.

very small matter, but to lose one's virtue is a very serious matter."[20] And
Zhu Xi took Cheng's ideas seriously enough to write to a disciple to urge
him to counsel his widowed younger sister not to remarry. He continues:

> ...let her understand that [just as when a dynasty falls,] the minister must re-
> main loyal, so too...the widow must remain chaste.... From the popular point
> of view, this is truly unrealistic, but in the eyes of a gentleman who knows the
> classics, and understands principles, this is something that cannot change.[21]

Confucian society did offer a few protections for women, prescribing
that a wife could not be divorced if she had no home to return to, if she
had performed three years of mourning for a parent-in-law, or if the family had risen from poverty or a humble station to wealth and a high station after the marriage.[22]

In the order of nature, the husband-wife relationship precedes even
that of the father-son, and certainly that of the ruler-subject. In the order
of social realities, however, the relationship of wife to husband was after
all patterned on that of the minister to the sovereign. After Sung times,
Chinese history witnessed an increasing centralization of state power in
the hands of the ruler, who regarded his ministers as servants rather than
partners, just as the women of his harem were all his concubines. Few
intellectuals dared to criticize such a system; real changes were only introduced in the twentieth century.

And the experience of women was in many ways shared by men, who
were themselves subject to fathers and rulers in a patriarchal society
which became increasingly "collectivized" without offering protection to
the individuals caught in the web. Confucian humanism was likewise
caught in the same web, serving the interests of the absolute state, which
slowly drained it of its humanistic content.

Being Humane (Ren): Respecting Human Rights

The United Nations Declaration on Human Rights, including a Preamble

---

[20] Consult *Er-Cheng quanshu* (*Complete Works of the Two Chengs*), SPPY edition; *Yishu*
(Surviving Works), 22B:3a.

[21] Letter to Chen Shizhong, in *Zhu Wengong wenji* (*Collected Writings of Zhu Xi*) Subu
beiyao edition, 26:26b–27a; consult Wing-tsit Chan, *Chu Hsi: New Studies* (Honolulu:
University of Hawaii Press, 1989), p. 540. Men were permitted to divorce their wives for
any of seven reasons: disobeying the parents-in-law, not bearing a son, adultery, jealousy,
incurable sickness, excessive talkativeness, or theft.

[22] Chan, *Chu Hsi: New Studies*, p. 539.

and some 30 Articles, was drafted very much under the influence of the Western nations, in particular the United States of America, at the end of the Second World War. The social and economic rights were included very much at the insistence of the Communist nations, which, however, did not become signatories. There has been, understandably, discussion and argument as to whether the statement of rights represents a Western conceptual construct with limited applicability, or whether it offers a solid core of principles that deserve the respect of all peoples and governments. I shall be discussing some of these problems later, but offer those parts of the Declaration that I have quoted as examples of what is considered to be the *content* of human rights. And these rights as "rights" are also considered—in the West—as universal and inalienable, to be enjoyed equally by all who are human, and indeed necessary for living a life deemed to be fully "human."

And here arises our problem. Is human rights mainly a Western ideological export (to accompany its trade delegations) bolstered by subtle claims of Western political and cultural superiority? What validity can it claim to have in non-Western cultures such as in the Chinese?

There is a problem, for example, with the word "rights": not just in Chinese translation, but also in Western languages. At first sight, the term represents legally protected entitlements of individuals in society. And many have the impression that certain rights taken for granted are a sacred legacy from the past.

We turn now to the term "human," since by *human rights* we are referring to the "rights of human beings." I shall not dwell on the definition of a human being, since even this could be controversial. Depending on whether we opt for the biological (for example, the full genetic code), the philosophical (rationality, free will, self-consciousness), or some other model, there will always be problems regarding boundary lines. For example, people question whether fetuses, or the comatose, should be considered human.

I would like to describe human rights as a creature of recent birth with a fairly long lineage. Its mother is liberal moral and political philosophy—the French Enlightenment and liberal English thinking, among other things; its father is international law; its midwife is revolution: first the Revolution of American Independence and then the French Republican Revolution of the late eighteenth century. Such papers as the American Declaration of Independence and the French Declaration of the

Rights of Man and of the Citizen may be considered its birth certificate. The ensuing Bills of Rights that became incorporated in many national constitutions worldwide, and especially the United Nations Universal Declaration of Human Rights (1948), might be described as its introduction to high society. But further back, its ancestry includes Stoic concepts of natural law and traditions of Roman civil law and Anglo-Saxon common law, to the extent that these lent protection to the rights of citizens and of individuals.[23]

Fa, the Chinese word for law, is a graph with a water radical and what could be a mythical animal (later symbolizing "justice") as a semantic component. Its etymology is difficult, but it represents a transcendent order.[24] Allegedly, in an ancient rite or ordeal, a bull was presented to the altar of the god of the soil, over which lustrations were sprinkled. The contestants then read their oaths of innocence; the guilty party was unable to finish, and was gored to death by the bull.[25]

It is interesting that a mythical animal instilling a sense of fear in contestants or litigants should serve as a symbol of justice. Justice, it would seem, inspires fear in the unjust, especially in those who seek, without merit, to take advantage of the system. Perhaps it is not surprising that the Chinese have traditionally and until our own days avoided law courts in their search for conflict resolution, preferring to avoid conflict, or at least to find arbitration to overcome conflict.

What the legendary ordeal also reveals is that the contestants are somehow presumed guilty unless proved innocent, which imposes not only the burden of proof but also the taint of suspicion on those who contest an issue or are detained by the authorities for alleged offenses.

In ancient texts, *fa* designates the law of Heaven to which sages look up, whereas another word, *xing*, with a knife radical, signifies penal law. And while the ancient concept of law was interpreted as belonging to the transcendent order, Confucian society regarded itself as being governed more by *li* (literally, "ritual," or ritual law), a term rooted in ancient re-

---

[23] There are many books on human rights. For example, Eugene Kamenka and Alice Erhsoon Tay, eds., *Human Rights* (London: Edward Arnold, 1978), includes international contributions from philosophers and legal experts.

[24] For *fa*, see Hsü Chin-hsiung, *Zhongguo gudai shehui wenzi yu renlei xue de toushi* (*Ancient Chinese Society: An Examination of Writing and Anthropology*), Revised Edition (Taipei, Commercial Press, 1995), pp. 542–543.

[25] Joseph Needham (ed.), *Science and Civilization in China*, vol. 2, p. 205, especially note (a).

ligion and presuming a distinction between nobility and commoners. *Li* may be described also as customary, uncodified law, internalized by individuals and governing gentlemen in their personal and social lives, in their behavior toward the spirits as well as the rest of the world. For that reason, *li* has the extended meaning of propriety or correct behavior. It was based on justice, righteousness (*yi*), even humaneness (*ren*). A classical education was an education in the rites, one that prepared the young nobles for life. *Fa*, on the other hand, referred to ritual customs, selected and codified, which became a penal code to be applied especially to commoners who had not the privilege of a ritual education.

"Not to do unto others what you would not have them do to you." This line, coming from Confucius himself, has been called the *negative* Golden Rule governing moral life. But how it is to be applied in different circumstances continues to be a puzzle. What if the individual finds himself or herself in conflict between responsibility toward the kinship group and responsibility toward the state? How should one choose?

Once told by a public official about a young man who testified against his father, who had stolen a sheep, Confucius replied: "In our village…, fathers cover up for their sons, and sons cover up for their fathers" (*Analects* 13:18).

This answer has been perplexing to many Western scholars, who are astonished to see Confucius' encouragement of deviousness, and concerned about the protection of one's family as the source of many problems in how society relates itself to the state. Certainly, such a statement appears naive in the case of someone who wanted to serve government; it can hardly endear the speaker to any ruler, and does not exemplify any kind of feudal loyalty on the part of Confucius.

That Confucius not only said it, but said so to a high official, is very relevant. It is indicative of the priority of natural relationships over artificial or contractual ones. In the course of time, as the country became unified, and as the state centralized all powers in its own hands, society could still resist the state's encroachments in the name of kinship duties, which the state, ironically, often had to support.

In its emphasis on the union between the moral and legal orders, the Chinese tradition has suffused the legal realm with a moral concern derived from Confucian philosophy, which is centered on the universal virtue of *ren* (humanity or benevolence), the practice of which renders a person perfectly humane.

But if incipient ideas of human equality and popular sovereignty arose very early in Chinese thought, they did not lead to a political structure which protects human rights. The twentieth century did not see the proper development of the institutions of participatory democracy which could assure human rights in China. Unfortunately, the danger remains that only another violent revolution could "rectify" the situation, and so far, revolutions have only replaced one set of ruling elite with another set.

The evolution of law in China may be described as the *devolution* of ritual (*li*) into law (*fa*) and of law into punishment.[26] For this reason, law is regarded as having played a mainly penal role in Chinese society, protecting the rights of the rulers and enjoining passive obedience on the part of the subjects. Unto this day the Chinese fear law, because law has been an arbitrary instrument in the hands of the rulers. Throughout history, Chinese law served public interest only insofar as it also served the interests of the government.

Even in political despotism, power is absolute only in theory. And many were the critics of power abuses in traditional China, including those in the inner circles of power itself. There were also other voices, of "dissidents," intellectual leaders. Long after the time of Mencius, critiques of power were increasingly made obliquely or in secret. A seventeenth-century thinker, Huang Zongxi, well known as a philosopher and intellectual historian, condemned the rulers for regarding their domains as their private property, and their subjects as their servants and slaves. He proposed that law (*fa*) be established for the interest of all rather than of the few, and that government be by laws rather than human beings. And he denounced those laws that enslave people as "unlawful laws."[27]

Unfortunately for China, Huang's ideas did not get the same reception as, for example, John Locke's in seventeenth-century England and beyond. But granted the historically alien character of the concept of human rights, could we still argue the validity of extending it to the Chinese situation, on the basis that there is enough in the culture that could accept it?

---

[26] Consult Sa Meng-wu, *Zhongguo fazhi sixiang* (*Chinese Thinking on Government by Law*) (Taipei: Yenbo Press, 1978).

[27] See *Mingyi daifang lu*, Subu beiyao edition, ch. 1–3; Eng. trans. by Wm. Theodore de Bary, *Waiting for the Dawn: A Plan for the Prince* (New York: Columbia University Press, 1993).

In the post-Christian West, liberal humanism, beginning as a revolt against theism and eventually influencing many believers in God, has offered a climate of openness for the assertion and discussion of universal moral values. In China, where a Western ideology, Marxist-Leninism, nominally reigns as absolute dogma, the population remembers a native humanist tradition going back more than two millennia to Confucius and even earlier.

Leading contemporary Chinese philosophers living outside China, where they breathe a fresher air, have agreed that traditional Chinese culture contains "seeds" for concepts like science and democracy which have come more directly from the West. I am referring to persons such as Carsun Chang, Mou Tsung-san, T'ang Chün-I, and Hsü Fu-kuan.[28]

In the West, the development of human rights also reflects the growth of individualism in the theory and practice of society. Socialists have criticized its development, and asked explicitly for economic and social rights. But presumably, Communist China followed the precedent of the Soviet Union as well as of the Chinese Republic of 1911 in eventually giving itself a constitution. China has promulgated several constitutions, three times (1954, 1975, 1978) before 1982. This reflects an effort to find a suitable instrument for legitimization, since each constitution lost credibility through its nonobservance by the party in power. Still, the impression is that a government should exist for the protection of the people's rights. So the 1982 constitution gives due regard to "citizens' freedom of speech, of the press, of assembly, of association" and even describes such freedom as "inviolable." In fact, article by article, we can compare the 1982 Constitution with the United Nations Universal Declaration and find real parallels.[29]

---

[28] Consult "A Manifesto for the Reappraisal of Sinology and Reconstruction of Chinese Culture," in Carsun Chang, *The Development of Neo-Confucian Thought* (New York, Bookman Associates, 1963), vol. 2, Appendix.

[29] Articles 35 and 37 of the 1982 Constitution. Consult Julia Ching, *Probing China's Soul: Religion, Politics, Protest in the People's Republic* (San Francisco: Harper & Row, 1990), p. 168. However, certain rights permitted earlier were struck out, such as the right for workers to strike, and the right of airing grievances on wall posters and of privacy in correspondence. Consult also Andrew Nathan, "Political Rights in the Chinese Constitutions," in R. Randle Edwards *et al.*, eds., *Human Rights in Contemporary China* (New York: Columbia University Press, 1986), p. 79.

A Vision of Peace (*Taiping*)

Confucius gathered about himself a small group of disciples, many of whom shared his life, travels, and tribulations. (Contemporary scholars dispute the traditional number of 3,000 and prefer a smaller figure, perhaps 72.) He was a fatherly figure in their midst, even if some of the disciples were only a few years younger than himself, and a few were even older. He practiced what may be called the art of spiritual guidance, exhorting his followers to moderate the excesses of their temperaments by certain efforts of self-control aided by the practice of self-examination. He gives this general advice: "When you meet someone better than yourself, think about emulating him. When you meet someone not as good as yourself, look inside and examine your own self" (*Analects* 4:17).

Moral education was Confucius' chief concern. He cannot be described simply as a pacifist. He talked about the need to give the people moral training for as long as seven years before leading them to war (*Analects* 13:29). Not doing so, and yet taking them to war, would be simply abandoning the people (13:30). Mencius added that

> Confucius rejected those who do their best to wage war....
> [We notice that] in wars to acquire territory, dead bodies fill the plains....
> Death itself is too light a punishment for warmongers. (*Mencius* 4A:15)

Mencius condemned King Hui of Liang as a ruthless man who "sent his people to war, making pulp of them, for the sake of gaining further territory" (7B:1). He also said that none of the many wars supposedly recorded by Confucius in the Spring-Autumn Annals—covering the years 722 to 481 BC in the small state of Lu, which was Confucius' home state—were just wars (7B:2). It shows that his standards for a just war were very high indeed.

The United Nations Declaration places primary importance on every *individual's* human dignity, and the sanctity of human life. In China, tradition claims that an ancient sage-king refrained from a war of conquest with the words: "I would not shed the blood of one innocent human being even if that could gain me the world." Whether that was actually said is not so important; the belief in the truth of the statement shows how important one individual human life was considered through the ages.

Confucianism has sometimes been described as an ethnic tradition. Actually, it has always had a universalist thrust, since it is at core an ethical humanism. And today, its influence is manifest in all of East Asia, stretching from China to Korea, Japan, and Vietnam. In his own days, Confucius had no aversion for other peoples. Indeed, he once expressed a desire to settle among the "barbarian tribes of the east." When someone asked, "How can you put up with their uncouth ways?" his answer was simply, "If a gentleman was to live with them, what uncouthness will there be?" (*Analects* 9:14).

Chinese utopian ideas have usually focused on time rather than place. The Chinese view of time has usually been described as cyclical and backward-looking, as shown in the preferred "utopian" description of a Golden Past, especially found in the section called *liyun* (Evolution of Rites) from the *Book of Rites*, which speaks of a remote past when the world "belonged to all," called the Great Unity (*datong*), and a time after that ruled by the early kings, called the Lesser Prosperity (*xiaokang*). This Confucian vision of peace and universal harmony is especially attributed to Confucius:

> When the Great Way was practiced, the world was shared by all alike. The worthy and able were promoted to office and all practiced good faith and lived in affection.... The aged found a fitting close to their lives, the robust their employment; the young were provided with an upbringing and the widow and widower, the orphan and the sick, got proper care.... This precluded conspiracies to do evil, as well as thieves and rebels, while people could leave their house gates unbolted. It was the age of Great Unity.[30]

The Spring-Autumn Annals was a more laconic text. It was elaborated by a narrative commentary, *The Annals of Tso*, and a catechetical commentary, the *Gongyang*, favorite commentary of the allegorical school. Following upon the philosopher Dong Zhongshu's suggestions, the scholar He Shiu (129–82 BC) elaborated on the "Three Ages" theory, which divided the 242 years covered by the Spring-Autumn Annals into three groups: the latest years were those personally witnessed by Confucius, and then, going backward, came those that he heard of through oral testimony, and those he learned of through transmitted records.[31] These "Three Ages" were subsequently described in chronological order as those of Disorder, Approaching Peace, and Universal Peace

---

[30] Eng. trans. adapted from W.T. de Bary, ed., *Sources of Chinese Tradition* (New York: Columbia University Press, 1960), p. 191.

[31] Dong Zhongshu, *Chunqiu fanlu*, ch. 1; Fung Yu-lan, *A History of Chinese Philosophy*, Derk Bodde, trans. (Princeton, New Jersey: Princeton University Press, 1953), vol. 2, p. 81.

(*taiping*).

Many reformers in history wanted to restore the age of Lesser Prosperity, and a few visionaries even looked back to the Great Unity. But the "Three Ages" theory has presented the possibility of projecting the past into the future in a different way: by claiming the possibility of progress through history, thus proclaiming a more linear view of time itself. This term, *taiping*, the great or universal peace, came to signify peace itself as well as a dream or an ideal to be realized through good government.

Both Dong Zhongshu and He Shiu belonged to the Modern Script School, which had much tolerance for apocryphal literature and sought political influence in proclaiming their flamboyant reading of the classics. Their ideas were resurrected in the late nineteenth century by the controversial scholar and reformer Kang Yuwei, who promoted their "utopian" theories to advance his own sociopolitical agenda—an eclectic Confucian, Buddhist, and even anarchist vision of a universal human community.

The problem was that traditional Chinese political thought always assumed that monarchy was the best form of government, as it looked back to a Golden Past of sage-kings who allegedly ruled. Confucianism obviously preferred benevolent monarchs and had no use for tyrants, but Confucian ministers were unable to keep tyrants from the throne. There were changes in the dynastic cycle but the individuals who acquired power were often of the wrong kind, even if they did so in the name of the Mandate of Heaven. In the light of events, this doctrine became understood by many as a kind of historical determinism governing the rise and fall of political dynasties. Besides, the sage-king ideal did not bring with it a carefully articulated program for good government. The Confucian text, the Institutes of Chou, presumed to contain a model for good government, offers mainly an idealized bureaucracy. Too much was expected of the personal, ethical qualities of the sage-king, and too little was done to regulate his rule, another reason for the ideal to become a generalized endorsement of benevolent despotism.

Conclusion

Why was it that the Chinese, very early, had articulated ideas about human dignity and equality, but were unable to establish a political system to protect this dignity and equality? This question has troubled the minds of many contemporary Chinese intellectuals. The disintegration of feudalism in Western Europe was eventually followed by the empowerment of the propertied classes, whose assertion of their own rights eventually contributed to the extension of like rights to the whole population. In China, however, a system of feudalism started very early and was disintegrating by the time of Confucius and Mencius. It came to a formal end when the country was unified by the sword under the First Emperor, a hated despot who burned books and buried scholars (c. 213 BC).

In contrast with Western Europe, power in China became increasingly centralized in the hands of the monarch, rather than shared. A titled aristocracy was strong during the classical period, at the time of Confucius and Mencius, when the country was divided into feudal states. Its powers and privileges were then dissolved by a suspicious absolute monarchy, never to be successfully restored. A government-controlled education system and a civil service examination promoted the principle of merit while monopolizing the supply of bureaucrats, who were mere advisors and administrators and, as the propertied class, never threatened rebellion. Eventually, even the position of prime minister was abolished in the fourteenth century, so that power-sharing at the top occurred more often with eunuchs than with competent ministers. There was never an independent judiciary, although a Censorate served to channel policy criticisms.

The Confucian doctrine of benevolent government from above was not sufficient to guarantee the rights of the subjects below, and the population was instructed more to serve social harmony than to assert their own rights. Power was more commonly wrested from one party by another through wars and rebellions, started in turn by the military elite or by the socially deprived who had nothing to lose. It was not properly distributed and structurally balanced.

Of course, democratic Western Europe is in many ways an exception on the geopolitical land mass of Eurasia, and in the world as a whole, in achieving democratic institutions after a mere period of nearly 2,000 years. Even there, it did not happen overnight. And the process evolved from the struggle for rights of the nobles and propertied to that for the rights of all. If China did not develop like institutions earlier, could she at least accept the importance of human rights as a concept and develop the necessary safeguards?

I think that philosophers like Mencius and Huang Zongxi demonstrate that the Chinese intellectual tradition was well prepared for accepting Western ideas regarding the legal protection of human rights. Witness the efforts of intellectuals in the late nineteenth and early twentieth centuries who sought to secure a constitutional form of government, first under a monarchy, and then under a republic. Their efforts failed not so much because they were introducing ideas considered alien, but rather because the country was not permitted by outside powers, both the West and Japan, to evolve peacefully.

Before the Communists took power, and in spite of great odds and many imperfections, the Republic of China had made halting progress with its judiciary system. Today we can find encouragement in those East Asian countries and regions where the record has improved vastly, even if it is still not perfect. We have in mind the situations in Japan (where the postwar Constitution is American-inspired) and more recently in South Korea and Taiwan, which have all been influenced by the teachings of Confucian humanism. These countries and regions have experienced rapid economic modernization, accompanied by democratization and the more conscientious enactment and observance of human rights legislations. Taiwan, which also calls itself the Republic of China, is a bastion of Chinese culture, distinct from Hong Kong, which has been a British colony and is only now experimenting with a democratic legislative structure which the mainland government has threatened to dismantle, and from Singapore, an ex-British colony which likes to claim its own form of participatory democracy under a one-party government.

Has the wisdom of China yet something to offer us today—to China, and to the larger world?

My own answer is a cautious "Yes," where China is concerned, with the understanding also that there is as yet little other cultural option available. In the recent past, Chinese humanism has been tested by the invasion of Western values, purified by the fires of revolution, and challenged by the ideology of Marxism-Leninism. No longer orthodox or established, Confucianism has once more become a diffused teaching rather than a state system. With self-examination and self-criticism, it may yet find new life with which to reinvigorate a tottering civilization. And it will do so only in a pluralistic society, as one school among many others, the way it was when Confucius himself was alive and teaching.

Where the rest of the world is concerned—especially the West, which has so changed China's destiny—Chinese humanism has perhaps also a few things to offer: what some people call family values and the work ethic, but what may more simply be described as discipline and tolerance and a new harmony. Chinese observers of the West have also pointed out what the West could learn from the East. For example, they find excessive individualism, a litigious spirit promoting conflict rather than harmony, and especially in the United States, an unacceptably high crime rate. There is also an increasing gap between the rich and the poor in capitalist societies, a monopoly of political election campaigns by those who can afford them, and the social deprivation of various minorities.[32] Within China, religions and spiritualities have been enjoying a mini-revival of sorts during recent decades. And the ancient art of *qigong* or Chinese yoga, promoting the unity of body and spirit, has been recognized increasingly as a healing resource. The peaceful, disciplined, and thriving societies in East Asian countries with very dense populations outside of China demonstrate the people's sense of social harmony. East Asians value what they call humaneness, or human warmth, which they find lacking in a system where human relationships have lost a personal touch. East Asians are also beginning to learn to avoid pollution of their natural environment due to unbridled economic development.

For the twelfth-century Zhu Xi, as for other representatives of the mainstream of Chinese philosophy, the world, the natural universe, is not only the "environment" in which the human being finds himself or herself. It is also the archetype or the paradigm, of which the human being is an instance or manifestation. And it is above all the ontological model for human nature and existence. The world is knowable to us especially as an ontological model; it is important to us especially as such. The world and the human being are seen essentially as related, each to the other, incomprehensible except in terms of this relatedness. The world is macrocosm, the human being is microcosm. The eleventh-century neo-Confucian philosopher Zhang Zai has written this poignant piece, in which he offers his cosmology as a basis for his love of and concern for other human beings, especially the weakest among them:

> Heaven is my father; earth is my mother, and even such a small creature as I find an intimate place in their midst. Therefore that which fills the universe I regard as my body, and that which directs the universe I regard as my nature. All people are my brothers and sisters, and all things are my companions.... Respect the aged—this is the way to treat them.... Show deep love toward the or-

---

[32] Consult Kishore Mahbubani, "The Dangers of Decadence: What the Rest Can Teach the West," *Foreign Affairs* 72 (Sept./Oct. 1993), pp. 10–14.

phaned and the weak—this is the way to treat them…. Even those who are
tired, infirm, crippled, or sick; those who have no brothers or children, wives or
husbands, are all my brothers who are in distress and have no one to turn to.[33]

Today we may not subscribe with equal zeal to a line from the Western Inscription not included above, that "The great ruler (emperor) is the
eldest son of my parents," but we may adjust the line following to say that
"the great ministers [namely, the world's leaders] are also its stewards."
Yes, they are the stewards of the world's resources: servants, not masters.

[33] Chang Tsai, "Western Inscription," Eng. trans. adapted from Wing-tsit Chan, *A Source
Book in Chinese Philosophy* (Princeton, New Jersey: Princeton University Press, 1963), p.
497.

Working Toward a Shared Global Ethic: Confucian Perspectives

Mary Evelyn Tucker

Introduction: Responses to the Ecological Crisis

It is becoming increasingly clear that we are living in a period of enormous change and upheaval, especially due to the environmental crisis which is threatening life systems on the planet in drastic and often unexpected ways. From resource depletion to population explosion, from pollution excess to biodiversity decrease, we are straddling a precarious moment in human history. Indeed, the human community has never before faced such a challenge in terms of sustaining life and livelihood on the planet. As the scientist Brian Swimme has stated, "We are making macrophase changes on the planet with microphase wisdom." The cultural historian Thomas Berry has raised the question of whether or not the human is a viable species. In this vein he notes we have developed ethics for homicide and suicide, but not for biocide and ecocide. In other words, the moral restraints formulated by a comprehensive environmental ethics are still not in place. Hence we continue to destroy ecosystems and species at a staggering rate. We need not elaborate all the particulars of this destruction, as the statistics are well known; the scale, complexity, and urgency of the environmental crisis are, however, of such magnitude as to require radical rethinking of worldviews and ethics in order to halt this mindless destruction.

There are currently three significant movements in this direction.

The first includes efforts to describe the broad sweep of the epic of evolution and to articulate the role of the human in this process. The second is enunciated by Tu Weiming in his call to move beyond the Enlightenment project and draw on the spiritual resources of the world's religions. The third is the collaborative work on formulating an Earth Charter and a Global Ethics to be brought to the United Nations. This paper on Confucian ethics can be situated in both the second and third categories. Our thesis is that the spiritual dynamics of self-cultivation in the moral political philosophy and the ecological cosmology of Confucian tradition are important resources for overcoming our present alienation from one another and from the earth itself. We will briefly discuss the three movements mentioned above, and then outline the role of the potential contributions of Confucianism.

The Epic of Evolution. Those involved in developing the epic of evolution include Pierre Teilhard de Chardin, Thomas Berry, Brian Swimme, Eric Chaisson, Carl Sagan, E.O. Wilson, Loyal Rue, and Ursula Goodenough. In their book *The Universe Story*, Thomas Berry and Brian Swimme note that we need to situate humankind amidst some 5 billion years of earth's evolution and against the backdrop of some 15 billion years of cosmic evolution. This provides a sufficiently comprehensive worldview against which to formulate an ethics of ecological sustainability and biological integrity to counteract the forces of massive environmental destruction. By reorienting ourselves to this vast sweep of time and space, we have new grounds for an appropriate *anthropocosmic* perspective beyond simply anthropocentric preoccupations. It is here, for example, that the Confucian virtue of humaneness takes on particular significance, for it is a virtue that is understood to have both cosmic and personal dimensions. Thus, self-cultivation links the individual to others and to nature as a whole, identifying the microcosm and the macrocosm.

Beyond the Enlightenment Mentality. Harvard professor Tu Weiming contributes a second important dimension to this discussion in his efforts to move beyond the negative effects of the Enlightenment. Tu calls our attention to the unintended consequences of the Enlightenment project in its frequently unrestrained promotion of rationality, individuality, science, and technology. The objectification of knowledge as power has become a driving force behind viewing the material world as simply a collection of resources to be exploited. Tu suggests that we need to critique the Enlightenment mentality while nonetheless drawing on the positive aspects of the Enlightenment legacy. For example, we have inherited the Enlightenment ideas of liberty and equality, which emphasize the importance of the individual and of democratic systems.

On the other hand, the idea of fraternity may need rethinking in the West in light of communitarian and environmental ethics. How we understand fraternity may be key to our survival as a species and as a planet. Most traditional religions have been anthropocentric and divine-centered; postmodernists have been largely human-centered and politically oriented; communitarian ethicists have likewise been socially focused. All these perspectives are not fully adequate to the challenges we face. Our devotion to individual liberty, human equality, and justice has blinded us to broader possibilities of being communal. As Thomas Berry has observed, we have become autistic in relation to the natural world.

Yet several projects may offset these tendencies. One is Tu Weiming's proposal to bring forth the traditional wisdom of the world's religions for contemporary concerns. This needs to be done with a sufficient sensitivity to the broader cosmological context in which religions arise. In this vein we might observe that Mircea Eliade, who established the History of Religion program at the University of Chicago, was attempting to do precisely this in his efforts to link religious symbols with natural processes such as the fluctuation of day and night, the agricultural cycles, and seasonal rhythms. Similarly, over a three-year period, Tu Weiming convened a series of conferences at the East-West Center in Hawaii on the Dialogue of Civilizations, focusing on religious interactions. Scholars and practitioners came together to explore the resources of these traditions for contemporary concerns.

Another such project is the conference and book series on "Religions of the World and Ecology" at the Center for the Study of World Religions at Harvard University. From 1996 to 1998, eleven major conferences were held at Harvard, examining the resources of the world's religions to meet the environmental challenge.[1]

In this spirit, a number of people are recognizing the value of the Confucian tradition in that it does not have a metaphysics of radical transcendence. Rather, it embraces a profound sense of the recovery of

---

[1] The conferences were organized by John Grim and Mary Evelyn Tucker, who also serve as series editors for the books, published by the Center and Harvard University Press. See *Confucianism and Ecology: The Interrelation of Heaven, Earth and Humans* (1998).

relational resonances between humans and the natural world. It is based on a sophisticated understanding of macrocosmic and microcosmic relations. In short, it promotes correlative thinking in which the personal and the cosmic dimensions are continually interrelated.

The Earth Charter and Global Ethics. Currently, an Earth Charter is being drafted that will be brought to the United Nations General Assembly for adoption by the year 2002. This is a formidable task in an age which celebrates diversity, multiculturalism, and radical particularity. Whether the human species can agree upon a unifying framework of global ethics for a sustainable future remains to be seen. This process may require three dimensions to be fully effective. One is a sufficiently broad cosmological, evolutionary context; second is the means of deepening human-earth relations through enhancing patterns of interaction with the natural world; and third is a concreteness or embodiment of eco-justice perspectives in laws and institutions. The first calls for the overcoming of the dualism of matter and spirit, the second requires new modes of self-cultivation in relation to heaven, earth, and humans, and the third elicits the formation of a global ethics, covenants, laws, and institutions to embody this more embracing worldview. The overall aim is to set forth parameters and goals for establishing sustainable life and livelihoods for future generations. With this context in mind, we turn now to explore the resources of the Confucian tradition in relation to contemporary efforts to forge a comprehensive and inclusive global ethics.

Overview of the Confucian Tradition. The acknowledged founder of the Confucian tradition was the sage-teacher K'ung Futzu (551–479 BCE) whose name was latinized by Jesuit missionaries as Confucius. Born into a time of rapid social change, Confucius devoted his life to reestablishing order through rectification of the individual and the state. This involved a program embracing moral, political, and religious components. As a creative transmitter of earlier Chinese traditions, Confucius is said, according to legend, to have compiled the Five Classics, namely, the *Book of History, Poetry, Changes, Rites,* and the *Spring and Autumn Annals.*

The principal teachings of Confucius, as contained in the *Analects,* emphasize the practice of moral virtues, especially humaneness or love (*jen*) and filiality (*hsiao*). These were exemplified by the "noble person" (*chun tzu*) particularly within the five relations, namely, between parent and child, ruler and minister, husband and wife, older and younger siblings, and friend and friend.

Confucian thought was further developed in the writings of Mencius (372–289 BCE) and Hsün tzu (298–238 BCE). As a political philosophy, it was utilized during the Han period (206 BCE–220 CE) especially with the thought of Tung Chung-Shu (179–104 BCE). The tradition culminated in a Neo-Confucian revival in the eleventh and twelfth centuries which resulted in a new synthesis of the earlier teachings. The major Neo-Confucian thinker, Chu Hsi (1130–1200), designated four texts as containing the central ideas of Confucian thought. Called the Four Books, they consisted of two chapters from the *Book of Rites*, namely *The Great Learning* and *The Doctrine of the Mean*, and the *Analects* and *Mencius*. He elevated these to a position of prime importance over the Five Classics mentioned earlier. These texts and Chu Hsi's commentaries on them became, in 1315, the basis of the Chinese civil examination system which endured for nearly 600 years until 1905.

Chu Hsi's synthesis of Neo-Confucianism was recorded in his classic anthology, *Reflections on Things at Hand*. In this work, Chu provided, for the first time, a comprehensive metaphysical basis for Confucian thought and practice. In response to the Buddhists' metaphysics of emptiness and their perceived tendency toward withdrawal from the world in meditative practices, Chu formulated a this-worldly spirituality based on a balance of religious reverence, ethical practice, scholarly investigation, and political participation.

Unlike the Buddhists who saw attachment to the world of change as the source of suffering, Chu Hsi and the Neo-Confucians after him affirmed change as the source of transformation in both cosmos and person. Thus Confucian spiritual discipline involved cultivating one's moral nature so as to bring it into harmony with the larger pattern of change in the cosmos. Each moral virtue had its cosmological component. For example, the central virtue of humaneness was seen as that which was the source of fecundity and growth in both the individual and the cosmos. By practicing humaneness, one could effect the "transformation of things" in oneself, in society, and in the cosmos. In so doing, one's deeper identity with reality was recognized as "forming one body with all things."

To realize this identification, a rigorous spiritual practice was needed. This involved a development of poles present in earlier Confucian thought, namely, a balancing of religious reverence with an ethical integrity manifested in daily life. For Chu Hsi and later Neo-Confucians such spiritual practice was a central concern. Thus interior meditation became known as "quiet sitting," "abiding in reverence," or "rectifying the mind." Moral self-discipline was known as "making the will sincere," "controlling the desires," and "investigating principle." Through conscientious spiritual effort one could become a "noble person" who was thus able to participate in society and politics most effectively. While in the earlier Confucian view the ruler was the prime moral leader of the society, in Neo-Confucian thought this duty was extended to all people, with a particular responsibility placed on teachers and government officials. While ritual was primary in the earlier view, spiritual discipline became more significant in Neo-Confucian practice. In both, major emphasis was placed on mutual respect in basic human relations.

Neo-Confucian thought and practice spread to Korea, Japan, and Vietnam, where it had a profound effect on their respective cultures. Since 1949, the government of the People's Republic of China has ostensibly repudiated the Confucian heritage. However, the Confucian tradition is currently being reexamined on the mainland, often relying on new publications of Western scholars, especially Tu Weiming, Julia Ching, and Wm. Theodore de Bary. Furthermore, as Tu Weiming has noted, we may be entering a third epoch of Confucian humanism in terms of its revival in both East Asia and the West.

The Confucian tradition may make a significant contribution to a shared global ethic because of its broad anthropocosmic vision and its deep commitment to self-cultivation as a means of affecting the larger social-political-natural order. This tradition affirms the goodness of human nature and values the importance of education; at the same time, it is committed to social harmony and political stability. Two primary goals of the Confucian tradition are fostering individual moral and intellectual growth while trying to create appropriate familial structures and stable political institutions—constantly balancing self and society, the individual and the community. When Confucianism is judged by certain standards (especially contemporary Western democratic principles), it appears not always to be able to live up to its goals of achieving an effective balance at different points in Chinese history.

We acknowledge, then, the historical failures of Confucianism (like every religious tradition) to achieve its highest aims; at the same time, we recognize its significant achievement in perpetuating the stability and longevity of Chinese culture as well as in contributing to the cultural identity and social and political institutions of East Asia as a whole, and Korea, Japan, and Vietnam in particular.

Confucianism was often seen as an authoritarian political system, a hierarchical social system, and a repressive family system. While the tradition has been used for personal and political control, this is a distortion of its central teachings. Moreover, while the role of women in Confucian societies has not been seen as "liberated" by contemporary standards, this has been true for women in most pre-modern societies around the world. We will draw on the positive aspects of the Confucian tradition to address the question of its potential contributions to a more just and sustainable world order. For it is the broader principles and aspirations of the world's religions that need to be brought to bear on the constructive formation of a global ethics undergirding an equitable system of global governance. From many quarters such a call for a global ethics is emerging—for example, from Hans Küng's Global Ethics Foundation, Baird Callicott's work on environmental ethics, the drafting of an Earth Charter, and the long-term commitments of Global Education Associates to an Earth Covenant.

Working Toward a Shared Global Ethic
Peace and Security

> When things are investigated, knowledge is extended; when knowledge is extended, the will becomes sincere; when the will is sincere, the mind is rectified; when the mind is rectified, the personal life is cultivated; when the personal life is cultivated, the family will be regulated; when the family is regulated, the state will be in order; and when the state is in order, there will be peace throughout the world. From the Son of Heaven [Emperor] down to the common people, all must regard cultivation of the personal life as the root or foundation. (*The Great Learning*)[2]

Confucianism has a profound commitment to establishing a peaceful order through the transformation of the individual. *The Great Learning* indicates in a series of eight graduated steps that when one wishes to establish a peaceful society, one must first regulate oneself, then one's family, and finally the state. The text speaks of the need for understanding roots and branches in order to affect the interconnected network of individual, family, society, and country. Thus, carefully prioritizing and acting

---

[2] Chan, Wing-tsit, trans. *A Source Book in Chinese Philosophy* (Princeton, New Jersey: Princeton University Press, 1963), pp. 86–87.

in a reflective manner means that peaceful ends will be realized more readily. Again, while this is an ideal goal, the image of concentric circles spreading outward like ripples in a pond calls to mind the ability of the individual to influence change from oneself outward.

This model is central to all Confucian ethics, and would be a major contribution to a larger global ethics. It might be called the concentric-circle model of ethics, in which peace and security rest on the dynamic interplay between the individual and the key communities in which he or she is imbedded. This is not a dependency model, but rather a responsibility model which reflects the recognition of personal cultivation as the key to a peaceful society. This cultivation rests especially on the sincerity of will, which means avoiding self-deception and being watchful over oneself when alone. A rigorous reliance on moral individuals is the backbone of regulated families, stable societies, and peaceful nations.

This picture of individuals who are self-reflective yet contributing to and nurtured by communities is quintessentially Confucian. East Asian societies with these values have been described as "group-oriented societies"; the underlying implication of this terminology is often that such societies are somehow inferior to the highly individualistic societies of the West. However, it is precisely this group orientation which emphasizes the development of the person in relationship to others that is needed in today's world. This model encourages responsibilities to and cooperation with the larger social and political order, which is lacking in societies that place individual freedom unconditionally above public responsibility. Hence, we have great difficulty in the contemporary West to establish the grounds for a common good.

A peaceful and secure society is impossible without a minimal commitment to a communitarian sensibility, common aspirations, and shared ethical imperatives. It would seem that this is one of the most important contributions Confucianism can make to a shared global ethic in this regard. In short, peace and security are impossible without a greater sense of common good and shared destiny—of both humans and the earth. These links need to be forged by an ethic of concentric circles, where the individual has the security of being connected to interlocking communities and at the same time has the affirmation that his or her development as an individual will add to the flourishing of the entire community. In our times it is essential that the notion of community include not only humans but the earth as well. This communitarian consciousness is the basis of a lasting peace.

Economic and Social Justice

> Mencius replied [to King Hui at Liang], "Why must Your Majesty use the term 'profit?' What I have to offer are nothing but humanity and righteousness. If Your Majesty asks what is profitable to your country, if the great officers ask what is profitable to their families, and if the inferior officers and the common people ask what is profitable to themselves, then both the superiors and the subordinates will try to snatch the profit from one another and the country will crumble."
>
> Mencius answered [King Hui], "Even with a territory of a hundred *li*, it is possible to become the true king of the empire. If Your Majesty can practice a humane government to the people, reduce punishments and fines, lower taxes and levies, make it possible for the fields to be plowed deep and the weeding well done, men of strong body in their days of leisure may cultivate their filial piety, brotherly respect, loyalty, and faithfulness, thereby serving their fathers and elder brothers at home and their elders and superiors abroad. (*Mencius*)[3]

For the Confucian, economic and social justice depended on two key ideas: the importance of virtue over profit, and the value of benevolent government over despotic government. The critique of profit reflected in the passage above suggests that the virtues of humanity and righteousness are more important than profit. Indeed, Confucians looked down on profit that exploited others as problematic. For this reason, they valued the work of farmers and artisans above merchants. The former contributed to the common welfare, while the latter were more often interested in personal gain. Thus, what was seen as public-minded was valued, while what was viewed as only personally beneficial was regarded as suspect.

With respect to human government, it was considered the responsibility of the ruler to be a moral example for the people. Without moral righteousness, the king could be overthrown. When the ruler possessed moral power, it was said that the people would respond naturally to this kind of leadership. Similarly, if the ruler planned for the needs of the people, especially economically, then there would be order and stability in the nation. The ruler was urged to put his desires for pleasure or comfort aside until the basic needs for food, clothing, and shelter were met.

For Mencius, the doctrine of humaneness was developed with regard to its application to both government and the individual. These are the two complementary poles of Confucian thought, and Mencius wished to

---

[3] *Ibid.*, pp. 60–61.

describe how humaneness operates in both these spheres. In doing so, he expanded upon the ideas already evident in Confucius' teaching. With regard to humane government, he elaborated the first comprehensive plan for practical reforms. With respect to the individual, he stressed the importance of balancing the virtues of righteousness and humanity as a corrective to Mo-tzu's idea of universal love for utilitarian ends.[4] Righteousness in this sense simply means behavior appropriate to circumstances and within specific spheres, beginning with the family and moving outward to the society and the state. It is also implied that distributive justice was a key to establishing social harmony.

Humaneness in Government. Throughout his work, Mencius calls for benevolent government for the people. He points out how the ruler should share his pleasures with the people, who will, in turn, respect him (I:A:2). By seeing himself as father and mother of the people (I:B:7) he will act in a way that is responsive to their needs. Even more concretely, however, a benevolent or humane government can be established through the public responsibility of the ruler in carrying out practical social and economic programs. Mencius suggests measures for productive yet ecologically sound farming, fishing, hunting, animal husbandry, and sericulture (I:A:3,4,7; 2:A:5). Similarly, he devised specific plans for irrigation, taxation, labor, education, and land distribution. Mencius uses numerous examples of the early Sage Kings in setting forth programs by which government can operate both effectively and benevolently.

Mencius points out how these programs and laws are incomplete unless humaneness is practiced by the ruler. He writes that while "[g]oodness alone is not sufficient for government; the law unaided cannot make itself effective" (4:A:1). Thus, a balance of virtue and law is necessary, for when a ruler is indeed a person of humaneness, "people will turn to him like water flowing downward with a tremendous force" (I:A:6). Furthermore, they will respond to his virtuous nature, which they would not do to coercive measures or by surrendering their individual integrity. Rather, "when people submit to the transforming influence of morality they do so sincerely, with admiration in their hearts" (2:A:3).

Humaneness in the Person. Mencius believed that a person of humaneness was one who had retained the heart of a newborn babe, and that, in

---

[4] See *Mo Tzu: Basic Writings*, Burton Watson, trans. (New York: Columbia University Press, 1963), pp. 39–51.

a ruler, this would evoke the favorable response mentioned above (4:B:12). For a ruler or citizen to practice humaneness is to strive for purity of spirit like one's original, unblemished mind. Such practice means, above all, the elimination of all intentions of personal aggrandizement or profit. Mencius opens his work with a passage condemning motives for human action that are measured simply in terms of profit. He stresses that, instead, both the state and the individual should be governed by the principles of humaneness and righteousness. He writes, "Humaneness is one's peaceful abode and righteousness the proper path" (4:A:10).

Mencius elevates righteousness to a virtue comparable to humaneness for a number of reasons. First, he wishes to establish a moral principle to provide a foundation for the operation of humaneness that would be in appropriate contrast to the utilitarianism advocated by Mo-tzu. In so doing he formulates a compelling directive to purify one's intentions and be discriminating in one's actions. Thus, to practice humaneness for the sake of what is right means that one can set aside utilitarian or egotistical preoccupations, which interfere with sincerity of will. As Mencius writes of the result of such sincerity, "There has never been a person totally true to himself who fails to move others" (4:A:12).

Moreover, by linking humaneness and righteousness, Mencius provides an alternative to Mo-tzu's idea of universal love without distinctions. Mencius feels universal love is impractical and may lead to unfilial behavior through neglect of immediate family members. So, by stressing righteousness as a part of humaneness, he reaffirms Confucius' teaching that humaneness is rooted in the family and extends outward. For Mencius, these kinds of distinctions are important to the cohesion and coherence of the social fabric, and a discriminating sense of duty is an indispensable counterpart to the practice of humaneness.

Human Rights[5]

> There are five universal ways [in human relations], and the way by which they are practiced is three. The five are those governing the relationship between ruler and minister, between father and son, between husband and wife, between elder and younger brothers, and those in the intercourse between friends. These

---

[5] The important work of Julia Ching, Wm. Theodore de Bary, Irene Bloom, and Tu Weiming in this area should be noted, e.g., *Confucianism and Human Rights*, Wm. Theodore de Bary, Tu Weiming, eds. (New York: Columbia University Press, 1997).

five are universal paths in the world. Wisdom, humanity, and courage, these three are the universal virtues. The way by which they are practiced is one.[6]

Confucianism is a tradition which places primary emphasis on human relations and on the cultivation of virtue so as to enrich these relations and enhance social harmony. In terms of the five key relations mentioned above, it is said that between father and son there should be affection; between ruler and minister, righteousness; between husband and wife, differentiation; between older and younger brothers, proper order; and between friends, faithfulness.[7] The relations are meant to be mutual and reciprocal. Clearly, throughout Chinese history these ideals of mutuality and reciprocity have frequently been abused by autocratic rulers, oppressive bureaucrats, and tyrannical family situations; this should not be minimized.

However, the rights of humans in a Confucian society need to be seen in this context of mutual obligations and responsibilities with regard to human relatives. This is a different emphasis from a Western Enlightenment mentality, which proclaims human freedoms and rights as inalienable. This sense of individual freedom has been a distinctive feature of the emergence of democratic societies in the West, and a rallying call for many other societies in the West struggling to establish democratic constitutions with protection of minority rights. Some of this has resulted in an individualism of entitlement rather than an individualism of responsibility. Indeed, this has been carried to an extreme in the United States where "rights" border on a sacrosanct concept subject to few qualifications or possibilities for improvement. On the positive side, the protection of rights by law has been a distinctive feature of democratic societies. Political institutions and processes which defend the individual against the tyranny of the majority are highly prized in the West.

It has been argued by Wm. Theodore de Bary and others that while these Western concepts and institutions are critical to ensuring necessary freedoms, rites or rituals may serve some of the same functions in East Asian society. The argument has been made that civil society in East Asia has been maintained by elaborate systems of human interchange and community compacts that have helped people to understand their role and value within a larger configuration of society and political inter-

---

[6] Chan, Wing-tsit, *op. cit.*, p. 105.
[7] *Mencius* 3A:4.

actions. Rituals of exchange have been a social glue which allows for maintaining the dignity and self-worth of each person in the exchange. Ritual interchange is measured in language (levels of politeness), bodily movement (bows), gift-giving (end of year), seasonal celebrations (New Year, equinox, solstice), or artistic creations.

Ecological Sustainability

Only those who are absolutely sincere can fully develop their nature. If they can fully develop their nature, they can then fully develop the nature of others. If they can fully develop the nature of others, they can then fully develop the nature of things. If they can fully develop the nature of things, they can then assist in the transforming and nourishing process of Heaven and Earth. If they can assist in the transforming and nourishing process of Heaven and Earth, they can thus form a trinity with Heaven and Earth. (*The Doctrine of the Mean*)[8]

The Way of Heaven and Earth may be completely described in one sentence: They are without any doubleness and so they produce things in an unfathomable way. The Way of Heaven and Earth is extensive, deep, high, brilliant, infinite, and lasting. The heaven now before us is only this bright, shining mass; but when viewed in its unlimited extent, the sun, moon, stars, and constellations are suspended in it and all things are covered by it. The earth before us is but a handful of soil; but in its breadth and depth, it sustains mountains like Hua and Yueh without feeling their weight, contains the rivers and seas without letting them leak away, and sustains all things. The mountain before us is only a fistful of straw; but in all the vastness of its size, grass and trees grow upon it, birds and beasts dwell on it, and stores of precious things [minerals] are discovered in it. The water before us is but a spoonful of liquid, but in all its unfathomable depth, the monsters, dragons, fishes, and turtles are produced in them, and wealth becomes abundant because of it [as a result of transportation]. (*The Doctrine of the Mean*)[9]

As Tu Weiming has observed, Confucianism has a profoundly anthropocosmic sensibility, for Confucian cosmology situates the human within the dynamic, organic processes of nature, not above or controlling those processes. The aim of Confucian self-cultivation and social-political philosophy is to achieve harmony of humans with themselves, with one another, and with the cosmos itself. It is the human who completes heaven and earth and forms a triad with them. As *The Doctrine of the Mean* notes, it is the human who can assist in the transforming and nourishing process of heaven and earth.

---

[8] Chan, Wing-tsit, *op. cit.*, pp. 107–108.
[9] *Ibid.*, p. 109.

For Confucians the earth is seen as abundantly fecund, rich with resources, and resilient with seasonal change. Of course, there are passages
which acknowledge ecological problems, such as one in *Mencius* describing deforestation on Ox Mountain.[10] However, there is an abiding sense
that the concentric community in which the human is embedded includes the natural and cosmic orders. Indeed, harmony in these communities depends on the ability of the human to establish and maintain a
balance between the human and natural worlds. Numerous ritual structures and patterns of correspondence were set up to insure this connection, especially in Han Confucian thought.

Moreover, Confucian societies affirmed that ecological harmony was
not just in terms of reciprocal human-earth relations as a means of self-
cultivation. Rather, ecological sustainability depended on proper cultivation of the land itself. For the government to promote agriculture and
sericulture was essential. Moreover, to build appropriate technological
assistance for these endeavors was all-consuming. Hence huge irrigation
projects and massive public works were undertaken, including building
dikes and canals, and constructing storage granaries and roads for trans-
porting goods. All of this implied that ecological sustainability was primary. Confucian texts, especially *Mencius*, speak frequently of practical
learning to assist agriculture and to insure the good of the commoners.

Naturalistic Cosmology. As an example of the intellectual resources of
Confucianism, a more detailed discussion follows of some of its key ideas
regarding cosmology and ethics. Chinese naturalism as a primary ingredient of Confucianism is characterized by an organic holism and a dynamic
vitalism. The organic holism of Confucianism refers to the fact that the
universe is viewed as a vast integrated unit, not discrete mechanistic
parts. Nature is seen as unified, interconnected, and interpenetrating,
constantly relating microcosm and macrocosm. This interconnectedness
is already present in the early Confucian tradition in the *I Ching* and in
the Han correspondences of the elements with seasons, directions, colors,
and even virtues. Cheng Chung-ying has described the organic naturalism of Confucian cosmology as characterized by "natural naturalization"
and "human immanentization" in contrast to the emphasis on rationality
and transcendence in Western thought.[11]

---

[10] *Mencius* 6 A:8, p. 56.
[11] Cheng Chung-ying, *New Dimensions of Confucian and Neo-Confucian Philosophy* (Al-

This sense of naturalism and holism is distinguished by the view that there is no Creator God; rather, the universe is considered to be a self-generating, organismic process.[12] Confucians are traditionally concerned less with theories of origin or concepts of a personal God than with what they perceive as the ongoing reality of this self-generating, interrelated universe. This interconnected quality has been described by Tu Weiming as a "continuity of being."[13] This implies a kind of great chain of being, in continual process and transformation, linking inorganic, organic, and human life forms. For the Confucians this linkage is a reality because all life is constituted of ch'i, the material force or psycho-physical element of the universe. This is the unifying element of the cosmos and creates the basis for a profound reciprocity between humans and the natural world.

This brings us to a second important characteristic of Confucian cosmology, namely its quality of dynamic vitalism inherent in ch'i (material force). Material force as the substance of life is the basis for the continuing process of change and transformation in the universe. The term sheng sheng (production and reproduction) is used in Confucian texts to illustrate the ongoing creativity and renewal of nature. Furthermore, it constitutes a sophisticated awareness that change is the basis for the interaction and continuation of the web of life systems—mineral, vegetable, animal, and human. And finally, it celebrates transformation as the clearest expression of the creative processes of life with which humans should harmonize their own actions. In essence, human beings are urged to "model themselves on the ceaseless vitality of the cosmic processes."[14] This approach is an important key to Confucian thought, for a sense of holism, vitalism, and harmonizing with change provides the metaphysical basis on which an integrated morality can be developed. The extended discussions of the relationship of li (principle) to ch'i (material force) in Neo-Confucianism can be seen as part of the effort to articulate continu-

bany, New York: State University of New York Press, 1991), p. 4.

[12] Frederick F. Mote, Intellectual Foundations of China (New York: Alfred A. Knopf, 1971), pp. 17–18.

[13] See chapter 2, entitled "The Continuity of Being: Chinese Visions of Nature," in Tu Weiming's Confucian Thought: Selfhood as Creative Transformation (Albany, New York: State University of New York Press, 1985).

[14] Tu Weiming, op. cit., p. 39. Professor Tu notes, "For this reference in the Chou I, see A Concordance to Yi-Ching, Harvard Yenching Institute Sinological Index Series Supplement no. 10 (reprint; Taipei: Chinese Materials and Research Aids Service Center, Inc., 1966), 1/l."

ity and order in the midst of change. *Li* is the pattern amidst flux which provides a means of establishing harmony.

Clearly, this cosmological understanding of the universe as organic holism and dynamic vitalism is essential for the effective formation of an environmental ethics. Without this understanding of the interconnectedness of natural processes, it will be difficult to generate the appropriate sense of respect for nature not simply as a resource but as the source of life itself.

Cultural Identity and Integrity

> What Heaven (*T'ien*, Nature) imparts to man is called human nature. To follow our nature is called the Way (*Tao*). Cultivating the Way is called education.... Before the feelings of pleasure, anger, sorrow, and joy are aroused it is called equilibrium (*chung*, centrality, the mean). When these feelings are aroused and each and all attain due measure and degree, it is called harmony. Equilibrium is the great foundation of the world, and harmony its universal path. When equilibrium and harmony are realized to the highest degree, heaven and earth will attain their proper order and all things will flourish. (*The Doctrine of the Mean*)[15]

As one can see in this passage, to cultivate the Way is to educate. This meant watching oneself and being careful to express one's emotions appropriately. To actualize equilibrium and harmony in one's emotions is to allow all things to flourish. This is preserving and nourishing one's integrity in relation to humans and all life forms. Confucian cultural identity and integrity are based primarily on education and the values of moral cultivation of the individual.

It should be noted that this sense of cultural identity could also be carried to extremes in jingoistic nationalism. The Chinese characters for "China" signify "central kingdom," and frequently non-Han Chinese were regarded as barbarians, as were those peoples outside the middle kingdom (Korea, Japan, Vietnam). The same kind of cultural and nationalistic chauvinism has been evident in these border countries, who were deeply influenced by Confucian culture. For example, the debates regarding Japanese identity (known as *Nihonjinron*) are still raging today in sometimes disturbing ways reminiscent of prewar nationalist ideology.

Yet on the positive side, it can be said that Confucian cultural identity and integrity were maintained and fostered by education. Perhaps no other civilization has so highly prized education, making it central to its

---

[15] *Ibid.*, p. 98.

cultural continuity. Through both family structures and political institutions such as the examination system and local schools, education was encouraged. Indeed, as Tu Weiming notes, the cultural DNA of Confucianism has been ethical values of human relations and responsibilities carried on from generation to generation within families. Moreover, the political continuity of Confucian civilization in China has been assisted in part by the examination system, which ideally prepared young men to be capable and moral civil servants.

Conclusion

To summarize, then, some of the values of Confucianism which can contribute to the formation of a global ethics, we list the following principles.

1. Moral and spiritual self-cultivation can positively affect the larger social and political order.

2. A concentric-circle mode of ethics based on communitarian sensibilities needs to be fostered.

3. Economic profit needs to be subordinated to humaneness and righteousness (i.e., equity and distributive justice).

4. Humane government means government for the people, not only of and by the people.

5. Leaders need to put the public good and the common future above private gain and short-term interests.

6. Mutual responsibilities in human relations need to be valued as significantly as individual freedom.

7. Humans need to see themselves as part of nature, thus harmonizing with, not controlling, natural processes.

8. Education of future generations needs to be a primary commitment of contemporary societies aiming for a sustainable future.

ABRAHAMIC TRADITIONS

Judaism

Our Place in Creation: A View from the Jewish Tradition
by Philip J. Bentley

A Jewish Perspective on Global Issues
by Bernard M. Zlotowitz

Christianity

A Christian Perspective on World Order
by Eileen W. Lindner

Some Protestant Reflections on Religion and World Order
by John B. Cobb, Jr.

Development and Spirituality:
Personal Reflections of a Catholic
by Luis M. Dolan

Islam

Islam and Global Governance
by Saleha Mahmood-Abedin

Islamic Revivalism: A Global Perspective
by Abdul Aziz Said and Nathan C. Funk

Bahá'í Faith

Humanity's Coming of Age:
The Bahá'í Faith and World Order
by John Woodall

Our Place in Creation: A View from the Jewish Tradition

Philip J. Bentley

You are not required to complete the work, but neither are you free to abstain from it. (*Pirkei Avot* 2:21)

From Creation To Redemption

The Jewish view of the world and humanity's place in it might be called reverse entropy. Time proceeds from a chaotic beginning toward a perfect ending. The Talmud (an encyclopedic work that is the basis of Rabbinic Judaism, developed over many centuries and completed approximately 600 CE) warns us to be concerned only with what happens since that beginning up until the end. Of those who inquire into what was before and what will be after, we are told, "It would have been better had they never been born."[1] However, our traditional sources give accounts of Creation that seek to answer such questions in order to explain what our place in the world is. One such account comes from the Lurianic Kabbalah.[2]

We can know nothing of *Eyn Sof* (the Infinite) or why such a perfect entity would create time and space. The Kabbalah, the Jewish mystical tradition, teaches that *Eyn Sof* withdrew, creating a place where Infinity

---

[1] Babylonian Talmud, Mishnah, *Hagigah* 2:1.
[2] Kabbalah is the Jewish mystical tradition. The school of Rabbi Isaac Luria (1534–1572, Safed, Palestine) developed the Kabbalah into its most commonly accepted form.

was not, and brought space-time into being. Into space-time *Eyn Sof* introduced ten divine emanations in the form of light and made vessels to hold them. A cosmic accident occurred and the vessels shattered, causing the emanations to mix with the material of which the vessels were made. This material formed shells around the sparks of light, hiding them from their Creator. In order to restore these sparks to their source, a being empowered with free will had to be created—humanity. Free will is a paradox, as Rabbi Akiva taught: "All is foreseen, but free will is granted."[3] The physical world was created in which humanity could act as God's partner in this work, which is called *Tikkun Olam* (literally, "repairing the world").

Why, the Talmud asks, was all of humanity descended from one couple? Several answers are given, including one that says no one should be able to say "My Adam and Eve were superior to your Adam and Eve." Another says that this establishes the life of every human being as equal to an entire world. Thus we have the famous dictum, "One who destroys a single human life destroys an entire world; and one who saves a single human life saves an entire world." Human life in this world is considered the highest ethical imperative in Judaism. Every single human being who has ever lived, or who will ever live, must be thought of as made in the Divine Image and worth the life of the entire world.[4]

Anyone who takes this doctrine seriously must see in every human being a face of God. It then becomes impossible to intentionally harm or degrade any person.

The Flood and The Tower

If all human beings have one common ancestor and are made in the Divine Image, how has it come about that humanity is divided into so many national, ethnic, and religious groups? In the tenth generation, something had gone terribly wrong in the world. Everyone was against everyone else and the world was filled with violence and lawlessness. The Creator, who had already been all but forgotten, decided that a new start was needed, a reunification of humanity. This would be accomplished by a universal destruction that would preserve only one family of each species, including humanity.

---

[3] Mishnah, *Pirkei Avot* 3:15.
[4] Mishnah, *Sanhedrin* 4:5.

The family of Noah was chosen. Of him the Torah says, "Noah was righteous and innocent in his generation" (Genesis 9:9). This is understood to mean that only by the standards of his times was he righteous and innocent. Faced with the impending death of every human being in the world aside from his immediate family, Noah offered no protest, nor did he warn anyone of what was to come. He obeyed the divine commandment, building the ark and gathering the animals.

When the Flood was over and Noah emerged from the ark, God made a covenant with Noah and all of Noah's descendants, which was all of humanity. A basic standard of conduct was established in the form of seven laws. Six were prohibitions—not to murder, not to steal, not to commit incest, not to curse God, not to practice idolatry, and not to cut flesh from living animals for food—along with one positive commandment: to establish a system of justice. This is called the Noahide Covenant, and Judaism teaches that anyone of any nation or people who lives by it is worthy of a reward in the world to come. God promised never to destroy the world again with a flood. Some have noticed that there was no promise not to destroy the world by other means, and no promise that humanity would not destroy the world. The warning to Adam still stood: I have done all the creating that I will do; therefore take care, for if you ruin it no one will come after you to fix it.

Over time the world was repopulated, but all of humanity lived as one community, speaking one language. A king arose over them who ordered that a city and a tower be built to maintain the unity of humanity. God, however, was displeased by this project. Why? Franz Kafka wrote, "If it had been possible to build the Tower of Babel without ascending it, the work would have been permitted."[5] This paradox may refer to a teaching that when a man fell to his death at the construction site it was hardly noted, but when a brick fell and was shattered, everyone mourned.[6] The king was able to pervert human values for the supposedly higher purpose of unity—a unity that would exist under his rule. The penalty did not have to be as drastic as that suffered by the generation of the Flood, because in this generation humanity had at least learned cooperation and community.[7]

The penalty, from which we still suffer, was that humanity would be

---

[5] *Parables and Paradoxes.*
[6] *Pirkei de-Rabbi Eliezer* 24.
[7] *Avot de-Rabbi Natan* (version A) 16:32b.

scattered and divided into nations. Where they had all been able to understand one another's speech, they now spoke different languages and could not understand each other. The goals of a universal human language and a single human community in the world would have to wait for a time when humanity would also be able to resist the curse of a single tyrant ruling over all. Several men have since tried to conquer the whole world, and none has succeeded.

Abraham and His Children

What was needed was a vision of unity that could exist in the context of division. The great ancient empires and civilizations produced such visionaries as Akhenaten and Socrates, but they were rejected and their visions were changed or suppressed by others and did not survive.

Abraham was an exile from the great cities of the Babylonian Empire. Tradition says he was forced into exile because of his vision of a single divine being who ruled over everything and had created everything. Perhaps his vision survived to change the course of human history because he turned his back on the centers of power and on the values that governed life in the great cities. The Torah shows that he was far from perfect in his ways, but that he had strong ideals.

Abraham practiced hospitality. His tent would be set up at a crossroads with openings in all four directions so that passersby could not help but enter. Even when he was recovering from his self-circumcision, he personally attended to the needs of three strangers who came by. The Cities of the Plain, Sodom and Gomorrah, were notorious for their lack of hospitality; tradition says that persecution of strangers was the law there. The mob that attacked Lot's house, demanding that his two guests be turned over to them, were responding to the violation of that law by Abraham's nephew. Yet when God told Abraham that these cities were about to be destroyed for their wickedness, Abraham protested, "Shall not the Judge of all the earth do justly?" (Genesis 18:25). The thought that any innocent residents of those cities would die along with the guilty was intolerable to him, and he bargained with God until he extracted a promise that even ten innocent people could save the cities. Sodom represented everything Abraham hated, but he could not bear the thought of its destruction. Compare him with Noah, who said no word of protest at the annihilation of humanity; compare him with Jonah, who tried to run away from warning Nineveh to repent because he wanted to see that city destroyed. Abraham's vision of divine oneness meant a vision of human unity as well.

The idea of shared identity with all human beings, even those we have reason to hate, must be the basis of any hope for a world united. The ability to accept that idea even while identifying as a member of a particular tribe, nation, culture, or religion must also be a prerequisite for a united world. The human family need not, in fact should not, become homogenous in order to reach the goal of world peace and harmony; the differences and distinctions are important and enriching, and ought to be cherished. Finding a good balance between particularism and universalism would become a constant labor for Abraham's children.

Abraham's children are not just the Jewish people. He had two sons, Isaac and Ishmael, who inherited his blessing and his covenant. Ishmael's descendants, the Arab people, would eventually bring Abraham's vision and message to much of the world through Islam. Isaac also had two sons, Jacob and Esau. Tradition sees Esau as the ultimate ancestor of Rome, which symbolizes Christendom, and therefore he too would spread Abraham's vision and message to many parts of the world. Jacob became Israel and was the ancestor of the Jewish people, who would continue as a people apart and alone, a people whose continued existence would come to embody God's covenant with Abraham in a unique way.

Exodus, Redemption, and Revelation

Every year at Passover, the Jewish people sit down at family tables for a *seder* and remember their beginnings. We were slaves to Pharaoh in Egypt. Our ancestors were idol-worshippers. We began our history as a people as the least of nations: enslaved exiles. We cannot even say we freed ourselves. Neither Moses nor anyone else but God is credited with our liberation in the Haggadah. We cried out; God heard us; Egypt suffered a series of plagues until they threw us out; and we were free. That story is the basic myth of who we are, and it has inspired oppressed people all over the world and continues to do so. It is also a myth that teaches us many lessons.

At the *seder*, when we recite the list of ten plagues, we dip a measure of wine out of our cups for each one. The reason is that we are celebrating our liberation, but not the suffering of the Egyptians. We therefore lessen the wine to reduce our own happiness and pleasure because our oppressors had to suffer so that we could be freed. We are cautioned to remember that when we first came to Egypt we were fleeing from a famine, and Pharaoh generously allowed us to settle in his domain, saving our ancestors' lives and providing us with the setting in which we grew from a clan into a nation. When we were rescued at the Sea of Reeds, Moses sang a song of triumph; tradition teaches that when the angels likewise began to sing, God admonished them, "My children are drowning and you sing songs?"[8]

We are not allowed to forget the lesson of our time in Egypt. The Torah tells us no fewer than 36 times that we may not oppress or abuse the strangers among us because we know the heart of the stranger, having ourselves been strangers in the Land of Egypt. Our history, which was to spare us no degradation or atrocity, was not to set us against other peoples—even our oppressors—but was to be a continuing lesson in how not to treat people over whom we would have power.

When we left Egypt, we were told that we were going to occupy a land flowing with milk and honey, as was promised to our ancestors. Before we could make that journey, however, we were to go to a place in the wilderness where we would receive the terms of a covenant between God and our people in a unique event—a national theophany. Why did this take place in the wilderness, rather than at a holy site in the land promised to us? We are taught that this is because ultimately the Torah was for all of humanity, and therefore would enter this world in territory that was part of no kingdom or empire.

The Torah is a universal document written in human language. Tradition says it preexists Creation and is, in fact, the blueprint for Creation. What we read is merely the outer shell or garment; within are deeper and deeper layers of meaning. It is written in human language but hides within it infinite interpretations. As the Kabbalah puts it, we read the Torah as black on white, but when we can read it as white on black we will fully understand it.[9] The function of the Jewish study of Torah is to unpack all of Torah's meaning so that it can be read as the source of universal truth that it is. The particular people is a divine implement toward realizing the unification of all of humanity, as written by the prophet Isaiah:

---

[8] Babylonian Talmud, *Megillah* 10b.
[9] *Encyclopedia Judaica*, "Kabbalah" (by Gershom Scholem), Vol. 10, p. 624.

In the end of days it shall come to pass
That the mountain of the house of Adonai shall be established as the topmost
  mountain
And shall be exalted above the hills;
And all of the nations shall flow unto it.
And many peoples shall go and say:
Come and let us go up to the mountain of Adonai,
To the house of the God of Jacob...
And God shall judge between the nations
And shall decide for many peoples
And they shall beat their swords into plowshares
And their spears into pruning-hooks
Nation shall not lift up sword against nations
Nor ever again train for war. (from Isaiah 2:2–4)

The Lessons of Our History: The First Commonwealth

The Jewish religion cannot be understood without knowing the unique historical experience of the Jewish people. That history embodies our response to the tension between our tribal identity and our global vision. Our very existence defies the rules of history. Deutero-Isaiah commented 25 centuries ago, "Who can believe what we have heard?" (Isaiah 53:1). as an expression of amazement at our survival. A Jewish global vision of humanity has to grow not only out of its biblical traditions and mythology, but out of our peculiar historical experience.

The Land of Israel is situated between two ancient powerful rivals, Egypt and Mesopotamia (modern Syria and Iraq). For over 4,000 years and down to the present day, these two giants fought over the small territory that divided them. We suffered from the passage of huge armies through our land and sometimes we were pawns in international rivalry. In Jeremiah's day, Pharaoh convinced the King of Judah to rebel against Babylonia with a promise of support. The rebellion took place; no help was forthcoming; and as a result, Jerusalem and the Temple were burned to the ground and those people who did not escape to Egypt were exiled to Babylonia.

Thus, throughout our Scriptures, there is distrust of great cities, kingdoms, and empires. The powers of the Jewish king were always limited, because the king was to be subject to the law and ethics that ruled everyone else. In the Bible, the great warrior or athlete, or the person with great political power or wealth, is not regarded as a hero. The great person is the one who is just, kind, and learned. Our peculiar historical situation gave us a view of the world different from that of other peoples.

At first we lived in the Land as separate tribes: "Each man stayed in his own tent and did what was right in his own eyes."[10] We became prey to powerful neighbors who would invade the Land and oppress us until a leader arose, united the tribes, and drove the invader away. That leader would be named a judge and would rule over the united tribes for a time, but then the pattern would repeat itself. Finally the tribal elders came to Samuel, a highly respected judge, and demanded, "Give us a king!" They wanted Israel to be like the other nations around them. Samuel did not want to set up a monarchy, because this nation was not supposed to be like other nations. He warned them about taxes on both property and labor, and warned them that a king would demand a military draft, but they persisted in their demand.[11]

The monarchy began, as monarchies do, with kings who were men of great qualities but also of human weaknesses. Saul was a capable leader, but power made him fear the loss of power until he lost his sanity and became unfit to rule. David became king and was very much beloved by the people, but he too was governed by his emotions and suffered greatly from the quarrels among the children of his many wives. Solomon, known for his wisdom, inherited a kingdom whose enemies were in defeat and whose treasury was full. His wisdom did not allow him to see how he abused the love and trust of his people, so that in the days of his son, the kingdom divided in two.

The northern kingdom, Israel, came under the influence of the Phoenicians and later the Assyrians, who eventually destroyed the capital, Samaria, and dispersed its people, giving rise to the legends of the Ten Lost Tribes of Israel. The southern kingdom, Judah, continued to be ruled by David's descendants, but it was small and weak and became a pawn in the ancient rivalry between Egypt and Babylonia.

It was there that the idea of a messiah was born. Mashiah ("Anointed One") would be a king out of the house of David who would lead the people into an era of prosperity, security, justice, and peace. When it began, this vision referred only to the kingdom whose capital was Jerusalem, the City of David, but it became increasingly universal over time. The vision expanded to one of an end of time when Jerusalem would become the focal point for people all over the world. The blessings of the Messi-

[10] Judges 21:25.
[11] I Samuel 8.

anic Age would extend to all of humanity.

When political and diplomatic folly led to the destruction of Jerusalem and the Temple of Solomon, this vision allowed us to survive the condition that destroyed other civilizations: exile. The practice of exiling rebellious peoples was an effective imperial policy for ending their very identity. Virtually all peoples who suffered from this policy simply disappeared from history. During the Babylonian Exile, new institutions, most notably the synagogue, were created to allow Jewish tradition to survive. The doctrine of monotheism allowed for the belief that the destruction of Jerusalem, and even of the Temple, were divinely ordained but did not mean the end of the covenant between God and the Children of Israel. Even the greatest empires were merely God's instruments in history.

Belief in one God over one human family, working toward a time of redemption for all, allowed the exiles to see beyond their situation to a triumphant future. The prophet of the exile, Ezekiel, painted vivid word-images of the restoration of the Jewish people to its homeland and continuing on the path toward ultimate redemption of all of God's promises.

When the Persian Empire overwhelmed Babylonia and decreed the return of exiled peoples to their homeland, the prophets of that generation saw the fulfillment of the visions of Ezekiel and those who had come before him. The Babylonians and Persians were seen as acting according to a divine plan leading toward the Messianic Age. Isaiah even hailed Cyrus as "Messiah."[12] Jerusalem was restored and the Temple rebuilt under the aegis of the Persian Empire.

The Lessons of Our History: The Second Commonwealth

The coming of Alexander the Great and the Hellenistic civilization added new power to our universalistic visions. It also created a new problem, because we were now a small dissident tribe in the midst of a civilization that embraced the entire known world. In Egypt we had been an enslaved foreign element; in Babylonia we were unwilling exiles. Now we were in our own land and were invited to abandon our old "barbarian" way in favor of "civilization."

Some, especially the well-educated and wealthy, wanted to embrace this foreign civilization; others vehemently rejected it. At first we were

---

[12] Isaiah 45:1.

ruled by the Ptolemies in Egypt, who could afford to be patient and tolerant: the vast majority of their subjects were of one historical and cultural tradition. The Egyptian Jewish community, which had begun in the wake of the destruction of Solomon's Temple centuries before, prospered; and the Jews in and around Jerusalem were governed by leaders friendly to the Ptolemies.

When the Seleucids took the eastern part of the Ptolemies' holdings, including Jerusalem, everything changed. The Seleucid Hellenistic Empire stretched from the Mediterranean Sea almost to the Indus River and included many different peoples and cultures. For this empire, the Hellenistic civilization was a unifying factor that had to be imposed on its diverse subjects.

Eventually the virtual civil war in Jerusalem between the Hellenists and the Jewish traditionalists became too much of an irritant to Antiochus IV, a heavy-handed Seleucid emperor. He banned traditional Jewish practices and imposed an idolatrous emperor cult on this rebellious people. The result was the unification of all the Jews, who engaged in a successful rebellion, resulting first in the restoration of the right to follow their own tradition and later to political independence. The Jewish people and its traditions survived even while it adopted many aspects of Hellenistic culture. A minority civilization could maintain its identity within a world-embracing culture, but not without a struggle.

By the time the Romans came to rule, there were at least four schools of thought among the Jews; each was a way to respond to the challenge of the wider world. The Sadducees, who came mostly from the aristocratic and priestly families, held that Temple rituals were sufficient as a focus for Jewish identity. In all other things they promoted cooperation with the Romans. Even the High Priesthood became an office appointed at the pleasure of the Procurator.

The Pharisees were engaged in the work of teaching Torah as a way of life for all Jews, not just the priests. The law was determined as the result of study conclaves and debates among the scholars. Their purpose was to create a Torah that would be a way of life for Jews independent of the Temple and its rituals. They envisioned a way for Jews to live as a distinct people among non-Jews. That process would continue for centuries until the publication of the Talmud.

The Zealots, with origins in remote Galilee, were for driving the Romans out by force and reestablishing an independent Jewish commonwealth. These ultra-nationalists were hostile to all foreign influences and believed that the Torah and the Jewish people would survive only as an independent nation.

The fourth group was the Essenes, who sought a purification of Jews and Jewish institutions. They saw the priesthood and the Temple as corrupt, believed that Jews had no business trying to live among other peoples in the world, and developed a separate way of life for themselves based on how they interpreted Jewish traditions. They withdrew from mainstream society into communities that practiced their own spiritual disciplines, while awaiting the advent of the Messiah.

When a Zealot-led revolt ended in the destruction of Jerusalem and the Second Temple at the hands of the Romans, the Sadducees became irrelevant, as did the Essenes; both disappeared from history. The Zealots and their spiritual descendants were active in Judea and elsewhere in the Roman Empire for another two generations. Another vain attempt to drive out the Romans by force, under the false messiah Bar-Kochba, ended in a military disaster that brought that movement to an end.

The future of the Jewish people and its traditions now rested in the hands of the spiritual descendants of the Pharisees—the Rabbis. Their task was to prepare the Jewish people for a historical experience that would be unique. Jews would become a nation without a land, an army, or a centralized government. Our national religion, Judaism, would have to be practiced under all kinds of conditions that these rabbis could not have foreseen. What they did foresee was that for the Jewish people to continue its existence, in hope of the redemption of the divine promise of a return to the Land in safety, security, prosperity, and peace, the Torah would have to become portable. It would have to represent a way of life that could withstand both the pressures of persecution and the seductions of assimilation among the nations of the world. It would have to transcend both time and place.

The Lessons of Our History: The Diaspora

Before the rise of the modern state, Jewish communities existed everywhere at the pleasure of the local rulers. Often we were a tolerated foreign element that existed to fill roles not entrusted to people of the same nationality as the rulers. In medieval Christian Europe, Jews were not a part of the feudal system; we could not own or even work land, bear arms, or aspire to the aristocracy. We lived in towns and cities pursuing trades and filling the role of money-lender, which was forbidden to Christians. Under the Moslems we pursued trades and professions. Sometimes we became important figures in court: royal physician, finance minister, even prime minister. In Poland we were made tax and rent collectors. The reason for this was simple: no Jew could ever be a threat to the throne, no matter how much authority he was given.

When situations changed, we frequently suffered persecution or even expulsion. We became the scapegoats for every calamity. When the Pope sent the criminals of Europe on the Crusades as part of their penance, they looted or massacred every Jewish community they found along the way. When the Black Plague came to Europe in the fourteenth century, the Jews were accused of poisoning the wells and entire communities were massacred. When the long-suffering Polish peasantry revolted in 1648, their anger turned first on the Jews, who collected the taxes and rents that went to the aristocracy.

Through all of this, Jewish scholarship and culture flourished, both in prosperity and in adversity. We maintained every kind of communal institution, pursued knowledge, created works of art. Because there were Jewish communities everywhere from Portugal (until the expulsion at the end of the fifteenth century) to China that communicated with each other, there was a cultural and intellectual cross-fertilization unknown to almost anyone else. Jews spoke many languages and created new ones for their own use; they adapted to a wide variety of cultures, and therefore developed many different kinds of religious and cultural expressions. Yet all maintained a common identity, a common faith, a common language (Hebrew), and common ideals. We had become a world-embracing civilization transcending the norms of history. Later, of course, this would bring us new troubles.

Because of our peculiar situation, Jews were often in the vanguard of new developments. When printing was invented, Jewish presses were soon established because universal literacy and the spread of knowledge are valued among Jews. When explorers found new lands, Jews went with them and became early settlers because of the need to escape persecution. When capitalism created a means of success based on achievement rather than birth, Jews quickly became involved. When revolutionary movements arose to free people from the heavy hands of royalty, aristocracy, and established religion, Jews were often in the vanguard, having so much to gain.

The French Revolution in particular had a powerful effect on Europe's Jews. The Jews of France and, in the wake of Napoleon's conquests, those of the rest of Europe, became citizens of the lands they lived in for the first time. The founder of Habad Hasidism, Rabbi Shneor Zalman of Lyady, said, "Napoleon is good for the Jews and bad for Judaism."

In 1791, the revolutionary government stated the principle, "For the Jews as individuals everything; for the Jews as a people nothing." In 1807, Napoleon convened what he called *Le Grand Sanhedrin* to ask the French Jewish community whether it was willing to trade autonomy for citizenship. Would Jews send their children to French schools? Would the rabbis permit Jews to be married under civil law? The body of distinguished rabbis and laymen agreed. Most Jews in France and in the lands conquered by Napoleon embraced the rights and responsibilities of national citizenship.

The problem now was what to do with the nationalistic aspects of Judaism. Reform Judaism, a movement that began under Napoleon's rule, quickly discarded almost everything that made Jews feel foreign. They envisioned "a Jew at home and a citizen in the street." Judaism was to be a religion with synagogue worship modeled on the Protestant church services in Germany. References to Zion and Jerusalem were discarded, and much of the Hebrew was replaced with the vernacular. Reform soon arrived and flourished in the United States of America, where the citizenship of Jews was not an issue once the Bill of Rights with its First Amendment was enacted. To this day, the challenges to Jewish survival of freedom and citizenship are at the top of the Jewish communal agenda: assimilation and intermarriage.

Nationalists, however, often continued to see Jews as a foreign element whose loyalties were to a nation that dwells in many lands. The Jewish people in the modern era of nation-states began to suffer a new kind of scapegoating, one that accuses us of so-called dual loyalty. The Dreyfus affair, which split French society apart a century ago and is still controversial today, was especially shocking because this orgy of anti-Semitic bigotry took place in the birthplace of modern Europe (the term "anti-Semitism" actually comes from that time and place). The infamous historical forgery "The Protocols of the Elders of Zion" was contrived by the czar's government to justify its anti-Jewish policies. That work, along with Henry Ford's "The International Jew," is still being published today. They accuse Jews of engaging in a worldwide conspiracy to undermine

Western civilization. Many of those who oppose international law see
world federalism as part of this supposed Jewish plot.

Widespread distrust of Jews as cosmopolitan internationalists was an
important element in the Nazis' being able to carry out the utter destruction and near-extermination of Europe's Jews. The enormity of such a
program coming out of a nation so highly regarded for its culture and
civilization was compounded by the complicity of so many other nations.
Even the United States and Canada were home to powerful political
forces that prevented the rescue of Europe's Jews. Jews simply lacked the
political strength even to open the gates of immigration for the victims of
the Holocaust. Many Jews believe that the Nazis were so successful in
carrying out the slaughter of Jews because, in a world of nation-states,
Jews had no state of their own.

The Holocaust is a great challenge to historians and theologians
alike. How could a civilized nation accept and carry out such an irrational ideology and evil program? The Talmud says that an ordinary person is sometimes called a Sodomite (similar to the people of Sodom—see
above). The main characteristic of the Sodomites was their hostility to
strangers. The Nazi program called for the extermination of some people
(Jews, homosexuals, gypsies, and the mentally retarded) and the enslavement of everyone in the world who was not a member of the so-
called Master Race. Germans were told that their people was the standard by which humanity should be judged. In dealing with everyone else
there was no extreme of cruelty or violence that was out of bounds. This
was the evil of national chauvinism and racism carried to their furthest
degrees. It was all too easy for the average person to accept this doctrine,
and therefore the government policies that derived from it.

Nonetheless, there were many people who did not accept these ideas,
and some of them refused to cooperate with Nazi racial policies. I have
met many Jews who managed to survive the Holocaust. Without exception, every one of them did so with the help of at least one person who, at
great risk, defied and disobeyed Nazi laws. The effectiveness of nonviolent resistance has been nowhere more effectively demonstrated than by
the *Hasidey Umot HaOlam* (Righteous of the Nations of the World), a
term which includes the many non-Jews who, during World War II,
risked life and limb to save Jews. For example, during the Nazi occupation of France, the people of the Huguenot village Chambon-sur-Lignon,
led by pacifist pastor Andre Trocme and his wife Magda, saved the lives

of hundreds of Jews right under the noses of the Gestapo. The power of a moral vision that encompasses all of humanity was proven over and over again in every part of what Elie Wiesel called "the Kingdom of Night."

The Lessons of Our History: The Third Commonwealth

The First Zionist Congress took place over a hundred years ago. The idea of the need for a Jewish state had already been gathering power for a century. Not only was the idea proposed by philosophers, it was attempted by philanthropists and activists in Palestine, the United States, Argentina and elsewhere. Whether this Jewish state would be in our ancient homeland was a matter of debate until 1903, when the Sixth Zionist Congress hotly debated and then rejected Britain's offer to set up a Jewish homeland in what is now Kenya. In affirmation of that rejection, Theodore Herzl, the founder and leader of the Zionist movement, recited:

> If I forget you, O Jerusalem,
> let my right hand wither,
> let my tongue stick to my palate,
> if I cease to think of you,
> if I do not keep Jerusalem in memory
> even at my happiest hour! (Psalms 137:5–6)

The Zionist movement was not popular with all Diaspora Jews. On the one hand, many Orthodox Jews saw it as a blasphemous attempt to force the coming of the Messiah; there are some who reject the Jewish state for this reason even today. On the other hand, Reform Jews, especially in the United States, were disturbed by Jewish nationalism. "Let all the world be one Jerusalem," proclaimed Rabbi Isaac Mayer Wise, the first great leader of American Reform Judaism.[13] Asked his opinion of Zionism, Wise said that America was his Zion and Washington his Jerusalem. On the other hand, some American Jews supported it. Louis Brandeis asserted that there is no contradiction in an American Jew supporting Zionism: "Loyalty to America demands that each American Jew become a Zionist."[14]

Another group of Jews who were at least ambivalent about Jewish national aspirations were socialists, communists, and anarchists in East-

---

[13] *The American Israelite*, August 31, 1866.
[14] "The Jewish Problem," 1915.

ern Europe. Many of them vehemently rejected Zionism as a step backward in history. Others, however, immigrated to Palestine in the hope of building a Jewish homeland based on the revolutionary ideals of justice and human dignity. Their collective farms, *Kibbutzim*, would play an important role in the creation of the Jewish state.

The violent anti-Semitism of the first half of this century, culminating but not ending with the Holocaust, gave increasing power to the idea of setting up a Jewish state in Palestine. While many might deny it, the movement toward carving a Jewish state out of the British Empire served as model for many other nationalist movements seeking independence from European colonial powers. The difference, of course, was that the other new nations were the natives of their lands who had suffered under colonial regimes. The Jews who founded the State of Israel, the Third Jewish Commonwealth, were the traumatized descendants of an ancient people returning to their homeland in the wake of an attempted genocide.

The founding of a modern Jewish state created many new issues for the Jewish people. Zionist doctrine says that Judaism and Jews cannot live normal lives, or even survive, outside a Jewish state. Most Diaspora Jews would dispute that, even if they are self-identified Zionists. Accusations of dual loyalty are heard again from anti-Semites. How much of a claim does Israel have on the loyalty of Diaspora Jews? What should a Diaspora Jew do if Israeli policies or actions violate his or her conscience? Is public protest against Israel a moral action? These questions are still hotly debated among United States Jews today.

Underlying all of this is the issue of whether Israel should be "a nation like any other or a light unto the nations" (a pun in Hebrew: the two phrases sound quite similar). Should the Jewish state try to live up to the prophetic and messianic idealism enshrined in Israel's Declaration of Independence, or should it act in accordance with the rules of the "tough neighborhood" in which it must exist? The unique experience of Jewish history, going from nationhood to worldwide exile and then back to the creation of a state, raises many unresolved issues. It also illuminates many of the questions faced by those who envision humanity transcending nationalism in favor of a primary identity as human beings.

Israelis are caught between a vision of themselves as the surviving remnant of a persecuted people, and a vision of the Jewish state seeking to be a model society for the world. The result is a political spectrum which extends from blood-and-soil nationalism to universalistic idealism. Albert Einstein was a passionate proponent of world government, but also a fervid Zionist who was once offered the presidency of Israel. Israel is so hard to understand precisely because it is caught between the desire for a secure existence and an ardent yearning for peaceful relations with her neighbors. Scratch an ultranationalist settler and you will find an idealist; scratch a leftist dove and you will find a chauvinist. In the State of Israel, the age-old Jewish tension between parochialism and universalism continues to play itself out.

The Messianic Age: A Vision

Whether a Jew believes in a personal messiah or in the advent of a messianic age, the idea that humanity is working its way toward a perfected world is virtually universal among believing Jews. When will this vision be realized? What will this time be like? How do we get there?

Messianism has always been a problem for Jews. Times of crisis tend to produce messianic figures and movements. Christianity itself grew from one of many such movements in the first century of this era.[15] Rabbi Yohanan ben Zakkai, who witnessed the destruction of the Second Temple, said, "If you are planting a tree and someone says that the Messiah has arrived, first finish planting the tree, and then go out and greet the Messiah." Dozens of messianic figures have appeared among the Jewish people in the Diaspora, raising hopes and then dashing them. The idea of a messianic age without a personal messiah may well have been part of the inspiration for Marx's vision of history. Even Reform Judaism, which suppressed as much of the nationalist element in Judaism as possible, maintained faith in the idea of a messianic age. Zionism is a kind of secular messianism.

Should we wait passively for the Messiah, or should we work to force the coming of the Messianic Age? Traditionally, Judaism has taken a passive approach because of the dangers of messianic movements; social activism among Reform Jews is based on the belief that the birth of a messianic age requires our efforts. Another Kafka paradox says, "The Messiah will arrive only when he is no longer necessary."[16] Many Jews believe that the birth and survival of the State of Israel are the first signs

---

[15] E.g., see Acts 5:34–38.
[16] *Parables and Paradoxes*, p. 81.

of a messianic advent. This belief underpins the political positions of right- and left-wingers alike.

Since biblical times, the Messianic Age has been described in terms of *shalom*, a Hebrew word that means much more than "peace." It comes from a root that expresses the idea of completeness, wellness, and wholeness. The Messianic Age will be one in which there are no wars and in which no one prepares for war; humanity is at peace not only with itself but with nature; justice is perfect; people live without fear; no one is hungry, naked, or homeless. All of the peoples of the earth will recognize that God is One and that humanity is, in turn, one. It is through understanding that truth that the diverse peoples on this planet can resolve the tensions that are a universal aspect of human existence. How and when we can achieve such a world is in our own hands.

Religion and World Order

Being divided into many different ethnic, national, and religious groups is an essential aspect of humanity, and will continue to be so. Any attempt to unify humanity with one language, one culture, and one faith would deprive us of the diversity that is essential to the vitality of humanity as a whole. It would diminish the Divine Image in the world. A global community will continue to require human diversity.

Different kinds of people with differing views of the world, meeting with mutual respect, can work together to solve mutual problems. Many nongovernmental organizations (NGOs) as well as governmental organizations (most prominently the United Nations) are seeking to do just that.

The problem is that many such agencies, the United Nations among them, often carry out or advocate policies that exacerbate problems rather than easing them. It is not the role of seekers of justice and peace to take sides, even in the name of justice and peace. Too many of these efforts work to create a winner and a loser. Conflicting claims need to be resolved in ways that produce only winners. The harsh treatment Israel has often received at the hands of the United Nations has sown distrust in that agency among Israelis, and among Jews in general. The result is distrust of many international efforts for peace, justice, and environmental integrity, despite the fact that these are all basic Jewish ideals.

On the other hand, Israel and Jewish NGOs are prominently involved in humanitarian efforts all over the world. Israel was the first nation to accept Vietnamese boat people as immigrants. Organizations like the Joint Jewish Distribution Committee, founded to help Jewish refugees, works to help refugees of many nations worldwide. Jewish environmental organizations join with others to defend such causes as species diversity and protection of endangered ecologies. These organizations have proven again and again their eagerness to work in multireligious and multiethnic efforts. I do not doubt for one moment that the Jewish people stand ready to work for the kind of global community we all envision.

> If I am not for myself, who will be for me;
> and if I am for myself only, what am I;
> and if not now, when? (*Pirkei Avot* 1:14)

JUDAISM

A Jewish Perspective
on Global Issues

Bernard M. Zlotowitz

Introduction

T he purpose of this paper is to present a Jewish perspective—that
is, a perspective based on *halachah*, or Jewish law—on the important issues of peace and security, ecological sustainability, and
economic and social justice. Judaism's vision of a better world is embla-
zoned in the immortal words of the prophets and Rabbis. The words of
Isaiah (2:4) and Micah (4:3) about beating swords into plowshares and
spears into pruning hooks are incised in the hearts and minds of all righteous peoples. Their words, teachings, hopes, and aspirations are rooted in
the tradition of Judaism. Ours is the obligation and the responsibility to
fulfill their vision.

The story is told of a young child urging his father, who was reading
the newspaper, to come and play with him. The father said, "I will play
with you later," but the boy persisted. In exasperation, the father tore a
map into small pieces. "When you have finished putting the pieces of the
map back together, I will play with you," he said, and settled back to
read. But in 15 minutes the boy was back, with the whole map pieced
together. The father was astonished and asked, "How did you do that so
quickly?" "Oh, it was easy, dad. You see, there was a picture of a man on
the other side. I put the man together, and the world fell into place."

When you put the human being together, you put the world together. This is achievable by having a vision of what the future could be
like. To visualize a better world is easy; to accomplish it is hard. *Nil sine*

magno labore, "Nothing achieved without great labor," taught one of the ancient Roman philosophers. The Rabbis teach, "All beginnings are difficult." We must, however, not desist from working toward our goal. First we must look to our religious traditions for guidance, vision, and inspiration. It was Toynbee who declared that we need a spiritual vision to have a spiritual impulse. The original Latin meaning of "religion" is "to bind together," "to unite." If we do not unite, and care only for ourselves, redemption will not come. In the Reform Jewish liturgy there is a prayer which reads "May your children unite to do Your will: to establish peace and justice throughout the world." May it be so. This is our quest. The unity of the human family forms a basic axiom of all religions.

The ideals governing society have their origins in religious institutions founded by faithful adherents to God's teachings.

"It was evening and it was morning," says the Bible. The darkness gives birth to light. Out of chaos, God creates order and brings light into the world. Similarly, religion takes a person out of darkness and brings him or her into light. God inspires. Religion enhances. The teachings of God are the conscience of the universe, for they remind humankind of its responsibility to carry out God's mandate to improve the world (in Hebrew, *tiqqun ha-olam*): to make peace, not war, as God demands of us; to preserve the environment and make it a safer and more beautiful place in which to live; to deal fairly and justly in our relationships with our fellow human beings—both economically and as regards social justice.

Peace (Shalom)

Any discussion of peace in Jewish tradition must necessarily be multifaceted—for this is among the most important and widely discussed values in Judaism. The quest for peace has ever been the hope, desire, and wish of the prophets, the Rabbis, and the Jewish community. Never has a day gone by when prayers for peace have not been uttered by the Jewish people. In our sacred liturgy, we offer daily the prayerful words, "He [God] Who makes peace in the heavens above, may He make peace for us."

The wish for peace is also prevalent in daily conversation. Not only was it a biblical practice (see below), but it later evolved into a Rabbinic injunction to greet another individual with the word "peace": "It was related of Rabbi Jochanan the son of Zakkai that no man ever gave him greeting [with peace] first, even a heathen in the street" (B. *Berachoth*

17a);[1] for he made sure he was the first to do it. Indeed, so great is peace that the name of God is peace: "God is faithful...[and] the Name itself is designated 'Peace,' as it is written, and he called it, The Lord is Peace" (B. *Shabbat* 10b).

The Hebrew word for peace, *shalom* (literally, "whole"), has several meanings, as we will discuss below. In selecting our examples, we shall focus on the biblical period, the time of the prophets, and the Rabbinic period.

The Biblical Period. In the biblical period, peace was often taken to mean "prosperity" and/or "health." Two examples will suffice: "Oh that thou wouldst hearken to My commandment! Then would thy peace be as a river, And thy righteousness as the waves of the sea" (Isaiah 48:18); and "And seek the peace of the city whither I have caused thee to be carried away captive, and pray unto the Lord for it; for in the peace thereof shall ye have peace" (Jeremiah 29:7).

Peace was also understood in the sense of "well-being," as illustrated by the following. Jacob inquires after the welfare of his uncle, Laban: "And he [Jacob] said unto them [the shepherds], 'Is it well with him?' and they said, 'It is well....'" (Genesis 29:6); similarly, Joseph has not seen his father in over 20 years and is anxious to know how he is faring: "And he [Joseph] asked them [his brothers] of their welfare, and said: 'Is your father well, the old man of whom you spoke? Is he yet alive?'" (Genesis 43:27).

The Time of the Prophets. Peace, as opposed to war, was a dominant theme of the prophets of ancient Israel and was recognized as a virtue to be achieved, as we read: "Love ye truth and peace" (Zechariah 8:19); "I make peace ..." (Isaiah 45:7); and "Behold, how good and how pleasant it is, for brethren to dwell together in unity!" (Psalm 133:1).

The prophets preached a universal message of peace, declaring that all men will become one, worshipping the true God. At that time, there will be no more war. Micah preached:

> And He shall judge between many peoples, and shall decide concerning many nations afar off, and they shall beat their swords into plowshares, and their spears into pruning-hooks; nation shall not lift up sword against nation, neither shall they learn war anymore. But they shall sit every man under his vine and

---

[1] All Talmudic quotes are taken from the Soncino translation.

under his fig-tree; and none shall make them afraid; for the mouth of the Lord of hosts hath spoken." (Micah 4:3–4)

Though the prophets preached a Messianic message of peace, they also imposed an obligation on each and every individual to pursue peace in his or her own time and place: "In the case of peace...*seek peace* wherever you happen to be *and pursue it* if it is elsewhere." In fact, Israel followed this injunction. Although the Holy One, blessed be He, had said to them, "Begin to possess it, and contend with him in battle" (Deuteronomy 2:24), they chose to pursue peace: "And Israel sent messengers into Sihon...Let me pass through thy land" (Deuteronomy 2:26–27, Numbers [*Chukkath*] *Rabbah* 19:27).

The prophets also teach that not only will there be peace among peoples, but even the animals, the beasts of the field, will be blessed with peace:

> And the wolf shall dwell with the lamb, and the leopard shall lie down with the kid; and the calf and the young lion and the fatling together; and a little child shall lead them. And the cow and the bear shall feed; their young ones shall lie down together; and the lion shall eat straw like the ox. And the suckling child shall play on the hole of the asp, and the weaned child shall put his hand on the basilisk's den. They shall not hurt nor destroy on all My holy mountain, for the earth shall be full of the knowledge of the Lord, as the waters cover the sea. (Isaiah 11:6–9)

The Rabbinic Period. In the Rabbinic period, the Rabbis emphasized the importance of peace for all peoples—Jew and non-Jew alike. The poor of the heathen are not prevented from gathering gleanings:

> And when ye reap the harvest of your land, thou shalt not wholly reap the corner of thy field, neither shalt thou gather the gleaning of thy harvest. And thou shalt not glean thy vineyard, neither shalt thou gather the fallen fruit of thy vineyard; thou shalt leave them for the poor and for the stranger; I am the Lord your God. (Leviticus 19:9–10)

Provisions are also made for forgotten sheaves—"When thou reapest thy harvest in thy field, and hast forgot a sheaf in the field, thou shalt not go back to fetch it; it shall be for the stranger, for the fatherless, and for the widow; that the Lord thy God may bless thee in all the work of thy hands" (Deuteronomy 24:19)—and for the corner of the field (see above, Leviticus 19:9), in the interests of peace. Our Rabbis taught: "We support the poor of the heathen along with the poor of Israel...and bury the poor of the heathen along with the dead of Israel, in the interests of peace" (B. *Gittin* 59b and 61a).

And indeed, we learn that one may even tell an untruth for the sake of peace: "Rabbi Ille'a...stated in the name of Rabbi Eleazer, son of Rabbi Simeon, 'One may modify a statement in the interests of peace'" (B. *Yevamoth* 65b). Another tractate of the Talmud tells us: "Hillel said, 'Be of the disciples of Aaron [brother of Moses], loving peace and pursuing peace, loving thy fellow-creatures...'" (*Avot* 1:12). The Rabbis understood this to mean that you may tell an untruth, as Aaron would do, if it meant that peace would be forthcoming.

In another passage of the same tractate, the Rabbis teach that the world could not exist if peace were unknown: "Rabban Simeon, the son of Gamaliel, said, 'By three things is the world preserved—by truth, by judgment, and by peace; as it is said, Judge ye the truth and the judgment of peace in your gates'" (*Avot* 1:18), which is understood to mean that if there is peace within your borders, the world will also know peace.

So important was it to be on good terms with one's fellow that the Rabbis cautioned, "One should always strive to be on the best terms with his brethren and his relatives and with all men and even with the heathen in the street, in order that he may be beloved above [i.e., in heaven] and well-liked below and be acceptable to his fellow creatures" (B. *Berachoth* 17a), for that leads to peace in the world. Not surprisingly, the language of peace found a place in the daily vocabulary of both Arabs and Jews, who greet one another with the salutation "Peace unto you," to which the response is "Unto you peace."

The *Midrash* points out that so great is the need for peace that the priestly benediction ends with that very word. "The Lord bless thee, and keep thee; the Lord make His face to shine upon thee, and be gracious unto thee; the Lord lift up His countenance upon thee, and give thee peace" (Numbers 6:24–27; *Sifre* Numbers 6:26). Recognizing the necessity for reminding Jewish worshippers of the continual need to pursue peace, every service in a Reform synagogue ends with this benediction.

Despite the fact that idolatry is viewed as a heinous crime in Judaism, it is clearly subsidiary to the value of peace. "Rabbi [Judah the Prince] said, 'Great is peace, for even if Israel practices idolatry, but maintains peace among themselves, the Holy One, blessed be He, says..."I have no dominion over them"; for it is said, Ephraim is united in idol-worship; let him alone'" (Hosea 4:17; Genesis *Rabbah* 38:6). Thus, peace overrides the most vile of sins in Israel.

Unfortunately, while peace has been greatly desired, it has never truly been achieved. War, hatred, greed, all still exist—and have existed—throughout history and in different parts of the world. The prophet Jeremiah voiced it with an incomparable simplicity: "*Shalom, shalom, v'ayn shalom*—Peace, peace, and there is no peace" (Jeremiah 6:14). But hope for the Jew springs eternal. A time will come, in Messianic days, when the blessing of peace will assuredly arrive and peace will reign forevermore. We must never cease to strive for peace, for it is possible—working together as partners with God—to bring it about. People of all religions and faiths must join in the effort to achieve this noble goal for our own sake and for future generations, when no one will know war anymore and "each will sit under his vine and under his fig-tree in peace."

Ecological Sustainability

Uppermost in our minds today is the preservation of the world in which we live. The harmful effects of ozone depletion, the proliferation of nuclear weapons, the unchecked massacre of wildlife, the "greenhouse effect," the pollution of our cities, streams, and waterways—all bode danger to the survival of human and animal life on our planet.

The psalmist reminds us that "The earth belongs to Adonai [Lord] and all it contains, the world and they that dwell in it. For it was He who founded it upon the seas, and set it firmly upon the streams" (Psalm 24:1–2). Life on earth is God's gift to us. The earth is merely a loan from God and we have a responsibility to care for it—just as Adam was commanded to tend the garden in Eden: "And Adonai God took the man, and put him into the garden of Eden to dress it and to keep it" (Genesis 2:15).

Human beings are also given dominion over all that is on the earth:

And God blessed them, and said unto them, "Be fruitful, and multiply, and replenish the earth, and subdue it; and have dominion over the fish of the sea, and over the fowl of the air, and over every living thing that creepeth upon the earth." And God said, "Behold I have given you every herb yielding seed, which is upon the face of all the earth, and every tree, in which is the fruit of a tree yielding seed—to you it shall be for food; and to every beast of the earth, and to every fowl of the air, and to everything that creepeth upon the earth, wherein there is a living soul, [I have given] every green herb for food." (Genesis 1:28–30)

Adam was charged to care for the earth and all who live on it, be it human or animal or plant. So too are we commanded to care for what God has loaned us. A contemporary rabbi put it another way: "We do not inherit the world from our parents, instead we borrow it from our children."[2]

The responsibility for keeping the earth properly cared for was eloquently enunciated in *Midrash*:

> When the Holy One, blessed be He, created the first man, He took him and led him round all the trees of the Garden of Eden, and said to him, "Behold My works, how beautiful and commendable they are! All that I have created, for your sake I created it. Pay heed that you do not corrupt and destroy My universe; for if you corrupt it there is no repair after you. Not only that, but you will cause death to befall that righteous man [Moses]"

—i.e., you will bring death into the world as a punishment.[3]

Respect for the environment was so crucial that even in wartime, regard for God's earth was to be respected, and trees bearing fruits were not to be destroyed even during the siege of a city: "When thou shalt besiege a city a long time, in making war against it to take it, thou shalt not destroy the trees thereof by wielding an axe against them; for thou mayest eat of them, but thou shalt not cut them down; for is the tree of the field a man, that it should be besieged of thee?" (Deuteronomy 20:19). The prophet Isaiah enlarged upon this by declaring, "They shall not hurt nor destroy in all My holy mountain" (Isaiah 11:9).

This biblical law was later expanded by a Rabbinic injunction known in Hebrew as *bal tashchit*, mandating that we not destroy needlessly what God has loaned to us. Even one's personal property cannot be destroyed without a valid reason: "Just as one has to care for his body, not to destroy it, not to impair it, or to damage it...[he] who breaks a utensil, or tears garment, or destroys food or drink, or makes it filthy, or throws money away so that it is lost, or spills anything that people could enjoy, transgresses the commandment...."[4]

According to the Rabbis, everything was created for a purpose. No one thing is superfluous or unnecessary on God's earth. Each thing has a function in working to maintain the ecological balance:

---

[2] Quoted in Albert Vorspan and David Saperstein, *Tough Choices* (New York: Union of American Hebrew Congregations Press, 1992), p. 245.

[3] From the Soncino translation of Ecclesiastes *Rabbah*, 7:12 §1–13, §1.

[4] Abridged *Shulchan Aruch*, 190:3.

> Woe to one who stands on the earth and does not see what one sees, for every drop of water in the sea and every grain of dust in the earth have I created in its own image.... Of everything God created nothing was created in vain, not even the things you may think unnecessary, such as spiders, frogs, or snakes. Human beings were not created until the sixth day so that if their pride should govern them it could be said to them, "Even the tiniest fleas preceded you in creation."
> ...Why did God appear to Moses in the lowly bush? To teach us that nothing in creation is without God's holy presence, not even the commonest bush.[5]

The concept that God is in nature is probably at the root of Baruch Spinoza's theory of Pantheism, which forms part of the philosophical system developed in his *Ethics*.

Equally important was the mandate to improve our environment, beautify it, and maintain healthy surroundings. Sanitary conditions were to be maintained in all cities for the health and welfare of all the people. Thus we read: "They may not keep dung in it [originally applicable only in Jerusalem but later ruled for all cities] because of impurity" (*Tosefta Negaim* 6:7). Dung heaps, originally placed in public thoroughfares, were later prohibited because of the danger to public health. Jerusalem was also forbidden to have furnaces because of pollution: "They may not make furnaces in it [Jerusalem] because of the smoke" (B. *Baba Kamma* 82b).

In Jerusalem it was forbidden to have orchards and gardens (except for rose gardens, which existed from the time of the early prophets) because of the bad odor of manure and rotting leaves, which endangered the purity of the priestly classes. Nevertheless, in all other cities, "It is forbidden to live in a town in which there is no garden or greenery" (J. *Kiddushin* 4:12, 66d).

The concern for pollution was so strong that it was forbidden to have threshing floors in town; they had to be located outside the town so that the chaff carried by the wind could not dirty it. The law was also specific with regard to "carrion, graves, and tanneries," which had to be kept 50 cubits from a town (a cubit is equal to 18 inches). We read that "A tannery must be placed only on the east side of a town" (B. *Baba Bathra* 2:8,9), since the east wind is not a prevailing one. Thus, we see that the ancient Rabbis were very concerned with the ill effects of pollution.

Another overriding consideration of the Rabbis was their sensitivity

---

[5] In Vorspan and Saperstein, *op. cit.* p. 250; see also B. *Sabbath* 67a; and B. *Sotah* 5a regarding the comment on Moses and the bush.

for animals, teaching us that compassion for God's creatures is an integral part of Judaism. For example: "And whether it be a cow or ewe, ye shall not kill it and its young both in one day" (Leviticus 22:28). Another injunction with an equally compassionate view is expressed in Deuteronomy: "If a bird's nest chance to be before thee in the way, in any tree or on the ground, with young ones or eggs, and the dam sitting upon the young or upon the eggs, thou shalt not take the dam with the young; thou shalt in any wise let the dam go, but the young thou mayest take unto thyself, that it may be well with thee, and that thou mayest prolong thy days" (Deuteronomy 22:6–7).

Clearly, we have a moral responsibility to preserve what God has loaned us, keeping God's earth clean, pure, and whole. Nevertheless, the violence being done to our universe is staggering. The proliferation of nuclear weapons—which have the power to destroy men, women, and children as well as plant and animal life—should cause us grave concern. Other environmental concerns are equally troubling: global warming, acid rain, and ozone depletion (a possible cause of cancer), waste dumped in our rivers, oil spills—all are in violation of God's mandate.

Just as we inherited a beautiful world, so must we transmit the same beautiful world, or one even more beautiful, to future generations. This is God's command, for us to heed. May it be so.

Economic and Social Justice

The body of Jewish law dealing with economic matters is so extensive that it would require several volumes to convey. The *halachah* encompasses such subjects as business dealings, market ethics, advertising, supply-side economics, inflation, and philanthropy. Since a primary concern of this conference is human welfare—particularly, helping and serving the poor and indigent—I will address myself to those laws that deal with charity toward the less fortunate.

The term for charity in Hebrew is *tzedakah*, which literally means "righteousness." Who is righteous? One who cares for his or her fellow human beings. *Tzedakah* is a moral obligation upon every Jew. And when charity is dispensed, it must be given wholeheartedly and with respect for the recipient. If one gives charity condescendingly, it is tantamount to desecrating God's name: "Who so mocketh the poor blasphemeth his Maker" (Proverbs 17:5).

One must give with an open hand and a full heart. The Rabbis singled out Abraham and Job as models of philanthropy. Job was said to be very pious; like Abraham, he was occupied with charity. He built inns at the crossroads with doors opening on all four sides, so that wayfarers would have no trouble finding an entrance. And all who entered praised Job. Job would visit the sick, feed the poor, and care for the widow, the blind, and the lame. He never turned anybody away.[6]

The Rabbis went a step further when they declared, "It is fitting for the benevolent to seek out the poor" (B. Shabbath 104a). But in giving charity, the donor should not be haughty and condescending. He must be sensitive to the downcast position of the recipient. He must avoid embarrassing him, for as Rabbi Jannai taught: "It had been better that you had not given him [a poor person], than now that you have given him publicly and put him to shame" (B. Hagigah 5a). And Rabbi Eleazer taught: "A man who gives charity in secret is greater than Moses" (B. Baba Bathra 9b).

The amount to be given depends on the ability of the giver. A man of modest means who gives a small coin should not think his charitable act any less important than a large gift by a rich man. For "he who gives a small coin to a poor man obtains six blessings, and he who addresses to him words of comfort obtains eleven blessings" (B. Baba Bathra 9b).

The Bible is very explicit regarding our responsibilities to the indigent. "If there be among you a needy man, one of thy brethren, within any of thy gates, in the land which the Lord thy God giveth thee, thou shalt not harden thy heart, nor shut thy hand from thy needy brother; but thou shalt surely lend him sufficient for his need in that which he wanteth" (Deuteronomy 15:7,8). Therefore, some Rabbis contend that it is a greater mitzvah (good deed) to lend rather than simply to dole out money: "Rabbi Abba...said in the name of Rabbi Simeon ben Lakish, 'He who lends [money] is greater than he who performs charity'" (B. Shabbath 63a). The probable reasoning is that the recipient of a loan can thereby maintain his dignity and a positive image of himself.

Moses Maimonides (Rambam)—the brilliant twelfth-century Rabbi, philosopher, and physician—proposed that the greatest service a charitable person can perform for a poor man is to give him a loan, teach him a trade, or put him into business. By this means, poverty is prevented. Moses Maimonides made this the highest degree or step in his "eight de-

---

[6] Job 29:12, 13, 15, 16. See The Jewish Encyclopedia, Vol. 7 (New York/London: Funk & Wagnalls, 1904), pp. 200–201.

grees" of charity:

> Lastly, the eighth, and the most meritorious of all, is to anticipate charity by preventing poverty; namely, to assist the reduced fellowman, either by a considerable gift, or a loan of money, or by teaching him a trade, or by putting him in the way of business, so that he may earn an honest livelihood; and not be forced to the dreadful alternative of holding out his hand for charity. To this Scripture alludes when it says: And if thy brother be waxen poor, and fallen in decay with thee, then thou shalt relieve him; yea, though he be a stranger or a sojourner; that he may live with thee. This is the highest step and the summit of charity's golden ladder.[7]

Nevertheless, Moses Maimonides was realistic enough to understand that not everyone was capable of reaching this lofty goal and, therefore, included all levels of charitable giving as equally valid:

> The first and lowest degree is to give, but with reluctance or regret. This is the gift of the hand, but not of the heart.
>
> The second is to give cheerfully, but not proportionately to the distress of the sufferer.
>
> The third is to give cheerfully and proportionately, but not until solicited.
>
> The fourth is to give cheerfully, proportionately and even unsolicited; but to put it in the poor man's hand, thereby exciting in him the painful emotion of shame.
>
> The fifth is to give charity in such a way that the distressed may receive the bounty, and know their benefactor, without their being known to him. Such was the conduct of some of our ancestors, who used to tie up money in the corners of their cloaks, so that the poor might take it unperceived.
>
> The sixth, which rises still higher, is to know the objects of our bounty, but remain unknown to them. Such was the conduct of those of our ancestors, who used to convey their charitable gift into poor people's dwellings, taking care that their own persons and names should remain unknown.
>
> The seventh is still more meritorious, namely to bestow charity in such a way that the benefactor may not know the relieved persons, nor they the name of their benefactors, as was done by our charitable forefathers during the existence of the Temple [in Jerusalem]. For there was in that holy building a place called the chamber of the silent, wherein the good deposited secretly whatever their generous hearts suggested, and from which the poor were maintained with equal secrecy.[8]

Out of these idealistic suggestions grew the necessity of establishing

---

[7] From *The Union Prayer Book for Jewish Worship*, Part II (Cincinnati, Ohio: Central Conference of American Rabbis, 1942), p. 300. The original is found in Maimonides, *Yad, Mattenot Aniyyim*, 10:8–14.

[8] *Op. cit.*, pp. 299–300.

communal organizations to alleviate the dreadful conditions of the poor. Free employment agencies and *gemilut chasadim* (charitable) agencies as well as free loan societies came into being in every Jewish community. Such organizations still exist today in many Jewish communities, even lending money for college tuition without interest.

The Rabbis realized that in order to gain self-respect, one had to be gainfully employed. As already mentioned above, *tzedakah's* true meaning was righteousness. Poverty could be reduced, insisted the Rabbis, by universal education. For only by being educated and having certain skills can one escape from dependence on charitable acts of the community. Thus, strong emphasis was placed on education.

Until recent times, if a student could not handle academic subjects, the community saw to it that he was apprenticed to a tradesman such as a baker or carpenter to learn a trade. If, on the other hand, a student was qualified, he was encouraged to continue his studies and become a Rabbi or other religious functionary. It became a communal responsibility to provide the best schools possible. What better way to reduce poverty and at the same time perform a righteous act? The community also regulated market prices so the poor could buy food at reasonable prices. Lodging for wayfarers was arranged by the community as a hospitable act in imitation of Abraham and Job, whose doors were open on all four sides.

The concept of righteous behavior, which grew out of the biblical commandment "Thou shalt love thy neighbor as thyself" (Leviticus 19:18), undergirds the whole policy of social welfare programs, be they private or public. Acts of human kindness must govern human behavior. We are required to emulate God, *imitatio Dei*, a teaching enunciated in the Talmud:

> Rabbi Chama son of Rabbi Chanina...said, "What means the text, *ye shall walk after the Lord thy God?*" (Deuteronomy 13:5) Is it, then, possible for a human being to walk after the Divine Presence; for has it not been said, *for the Lord thy God is a devouring fire?* (Deuteronomy 4:24) But the meaning is to walk after the attributes of the Holy One, blessed be He. As He clothes the naked—for it is written, *and the Lord God made for Adam and for his wife coats of skin, and clothed them* (Genesis 3:21)—so do thou also clothe the naked. The Holy One, blessed be He, visited the sick, for it is written, *And the Lord appeared unto him by the oaks of Mamre* (Genesis 18:1); so do thou also visit the sick. The Holy One, blessed be He, comforted mourners, for it is written, *And it came to pass after the death of Abraham, that God blessed Isaac his son* (Genesis 25:11); so do thou also comfort mourners. The Holy One, blessed be He, buried the dead, for it is

written, *And He buried him in the valley* (Deuteronomy 34:6); so do thou also bury the dead. (B. *Sotah* 14a)

The act of kindness is a divine obligation and must be extended even to one's enemies: "If thou meet thine enemy's ox or his ass going astray, thou shalt surely bring it back to him again. If thou see the ass of him that hateth thee lying under its burden, thou shalt forbear to pass by him; thou shalt surely release it with him" (Exodus 23:4, 5).

The Rabbis did not simply read the Bible, but rather acted upon its commandments. They put it into practice. They set up employment offices so people should not fall into poverty and be a burden to the community. They inculcated the idea that it is better to take a menial job than not to work at all. One should "flay carcasses in the marketplace and earn wages and do not say, 'I am a priest and a great man and it is beneath my dignity'" (B. *Pesahim* 113a).

If no work is available, then the responsibility of caring for the poor falls upon the family first, and afterwards on the community. If a person suddenly becomes needy, he must first seek help from his family and friends (B. *Nedarim* 65b), who have an obligation to help him. The community has a right to coerce the family to fulfill its responsibility. Communal charitable funds were to be used for those who did not have friends or relatives to help them.

We must never lose sight of our ultimate goal—to raise the poor from the depths of poverty to the dignity of labor. In our complex society, the bulk of this responsibility must fall on the shoulders of the government. Today, individual religious communities hardly have the means or the wherewithal to implement and support programs for the poor. We may nevertheless gain our inspiration from Scripture and use the teachings and practices of the past as a guide.

The synagogue avails itself of its limited resources as best it can—Meals on Wheels, a meal-delivery service, for the needy; sleep-ins (simple rooms) with clean beds and showers in synagogue buildings, together with breakfast and luncheon. But the problem is beyond the capability of the synagogue alone to resolve. Government response is absolutely necessary and essential. Aaron Levine is correct when he says:

> With the aim of increasing employment opportunities for the poor, government support of the following programs is suggested: (1) improving information channels in the labor market to better facilitate the matching of employers with job-seekers; (2) monitoring the labor market and conducting research regarding

future trends in respect to job opportunities; (3) running job-training programs; (4) relocating families from depressed to viable economic areas; (5) subsidizing employers who hire difficult-to-place workers, i.e., the handicapped and individuals having criminal records; (6) extending interest-free loans to poverty households for the purpose of pursuing higher education.[9]

These programs will not eliminate poverty altogether, but they will go a long way toward reducing it considerably. The great leaders of Judaism understood that the key to world order is to have idealistic goals and strive toward them. A necessary ingredient to improve the world is to have a vision of the future, for a world without vision will perish. Our responsibility is to inculcate these ideals in our young, not only by teaching them but by practicing them as well. By becoming role models and imbibing these ideals we can best transmit them to our children. We have to act to others as we would want them to act to us. We are required to fulfill the biblical injunction of "You shall not hate your brother in your heart" (Leviticus 19:17) and above all "You shall love your neighbor as yourself" (Leviticus 19:18).

To love the stranger (Leviticus 19:34) is a great *mitzvah* (good deed). To love regardless of differences, and to respect the beliefs of others, paves the way for a more secure and better world. This should be our clarion call. If each of us acts righteously one to another, then this will have a ripple effect for good. This vision can be achieved and will be achieved if we will it. It need not be a dream; it can become a reality. In this way the world will be renewed, enriched, and enhanced, and know peace, economic stability, and social justice.

May God help us in our endeavors. "Except the Lord build the house, they labor in vain that build it. Except the Lord keep the city, the watchman waketh but in vain" (Psalm 127:1).

---

[9] Aaron Levine, *Economics and Jewish Law, Halakhic Perspectives* (Hoboken, New Jersey: Ktav Publishing House, Inc. and Yeshiva University Press, 1987), p. 131.

CHRISTIANITY

A Christian Perspective on World Order

Eileen W. Lindner

Introduction

> Then I saw a new heaven and a new earth; for the first heaven and the first
> earth had passed away and the sea was no more. And I saw the holy city, the
> new Jerusalem, coming down out of heaven from God, prepared as a bride
> adorned for her husband. And I heard a loud voice from the throne saying,
> "See, the home of God is among mortals. He will dwell with them as their
> God; they will be his peoples, and God himself will be with them; he will wipe
> every tear from their eyes. Death will be no more; mourning and crying and
> pain will be no more, for the first things have passed away." (Revelation 21:1–4)

This triumphant finale of human history as depicted in the concluding chapter of the Christian canon shapes Christian eschatological hope. As such, it is determinative in forming Christian
striving and historical imaging. The future of the cosmos resides within
God's keeping. World order and all created matter lies within and is subject to God's sovereignty.

Given such bold hope in a God who acts in human history, one might
easily conclude that Christianity, as a world religion, has little interest in,
and less to contribute to, any consideration of "Religion and World Order." Yet, it is not only the eschatological hope of Christian faith that
informs the believer but the whole incarnational life and witness of Jesus
that instructs. Moreover, the 2,000 years of lived experience of the
church offers ample illustration that Christianity brings a proactive and
faith-based stance to the questions of life in and for the world.

The very complexity and diversity of the Christian experience over the course of two millennia means that no one "Christian perspective" on world order can be said to exist. Differences of culture, tradition, race, ethnicity, theology, age, gender, and status will give rise to a variety of viewpoints, all of which can be said to take Christian teaching as their point of origin. The modest reflection which follows offers but one view of the role of religion in relation to world order from the perspective of Christian faith and theology.

Toward a Shared Global Ethic

Theology itself is broadly defined as critical reflection about the meaning of human existence and the nature of the created universe. Christian theology takes as its base position the revelation of God in the person of Jesus the Christ, as recorded in scripture and in dialogue with the church's historical experience, as well as in the context of contemporary human experience and in dialogue with those of other faiths and world-views. Any Christian contributions to an emerging global ethic will grow out of the dynamism of a theological inquiry shaped by the experiences of individuals and communities of faith.

Perhaps most central to Christian thinking about a global ethic will be the place and understanding of *community* itself within Christian thought. The place of *koinonia* or community is well-established in Christian tradition. While Christian practice has often fallen short of a biblical understanding of *koinonia*, the value of community as an all-inclusive source of and context for human well-being is a venerable aspect of Christian thought. The extension of this concept of community to encompass the whole world or the *oikumene* is a value that undergirds Christian participation in discussion of global life together. The essential unity of the family of God, joined both to God and to one another within the created order, is the belief upon which Christian discussion of world community is predicated.

Development of a shared ethic on a global basis will require a process in which values are explicitly identified and articulated. Relative to other faith traditions and belief systems, Christianity has, for most of its history, benefited from highly articulated values codified in scriptures, creeds, prayers, texts, and formed theologies or ethical discourses. The mere existence of written text, however, does not convey primacy or assure usefulness. While Christian values have much to contribute, the world community can only be developed around values that are truly held and utilized by all those participant in community life. Christian values of peace, justice, kindliness, mercy, and unity can be offered in a spirit that seeks to find points of consensus, or at least convergence, in the values of other belief systems.

Peace and Security

Perhaps no text better outlines Christian teaching regarding peace and security than that which Christianity has drawn from Hebrew scripture:

> No more shall there be in it an infant that lives but a few days, or an old person who does not live out a lifetime; for one who dies at a hundred years will be considered a youth. And one who falls short of a hundred will be considered accursed. They shall build houses and inhabit them; they shall plant vineyards and eat their fruit. They shall not build and another inhabit; they shall not plant and another eat; for like the days of a tree shall the days of my people be, and my chosen shall long enjoy the work of their hands. They shall not labor in vain, or bear children for calamity; for they shall be offering blessed by the Lord—and their descendants as well. Before they call I will answer, while they are yet speaking I will hear. The wolf and lamb shall feed together, the lion shall eat straw like the ox; but the serpent—its food shall be dust! They shall not hurt or destroy on all my holy mountain says the Lord. (Isaiah 5:20–25)

The peace envisioned in this prophecy is notable for its insistence on not only the peacefulness of the whole holy mountain, but also the security of each individual member of it. New Testament teaching reinforces this tendency, extending its typical greeting of peace not only to its own members but to "those who are far off..." (Ephesians 2:17).

Peace and peacemaking are central to Christian theology and to scripture. The admonitions of Jesus, "Blessed is the peacemaker..." (Matthew 5:9) and "be at peace with one another" (Mark 9:50), culminate in his weeping over Jerusalem in lament, saying, "If you, even you, had only recognized the things that make for peace!" (Luke 19:42). Pauline theology likewise gives centrality to peace and peacemaking: "Let us then pursue what makes for peace" (Romans 14:19), "for God has called us to peace" (I Corinthians 7:15) and "aim at righteousness, faith, love, and peace..." (2 Timothy 2:22).

Modern history has concerned itself more with peace between nations than the security of individuals. Christian teaching and the historic witness of the church provides ample material for a more thorough exploration of the nature of and need for human security. Christian social witness has long recognized the need for human security and has sought to assuage this need in the poor, widowed, orphaned, and sick, as well as in ministries to the homeless and refugee. Any emerging global ethic will be challenged to define peace and security in human as well as geopolitical terms.

Economic and Social Justice

The Christian Church has not always identified itself or its interests with economic and social justice, any more than with peace and security. Yet church practice and Christian theology are not one and the same. Also, it remains true that those acting in Christ's name have witnessed powerfully, at times heroically, to the gospel call to economic and social justice.

Biblical teaching is replete with an insistence on concern for the common good and mercy toward the poor. Jesus' own occupation with the poor is filled with injunctions to "give to the poor" (Matthew 19:22), "preach good news to the poor" (Luke 4:18), "when you give a feast, invite the poor" (Luke 14:13), and "bring in the poor" (Luke 14:21). This preferential option for the poor is at the very heart of Christian teaching. Two examples from this hemisphere and century (the Social Gospel movement in North America and the Liberation Theology movement in Latin America) give contemporary witness to this Christian teaching. Around the world, other Christian communities have sought to address the widening gap of economic injustice and issues of disparity in social justice. Such experiences have taught the church important lessons about the intractable nature of injustice and the complexities of economic planning.

An emerging global ethic will be confronted not only with the necessity of addressing individuals and nation-states concerning the standards of economic and social justice, but will need to address the practices and procedures of multinational corporate structures which hold vast discretionary powers over the economic well-being of the world's people. In many ways the infrastructure for discussions between governments is extant, while ways to address business interests remain illusive.

Human Rights

Christian teaching, with its tradition of high anthropology—placing a priority on human existence over that of other forms of life—has a theological basis for the support of human rights. Dispersed as it is throughout numerous and diverse cultures, the Christian community has internally held opposing views with regard to human rights. The Christian West has often joined with those who define human rights in individualistic, democratically based formulations. The Christian East has often joined with those who give definition to human rights in more corporate and economically oriented fashion.

An emerging global ethic will need to be forged in the area of human rights which incorporates the insights of both perspectives and can be culturally supported in diverse societies. Christian teaching might well lend itself and its moral authority to a more comprehensive view of human rights.

If Christian teaching has the potential to be supportive of a more broadly drawn approach to human rights, Christian practice, like that of the world community as a whole, gives little room for confidence in the potential success of such an ethic. Historically, Christianity has found itself co-opted by, and even contributing to, massive violations of human rights, even within societies which enjoyed Christian majorities. The long Christian sanction and blessing given to chattel slavery in the United States and the continued apparent peaceful coexistence of the church within cultures that deny women full human rights are but two examples. It is not that the church entirely lacks the capacity for leadership within the area of human rights; even in the twentieth century, those acting upon self-conscious Christian convictions participated and gave leadership to the struggle for human rights in South Africa and Central America. Nonetheless, the Christian community might well approach the development of a global ethic of human rights chastened and humbled by its own history and alert to the contributions of others.

Ecological Sustainability

The Christian proclamation of a creating and sustaining God who loves the whole of the cosmos (Genesis 1) offers a sound base for contributions to the ethical and practical formulation of attempts at establishing ecological sustainability. In recent decades, Christian ethicists particularly have developed increasingly thoughtful explorations into the meaning of the Christian belief in the inherent holiness of the creation and their responsibility within it.

Any global ethic that develops around the issues of ecological sustainability will need to take into account the ways in which the preservation of the environment is directly linked with economic justice. Work in the United States in the last decade, and in the larger world during the last several decades, has indicated that issues of environmental protection and sustainability are often resolved in favor of those with economic capacity. Particularly for developing nations, the ethical dilemmas have been excruciating ones of preservation of the natural environment at the expense of the well-being of people. In a true world community, such a situation represents a false dichotomy. The overwhelming disproportion of the world's resources consumed by post-industrial nations must be considered carefully in the development of plans and programs for preservation of the natural environment. Understandably, developing nations harbor a great deal of suspicion about a commitment to environmental preservation in the contemporary setting.

Cultural Identity and Integrity

In the contemporary world, which seems increasingly insular and xenophobic, the issues of cultural identity and integrity present an enormous challenge. Post-industrial nations, particularly the United States, carry out commerce and communication in ways that have the unintended effect of eroding cultural identity and undercutting the integrity of traditional societies. In particular, new communication capacities and technologies have helped create what is sometimes called a "CNN worldview." Such a perspective does much to undercut and compromise other existing worldviews and perspectives. It is this process of erosion that many traditional societies have in mind when they close their borders and media outlets to foreign materials.

The erosion of culture only begins with the issues of news coverage and the materialism that often accompanies such messages. The fabric of traditional culture, along with its religions, systems of authority and accountability, and even family structure, is often laid waste by the seductive and attractive introduction of Western culture with its numerous goods and services.

During the last quarter-century, the global "Westernization of culture" has been viewed by some as a new form of colonialism. In the wake of such an invasion, we have seen the rise of a reaction that has entrenched traditional cultures, often at the expense of the human and social rights of their people. This counter-reaction is likewise disruptive to civil society and problematic for the development of a global social ethic.

Careful and candid discussions and deliberations will need to be held to find ways to, on the one hand, provide access and information as promptly as possible, and on the other, preserve cultural identity and the fabric of society.

Toward Global Governance
Global Civic Society

The Christian community might well find in a global civic society the need to advocate for persistent guarantees of human dignity within the context of cultural pluralism. An insistence on the rights of individuals will, in many cultural settings, run headlong into cultural practices and values at variance with such a perspective. Women and children, racial or religious minorities, and ethnic enclaves often become the object of their own society's bias. Moreover, nation-states which continue environmental exploitation, geopolitical militarism, and abuse of internal political debate will continue to pose a threat to the development of a global civic society. A bill of particulars must be developed internationally and affirmed globally in order to assure the most basic right of all the world's citizens.

Global Structures and Systems

We need to develop global policies of aid and trade that reward national behaviors contributing to the common good, and that serve as a disincentive to those nation-states that fail to serve environmental sustainability. Such practices must gain the weight and force of law to be effective instruments in establishing global governance.

Local Initiatives

While transnational initiatives will be central to the creation and maintenance of policies and systems capable of establishing and maintaining global governance, such initiatives will not be effective in assuring the full participation of world citizenry. Local initiatives are better able to assure full participation and provide the needed feedback to evaluate the ways in which international policies are (or are not) responsive to local need. The vast diversity of the world's cultures argues for the establishment of goals to be achieved by such local initiatives, while permitting the broadest possible cultural diversity in achieving those goals.

Balancing Tensions

The tensions outlined in the guideline document provide the best evidence of the nature of the challenge confronting any attempt to be intentional with regard to the shaping of a future global ethic and world order. The United Nations must be enabled to become a venue of discourse which will allow for the identification of such tensions and their ultimate resolution. Many additional tensions will exist within particular cultures, and many cultures will be resistant to the legitimacy of countervailing values in such discussions. It is perhaps necessary for the UN to sponsor or be related to regional centers which would provide a venue for the discussion of such tensions as private-sector and public-sector responsibilities. Other tensions, such as national and global sovereignties, do not lend themselves so clearly to a regional settlement and would need to continue to be addressed on an international basis.

Religious Resources for Global Governance

Three factors are central to the role of religions in shaping the world order: *context*, *capacities*, and *process*.

Context

1. Many of our religious traditions in communities are much more venerable than most present forms of governance, and certainly than the modern nation-state. In this demonstrated capacity for longevity, religious communities are themselves a model of sustainability.

2. Religious communities and institutions might be conceived of as the interstitial membranes within the body politic: elastic, permeable tissues that lie between and around the governmental organs. While interstitial membranes cannot carry out the specialized functions of the organs, their existence is essential to the coherent functioning of the organism.

3. Taking Robert Traer seriously [see Traer's "Religion and..." in this volume], I am no longer comfortable with looking upon religion as a *resource* for global governance. Yet neither am I satisfied in this context to look upon religion as a *source* for global governance, inasmuch as human history is littered with disastrous examples of various religions' attempts to serve as a source for governance. I prefer to address

religion as a *catalyst to*, and *for*, global governance. (I am also grateful for the formulation of our questions in terms of *global* rather than *international* governance. "International" relates to "between nations"; "global" better captures the notion of governance between peoples.)

Capacities

Religion brings three essential capacities to its function as catalyst to global governance. (I speak from my own Western Christian tradition; others may judge whether these capacities apply to other religious communities. My experience in the Middle East leads me to believe that, to a degree, they apply to Islam as well.)

1. *Educative Capacity.* The very processes which have maintained the faith, belief, and doctrines of our communities over the centuries can be instrumental in the birthing of global governance. Here "educative capacity" is used rather than "educational institutions" because I believe that the educational tasks in bringing forth global governance will go well beyond the education of the elite associated with institutional educational practices. Educative capacity includes not only institutions and practices of primary, secondary, and higher education, but also the practices of spiritual or faith formation, informal educative enterprises on a congregational basis, and educative processes associated with, for instance, "barefoot doctors," midwives, community organizers, and so on.

2. *Infrastructure.* The infrastructure of our religious communities is sometimes explicit, often implicit. In many religious communities it is very highly developed, with institutions of healing, teaching, and service, and the capacity to interact with other sectors at the highest level of their national governance. In communities around the world, especially rural hamlets and frontier areas, governmental infrastructure is often noticeably absent; the church (and sometimes other religious institutions) supplies whatever infrastructure exists. Taken in the aggregate, I believe the infrastructure of religion will be an essential capacity in helping to bring into reality global governance.

3. *Moral Authority.* The faith, confidence, and goodwill of its membership are of course the greatest assets of any religious community; the capacity of moral authority of the religious body and its leadership derives directly from them. The capacity of moral authority to vali-

date, credential, authenticate, and foster inquiry into the moral and ethical necessity of global governance will be perhaps the greatest capacity religion has to offer the emergence of global governance. The use and application of this moral authority allows our communities and nations to rise above mere self-interest to seek out the common good; indeed, it is this moral authority that can provoke the necessary sustained debate about the urgent need for global governance.

Process

What is the process by which these capacities might function, within our present context, to bring about a movement toward global governance? The last half-century teaches many lessons about the role of religions in relation to global governance. Obvious examples include Gandhi and the Dalai Lama; I will concentrate on examples from the Christian tradition of ways in which the moral authority of the church, when combined with its infrastructure and educative capacity, can provide for real and enduring changes in governance.

- Shortly after his elevation to the Papacy, Pope John Paul II planned to visit Poland. To its everlasting regret, the Communist government of Poland chose not to itinerate him, so the job fell to the Catholic Clubs of Poland. In the aftermath of His Holiness' visit, the network established to provide for his visit quickly converted itself into the movement we know as Solidarity, which was instrumental in bringing down the government.

- Christian organizations in the USSR and the United States maintained difficult but important relationships throughout the cold war. Although the achievements of these relationships could not be made public at the time, it is now known that through them, the names of Jewish and Pentecostal dissidents were spirited out of the Soviet realm into the West. Along with other achievements, this ultimately contributed to the revision of governance in Central and Eastern Europe.

- Let us recall the role of Archbishop Desmond Tutu in the dismantling of apartheid in South Africa; the role of Dr. Martin Luther King, Jr., in bringing the moral authority of the church's witness to bear on the struggle for civil rights in the United States; the work of Dom Helder Camara and Archbishop Oscar Romero in Latin Amer-

ica; and on and on. Lest we think such leadership involves only religious leaders in hierarchical churches, let us remember those motivated by Christian teaching who played an important role in the US
civil rights movement, for instance, Fannie Lou Hamer and Rosa
Parks. On the other hand, we must also remember the most striking
failure of the twentieth century, at least from the perspective of the
Christian community: the story of the Barmen Declaration and the
Confessing Church during Germany's Third Reich should give us all
pause. The words of moral authority must be matched by the brave
deeds of moral witness.

In order to maximize the benefit of the role of religious communities
in the creation of a more just and peaceful world order, an international
venue of world religions must exist. Such a potential could be realized
either through existing world religious structures, or be created as a parallel to the United Nations. As a first order of business, such a venue
would need to provide the opportunity for the diminution of religious
hostilities which now abide, replacing them with a fuller trust and confidence between religious communities. Ways must be sought to develop
the means to adjudicate conflicts that arise between religious communities and their governments, and between religious communities and business communities, if all three sectors are to play a constructive role in the
world order that is envisioned. Religious entities hold an unusual capacity
to legitimize and encourage confidence in international organizations,
policies, and systems. To be effective, any emerging world order will require the best effort from religious infrastructures, as well as the moral
authority that religious organizations are able to exercise.

Collaborating with the United Nations
and Its Specialized Agencies

The member churches of the National Council of Churches of Christ
USA, and many of their partner churches around the world, have long
experience in working with and in conjunction with the United Nations
and its specialized agencies. Many churches and religious bodies maintain
offices at, or adjacent to, the United Nations and participate in committee structures on various issues before the UN. During the UN's 50-odd-
year life, religious leaders have worked in conjunction with UNESCO
and UNICEF as well as the agencies dealing with refugees in particular.

A detailed report of the involvement of churches with the United Nations goes well beyond the scope of this paper. In general, these relations have ranged from highly effective to woefully inadequate. It is not uncommon for church organizations to find the UN, and particularly its specialized agencies, slow in responsiveness and at times insensitive to cultural and religious values at stake in the administration of programs.

The status of the United Nations within the various nation-states, and its chronic underfunding, have rendered it less useful than it might otherwise be. An example of this can be illustrated in UNICEF's response to the rapidly expanding area of child sexual exploitation and the world pandemic of child pornography available on the Internet. While UNICEF has been a staunch advocate for children, it has found its resources and structure far too limited to respond in an effective and timely manner to this rapidly expanding threat to children. With the cooperation of (but without the leadership of) UNICEF, the queen of Sweden was able to sponsor the world's first Congress on the Commercial Sexual Exploitation of Children. In order for this issue to be addressed effectively, cooperation will be required not only from the United Nations and particular nation-states, but from Interpol, the world's religious communities, and the travel and communications industries. At present the United Nations does not enjoy enough public prestige or financial resources to give leadership to such a multifaceted campaign.

Developing Multireligious Initiatives

Any number of multireligious or interfaith initiatives might be undertaken as a means for introducing a global conversation concerning the emergence of a just and human world order. World religious communities might even model the potential for such a world order by the emergence of an international multifaith agency to serve as an ongoing source of discussion among world religions concerning the development of a global ethic. Religious communities and structures with which I am well acquainted (the Vatican, the World Council of Churches, the World Evangelical Fellowship, Lambeth Palace, etc.), as well as the World Muslim League and international Jewish organizations, enjoy sufficient infrastructure and experience to enable the formation of such a place and basis for dialogue. Two hurdles which need to be overcome to enable a broader discussion include identification of (1) the appropriate initiating body and (2) the appropriate partners for such a discussion among the world's religions. Until such obstacles are overcome, the religious community will be stymied in its ability to contribute productively to either the process or the substance of an emerging world order.

Conclusion

Let us recall those of many traditions who have gone before us and modeled the way of justice and peace. Those to whom we look as exemplars knew how to utilize the context, the capacity, and the process of the religious community's role in service to social justice, even in the face of powers and principalities which were far more powerful. Each religious community, and certainly all the religious communities taken together, constitute a good and great force in service to the development of a global system of governance.

I would like to conclude with a story that, for this occasion, I will pry loose of its Christian moorings.

A man had done an exceedingly good deed, and the god of the universe sent an angel to him. The angel told him that the god wished to grant him a request as a reward for his good deed; however, the god's heart was troubled by an enmity that the man had long harbored against another, and so the god had directed that whatever the man chose for his own reward would be given twofold to his enemy. The angel departed, allowing the man time to think this over.

The man pondered: "Perhaps a bag of gold? No, then my enemy would have two bags of gold...perhaps a huge farm with crops and livestock? No, no; then my enemy would have a farm twice as large." And so it went. Finally, the angel reappeared, saying it was time to decide. Troubled, the man continued to weigh grace versus enmity, enmity versus grace. In the end, unable to free himself from enmity in order to accept the god's graciousness, he sadly told the angel, "Make me blind in one eye"—knowing that this would plunge his enemy into total darkness.

In many ways, the world community faces such a choice. Will we give up our own enmity in order to accept the grace that is ours for the asking? It remains an open question. I personally believe the religious communities of the world, acting in concert, have much to contribute to the potential of the world community—choosing grace.

CHRISTIANITY

Some Protestant Reflections on Religion and World Order

John B. Cobb, Jr.

Working Toward a Shared Global Ethic

The need to bring moral commitments and religious perspectives to bear on the shaping of world order is evident. A major problem has been that diverse religious communities have found it difficult to speak together, often seeming instead to counter one another's potential influence. In religiously plural societies, communities of faith are, thereby, often divisive rather than unifying. Partly for this reason, politicians have often looked for guidance to the masters of technical reason, instead of religious leaders. Unfortunately, purely technical solutions are often dehumanizing, having adverse consequences for individuals, for their human communities, and for the Earth itself.

One important counter to this unhappy situation has been the formulation of shared beliefs under the leadership of Hans Küng. This has proved remarkably successful. Küng has demonstrated that leaders from highly diverse religious traditions can now agree on a wide range of principles partly because their traditions' teachings have always overlapped extensively, and partly because all the great religious Ways have assimilated much of the spirit of the Enlightenment and contemporary movements for justice and environmental protection. At best, however, each community finds that the account of overlapping teachings abstracts from the rich and motivating context found in the fullness of its faith.

Alongside the flattening trend resulting from globalization's demands is another accenting the particularity of each community and its way of life. For example, some assert that religious traditions are cultural-linguistic systems in which each idea gains its meaning from its interconnection with others so that no element of one system can be equivalent to an element in another system. From this point of view, whatever is formulated as common is either illusory (the words standing for different meanings in diverse systems) or a secondary language distinct from all the primary religious ones.

The history of the ecumenical movement in Protestantism illustrates a third way of dealing with diversity. Historic suspicions among Lutherans, Calvinists, and free churches were not dealt with primarily by minimizing differences and identifying the points of agreement; but equally, the denominations were not left each to itself simply in its uniqueness. Instead, each explained itself to the others, and each listened.

Representatives of traditions that stressed the preservation of the purity of doctrine and practice by authoritative leadership heard and respected the witness of those who stressed the equality of all believers and the autonomy of local congregations. The latter came to appreciate the importance of the inclusive church and the need for structures that represent and maintain that inclusivity. The two groups did not merely come to accept the authenticity of one another's faith; they also rethought their own teachings so as to reflect what they had learned from the others. This did not lead to institutional union or the abandonment of particularity. But it did generate a deeper sense of unity and enhance the possibility of a common witness.

This mutual transformation has extended to relations between Protestants and Catholics. Among the teachings that had long separated us were the Protestant emphasis on scripture alone and the Catholic emphasis on tradition. Through dialogue, Protestants came to recognize that the Bible is in fact part of our tradition and that all of us are informed by an ongoing and developing tradition in which we are participants. Catholics came to recognize the value of highlighting scripture as providing critical norms for the evaluation of traditions and for directing the development of tradition in the present. Protestants remained Protestant; Catholics, Catholic. But the self-understanding of both has been changed, and our ability to work together has been greatly enhanced. There has been a creative transformation of both.

We can propose that collaboration among our great religious Ways take on a similar character. To some extent it already has: for example, through Buddhist-Christian dialogue, some Christians have learned (with varying degrees of understanding) the truth and value of viewing things non-dually in their mutual constitution or dependent origination. Some Buddhists have come to appreciate the value of a greater historical consciousness in guiding their application of Buddhist wisdom in the transformation of the world. Buddhists remain Buddhist; Christians, Christian. Both are enriched, and our capacity to work together is enhanced.

This is a slow, never-completed process of mutual transformation toward greater sharing of wisdom and values. It should be accompanied by efforts, such as that of Hans Küng, to articulate existing overlaps in our convictions. Working together on the basis of those overlaps will also lead to mutual transformation.

Protestants have a more ambivalent relation to ethical or value systems than most religious communities. We distinguish the life of faith from the moral life quite sharply, tending to disparage the latter ("All our righteous deeds are like a filthy cloth": Isaiah 64:6). Apart from love, we understand even heroic morality (such as giving away all of one's possessions: 1 Corinthians 13:3) to be empty of true spiritual meaning.

Ideally, we affirm that the life of faith expressed in love of God and neighbor far transcends the requirements of mere morality. ("Unless your righteousness exceeds that of the scribes and Pharisees, you will never enter the kingdom of heaven": Matthew 5:20.) Unfortunately, we know that in practice the belittling of morality can lead some Protestants to moral laxity instead of to sacrificial love. To many, freedom from the law is not experienced as freedom to go beyond the law but as freedom to be casual about morality. We also know that many Protestant groups, recognizing the practical importance of rules for governing life in Christian community, develop legalisms that are more arbitrary and divisive, and more likely to generate self-righteousness, than those in traditions that affirm the religious importance of rule-bound behavior.

The distinctive history of English-speaking Protestants is nowhere clearer than in our relation to the Enlightenment. Whereas most religious traditions, including the Catholic, continue to experience the Enlightenment as an external challenge, we experience it as a part of our internal history. In this history its ethical systems and values have been virtually identified with those of the Bible. Our struggle is to recover an authentically biblical witness over against the rationalism, nationalism, individualism, and anthropocentric dualism that mar the authentic humanistic achievements of the Enlightenment.

Our distinctive contribution to the formulation of our shared convictions may include clarification of the Christian roots and substance of the Enlightenment. In many ways the Enlightenment was an attempt to work out the meaning of love of God and neighbor over against religious and political practices and structures that demeaned people and restricted their proper freedom. As such, we continue to affirm it. But we also see that as it separated itself from its initial theistic context, it brought about a fragmentation of thought and society. It also subordinated reasoning about ends to reasoning about means and, thereby, moral and spiritual values to economic ones. We repent of our tardiness in recognizing and naming the profoundly heretical and demonic character of this atheistic version of the Enlightenment.

Despite all of the associated problematic, our distinctive contribution to the conversation among religious communities must remain that of witnessing to the primacy of faith and love over structure and law. From this point of view, the Protestant perspective on specific contemporary concerns can be articulated.

Peace and Security

The love we see incarnate in Jesus certainly affirms peace and security as important contributions to the well-being of all. It shares this affirmation of peace and security with all the great faith traditions and with many others. The distinctive contribution of Jesus, here, may be the emphasis on love of the enemy. (Matthew 5:43–48. Scholars debate which of the teachings attributed to Jesus in the gospels were his actual words. In this essay I reference only verses which, I believe, probably express his thought. In any case, these are verses that have been taken by Protestants over the centuries as the words of Jesus.)

From this perspective, there is a danger in too great an emphasis on security. It tends to accent the security of each community over against others. In the United States it has been used to justify huge armaments and "first-strike" capability in nuclear arms. Peace is aimed at through a Pax Americana which is also justified by the importance of our security.

The distinctive Protestant witness, all too muted in this country, must be that those against whom we secure ourselves are equally loved by

God and have an equal right to security. When we secure ourselves by means that threaten them, we profoundly violate Christian teaching as we understand it. We must advocate policies that lead to peace based on the equal security of all. This means we should emphasize those means of insuring our own security that do not constitute a threat to others.

Economic and Social Justice

At least today all faith communities and many others will affirm economic and social justice as desiderata. Many American Protestants identify this concern as central to their efforts to work with God toward a world in which God's will is done. We find special inspiration in the Hebrew Prophets, and we locate Jesus and the kingdom he proclaimed in that tradition. For 50 years, from 1890 to 1940, this self-understanding expressed itself in what we call the Social Gospel. This collapsed because it failed to appreciate its own limits, its naive optimism, its excessive identification with Enlightenment values, and its failure adequately to emphasize God's transcendence of history. But the more basic commitment to God's kingdom for whose coming we regularly pray, a world in which God's will is done, continues to inspire and energize us.

If Jesus not only inspires us to seek justice but also provides us with an insight into what justice is and how it is to be sought, the key element is his emphasis on "the least of these" (Matthew 20:40–45)—those who have the least power and status in society. We assume that what we do to all our neighbors is important to the God whom Jesus called *abba*, but his explicit words highlight that it is what we do to the least of these that we are doing also to him. Catholics have recently taught us to translate this into "the preferential option for the poor." If we are to move toward justice in the present situation, it will be by empowering the disempowered to have a major voice in determining world order.

Human Rights

We experience the affirmation of human rights as a way of proclaiming our faith. To love our neighbors is to recognize their dignity, their valid claim to self-determination, and, therefore, the importance of limiting the power of society or the state to interfere in their lives. We also believe it appropriate to love ourselves and to assert ourselves against the tyranny of society, church, or government. Although this is especially true when our conscience requires such assertion, our rights go beyond the freedom to obey God rather than human authority to the freedom to enjoy our share of this world's opportunities and goods.

We realize increasingly, however, the one-sidedness of our long emphasis on individual rights and the resulting imbalances and distortions. Although we have always associated the rights of others with our duties toward them, the rhetoric of our culture has lost the strong emphasis on the claim of others upon us. We need to restore the balance. Also, the emphasis on individual rights developed in a context in which social pressures and ecclesiastical and governmental authority were strong. Combined with market economics, it has now generated a situation in some parts of the world in which the taken-for-granted strength and authority of community are threatened.

Individualism has thus become a demonic force in the world. This does not warrant the abrogation of individual rights, but it does require a different paradigm from that which initially led to the emphasis on individual rights. The rhetoric of "person-in-community" is more biblical and more promising.

As Paul (and the Pauline school) pointed out, we are members of one another, jointly constituting the body of which Christ is the head (Colossians 1:18). Each part has equal dignity, deserving the respect of all the others and thus rightfully demanding that its rights be respected (I Corinthians 12:14–27). But each exists only in and through its relations with all the others. None can thrive if the body as a whole sickens. Thus each should exercise its rights with attention to how the whole is affected. The whole has rightful claims on every part.

Ecological Sustainability

Like many others, Protestants long took the natural context for granted. We participated in the Enlightenment dualism of the human and the natural, and the anthropocentric justification of the objectification and exploitation of nature for human purposes. Under the influence of Immanuel Kant, we carried this dualism to an extreme, separating the study of human phenomena radically from the study of nature. We saw history as the context of all meaning, with nature, at best, as a stage on which the historical play is enacted. We were blind to the destructive effects of our historical actions on the natural stage. We reduced the biblical doctrine of creation to an existential relation of human individuals to God.

We ignored the rare prophets who warned us of our self-destructive ways.

Finally, it was a Presbyterian layman, Lynn White, Jr., who shocked us, toward the end of the 1960s, into some measure of awareness. In defending ourselves against his charge of our culpability for the ecological crisis, we began to recover the biblical doctrine of creation. By 1975, the World Council of Churches was ready to affirm the central importance of ecological sustainability. In 1982 it committed itself to the "integrity of creation."

If Protestantism has a distinctive contribution to make in this area, it is by the extension of love to every creature. This is a different basis for ecological concern from that expressed in most secular approaches, and perhaps most religious ones as well. It does not depend on establishing either kinship or interconnection with other creatures, although the reality of this kinship and interconnection are affirmed. Otherness and separateness are not reasons for withholding love.

The argument for us is quite simple. In the first chapter of Genesis we are told that God sees that other creatures are good, quite apart from their use to human beings. In contemporary language, they have intrinsic value. The story of the flood (Genesis 6–8) brings out God's concern for species as species. Jesus tells us that God's care can be seen in the lilies of the field (Luke 12:27–28) and that God attends to each individual sparrow (Matthew 10:29). If God sees the intrinsic value of all creatures and cares for them, then we are called upon not to restrict our love to human neighbors but to extend it to other creatures as well. God "knows" them in the rich Hebrew sense of knowing. When we cause them suffering, God suffers with them.

This Protestant argument opposes the view of some who call themselves "deep ecologists" that all creatures have equal value. Jesus tells us that although God cares for the sparrow, we are of far greater importance to God than sparrows. All creatures have intrinsic value, but they do not all have equal intrinsic value. We are not wrong to care more for a dog than for the fleas and ticks that torment it. We are certainly not wrong to care more for fellow human beings than for the bacteria that sicken us.

One may argue that support for ecological sustainability does not require concern for other creatures in themselves. Human self-interest, it is supposed, when sufficiently enlightened, suffices. But this is probably not the case. Those interested only in human well-being simply do not attend sufficiently to what is happening to other creatures to be aware of long-term threats to sustainability. The requisite sensitive attention depends on love that extends beyond human beings to all creatures.

Cultural Identity and Integrity

In its origins, Christianity broke radically with the association of religious faith and a particular culture. "There is no longer Greek and Jew, circumcised and uncircumcised, barbarian, Scythian, slave and free; but Christ is all in all" (Colossians 3:11). Even the distinction between male and female is transcended in Christ (Galatians 3:28). Of course, Christianity generated its own culture to some extent, and it tended to identify faith with that.

Protestantism in theory renewed the emphasis on the transcendence of faith over culture, but in practice it has usually failed to live by this understanding. In fact there is a Protestant culture with which Protestants easily identify faith. Especially in the English-speaking world, this culture has been one form of the Enlightenment, so that it has been difficult for Protestants to bring the biblical perspective to bear in a critical and prophetic way against the failures of the Enlightenment.

Nevertheless, the conviction that faith transcends culture plays a considerable role. Protestants emphasize the importance of indigenization of Christianity in diverse cultures. In principle, thus, faith can unify across cultural boundaries without erasing those boundaries. But this may not be a contribution to the political issue of attaining sufficient unity while respecting cultural identity and integrity. Unity in faith does not provide for unity with persons of other faiths.

The one way in which the emphasis on the transcendence of culture by faith may help is by its relativization of one's own culture. Protestants know that the values of their cultures are real but limited, that other cultures also have real but limited values, that no culture defines what it means to be authentically human. In principle this opens Protestants to seek political arrangements across cultural lines that respect the relative values of each culture.

Working Toward Global Governance

Global governance was not an issue among the writers of the Bible. In the time of the New Testament, the Roman Empire was taken for granted as providing inclusive governance. Both positive and negative attitudes to that empire are expressed, but the authors do not think of themselves as having any ability to influence the imperial government or propose alternatives. If they think of an alternative at all, it is in apocalyptic terms, which means that the transformation is in the hands of God.

In subsequent centuries, when the church became politically powerful, it did deal with questions of governance over large regions. These were not, of course, global, since the people living around the Mediterranean were ignorant of much of the globe. Later in Eastern and Western Europe two patterns of dividing responsibility between church and state developed. In both cases the church concerned itself with large segments of social life.

It is difficult, however, to extrapolate from medieval Europe to our present needs to reflect on global governance. In that period, a single ecclesiastical institution was overwhelmingly dominant. Today many religious communities exist, and none is willing to submit to the hegemony of another. The issue of global governance must take account of religious pluralism, but other issues are primary.

Protestantism has not concerned itself with global governance any more directly than have other forms of Christianity. Nevertheless, because its historical experience is different, its perspective on the issues is distinctive. Because of its disconnection of faith from culture and morality, it does not have a "core set of values" to offer. On the other hand, it does have convictions relevant to global governance.

As noted, its primary commitment is to loving God and neighbor—understanding the neighbor as other people regardless of their friendship or enmity, their cultural differences, or their personal virtue. Recently, we have reemphasized that all people are members one of another (this is language applied by Paul to Christians only: Ephesians 4:25) and that our love is to be extended to all creatures. From these convictions some general principles can be drawn regarding global governance, recognizing that they need to be associated with other principles in each time and place in order to generate concrete proposals.

Global Civil Society

To love another human being is to treat that person as one wishes to be treated oneself (Luke 6:31), that is, with respect. It is to seek a situation in which people can participate in making the decisions that shape their lives and have confidence that their freedom of self-determination will

not be arbitrarily revoked. Equally, it is to insure that all have access to
the goods they require for a decent life and the opportunity to make their
own respected contributions to society.

As we realize the importance of community for individual well-being,
we recognize that love for others involves also concern for the health and
well-being of the communities in which they live. Efforts to improve the
lot of individuals must not be at the cost of breaking up viable communities or rendering the development of new communities more difficult.
Measures of well-being that ignore the health of human communities are
abstract and misleading.

We now know that human communities are inextricably connected
with local ecological systems. These ecological systems are composed of
creatures of individual worth. Their individual well-being, in turn, is
wholly dependent on the health of the system. For the sake both of human beings and of other creatures, the ecosystems in which we all live
require sensitive attention and often regeneration.

Global Structures and Systems

There is no Protestant doctrine as to what global structures and systems
are best. The question is what structures and systems will best serve the
interests of individual people, human communities, and ecosystems. The
problems to be dealt with are increasingly global, which suggests the importance of concentrating power increasingly at the global level. On the
other hand, removing control so far from individuals will accentuate the
powerlessness and alienation that already affect so many. Furthermore,
the planetary environment will always also be the result of many local
ecosystems, each of which requires local preservation and regeneration by
those sensitive to their uniqueness. The homogenization inherent in most
forms of globalization is destructive of both human communities and local ecosystems. We need a system that emphasizes both the unity of the
globe and the singleness of every part, that empowers local communities
while enabling them to act together effectively at the global level.

Protestants in North America have long struggled with a similar
problem on a much smaller scale. Our solutions have varied. Nevertheless, on the whole, we now recognize the local congregation as the foundational unit of the denominations. Congregations select representatives
to meet with representatives of other congregations to make decisions
about church life in the larger region. These in turn select representatives

to still larger regions and finally to the national or global body. What decisions are made at what level varies from denomination to denomination. There are strengths and weaknesses in each system.

In this system, congregations give authority to institutions and leaders at various levels to exercise certain authority for the sake of achieving goals that cannot be attained by congregations acting independently. They also give to the larger organization some authority to maintain standards which all local congregations must meet. If a congregation begins to espouse patently unchristian ideas, such as racism, other congregations expect the larger organization to intervene and, in the extreme case, expel the erring congregation.

We may think of each congregation as a community and of the regional institutions as expressing a community among communities. The national level can be viewed as a community of communities of communities. If there is also an international level, the same general understanding applies to it.

This image can be proposed for consideration also in the political sphere. Here, of course, the local communities include all the people living in a locality instead of those who participate voluntarily in a local congregation. These may be conceived as the primary political units. Since many of their needs cannot be dealt with at the local level, they recognize their community of interests with neighboring localities with whom they constitute a community of communities, to which they assign certain responsibilities and sufficient power to carry these out. These in turn grant power to communities of communities of communities up through the national level and culminating in the global one.

Among the responsibilities of governments representing more inclusive communities will be setting minimum standards for the smaller units. For example, localities must function as genuine communities. They cannot be allowed to exclude unpopular or weak minorities from full political participation. Also, they must deal with their problems in ways that do not impose extra burdens on their neighbors. For example, they cannot be allowed to deal with their pollution by building smokestacks that improve the quality of local air by exporting poisons to other localities.

In any case, this proposal has implications for the five topics considered above.

Peace and Security

The distribution of authority and the power to exercise it over many levels should reduce the danger of both tyranny and large-scale wars. Each locality would have primary responsibility for maintaining order in its own boundaries. If it fails to do so, or does so in a way that grossly oppresses parts of its population, the community of communities may need to intervene. Similarly, if a locality violates its neighbors, intervention may be needed. On the other hand, enforcement power should not be so concentrated at the larger level that it easily overrides local liberties.

In the same way, there should be sufficient military power at the global level to restore peace and security in troubled nations and to stop aggression. But much of this power should be provided voluntarily by the nations making up this inclusive community. We do not want all military power concentrated in the hands of a single global army, control of which would make possible a global tyranny.

Economic and Social Justice

No structure can insure economic and social justice. This depends on the will of all those involved and remains always and everywhere an illusive goal. Vigilance must be exercised at every level to establish minimum standards that will be enforced, when necessary, from larger levels of government. Smaller units must be equally vigilant to prevent larger ones from assuming excessive power or being unduly influenced by special interests. The challenge is to establish and enforce minimum universal standards in a way that does not disempower local communities or destroy the unique values of diverse cultures.

Two general principles can be formulated that should apply at all levels. The political structures must allow for the relative autonomy of various spheres of activity, such as the economic, the legal, the medical, the educational, the artistic, and the scientific. Those who understand particular aspects of life best must be safeguarded against too-quick interference by popular prejudices. Their connections will often be with persons in other localities. This will insure, also, that there will be important communities that cut across political boundaries and have authority and power of their own.

This relative autonomy is especially important in the sphere of religion. Some faith communities affirm an ultimate loyalty to God that political units should respect in a way that is not true of other social spheres. Freedom of religion is not just one expression of human freedoms generally.

Of course, this freedom cannot be absolute. People cannot be allowed in the name of their obedience to God to harm others. Religions must be accountable to the most basic needs of the inclusive community and its natural environment. Nevertheless, the fact that human beings are validly committed to goals that transcend the political sphere and have the right to express this commitment individually and in communities should be acknowledged and affirmed.

The second principle is that political life should not be subordinated to any other sphere. In some countries this means that the people as a whole must be able to express the full range of their concerns through political processes without being restricted by religious leaders from doing so. In the North Atlantic countries, and indeed generally outside the sphere of Islam, religious authorities are not today the major threat to freedom. The sphere that now threatens the autonomy of the political one is the economy. Today governments at many levels are subservient to economic institutions.

These institutions include national and transnational businesses on whose investments local communities are dependent. They also include public institutions such as the International Monetary Fund and the World Bank, which have imposed structural adjustment on many of the countries of the world, as well as the World Trade Organization, which overrules national policies that it sees as restraining trade unfairly. The ability of governments to balance the many competing concerns of their people is also restricted by the influence of money in democratic elections and in shaping public opinion through the media.

Protestants join with all other religiously concerned people in holding that economic values are only one of many types of value. Certainly it is crucial that the physical necessities of life be provided for all, and it is highly desirable that all participate in a standard of living that goes beyond mere subsistence. But it is also highly desirable that people have a meaningful role in healthy communities, that they participate in shaping the policies that determine their destiny, that they enjoy natural and artificial beauty, that they are free to think and stimulated to think well, that they have stable and happy families, and that they are able to express their deepest convictions in prayer and worship. When all aspects of life are subordinated to the economic, much of this is truncated. A society that is primarily devoted to the generation of material wealth is unacceptable. The New Testament tells us quite directly that we cannot serve both God and wealth (Luke 16:13). To organize society as a whole in the service of wealth is unacceptable.

This means that political units which have at least the possibility of serving multiple values must not be subordinated to economic units that are designed only for the service of wealth. Structurally this requires that economic units operate within political boundaries. If the economic units are local, they can be regulated by local governments; if they are national, by national governments. Transnational economic units require regulation by transnational government. This cannot be, as at present with the World Trade Organization, governmental institutions created only to promote the economy. It must be a government that is concerned about the whole range of human needs and values.

This principle requires either the great strengthening of the global level of governance or the reassertion of national control over economic actors. It is the rejection of the ideal of a global market transcending all political control. If we are to avoid concentrating political power at the global level, we must reverse recent trends that free economic actors from national control.

Human Rights

Every type of structure, and every level of government, is capable of distortion that infringes on human rights. Only a deep and widespread commitment of people everywhere to the maintenance of such rights can preserve them. Nevertheless, the structure here proposed may be helpful.

A major problem with local autonomy is that in many instances it allows a local majority to oppress local minorities or an elite to disempower the majority. In general, public opinion in other locations is critical of these abuses. Hence, government at larger levels is likely to give support to correcting them. This is a major reason for concentrating power at higher levels of government. The proposed structure of governance takes this into account.

On the other hand, human rights should be balanced by felt obligations to community, which cannot be effectively enforced by higher levels of government. Concentration of power at those levels tends to weaken the local community feeling which generates the awareness of obligations. Thus, it is important not to give up localism for the sake of implementing universal standards of justice and human rights. The model proposed tries to maintain a balance between the need for local participation and the enforcement of standards from higher jurisdictions.

Ecological Sustainability

Ecological issues need to be addressed at all levels. Some are truly global. Global warming, the reduction of the ozone layer, and the pollution of the oceans are examples. There is also a strong global stake in the preservation of biodiversity. Global government should have sufficient authority to deal with matters of this sort.

On the other hand, local communities know, or can learn, about their immediate environment and its needs in their specificity. Often the imposition of rules from higher levels of government does not work partly because local conditions make them inappropriate, and partly because local people do not feel any ownership of them. The structure proposed here is designed to encourage people everywhere to be concerned with and take responsibility for their local environments. As they try to do so, their interdependence with other localities becomes clear and they are more willing to allow many decisions to be made at higher levels.

Cultural Identity and Integrity

To whatever extent cultures are local, the structure here proposed is favorable to their ability to maintain their integrity, as long as this does not abuse others. The problem is more difficult when, as today, even small localities are likely to be multicultural; then it sometimes helps to think of even the single locality as a community of communities. Even so the danger of domination by one cultural group over others arises. There is need for power at higher governmental levels to check such domination.

This need is present at many levels. One reason for strengthening the power of global government is to check the tendencies of nation-states to oppress minorities. Nation-states often need to intervene in regions where such oppression occurs. And those regions, as noted, may need to intervene to prevent local oppressions.

The opposite danger is that the principles employed in determining the minimal standards of justice and rights to be enforced are themselves derived from one culture and then imposed on others. To check this requires constant discussion among representatives of the several cultures involved to determine principles on which general agreement can be reached, and whose implementation all can support. The importance of ongoing interaction among leaders of cultures and religions is demonstrated at this point.

Local Initiatives

Without strong support from people all over the planet, there can be no happy solution to issues of global governance. There must be widespread agreement as to the importance of such governance. Even when there is disagreement in detail about the interventions that larger governments exercise locally, there must be recognition of the necessity of such interventions in general.

But dependence on leadership from higher levels of government is enervating. As much power as possible needs to remain local. This requires that much of the economy be local as well. Local initiatives to strengthen the local economy and minimize control of the economy from distant centers are one important type of local initiative.

Also, local initiatives may be needed to protest decisions made at higher levels that are insensitive to their local consequences. Many nongovernmental organizations have their rise in such protests, and their voices are important to counter the excessive influence of special interests, particularly global economic ones, at higher levels of government.

It is highly desirable that local communities have greater freedom to experiment with educational systems. At present, authority over education in the United States is centralized at the state level. It is appropriate that some standards be set at state and national levels, but the current loss of close ties between school and local community is too high a price to pay.

Balancing Tensions

Most of what needs to be said in responding to the problems of balance listed here is implicit, or even explicit, in what has been written above.

Individual Good and Common Good

If we understand ourselves as persons-in-community, the real good of the individual person requires the well-being of the community. On the other side, the community is made up of individuals, so that it is meaningless to suppose that it thrives if the individual persons who make it up do not.

The tensions arise, in general, from inaccurately defining what is good for individuals and communities. If we define the good primarily in economic terms, it is possible to suppose that an individual gains by amassing a higher and higher percentage of the communal wealth despite the resulting decline of the community. This is one more reason for rejecting the primacy of economic measures.

Similarly, if we define the community good chiefly in terms of harmony, then dissident individuals appear to be working against the good of community and have to be suppressed and oppressed for the good of community so defined. But this is to misunderstand what makes for the real good of community. The community benefits from internal diversity as long as the members continue to respect and listen to one another.

There may also be cases in which there is real conflict between the good of certain individuals and the good of the community. Some individuals may have values and concerns so at odds with the majority that no reconciliation is possible. If these individuals remain part of the community, they must sacrifice in order to hold the community together. The alternative is that the community is fractured in order to allow diverse interests to be realized.

No theory or structure can prevent such tensions from arising. What can be done is to help both individual persons and communities to develop understandings that show their community of interests. Individuals can grow as they appreciate the values for themselves of participation in community. Communities can grow as they recognize the positive contribution of protest and diversity. But no structure can prevent tensions from leading to rupture in some cases. Nor should we suppose that better solutions are always possible.

Rights and Responsibilities

The Bible, like most scriptures, places primary emphasis on responsibilities. The call, especially in the New Testament, is more often to sacrifice for others than to assert one's own rights. Many today protest that they were taught by Christianity to allow themselves to be abused and oppressed rather than to assert themselves and resist tyranny.

The history of the church is mixed on this point. By encouraging people to believe that they are loved and affirmed by God, the church has

supported a self-esteem that has sometimes led to self-assertion or assertion of claims by oppressed groups. On the other hand, by reminding us
that our self-centeredness and claim to special consideration are sinful, it
has led us to think that our suffering is merited. Women and those who
have been colonialized and enslaved suggest that the emphasis on self-
esteem has been largely arrogated by elite white males, whereas others
have been taught their obligations and passive acceptance of their condition of servitude.

The Enlightenment lifted up the claims of individual persons against
the state, the church, and the community. Of course, Enlightenment
thinkers also had a strong sense of obligation and duty. But this tended to
be duties to other individuals more than those that arise from participation in community; these continued to be taken for granted.

Today we are struggling to understand rights and responsibilities
more integrally. To participate as an individual person in community in-
sures that the community gives one space to be a person whose decisions
and contributions are respected and affirmed. On the other hand, it also
means that concern for the well-being of the community as a whole informs one's decisions and actions. Failure in either direction leads to
weakening both of personhood and of community.

Private Sector and Public Sector

Within any healthy society, most of life and social activity takes place
independently of the government. For the public sector to expand into all
spheres of life and thought is totalitarianism. Protestant churches have
always opposed such expansion, first and foremost because they claim the
right to manage their own affairs and to proclaim the Word of God as
they understand it, regardless of governmental approval or disapproval.

At the same time, there are many functions important for society
that can be performed only by governments. Protestant churches have
always recognized and affirmed this. Hence, issues arise only around the
question of which functions are best performed by the government under
what historical circumstances, whether the government should play an
exclusive role in these functions, and the extent to which activities that
are essentially private nevertheless sometimes require restriction and intervention by the government.

Social services are an example of a borderline area. These were once
performed chiefly by the churches and other voluntary groups. As needs

came to exceed the capacities of these groups, governments began to play an important role and eventually the overwhelmingly dominant one. The result is bureaucratization, with all its problems. Hence the question arises as to whether churches and other institutions in the private sector should recover a large role in this area. Since no one wants to exclude private agencies altogether and no one supposes that the government can abandon all responsibility, the issue is one of balance. "Liberal" Protestants tend to emphasize the responsibility of government; "conservatives," that of the private sector.

The most important tension between the two sectors today is between government and business. The American people as a whole are convinced that economic freedom is an important value, and that government interference leads to reduced efficiency in the economy. On the other hand, most people want workers to be paid properly and provided with safe working conditions. They want to be protected from pollution and want endangered species not to be casually wiped out. Hence, in fact they want considerable regulation of business. Among Protestants, liberals usually support stronger governmental regulations; conservatives, more freedom on the part of business. It can be argued, however, that business is free to act morally only when other businesses are also required to do so. Hence in some respects the freedom of business depends on government establishing the common rules by which all abide.

Today the most important questions concern the relation of transnational corporations to national governments. The commitment of national governments to "free trade"—meaning transnational corporations' freedom from control or interference by national governments—has thrown the balance of power to the private sector. The ability of national governments to shape their peoples' economic life is severely restricted. This means that economic growth becomes the dominant value and goal, with all other sectors of society subordinated to its pursuit. Although many Protestants do not yet understand the issue, in principle this situation is unacceptable from the Protestant perspective.

Long-Term and Short-Term Objectives
Economic and Environmental Needs

I am combining these two topics because the general issue of long-term and short-term objectives is most importantly illustrated in the tensions between economic and environmental needs. Within economic policies, the issue is more often formulated as the alternative of distributing the fruits of industry now, or reinvesting so that there will be more to distribute in the future. For the sake of long-term gains, it is often argued, "belt-tightening" is required in the present. Since those who must tighten their belts are often the poor, the present suffering required for anticipated long-term gains can be quite acute.

The problem is complicated by the fact that the long-term growth for which this suffering is demanded almost always adds to stress on the environment. Thus, supposed long-term economic advantages are in tension with long-term environmental health. Protestants are beginning to recognize that without a healthy environment, the economic growth that our society so prizes will fail to deliver on its promises.

This means that in general (there are exceptions, and each situation should be considered individually), the tension introduced by economic thinkers between current distribution and economic growth is misplaced. Present suffering is being demanded for the sake of long-term advantages that can never be realized. True long-term advantages based on healthy human community in a larger healthy ecological system can best be realized in ways that meet human needs now as well. Desirable community development programs do not promise great future economic luxury or wealth, but, on the other hand, do not call for acute sacrifice in the present. They treat economic matters as only one of the important considerations of true development, and it is improvement in the larger picture, including the economy, that is sought. The tension between short-term and long-term objectives does not disappear, but it is greatly muted in comparison with typical economic thinking.

Local, National, and Global Sovereignties

Enlightenment political theory has thought it necessary to identify some one level of absolute political sovereignty. It has recognized that the sovereign can delegate power to other levels of government; but the sovereign is thought to be in a position to revoke what is delegated.

In fact, of course, the real situation rarely fits the theory. In the founding of the United States it was held that the states were sovereign units, and this rhetoric still persists. However, states that have appealed to this sovereignty to justify withdrawal from the federal union have met with strong opposition from the federal government. From the perspective of state sovereignty, what is usually called the Civil War was the War

Between the States. But after the North's victory, no one seriously supposed that states have the kind of sovereignty they previously claimed. Still, they are sovereign in some respects, especially in relation to the lower levels of government within them. The reality is that sovereignty is divided between state and federal levels with some minor elements being delegated to local governments and international institutions.

The proposal made in this paper is that distribution of sovereignty go much further. Every level of government should have some sovereignty. The sovereignty of every level of government should be qualified by the sovereignty of others.

If we are to speak of a unique sovereignty at all in this system of global governance, it belongs to the people and to the local communities in which they directly participate. But because these are dependent on others, this sovereignty is immediately qualified by the acceptance of the authority of larger levels of government. The nation is one, important, larger level of government. But it derives its authority from the people and their local communities through the states, and it must immediately acknowledge the necessity of giving some of its authority to the global community of nations.

In fact it is better to give up the notion of sovereignty altogether. No one and no institution has sovereign authority. If there is any rightful sovereign it is God, and for some Protestants even that language theologically misrepresents the relation of creatures to God. Let us speak instead of the responsibilities of each level of government and insure that each has the power necessary to carry out these responsibilities.

Religious Resources for Global Governance

Protestantism in the past has been prolific in the creation of institutions. This is especially true in the United States. Protestants were once the main source of the educational and medical systems in the country, and the chief provider of social services. Protestant missionaries created numerous institutions of these types in Asia, Africa, and Latin America.

The question here, however, is not about the role Protestants have played in the past. It is about the ability of Protestants to make institutions of these sorts serve toward the development of desirable forms of global governance. The answer here must be more modest.

Over the centuries, most institutions established by Protestants have become autonomous. The once-Protestant universities, such as Harvard,

Yale, Princeton, and Chicago, are now secular institutions in which Protestantism has very little influence. Most of the hospitals established by Protestant churches have also become secular institutions. Protestant social agencies are quite minor factors on the national scene.

This process of secularization has not been opposed by Protestants. On the contrary, Protestants have given strong support to the idea that state and national governments should ensure, in ways the divided churches cannot, that education, medical care, and social services be available for all. As governments have moved into these fields, Protestants have largely withdrawn.

Today some Protestants have concluded that this concentration of responsibilities in the hands of governments has been a mistake, and they are supporting legislative changes that reduce the role of government and increase the role of the churches. On the whole, the old-line Protestant churches, which have been chiefly in view in this essay, are opposing this trend; they know they do not have the resources to deal with the magnitude of contemporary problems.

Even so, clear decisions by the Protestant churches in the United States that they had the responsibility to promote global governance of a particular type *could* lead to significant support. There are liberal arts colleges with close ties to these denominations that *could* orient themselves to preparing people for service in the global scene and supporting research relevant to global governance. Denominational publishing houses could encourage books and magazine articles to move thinking in positive directions. And, of course, local congregations and councils of churches could contribute to creating a favorable climate of opinion.

Developing Multireligious Initiatives

There are three levels at which work needs to be done. First, representatives of the several religious Ways need to get acquainted and discuss with one another, just as we have done in the Maryknoll meeting. Many dialogues are taking place all around the world among representatives of two or three communities; these contribute to the possibility of more inclusive meetings such as ours. These activities build mutual understanding and trust.

Second, representatives of these traditions need to determine whether they can reach consensus on the kind of global governance they favor. Our meeting moved in that direction, but for serious proposals to be formulated requires far more intensive and extensive discussion. Equally important to coming up with proposals would be getting these proposals seriously critiqued and modified from wider segments of the communities whose representatives have participated in the drafting. The processes that have been followed by Hans Küng and in the preparation of the Earth Charter may provide models. But the proposals I envisage may be more difficult to boil down into brief statements. They may require more sustained study in religious groups all over the world before they can play a role as expressive of religious consensus.

Third, the growing community of thought and concern among religious leaders needs to find expression in some ongoing institution that can speak for it. The closest approximation among Christians is the World Council of Churches. This is based on the official participation of many denominations. Whether the World Council of Churches could, as a unit, work with similar bodies representing other religious traditions, or whether the individual members of the WCC should be individual members of a multireligious institution, I do not know. However, the former approach would express the "community of communities" pattern affirmed in this paper, and hence would be my first choice. A third option is an organization more like the Parliament of Religions, made up of individual religious leaders who speak for themselves.

From my Protestant perspective, the issue of how to develop an agency able in some way to speak for the religious communities is a practical one. If all that is now possible is an agency made up of individual leaders, that should be developed. If it is possible to develop an institution that can speak more authoritatively for all the great religious Ways, that would be better. If such an agency could promote discussion throughout the world and advance reflection on urgent issues, as is done by the World Council of Churches, that would, indeed, be a great contribution.

CHRISTIANITY

Development and Spirituality: Personal Reflections of a Catholic

Luis M. Dolan

In this paper I concentrate on two points of the Guideline Questions: question three, "Collaborating with the United Nations and its Specialized Agencies," and question four, "Developing Multireligious Initiatives." I endeavor to reflect on these points as a Catholic. The perspective from which I write is on one hand that of the United Nations, with whom I have worked as an NGO, consultant, and religious advisor for over 30 years; on the other hand, my experience working on religious and interreligious programs in over 85 countries around the world. I am writing in my own name, not as an official of any office in the Catholic Church.

I will reflect on the following points:

1. Looking at the United Nations as a Catholic: what the UN offers, and questions it raises;

2. Elements that can contribute to the formulation of a process on religion and world order;

3. A program that offers a model on religion and world order.

Looking at the United Nations as a Catholic

The UN came into being in 1945 to seek peace among nations. To achieve this, the whole UN thrust was to work within the context of development.

But what development? The model of civilization presented at the time the UN began, and until the Group of 77 and the Group of Non-aligned Nations were formed, was the model of advanced, "developed" countries like those in Europe and the United States, or "Western European and other states."[1] This meant that development was equated with economic progress. As the UN progressed, this notion was expanded.

Two current definitions of development are used in the UN:

Sustainable Development. "Development" and "sustainable development" are interchangeable. Sustainable development is "[the] development that meets the needs of the present without compromising the ability of future generations to meet their own needs."[2] (Use of "sustainable" does not necessarily entail environmental protection.)

Human Development. "Human development is a process of enlarging people's choices. The most critical ones are to lead a long and healthy life, to be educated, and to enjoy a decent standard of living. Additional choices include political freedom, guaranteed human rights, and self-respect."[3] (This is the "human capital" Mahbub Ul-Haq speaks of as being more relevant than GNP.)

More insight into the centrality of development comes from scanning two documents by H.E. Boutros Boutros-Ghali, *An Agenda for Peace* and *An Agenda for Development*, in which it is stated that the twenty-first century should be the Development Century;[4] development is the most important task facing humanity today,[5] but this concept of development is complex and multifaceted; development must be seen in its own right;[6] what is development, and what is "non-development"?[7] Development looks at times like something mainly economic, but it is much more; therefore a common or new framework to carry out resolutions, etc., by

---

[1] See *Journal of the United Nations*.

[2] World Commission on Environment and Development, *Our Common Future*, Part I, Chapter 2, p. 43.

[3] *Human Development Report '90*, Chapter 1, p. 10.

[4] *Agenda for Development*, p. 10.

[5] *Ibid.*, p. 1.

[6] *Ibid.*, p. 7.

[7] *Agenda for Peace*, p. 24.

UN conferences is necessary to embrace the full notion of development.[8]

A religious perspective on the UN means for me a view of political realities in the world—and the UN expression of those realities in documents, declarations, conventions, etc.—from the standpoint of the inspired books that are part of the arsenal of humanity and of the major religions and spiritual traditions. From this perspective we can see what ethical and moral issues and problems need to be addressed today which, though politically delicate or even dangerous, would benefit nevertheless from the illuminating teachings of these same holy traditions.

Since the beginning of my exposure to the UN I have been intrigued by an apparent inconsistency in the UN: on the one hand the centrality of the issue of development, and on the other, the overt exclusion of religion and spirituality as essential elements to express the totality of development. This apparent inconsistency gave me my focus for the issues I have followed, and continue to follow, with the UN. My research and work with members of the UN diplomatic corps, NGOs, and international civil servants convinced me that sooner or later we would have to address the key issue of spirituality and development, religion and development. I saw that there was a great deal to learn from the wisdom and political vision of the UN's founders in making development the central focus of a global organization whose purposes include maintaining peace and security, developing friendly relations among nations, achieving international cooperation, and being a center for harmonizing the actions of nations to attain these ends.[9]

But because development *per se* is rarely mentioned in the Charter,[10] I decided to work on spirituality and development in the UN in order to see whether (and how) the UN dealt with religious, moral, and ethical issues affecting nation-states. Why? Because it was evident that there was a need to look at the connection between development, peace, security, and human rights, and to focus on several difficult questions: Does religion have anything to contribute to development? Is religion merely a cultural expression of a country? Is religion, as expressed in countries where UNDP, UNICEF, and other UN agencies organize programs, an obstacle or even a deterrent to development?

---

[8] *Ibid.*, p. 35.

[9] *Charter of the United Nations*, Chapter I, Article 1.

[10] E.g., Chapter II, Article 73, and indirectly in Chapter IX, Article 55, Para. 1A.

Coming to a religious perspective on the UN, I will make the general comment that, theologically, the UN has given the world new insights into what in several religions is called the Kingdom of God. These new insights come from the fact that in the UN all nations have a "home"; and even though it is a political "home," to formulate laws and propose forms of legal cooperation, the UN still offers a view of what is possible if there are united nations. This information can provide what is called by some Christian theologians a view of "the signs of the times," i.e., how God is working in the world today. If this material were compiled in a treatise on spirituality and development as seen at work in UN documents, conferences, committee meetings, etc., it would lead to new insight into "the Kingdom of God."

I believe that the UN offers us the first scripture written by communities rather than by a single inspired author. This scripture is the composite of all the basic documents of the UN, starting with the Charter and including the relatively recent *Agenda for Development*; all the plans of action, declarations, and conventions agreed on over 50-odd years; the frequent conferences; the unique symposia or consultations of UNESCO, UNDP, UNITAR, etc. It is a scripture because beyond all politics—and perhaps even because of all politics—we have for the first time a compilation of inspired documents dealing with nearly all the problems that affect living organisms. It does this through a long, painful, tedious consensual process among representatives from over 180 countries. It does this to offer national governments, as well as regional political bodies, a background and a context from which can be enacted new laws for the good of people. All documents are couched in UN jargon, i.e., legal terms for an international political audience, but the voices of the people are there, and these are "signs of the times" for all who believe that God is continuing to speak to us today.

The UN has also given us the first global forum: a venue in which all problems can be addressed. A simple study of the titles and sequence of UN conferences since 1945 will undoubtedly show this. The annual documents produced by the UN bring us up to date on the global voices of God. The UN meditation room, and the minute of silent prayer or meditation at the beginning of each UN General Assembly, place "the greatest gathering of nations...under the symbol of silent prayer or meditation," in the words of U Thant.[11] The UN is where "moral and ethical issues are being brought one after the other to the world organization." The UN is creating codes of ethics and conduct, one of the greatest being the Charter itself. The UN "extends the power of our hearts and souls." The UN thus has become "a cathedral where we can worship what is best in each other." "Little by little a planetary prayer book is being composed (at the UN) by an increasingly united humanity seeking its oneness."[12] Knowing this spiritual side of the UN led U Thant to say that the most significant event of our times was the signing of the UN Charter. This spiritual side of development, and therefore of the UN, was clearly stated by Mr. Joao Da Costa, executive secretary of UNCSTD (the UN Conference on Science and Technology for Development) in 1979:

> Development must be total, i.e., it must transcend the purely economic domain, to include the social, cultural, political, and spiritual dimensions.

See also:

> The ultimate end of development is a civilization of love.[13]

A religious perspective is something relatively new in UN discussions because the UN has been far too dominated by outdated models of civil society which have taken for granted that nation-states must either have total separation of church and state—without studying the full meaning of such a metaphor—or be a theocratic nation-state. This error must be corrected. I believe there is a need for research, critical analysis, and dialogue among the different disciplines, so that we may find out whether it is realistic and futuristic to speak of a religious perspective on the UN that can be put side by side with an economic perspective, a parliamentarian perspective, a humanistic-ethical perspective, a perspective as shown in annual reports of the secretary-general and heads of UN agencies, and a perspective from individual religions or spiritual traditions. This would offer a venue that addresses all issues affecting human beings and the world from a fully comprehensive context. I firmly believe, though, that for a religious perspective to be realistic, fit for a political environment, and of a caliber that can be studied at universities, meet-

---

[11] R. Muller, *Meditation at the UN*, p. 26.

[12] *Ibid.*

[13] See encyclical *Dives in Misericordia*, pp. 72–73.

ings of transnational corporations, and so on, this perspective needs to come from what I call a "religious spirituality" vantage point.

> I mean by religious spirituality a very deep and universal form of spirituality that expresses the essence of religion by connecting the transcendental with the immanent, the eternal with the temporal, through a series of significant and re-vealing prayers, values, beliefs, rituals, and offerings that were learned from one of the original religions. I call it religious spirituality to distinguish it from spiri-tuality per se, which has inundated the Western world in recent decades and is characterized by a series of values, actions, rituals, and lifestyle that are usually partially or totally separated from any known religion in the world.

> It is universal. I have seen it in animist, Buddhist, Christian, Hindu, Jew-ish, Muslim, and other believers, especially including those impregnated with a strong indigenous spirituality.

> It is behind all religions. It is not necessarily overtly a part of the creed, worship, or institutional life of a religion, but people have it from the present or past practice of a religion and it is embedded in their unconscious, to say the least. It cannot be understood without religion. If directed gently and respect-fully, it will even lead many people back to their religion of origin.

> It is the greatest expression of what the secretary-general of the UN once called the "resilience of the Spirit" that continues to tell the UN researchers, the leaders of government and economic institutions, that their job on devel-opment is still not complete because "the Spirit" has not yet been given its proper place in global documents.

> It is manifested by a childlike attitude, rational knowledge combined with a quasi-mystical approach to reality, and more frequently than not with growing interreligious activities. Because of these characteristics that manifest it and make it different from spirituality per se, it is religious spirituality that keeps open the doors for further flowering of development, challenges the present limits of human development, and is starting to channel the clamors of the Spirit coming out of the nascent experiences of interreligious dialogue and co-operation.[14]

Development UN-style experienced an explosion 50 years after World War II,[15] to the extent that today it makes us understand that "values" and "spirituality" are elements of development crying out for recognition. The questions raised today at UN conferences and peacekeeping missions by the values and spirituality aspects of develop-ment touch the core of postwar conflicts and clashes; they also offer a

---

[14] See L. Dolan paper, "Religious Spirituality: The Soul of Development and Change," UNDP Round Table on Global Change, Bucharest, 1992.

[15] See U. Kirdar, *People: From Impoverishment to Empowerment* (New York: New York University Press, 1995), pp. 210–216.

powerful ray of light to illuminate what is needed to touch the heart of people in such a way that conflict will change into conversation, and political confrontations into artful discussions on how to live with a political problem, knowing we will not or cannot solve it.

A few examples:

- Six decades after the Easter Uprising, the centuries-old Northern Ireland problem, which started with famine and opposing religious views and was mired in what seemed to be political issues, has given way to painful steps toward "understanding" one another, looking deeper than the stereotyped boundary and confessional issues; it is now beginning to address spirit, justice, and equity issues such as how to create an environment in which people live together, where loyalty is accepted toward London or Dublin. It is becoming a discussion of the spirit.

- In ex-Yugoslavia, after the iron grip of Communism was lifted, the people and countries involved realized that the deeper issues of one's religious and ethnic values had never been addressed. And so today, after bloody warfare and after NATO, the UN, and even religions have shown their inability to stop the war, what is slowly, painfully, falteringly but unmistakably emerging is the absolute need to accept both the fact that some people in the Balkans are and will remain Orthodox, others Muslims, and others Catholic, and that the factual territorial issues will remain real, delicate, and alive in the region. Through it all there comes the question: how can we live together? Noble and painstaking efforts by the UN, by churches and mosques, by Muslim and Orthodox and Catholic "countries" were needed, sorry to say, to highlight the enormous and centuries-old complexity of the issues, so that people, religions, nations, and international organizations would get down on their knees and pray for a different view of the issue.

- Political issues in Liberia, Sudan, Algeria, India/Pakistan, Punjab, Sri Lanka, and the powerful questions in Iran, Iraq, etc., on whether I'm a Sunni or a Shiite, a defender of the Islamic worldview, fundamentalist, or fanatic—are a piercing cry to feel the sacredness of Islam. The devastation of the Ayodya Mosque in India, together with the assassination of Gandhi, then of Indira Gandhi and her son, are very enigmatic and dramatic cries for a deeper understanding of values, religious rituals and cultural mores, and the teaching of history.

- In Europe, Bulgaria fears the Turkish menace. Turkey has not pardoned Russia for taking Central Asia. Germans and Poles are at loggerheads. Hungary wants a part of Romania. Slovaks got separated from the Czech Republic. The Irish do not want the British in Ireland. The Basques do not want Spain as it is. Romania wants Moldavia, and so on. Still, there are definite moves today toward a "United States of Europe," going far beyond economic or political union into some sort of "new" Europe.

Another issue that has recently come to the consciousness of the UN is the concept of global governance. It is a question that naturally arises because of the nascent global civil society. It presents questions for pursuers of development because it makes the world see that every institution has a contribution for development, and that development can only be real if it calls all peoples and governments to a sense of human solidarity. Global governance calls for a new vision, challenging people as well as governments to realize that there is no alternative to working together to create the kind of world they want for themselves and their children.[16] Unfortunately, and similarly to its treatment during 50-odd years of UN development work, the spiritual and religious contribution to global governance is excluded, or mentioned in very cautious terms. Global governance is portrayed as essentially a civil ideal. It will not work, though, unless it is also presented as a religious ideal.

Elements That Can Contribute to a Process on Religion and World Order

What elements are needed to translate a religious perspective on the UN into a movement toward greater development, peace, and global justice in the world? More specifically, how do we envision a world order in which the "Catholic voice" in the UN would help member states, NGOs, and other international institutions to contribute toward this movement, and in which the "Catholic voice" would at the same time be influenced by them in Catholic teachings and positions?

I mean by "Catholic voice" the very rich teachings and guidelines

---

[16] *Our Global Neighborhood*, the report of the Commission on Global Governance, Oxford University Press, p. 336.

coming from (1) recent popes, starting from the epochal appearance of Pope Paul VI at the UN, all the way to the very powerful speech of Pope John Paul II to the UN on the occasion of its fiftieth anniversary in 1995; (2) the teachings in official church documents; (3) the strong and very influential activities of Catholic NGOs throughout UN history, including the enormous influence of some outstanding Catholics who through their powerful example inspired some of the most challenging movements alive today in the UN, including le Père Joseph, who created "Le Quatrième Monde"; the founder of the International Catholic Child Bureau; the Franciscan eruption into the UN with the special charism of Francis for peace, justice, and a great love for the environment; the different educational and humanitarian Catholic NGOs; and so on and so forth.

To energize the movement toward a better world order mentioned above, the Catholic Church, like all other religious groups, needs to create a process born of an attractive, Catholic, global vision for the twenty-first century, sufficiently comprehensive to include all Catholic voices throughout the world. To make this process realistic and attractive, there is a need to diagnose again and again the role of religions and spiritual traditions today, the increasing contributions of interreligious dialogue and cooperation, and the unique contribution of Christianity.

This paper cannot be a total presentation of such a process. I will point out six key elements that need to be incorporated and inspire the process. I hope this will help to stir all concerned to give the world and the UN an uplifting future-oriented "Catholic voice" in the UN and other international organizations.

The Context

I believe that the theological context for this process should be how the church is trying to work for the coming of the Kingdom of God, and what it needs to be more Kingdom-oriented; how the mystery of the Incarnation can become a true human universal, reaching and benefiting all 6 billion people in the world; and how this search of the Catholic Church can become incarnated in different parts of the world.

This theological context, though, needs to be inserted into a global political context within which to address these key issues; and this political context needs to be born primarily, though not exclusively, from the plans of action formulated at recent UN conferences, which show a shift in the UN direction from ways to foster predominantly economic development so that there may be no more "developing" countries, to a world created by concentration on social development, with the challenging and life-giving new role recognized for the environment in the formulation of world plans. The UN needs to be congratulated for making social development the center of future concerns and plans.

The Basic Questions

The basic questions that arise regarding what can inspire a comprehensive world order are, in my opinion, the following: What is the appropriate relationship of the human person with the Creator, with other human beings, and with the environment? What needs to be affirmed or changed in the beliefs, teachings, and practice of world religions, so that this vital relationship will bring about new concepts of what a country—a nation-state—can mean in the future?

I would like to offer six of the elements to be included in the process that will lead to greater respect and love for the contributions of the church to a new world order, and that need to be included in the formulation of a "Catholic voice" for the future. (I leave for a future paper the formulation of an entire process.)

- *Knowledge and Application of Key Church Documents.* The first element is the knowledge and application of some key church documents, in order to portray how the teachings they contain will contribute to a better world. I personally have always found inspiration, challenge, and above all intellectual stimulation and security in the major documents resulting from papal letters, encyclicals and speeches, as well as from the Pontifical Committee "Justitia et Pax" and the Pontifical Council on Dialogue among Religions. These documents are born from a global context, they cover extremely interesting, difficult, and at times new religious areas, and they give one an intelligent and well-formulated Catholic view of the subjects dealt with. As I write, I have before me several copies of *Pro Dialogo*, the official magazine of the Pontifical Council on Dialogue among Religions, which offers current speeches by the Pope and information on interreligious conferences and consultations. I also have a pile of documents from "Justitia et Pax," because they too deal with issues that are on the cutting edge of society today.

A process for the future requires that these documents be put into curricula for Catholic schools and programs at the level of parishes, dioceses, seminaries, retreat houses, and so on, so that our people can better understand the magisterial aspect of the Catholic voice and hopefully commit themselves to a Catholic view of global events.

- *A Catholic Voice on the Economy.* The second element to be included in a future process is a Catholic view of today's economy. I do not mean only a moral appraisal of economic trends, which is very important, but an insertion into the basic realities of the modern economy, and from this practical basis to give the world a "Catholic voice" on the economic trends that so profoundly affect the life of every person on earth. The problem is how to do this. For example, in the Commission on Global Governance document *Our Global Neighborhood: The Basic Vision*, it is stated that economic well-being is of fundamental importance for all human beings.[17] Because the Group of Seven is not recognizing this, the document suggests the establishment of an Economic Security Council which could have the same importance as the UN Security Council.[18]

  We need a Catholic voice on economics. I am fully aware of some of the papal and episcopal teachings on this matter, and of some of the excellent contributions of Catholic economists, but I feel the church needs to express spiritual and moral values in economic language, accepting the reality that the first principle of global economy is the law of supply and demand. If spiritual and moral values do not become components of the world economy, global civilization will increasingly be a form of neocolonialism in which the northern countries will undermine the southern countries—in other words, in which the poorest nation-states will be excluded from international economic processes, as they are at present. We need Catholic voices that are realistic, moral, and hope-giving to the poorest of the world.

- *A Future-Oriented Model of the Church.* The third element is the model of a church we need to help create the future world order. In my many years of work with interreligious and/or international political groups, I have found this probably the Catholic voice's greatest need in order to be more credible. The church of the future needs to come across primarily as a community of believers, rather than as an

---

[17] *Ibid.*, p. 31.
[18] *Ibid.*, p. 31.

institution with a hierarchical structure. I believe ours is a hierarchical church, and I love and respect it, but in my experience I have seen this aspect over-stressed to the detriment of other Catholic believers who have an enormous contribution to offer the world. At times this is also expressed by overly emphasizing the teachings on the charism of each group that pertains to the church: laity, religious, clerical, hierarchical. It makes it appear as though that distinction gave credence to what is said by members of each group, rather than what is said by the community of believers, or some of its prophets "not accepted by their own."[19]

A consequence of this is the Vatican's apparent fear of theologians; its occasionally belligerent attitude at UN conferences; a certain defensiveness; and an overemphasis on ideology, which I believe sometimes leads to unnecessary and painful divisions, and to the decrease of a challenging Catholic voice in the marketplace and in other intellectual and political environments.

We increasingly need a church that is not centered on itself, but is ever finding new ways of expressing the fact that it exists only to point people and countries toward the Kingdom. There are extraordinary examples of the church doing this, especially in the field of humanitarian help and the search for justice and freedom of religion; but, like other institutions, the church needs over and over again to find ways of dealing with some of the crucial trends and realities that will mark the society of the future. It is not an easy role.

- *A Model of the Church as Seeker of Truth.* The fourth element, one of the burning issues of today, is for the church to find, and find again, ways of dealing with other religions as equals. I know the theological implications of this point; I also know the enormous growth that has occurred in the church since interreligious dialogue became a daily component of Catholic life. I still insist, though, that our church needs to appear not as an owner of the truth but as a seeker of the mystery of God on earth, together with believers of other religions. In this sense there was a remarkable assertion in a Vatican document: that the church cannot impose itself, that it needs to be a disciple seeking the total truth.[20]

---

[19] See "The Catechism of the Catholic Church," Part Three, Article 9, Paragraph 3.
[20] See "Declaration of Religious Freedom" #1, Vatican II Documents.

Many in the church are working with this mentality, but I would
like to see our church express more and more the fact that Catholics,
no differently from members of other faiths, have also at times sullied
the truth and the search for truth; how we have sometimes assented
intellectually to a specific ideological or dogmatic point without
linking this assent to a vital way of seeing the relationship of truth
with love. In my interreligious work I have found this particularly
noticeable and at times painful. I firmly believe that a very delicate
issue is how belief in a truth is expressed (as if only one group of believers owned it). The search for truth sets all believers on journeys
that periodically raise questions not easily answered, which therefore
can become apparent or real distortions of the truth.

- *An Examination of Syncretism and Irenicism.* A fifth element to be included in a process for arriving at a safe world order is the issue of
how the church deals with syncretism[21] and irenicism.[22] I thank our
church for clear teachings on this subject, as seen *inter alia* in two recent pontifical letters.[23] In my experience of working with "new age"
groups, with people searching for a personal identity they could not
find in their religion, and so on, I have seen dangerous expressions of
syncretism and irenicism, as, for example, in the "cafeteria" type of
personal religious life that includes a mishmash of different religions;
in an overemphasis on spirituality and a de-emphasis on religion with
its doctrinal teachings; in considering that the Christian religion is
only a cultural expression of a people and not a religious commitment
to discipleship to Christ. I have seen people struggle with the issue of
"the obedience of faith," which at times requires the submission of
one's intelligence and will to God who reveals.[24] In my own personal
life, the more I become involved in interreligious work, the more I
feel the need of the Eucharist, the sharing of Jesus, the enlighten-

---

[21] Syncretism: A combination, reconciliation, or coalescence of varying, often mutually
opposed beliefs, principles, or practices, especially those of various religions, into a new
conglomerate whole typically marked by internal inconsistencies.
[22] Irenics: the doctrine or practice of promoting peace among Christian churches in relation to theological differences.
[23] See the encyclical "Ut Unum Sint" on Ecumenism, May 25, 1995, especially Article 18;
and the apostolic letter "Tertio Millennio Adveniente" of November 10, 1994, especially Article 53.
[24] See "The Catechism of the Catholic Church," Part One, Chapter 3, Article 1.

ment of the Magisterium, the quietness of prayer.

Having said this, I still believe that in this twenty-first century we need a congress on syncretism in which the participants will not just be members of the hierarchy—leaders from different religions, theologians, academicians—but representatives of the common folk who in their daily devotional life may be practicing syncretism or irenicism, even though they do not even know the meaning of the concepts, much less fathom the depth of its consequences.

We need in that congress to ask questions such as: What is syncretism today? Is syncretism a natural consequence of living in a secularized world? Should we see the adoption of different forms of Christianity by indigenous peoples, with their veneration of ancestors and their love of nature, as a form of syncretism? Who is God and who is Jesus? What does Incarnation mean for 6 billion people? What does the fundamental principle put forward at the World Day of Prayer for Peace in Assisi, "to be together to pray but not to pray together," mean in today's stage of interreligious dialogue? What is the connection between prayer and/or meditation and the deepening of the sense of the ultimate Reality?[25] Let no one fear the supernatural power of such a conference on syncretism: it will deepen each one's faith and allow all to enter more deeply into the heart of "the other"; above all it will give an essential element to the future world order that only religions can give.

- *A Clear Teaching on Human Sexuality.* A sixth element for a vibrant contribution of the church to the society of the future is a clear and ever-richer teaching on human sexuality. My work with different religions and with diplomats has convinced me that one of the most important, though difficult, tasks of the church today is to be a bright moral voice on the issue of human sexuality. The discussion of this essential expression of human life has entered the social consciousness of the world as unexpectedly as an erupting volcano.

In recent UN conferences this matter has proven to be one of the most controversial and most debated issues. The church has taken a clearly stated position. The encyclical "Evangelium Vitae" of March 25, 1995, presented, in four illuminating chapters, the teachings of

---

[25] See Pope John Paul II's inaugural address at the World Day of Prayer for Peace in Assisi, October 27, 1986.

the church on all aspects of life, including sexuality. Earlier (November 1, 1983), the church had done the same in the document "Educational Guidance in Human Love." I believe Catholics need to understand this teaching in a spirit of faith. By that same token, I also believe that because this issue has blown into UN conferences with the force of a summer storm for which no one—neither politicians, nor diplomats, nor governments, nor church leaders—was prepared, there has resulted a sense of defensiveness, of limiting the discussion on human sexuality to stands on abortion, etc. rather than inspiring a search for more enlightenment on this issue.

At times I have wished that official representatives of our church at international meetings would show less defensiveness and more understanding of countries, organizations, and individuals holding different opinions. Having said this, it is my belief that, as the new world order takes concrete forms, the church will be looked to as one of the main champions on education for a healthy human sexuality. For this, all church members need to be better educated on all aspects of human sexuality and concentrate more on the long-term respectability of the church's position, rather than reacting defensively or belligerently in order to refute attacks or insults from some international groups who think they alone have the truth in this matter. If the church does not take this long-term approach, I fear there will be many more discussions and debates, and name-calling meetings rather than the meeting of minds, and that this will cause considerable delay in giving the world more future-oriented norms on human sexuality.

These are some basic elements I believe the Catholic Church can contribute, both to help the world define shared global ethics and to add religious components to global governance. These elements need to be discussed, corrected, and, most of all, seen within a broader context of religion and world order. I hope they will also be coupled with contributions from other religions and spiritual traditions.

A Program That Offers One Model for Religion and World Order

The last point of this paper is an offering of the Catholic Church's program to prepare for and celebrate the new millennium. The program is contained in an apostolic letter of Pope John Paul II to members of the

Catholic Church.[26] I believe this letter can be a starting point for the elaboration of an interreligious model on religion and world order.

The apostolic letter is centered, of course, on Jesus Christ. This centering, though, is formulated as a modern presentation of the mystery of Incarnation of the Word to shine forth and illuminate the twenty-first century,[27] and the presentation of a Jubilee 2000 as a hermeneutical key to the Catholic Church's opening of the twenty-first century.[28] The Pope states that we need a vision for the twenty-first century, and he offers one that comes out of "God's intervention in human history."[29] He further states that the world, and the Catholic Church, need purification and a conversion.[30]

The Pope goes on to show how in the Vatican II Council, the church questioned herself and her own identity.[31] He shows, too, how the church followed up on this questioning attitude by organizing special synods in which specific issues were discussed as seen on different continents.[32] He gives guidelines for a new world order. Some of the guidelines are the formulation of doctrine on social teachings against the background of the danger of nuclear war;[33] the validity of the papal journeys; the annual papal messages on peace since 1968. He forcefully points out that the year 2000 requires an examination of conscience for everyone in the Catholic Church.[34] He emphasizes the need for forms of dialogue with different religions, which he calls "circles of dialogue of salvation."[35]

This program is, of course, a Catholic one; for it to be used in a more international and interreligious context, it will have to be coupled with programs from other religions and UN agencies. The program does, though, help people see how to move toward religion and world order.

---

[26] "Tertio Millennium Adveniente," apostolic letter of November 10, 1994, available from Pauline Books and Media, 150 East 52nd Street, New York, NY 10022, USA.

[27] *Ibid.*, articles 1–4.

[28] Article 22.

[29] Article 17.

[30] Article 18.

[31] Article 19.

[32] Article 21.

[33] Article 22.

[34] Article 34.

[35] Article 56.

Islam and Global Governance

Saleha Mahmood-Abedin

Introduction

The close of the twentieth century marks the end of a tumultuous period in the recorded history of the human race. This century has seen the worst of human nature through wars of attrition involving ethnic and racial genocide, religious conflict, and political strife. It has also seen the best of human reason and intellect through phenomenal advancements in learning, science, and technology.

Religion seems to have played a major role in both respects. It has generously contributed to festering social and political conflicts, and in collaboration with race and ethnicity, which usually accompany religious identity, it has made the world witness the bloodiest of human acts and the fiercest of atrocities—well matched by its record in previous centuries, and even exceeding it with the aid of modern technology, which has provided the most efficient instruments of human extermination and mass destruction.

Religion has also been credited with providing the drive and motivation for major social and cultural transformations. The celebrated example in recent history is the Protestant Reformation, which, among other things, generated the proper work ethic, led to the rise of capitalism, facilitated industrialization, and accelerated technological advancement.[1]

---

[1] See Max Weber, *The Theory of Social and Economic Organization* (New York: The Free Press, 1947); see also Hans Gerth and C. Wright Mills, *From Max Weber: Essays in Sociology* (New York: Oxford University Press, 1946).

However, preceding these developments, history records the Golden Age of Islamic civilization, which spanned almost a millennium from the eighth to the eighteenth centuries.[2] As heirs of the Greco-Hellenistic tradition, Muslim scholars synthesized the ancient sciences of the Mediterranean peoples along with Oriental elements from China and India. The flowering of science and civilization in early Islam provided the impetus for European civilization to extricate itself from the Dark Ages and build upon its enriched heritage—a heritage that was preserved through the efforts of Muslim scholars, whose contributions to astronomy, cosmology, geography, natural history, physics, metaphysics, alchemy, and medicine provide the essential foundations of contemporary science. No less significant are their contributions to human sciences such as anthropology, social ethics, history, philosophy, and the philosophy of history. Names such as Al-Farabi, Averroes, Avicenna, Al-Biruni, Ibn al-Haytham, Ibn Khaldun, Rhazes, all remain Newtons in their respective fields.

The Role of Religion. The contemporary phase of phenomenal growth and development in the Western world was ushered in by the combined forces of religious reformation and political, social, and cultural revolution, backed by the values of liberty and equality as the fundamental basis of human rights, individual freedom, and social justice. That today some remain "more equal than others" is a different story. Nevertheless, what Western civilization has achieved so far in science and technology inspires the awe as well as the envy of the rest of the world. In spiritual and religious matters, however, there are lessons to be learned and taught on all sides of the great divides that separate people along religious and denominational lines.

That religion has played a significant role in the development of events that mold the history and character of nations and peoples is without dispute. To what extent its contribution has been positive and to what extent it has added to political strife and social conflict remains a matter of great controversy and begs serious discourse.

The term "religion" in social sciences is often defined in terms of the function it performs. Roberts states, for example, that religion means "to

---

[2] Seyyed Hossein Nasr, *Science and Civilization in Islam*, second edition (Cambridge: The Islamic Text Society, 1987).

unify," "bind together," and "make whole."[3] So, religion is what it does?[4] Government systems, family structures, and economic organizations differ in form and content but more or less serve the same function, providing political stability, personal security and fulfillment, and basic means of sustenance, respectively. Religions differ not only in form and content, but also in their focus on the functions they perform. Some focus on salvation of the soul as the main function and objective of religion (as in Christianity, Hinduism, and Buddhism); others focus on the realization and actualization of the Divine Order, the fulfillment of the Divine Command which forms the main purpose and function of religion (as in Judaism and Islam). This difference in approach has produced different modes of response and adjustment and yielded different worldviews, which in turn would bring distinctive approaches to the issues of global governance.

Religion and World Order. The Religion and World Order Program of Project Global 2000 has courageously taken on the task of inviting religious faith traditions to engage in an exercise of self-evaluation and self-examination with the objective of addressing the challenges faced by all faith communities. These challenges are intensified due to the need for collaboration with secular organizations to participate in promoting education, research, and community projects for the establishment of "a more just, participatory, and ecologically sustainable world order." In this increasingly a-religious world, the conveners of this Conference have reminded us that religion acts both as a cause and catalyst for social change and transformation. They have pointed out that the role of religion has not always been positive in society, and that "organized religion has sometimes been...a powerful force in war and human destructiveness."

However, while defining religion and spirituality as a unitive experience of "the holy," "the ultimate," "the sacred," "the unknowable," they point out that it is also a means of interpreting life, developing morality, and establishing practices which help followers deal with problems of meaning, suffering, and injustice. They rightly maintain that if religion is and does all this, then religion is still relevant to the emerging world or-

---

[3] See Keith A. Roberts, *Religion in Sociological Perspective* (Homewood, Illinois: The Dorsey Press, 1984).

[4] See Milton Yinger, *The Scientific Study of Religion* (New York: Macmillan, 1970), pp. 1–23.

der and in fact forms its deepest core of interest, experience, and concern. I find this position and statement much in harmony with the concept of faith and religion in Islam, where there has never been a tradition of separation between this world and the other world, between sacred and profane, the "world of Caesar" and the "world of Christ." All matters of this world, from the most complex to the most mundane, are subject to religious concerns. In that sense, everything is sacred, and religion is part of everyday life and not a ritual confined to specific acts on specific days. Nevertheless, the French sociologist Emile Durkheim maintained that religious phenomena emerge when a separation is made between the sphere of the profane—the realm of everyday utilitarian activity—and the sphere of the sacred: the numinous and the transcendental. He declared that religion itself is a system of beliefs and practices relating to the sacred.[5] This position, though familiar to Christianity, is very different from the Islamic approach to religion and society.

What Is Islam? Islam is the third and last of the three revealed religions, following Judaism and Christianity. The Qur'an, as revealed to Prophet Mohammed in the seventh century AD, is the bearer of the final message and last revelation from God, according to Muslim belief. The message in the Qur'an is the completion of the earlier messages brought by Moses and Jesus, and neither negates nor contradicts the original messages in their pristine forms.

Further, the root of the word Islam is *silm*, i.e., "peace"—peace with God and man. Islam means surrender to the will of God, and a Muslim is one who submits to His will. The objective of this submission is not as much the personal salvation of the individual believer, but the successful execution of the Divine Plan and the implementation of a just and harmonious social order. Islam is essentially a social religion. All rites, rituals, and religious duties involve a social content and facilitate a social purpose. The five obligations that establish the criteria of a Muslim are:

1. A declaration and acceptance of the oneness of God (*tawheed*) and the Prophethood of Mohammed (*shahada*). The great social significance of *tawheed* is that if God is one, so is all of His creation, and all the messages sent by God through different prophets were true messages—the message brought by Prophet Mohammed being the final message to

---

[5] Emile Durkheim, *The Elementary Forms of Religious Life* (New York: The Free Press, 1954), p. 47.

mankind.

2. Prayer five times a day is a fundamental duty of a Muslim which also has a social role and significance. When the prayer call is made, all Muslims pray at that time wherever they are, and if they go to the mosque to join the congregation for any or all of the five duty prayers they get an additional reward. This is meant to promote unity and solidarity, as well as sociability.[6]

3. The third duty of a Muslim is to pay *zakah* or obligatory charity, generally 2 1/2 percent of one's wealth annually. *Zakah* in Islam is a method of wealth redistribution and a manifestation of believers' concern for their fellow beings and local communities. In general, Muslims are encouraged to be generous and charitable to their family, friends, and society.

4. Fasting from dawn to dusk for 30 days in the month of *Ramadhan* is a great spiritual as well as social reinforcement exercise. Like the time for prayers, the time to start and end fast are predetermined and shared by all in the local community. This enhances a spirit of sharing, generosity, and social solidarity. Although fasting is meant to be a spiritual exercise, its social benefits are manifest to the most casual observer.

5. The fifth duty of a Muslim is to perform pilgrimage to Makkah once in a lifetime, if one can afford to do so. Again, pilgrimage is not a tourist activity engaged in any time of the year; like all other Islamic religious requirements, the *Hajj* has its specific time. Fasting, for example, is performed through the month of *Ramadhan*; prayers are performed at fixed times of the day according to the position of the sun; *zakah* is given out once a year in *Ramadhan*. Pilgrimage is performed during the five days spanning the 8th to the 12th of the month of *Dhul Hijjah*, when pilgrims from around the world gather in the plains of Mina and Arafat, outside Makkah. In recent years the number of pilgrims during the week of *Hajj* has exceeded 2 million, and forms an impressive gathering of Muslims, truly reflecting and celebrating the variety of nations and peoples in Islam.

Strictly speaking, the only "rituals" in Islam are the obligatory prayers five times a day, and the annual pilgrimage to Makkah to perform the *Hajj*. But Islam is more than prayer and pilgrimage. In a sense, all that

---

[6] M. Al Khuli, *The Light of Islam* (Riyadh, Saudi Arabia, 1982).

Muslims do, or ought to do, in their daily lives and dealings with fellow beings remains relevant to religious concerns. In the course of living their daily lives, they constantly face rewards and punishments and encounter prescriptions and proscriptions as laid down through Divine guidance in the revealed text, the Qur'an, in the Traditions of Prophet Mohammed, and in the interpretations of these two sources by learned and informed scholars and individuals.

Islam, therefore, is a religion as well as a way of life that promotes social harmony and solidarity through its sacred texts as well as its traditional and ethical systems and lived experiences. That things have been less than ideal in Islamic societies, as in societies of other faith traditions, is a well-recognized fact of contemporary life. Many theories can be propounded as to what went wrong and how that can be righted. At the end of a momentous era, it is once again appropriate to address this issue.

Islam, Religion, and Society. The Islamic perspective on religion and society differs from others in the sense that religion is not treated as a product of society, as in the social sciences, which explain the origin of religion in man's search for meaning and security and treat it as purely a social phenomenon. In the Islamic perspective, religion precedes life and society itself. God is the Creator of all life and all forms, and has created things with a design and a plan. Man's effort to live in accordance with the requirements of God's plan constitutes religious obligation and expresses his religiosity.

Thus in Islam religion is not simply what it *does*, but what it *is*. Essentially, it is surrender and submission to the will of God. Religion antecedes man and society. Religion is not the creation of man's imagination, nor is it a social creation, nor simply, as in Durkheim's words, "society divinized."[7] In Islam, religion is that blueprint, that grand design which has been formulated by the Creator and Sustainer of all, the Lord of heavens and earth, Who alone is responsible for the emergence and existence of all phenomena known and unknown to human beings with their limited powers of observation and comprehension.

Marett claims that ritual and emotion are primary to religion, and belief is only secondary.[8] To this idea Kluckhon adds that emphasis on

---

[7] Lewis A. Coser, *Masters of Sociological Thought* (New York: Harcourt Brace Jovanovich, 1977), p. 138.

[8] R.R. Marett, in *The Threshold of Religion* (London: Methuen, 1914), p. XXXI.

belief is a Western bias.[9] In Orthodox Islam, however, ritual is minimal, emotion is certainly not the primary accompaniment of the religious experience, but belief is central to the entire exercise of faith. A Muslim's declaration of his belief in God and His Omniscience is the defining moment that bestows on him his religious identity. Belief, therefore, is central in Islamic faith.

Niebuhr points out that all belief systems, such as nationalism or science, are religions, but they are inferior systems.[10] Islam, on the other hand, starts with faith and spirituality and culminates in belief: I have faith and so I believe. Niebuhr's "belief systems" operate at the cognitive level (of beliefs) and only secondarily generate the emotive state of faith. As I understand Islam, it starts with the premise of faith from which will flow beliefs, rituals, and emotions. Thus in Islam the component of faith and spirituality is central to its character and concerns.

Patricia Mische, in her introduction to this volume, refers to Toynbee's conclusions about the importance of spirituality and religion in the rise and fall of civilizations. Earlier, Auguste Comte also alerted us to the dangers and difficulties of transition from one stage to another through theological, metaphysical, and positive stages under his "Law of Human Progress." It would be a mistake, Comte asserted, to expect the new social order to emerge smoothly from the throes of the preceding order.[11] Contemporary history has reaffirmed the tribulations encountered by societies in transition. Comte recognizes the increasing diversity and complexity spurred by population growth and division of labor as powerful instruments of social progress.[12] These changes are taking place everywhere, affecting peoples of all faith communities and creating for them singular challenges in the context of their respective traditions.

Working Toward a Shared Global Ethic

The creation of a peaceful, equitable, and sustainable future is not just a matter of economy, planning, and politics. Without the infusion of the

---

[9] Clyde Kluckhon, "Myths and Rituals: A General Theory" in *Reader in Comparative Religion: An Anthropological Approach*, 3rd ed., William A. Less and Evon Z. Vogt, eds. (New York: Harper & Row, 1972).

[10] See H. Richard Niebuhr, "Faith in God and in Gods," in *Radical Monotheism and Western Culture* (New York: Harper & Row, 1960), pp. 114–126.

[11] Lewis Coser, *op. cit.*, p. 8.

[12] *Ibid.*

ethical and the spiritual, the entire edifice will crumble and deteriorate. So how do we bring spirituality back into the central arena? The question is difficult to address across the board, purportedly covering the entire spectrum of faith traditions. Perhaps the best results will be obtained when each faith tradition approaches this as a home mission and works at the problem from within.

However, the increasing heterogeneity created by burgeoning populations and greater geographic mobility, and the sharpened sensitivities toward roots and identities in an increasingly pasteurized and homogenized world at the mercy of the multimedia, make the task of addressing the spiritual and the moral even more challenging. Never in history was there greater awareness of the variety in races and nations, and never before was the vast segment of humanity exposed so graphically to man's inhumanity to man, conveyed vividly in tabloids and on television screens in living rooms across North and West, and in community huts and tea-shops across South and East. We see more and yet remain ignorant; we are surrounded and yet remain alone. The alienation in modern urban society, the sense of frustration and deprivation among the majority of the world's peoples and communities, has created an atmosphere of alarm, distress, and distrust. Humankind was never so advanced technologically and affluent materially, yet it was perhaps also never so ravaged emotionally and impoverished spiritually.

This is indeed the time for us to ring the alarm bells. It is appropriate that we use the turn of the century and the beginning of the new millennium as an excuse to take account of ourselves and come up with "new millennium's resolutions" that are not only serious but also sustainable.

We have been asked to address five important issues in the context of our respective sacred texts, ethical systems, teachings, traditions, history, and lived experience. A fair and comprehensive discussion of these issues is indeed a tall order; it would take volumes to address each one in the six wide and varied contexts identified above. I will briefly state some introductory points reflecting the Islamic perspective, focusing on the sacred text of Islam, the Qur'an, although my paper will not even approach a definitive statement of the Islamic position.

Peace and Security

The very word "Islam" denotes peace. Islam also means submission to the Divine Will and, by derivation, submission to the Rule of Law. The Holy

Qur'an in numerous verses exhorts believers to refrain from war and violence. The Qur'an encourages peace; the only war that is encouraged is the war of defense to protect faith and religion, person and property, and only if threatened with aggression. The Qur'an says:

> God only forbids you to turn in friendship towards such as fight against you because of [your] faith, and drive you forth from your homelands, or aid [others] in driving you forth. (Qur'an: 60:9)

> And fight in God's cause against those who wage war against you, but do not commit aggression—for, verily, God does not love aggressors. (Qur'an: 2:190)

> But if they incline to peace, incline thou to it as well, and place thy trust in God: verily, He alone is all-hearing, all-knowing! (Qur'an: 8:61)

The misuse of the word *jihad* as a holy war of conquest and aggression must be rectified. The Arabic word *jihad* literally means "struggle," either in physical terms as in war and political conflict, or, more importantly, against sin and oppression, greed and exploitation—a struggle with one's base spirits. There is much encouragement in the Qur'an as well as in the Traditions of the Prophet to engage in this latter kind of *jihad*.

Respect for human life and personal property is the fundamental ethical principle of Islam. It teaches respect for sanctity of the home and privacy of the individual. The Qur'an instructs even members of the family to:

> ...ask leave of you [before intruding upon your privacy]. (Qur'an 24:58)

The Qur'an recognizes the individual's right to ownership of property and specifies clear measures for the transfer of property among family members and between individuals and communities. Islam is particularly careful about ensuring accuracy and justice in all forms of transactions, and ensures this through prescribed means, for example, witnessing and documentation. The Qur'an says:

> O you who have attained to faith! Whenever you give or take credit for a stated term, set it down in writing. And let a scribe write it down equitably between you; and no scribe refuse to write as God has taught him: thus shall he write. And let him who contracts the debt dictate; and let him be conscious of God, his Sustainer, and not weaken anything of his undertaking. And if he who contracts the debt is weak of mind or body, or is not able to dictate himself, then let him who watches over his interests dictate equitably. And call upon two of your men to act as witnesses. (Qur'an 2:282)

The fairness of a deal is further ensured by requiring the witness to agree to witness a transaction only if it is fair, just, and legal.

The two most sensitive areas of human relations are political conflict leading to aggression, and war and economic exchange leading to exploitative transactions. Together they form the most nagging source of inter-group conflict. Application of the Islamic principles to maintain peace, obey the law, and respect the sanctity of individual privacy and personal property will certainly contribute to an atmosphere of tranquillity, peace, and security in society.

Economic and Social Justice

Islam is not just a religion, but a way of life which represents a complete system encompassing the social, the private, and the individual. In Islam all humankind is but one community, and as such it shares common interests and concerns. The individual, however, is guaranteed rights and freedoms "in accordance with the principles of social responsibility and solidarity as stipulated by the Islamic law."[13] However, the Qur'an places on the individual the responsibility to maintain truth and social justice. As the Qur'an says:

> O you who have attained to faith! Be ever steadfast in upholding equity, bearing witness to the truth for the sake of God, even though it be against your own selves or your parents and kinsfolk. Whether the person concerned be rich or poor, God's claim takes precedence over [the claims of] either of them. Do not, then, follow your own desires, lest you swerve from justice: for if you distort [the truth], behold, God is indeed aware of all that you do! (Qur'an 4:135)

Provisions in the Qur'an and the Traditions of the Prophet, from which Islamic jurisprudence is derived, cover all aspects of the economic system, which is founded on the combined principles of free enterprise, individual responsibility, and social justice. For example, Islam explicitly prohibits usury and other methods of obtaining wealth that are exploitative and speculative. It also prohibits gambling and games of chance. The Qur'an says:

> O you who have attained to faith! Intoxicants, and games of chance, and idolatrous practices, and the divining of the future are but a loathsome evil of Satan's doing. Shun it, then, so that you might attain to a happy state! (Qur'an 5:90)

In the Islamic economic system, all gains should accrue from personal

---

[13] International Commission of Jurists, *Human Right in Islam* (Morocco: 1982).

effort or hard work, or as a result of risk-taking in investment. Guaranteed return is seen as exploitative and is forbidden. This is a confirmation of Islam's deep regard for the principle of social justice.

Islam respects individual rights of property ownership and encourages gainful employment to ensure comfortable living for oneself and one's family. However, Islam prohibits hoarding of wealth, and adopts measures through *zakah* and charity, and through encouraging generosity, to redistribute wealth. The Qur'an says:

> Believe in God and His apostle, and spend on others out of that of which He has made you trustees. For those of you who have attained to faith and who spend freely [in God's cause] shall have a great reward. (Qur'an 57:7)

It is the fundamental duty of the Islamic state to ensure that these basic economic principles are enforced and respected. The state must supervise the market to prevent and eliminate economic crimes and exploitation. Murad Hoffman points out that "Islam may be...the only ideology which brings the individual and the state into a balanced relationship."[14]

Islam is also perhaps the only religion that constantly relates the here and the hereafter, and measures piety not only in terms of worship but also in terms of service to humanity. The Qur'an says:

> True piety does not consist in turning your faces towards the east or the west—but truly pious is he who believes in God, and the Last Day, and the angels, and revelation, and the prophets, and spends his substance—however much he himself may cherish it—upon his near of kin, and the orphans, and the needy, and the wayfarer, and the beggars, and for freeing of human beings from bondage, and is constant in prayer, and renders the purifying dues, and truly pious are they who keep their promises whenever they promise and are patient in misfortune and hardship and in time of peril: it is they that have proved themselves true, and it is they, they who are conscious of God. (Qur'an 2:177)

Social justice remains central to a system that treats the individual as an integral part of the symbiotic community. The Prophet said that the *ummah*, or community of believers, is like one body: if one part suffers, the whole also suffers the pain and injury. Social justice is the best insurance against social malaise. If individuals are treated justly and fairly, society will derive the direct benefit in terms of social peace and harmony.

The fundamental basis of justice is equality and equity. Equality of

---

[14] Murad Hoffman, *Islam the Alternative* (Reading: Garnet Publishing, 1993), p. 101.

individuals is assumed to be the norm in Islam. Although God has created different nations and peoples, they are all on the same level in the degree of their humanity. One individual is superior to another only in their degree of piety and closeness to God. The Qur'an says:

> ...Behold, We have created you all out of a male and a female, and have made you into nations and tribes, so that you might come to know one another. Verily, the noblest of you in the sight of God is the one who is most deeply conscious of Him. Behold, God is all-knowing, all-aware. (Qur'an 49:13)

There is no superiority of one person over another, of the rich over the poor, one social class over another, or one race over another. All people are equal in the eyes of God; only those who excel in piety and charity and work in the cause of Allah are the successful ones, and theirs will be the best rewards.

Human Rights

Islam accords much emphasis to human rights as the basis of social solidarity as well as stability. No society can prosper or be harmonious without giving adequate attention to the protection and preservation of human rights. Islam teaches that all human beings have the right to life at conception, and, after birth, a right to full opportunities to lead a rewarding and satisfying life. God says in the Qur'an:

> Are you not aware that God has made subservient to you all that is in the heavens and all that is on earth, and has lavished upon you His blessings, both outward and inward? (Qur'an 31:20)

> And He has made subservient to you, [as a gift] from Himself, all that is in the heavens and on earth: in this, behold, there are signs indeed for people who think! (Qur'an 45:13)

> ...and do not kill your children for fear of poverty—[for] it is We who shall provide sustenance for you as well as for them. (Qur'an 6:151)

Even in matters such as the selection of a name, parents are instructed to choose the best name with the best meaning with which to address the newborn. The child has the right to proper care and nurturing, to education and schooling. As an adult, each individual has the right to earn a living and own property, which he or she may inherit or acquire through personal effort such as trade or other forms of legitimate acquisition. Yet rights come with responsibilities. The Qur'an warns:

> [On the Day of Judgment,] every human being will be held in pledge for what-
> ever [evil] he has wrought. (Qur'an 74:38)

Each person is responsible for himself, yet each person is like a shep-
herd to his flock, responsible for its welfare—encouraging others to do
good and discouraging them from doing that which is harmful and prohibited. The Qur'an says:

> And [as for] the believers, both men and women—they are protectors of one
> another: they [all] enjoin the doing of what is right and forbid the doing of what
> is wrong, and are constant in prayer, and render the purifying dues, and pay
> heed unto God and His Apostle. It is they upon whom God will bestow His
> grace: verily, God is almighty, wise! (Qur'an 9:71)

Islam laid down a charter of human rights 14 centuries earlier than
the contemporary Universal Declaration of Human Rights. However,
human rights in Islam are not just based on human nature, or established
through human reasoning which hammers out a system of "just" and
"fair" rights. In Islam, human rights are bestowed by God on humans and
are inalienable as well as irrevocable. These rights are not obtained after
a struggle: they are given as a birthright. However, as in the system of
negative marking, some of these rights are taken away by state and society in violation of the principle of justice and respect for the rights of man
as guaranteed by God, which forms the fundamental basis of true spirituality in Islam.

Islam tells us that every person is born free in the *fitrah* or pure state
of nature. The individual's right to freedom is sacred, unless he or she
violates the law of God or desecrates the rights of others. There is no
concept of original sin in Islam. Every child is born pure and clean. He or
she does not inherit inferiority because of ancestry, social class, religion,
or ethnicity. The Islamic concept of individual freedom is based on the
principle that (1) human conscience is subject to God only, to Whom
every man is directly responsible; (2) there is personal accountability for
all of one's deeds, and the actor alone is responsible for the consequences, derives the rewards, and receives punishment; (3) God has
delegated to humans the responsibility to decide for themselves and make
rational choices, for humans are free agents, endowed with free will, and
that is why, unlike the angels, they remain accountable for their deeds.

These are the natural rights of humans, which constitute their moral
prerogative. Within this framework of Islam, religious persecution and
class and social conflict have little room to operate. The related concept

of equality of all human beings ensures freedom and justice for all.

The respect for leadership and the right to free expression, as well as the necessity for consultation, provided the model for participatory government of the people by the *shoura* (consultation) method. This form of government ensures democratic exercise of human rights and civil liberties. The Qur'an says:

> O' you who have attained to faith! Pay heed unto God, and pay heed unto the Apostle and unto those from among you who have been entrusted with authority. (Qur'an 4:59)

> Make due allowance for man's nature, and enjoin the doing of what is right; and leave alone all those who choose to remain ignorant. (Qur'an 7:199)

God tells us in the Qur'an that the more enduring reward of the hereafter will be given to those who:

> ...are constant in prayer; and whose rule [in all matters of common concern] is consultation among themselves. (Qur'an 42:38)

Indeed, women's rights are human rights, which are also Islamic rights. Fourteen centuries ago, Islam bestowed special rights and privileges on women, including economic and conjugal rights. But these rights come with special responsibilities, which have often been applied selectively and oppressively by society's vested interest groups. In Islam itself, in matters of faith and spirituality, economic justice, and individual rights and freedoms, there is the principle of equity and, wherever applicable, equality between men and women. The Qur'an says:

> Men shall have a share in what parents and kinsfolk leave behind, and women shall have a share in what parents and kinsfolk leave behind, whether it be little or much—a share ordained [by God]. (Qur'an 4:7)

> ...the rights of the wives [with regard to their husbands] are equal to the [husband's] rights with regard to them. (Qur'an 2:228)

That Muslim women remain deprived of these rights is part of the universal story of gender discrimination worldwide. Islam gave women the right to property ownership, inheritance, freedom of speech, and participation in the economy, in addition to specific conjugal rights, at a time when these were unthinkable under other faith traditions. However, as with most of their counterparts, Muslim women remain deprived of their rights because of their own general backwardness and lack of education, which renders them incapable of understanding, let alone demanding, their rights—thus excluding them from active participation in economic, civic, or political spheres.

Islam specifically identifies the rights of the child, and makes not only the parents but the community and the society responsible for securing adequate maintenance, education, and welfare. Islam surely recognizes that "it takes a village to raise a child"; however, Islam also places specific responsibilities on the child, especially in regard to matters of religious practice (from which the child is not exempt) and parental respect and obedience (for which the child is duly responsible).

The rights of non-Muslims living in Islamic societies (al dhimmi) are also identified specifically and elaborately. The Islamic state is to guarantee the freedom and protection of all ahl al dhimma with full respect for their religion and social and cultural heritage, as well as their rights to own property, engage in business, and make a living, and their freedom of movement and liberty.

Contrary to current media misrepresentation, Islam has never lent itself to large-scale religious persecution, nor has any Islamic country through history engaged in religious/ethnic "cleansing"—though they have frequently been the victims of genocide, such as lately in Bosnia, Chechnya, and Eastern Turkistan, among others. Perhaps the main reason that the image of violence has become associated with Islam and Muslims today is the deliberate and popular use of the term "Islamic fundamentalism." This term is both applied to, and self-applied by, groups that are nothing more than political/ideological factions comprised of extremists and terrorists who use the cloak of Islam to achieve, so they think, an air of legitimacy. These groups have done the most harm to Islam's image in the contemporary world. Similar groups and movements are found in almost all other major religions today but, for reasons too complex to get into here, have not had equally damaging consequences for the reputations of their faith traditions.

Ecological Sustainability

Human ownership of land, natural resources, and all material property is based on the Islamic principle that ultimate ownership belongs to God alone. The Qur'an says:

> Unto God belongs all that is in the heavens and on earth. Verily, God alone is self-sufficient, the One to whom all praise is due! (Qur'an 31:26)

All that is in the heavens and on earth extols God's limitless glory: for He alone is almighty, truly wise! His is the dominion over the heavens and the earth; He grants life and deals death; and He has the power to will anything. He is the First and the Last, and the Outward as well as the Inward: and he has full knowledge of everything. He it is who has created the heavens and the earth in six eons, and is established on the throne of His almightiness. He knows all that enters the earth, and all that comes out of it, as well as all that descends from the skies, and all that ascends to them. And He is with you wherever you may be; and God sees all that you do. His is the dominion over the heavens and the earth; and all things go back unto God [as their source]. He makes the night grow longer by shortening the day, and makes the day grow longer by shortening the night; and He has full knowledge of what is in the hearts [of humans]. (Qur'an 57:1–6)

People's right to ownership is legitimized through proper means of acquisition (inheritance, work, or risk-taking) but restricted to the extent that their use of their own property does not permanently damage or deplete the resources.

Here indeed is the earliest expression of concern for sustainable development and conservation of resources that guides the entire approach of Islam to economy, society, environment, and resources. The Qur'an teaches the importance of respecting the environment and the natural resources which humans may use for their benefit, but only to the extent that they satisfy legitimate needs and are not consumed in excess or acquired through unfair means. While encouraging the "good life" for believers, the Qur'an also emphasizes moderation in consumption. The Qur'an says:

Children of Adam! Beautify yourselves for every act of worship, and eat and drink [freely], but do not waste: verily, He does not love the wasteful! (Qur'an 7:31)
...and who, whenever they spend on others, are neither wasteful nor niggardly but [remember that] there is always a just mean between those [two extremes]. (Qur'an 25:67)

In fact, discouraging both miserliness and excesses of generosity, the Qur'an admonishes:

And neither allow thy hand to remain shackled to thy neck, nor stretch it forth to the utmost limit [of thy capacity], lest thou find thyself blamed [by thy dependents], or even destitute. (Qur'an 17:29)

Islam recognizes the importance of environmental safety and protection. Maintaining a clean environment is the basic civic duty of believers which will contribute to pollution control and a healthier environment. The Prophet encouraged the planting of trees, the preservation and conservation of resources, the careful use of water and other environmental resources, and safety in the environment when he described acts such as the removal of a harmful object from the way of the people, as charity worthy of Allah's reward. However, the principle of balance and moderation remains central to Islamic teachings.

Man is neither deified with perfect qualities nor vilified as base and sinful. Furthermore, Islam rejects hedonism as well as asceticism. Islam is not concerned primarily with this world (secular) or with the other world (sacred). It addresses itself to both the human condition here and human destiny in the hereafter. The Qur'an says:

> Seek instead, by means of what God has granted thee, [the good of] the life to come, without forgetting, withal, thine own [rightful] share in this world, and do good [unto others] as God has done good unto thee; and seek not to spread corruption on earth: for, verily, God does not love the spreaders of corruption! (Qur'an 28:77)

It would devalue life on earth only relative to life in the hereafter,[15] which is everlasting and where the rewards are even greater. God says in the Qur'an:

> Behold how we bestow [on earth] more bounty on some of them than on others: but [remember that] the life to come will be far higher in degree and far greater in merit and bounty. (Qur'an 17:21)

Humans hold the vice-regency of God on earth (Qur'an 2:30). They are therefore responsible for the protection and preservation of that which has been entrusted to them by God. All life is to be respected, so there is no hunting or killing of animals or keeping them in captivity for pleasure and profit. Waste is to be avoided and so is excessive use of resources. The Prophet advised Muslims to consume in moderation, yet without self-denial. Humans are not to forgo the good things of life that God has provided for them. The Qur'an says:

> Say: Who hath forbidden the beautiful (gifts) of God, for his servants, and the things, clean and pure, (which He hath provided) for sustenance? Say: they are, in the life of this world, for those who believe, (and) purely for them on the day of Judgment. (Qur'an 7:32)

---

[15] Hammudah Abdalati, *Islam in Focus* (Indianapolis, Indiana: Islamic Teaching Center, 1977), p. 50.

However, natural resources such as air, water, and minerals from the soil cannot be the private property of the individual, but may be leased from the state, which is to oversee the fair and proper use of these resources, with particular care for conservation and preservation of diminishing resources. These Islamic injunctions to the faithful provide the first principles of "sustainable development" as they facilitate the maintenance of a healthy environment and a prosperous and peaceful society.

Cultural Identity and Integrity

Islam recognizes the variety and differences among nations and peoples and accords no superiority to one over another, for all people are the creation of God and are deserving of equal respect. Islam does not extol uniformity, and in fact celebrates differences among peoples as signs of God's power of creation. The Qur'an says:

> And among His signs is the creation of the heavens and the earth, and the variations in your languages and your colors: verily in that are signs for those who know. (Qur'an 30:22)

In this context, Muslims are even encouraged to marry outside their immediate community so that it will help extend their circle of social contacts, expand their knowledge of different cultures and peoples, and increase access to wider resources. However, all religions are to be respected and all places of worship protected and treated with dignity and care. The Qur'an instructs Muslims to make the following declaration:

> Say: "We believe in God, and in that which has been revealed to us, and what was revealed to Abraham, Ishmael, Isaac, Jacob, and the tribes, and in (the Books) given to Moses, Jesus, and the prophets from their Lord: we make no distinction between one and another among them, and to God do we bow our will (in Islam)." (Qur'an 3:84)

All men come from the same source and are the beneficiaries of guidance from their Creator. All people who obey God and do good deeds will be rewarded. Heaven is not just reserved for good Muslims, but is available to:

> Those who believe [the Muslim] and those who are Jews, Christians and Sabeans—all who believe in God and the Last Day and do righteous deeds shall have their reward with their Sustainer; and no fear need they have, and neither shall they grieve. (Qur'an 2:62)

Variations of culture and language are to be respected and celebrated, not despised and eradicated. Islam does not enforce or encourage uniformity in outward expressions of cultural forms. There is no mark, symbol, dress, or form that designates Islam or Muslims. The message is eternal and universal for all humankind and not for a particular people at a particular time. Since no one cultural form is recognized as superior or dominant, all cultures are respected as legitimate and wholesome—as long as they neither threaten nor violate the universal principles of faith. People of different cultures are not to be challenged or confronted unless they violate the Divine laws. And even then, Muslims are asked to tell them, "To you your religion and to me mine" (Qur'an 109:6). Because as God says in the Qur'an: "Let there be no compulsion in religion" (Qur'an 2:256).

The Qur'an also lays down the general principle to guide Muslims in their choice of conduct:

> Help one another in righteousness and piety, but help not one another in sin and rancor. (Qur'an 5:2)

This principle allows Muslims as believers to cooperate in any effort toward the promotion of the good that will enhance peace, tranquillity, harmony, and enrichment of the quality of life in society.

Working Toward Global Governance

Trends in contemporary society clearly indicate that there will be far-reaching changes in the way we live and organize ourselves. With the shrinking and crowded globe resulting from technological advancement and population proliferation, not only have our problems intensified, they have also multiplied and spread across regions and continents without respecting state boundaries, national sovereignty, and territoriality. The world is indeed a global village. Within this wider playing field, game plans designed with a localized and limited perspective may have to be revised and adapted. The Islamic tradition, in spirit as well as in practice, has always been global. As a universal religion neither confined to a nation or people nor restricted to a single issue, message, or individual personality, Islam taught universal values and principles that are applicable to all people at all times.

Global Civic Society

The Islamic value of respect for the law and obedience to the highest authority provides the ethos and the environment for a global civic society. The criteria for global citizenship fit the criteria of the believer who accepts the will of God, obeys that will, seeks to understand to his or her best reasoning ability the relevant rules and obligations, and attempts to fulfill these obligations and achieve the accompanying privileges to the best of his or her ability. Faith, then, would be the ultimate criterion for effective global citizenship. Faith facilitates our understanding and acceptance of our duties as members of a community and citizens of a global society.

Global Structures and Systems

The Islamic concept of *ummah* (the community of believers) is truly a global concept which provides a global structure to operationalize a civic society. The *ummah* in Islam is not fractured by national boundaries and territorial sovereignty. It is not exclusive to particular peoples, races, or classes. The only criterion for membership in the *ummah* is one's adherence to the Islamic faith. With such a tradition of universality, extending beyond Islam to reach out to peoples of all other faith traditions is but an exercise on familiar territory; for if one can transcend all barriers of language, culture, and lifestyle and discover the essence of unity and brotherhood in Islam, one can move further and stretch to include all humankind, which the Qur'an tells us was initially one, and only later developed differences in views and approaches. Furthermore, the *ummah* is not supposed to be inward-looking; it is recognized to be part of a global community, and relations with this larger community are valued and recognized through clear instructions on dealing with it in political, economic, and social matters.

Local Initiatives

Local initiatives are essential to the success of any form of global governance. The establishment of local mosques in every neighborhood, where people congregate on a daily basis, is the basic structural design for providing opportunities for "bottom-up" initiatives to launch programs of community welfare. The mosques have traditionally been the centers of learning and social services, as well as civic and social activities.

On a transnational level and among countries of differing faith traditions, the local communities of citizens' welfare groups based in mosques, churches, temples, and synagogues can cooperate and develop a program of activities to be implemented within the limits of their immediate resources and shared with other communities interlinked by economic, political, or environmental interdependencies. Some of the most active and effective grassroots organizations have been operational at this level. They can link up together to form a global chain and thus serve the larger humanity.

Balancing Tensions

Balancing tensions should come easily under Islam, for it is a religion of "the middle way" which teaches moderation. It provides safeguards for the protection of individual good, without sacrificing the common good. What is good for all will be good for the individual, but what is good for the individual may not be good for all. Yet the individual's right to his or her own good is not denied as long as its exercising does not deprive others of their rights nor affect the common good. Rights in Islam are always in direct relation to one's obligations and responsibilities, for Islam recognizes the basic logical principle that one person's rights are derived through the fulfillment of obligations on the part of another. Thus, in order to obtain our rights, we have to fulfill our responsibilities, which are essentially the rights of others in worldly matters, and the rights of God in matters of faith and spirituality.

The private sector is that aspect of the economy operating on resources invested by individuals, in which capital belongs to the individual, and risks and benefits also accrue to the owner/s of the capital. The public sector has at stake public funds raised through taxes or other income generated by the civic authority. Islam encourages individuals (i.e., the private sector) to operate in such a way that the public sector also benefits. Circulation of funds and resources is encouraged to keep money moving from private to public domains through donations, gifts, investments, and the payment of obligatory charity, the zakah. The capital thus generated will come back to the individual through trade and earned wages, thus reentering the private sector. Thus, a healthy circulation is maintained in the movement of resources between the two sector domains.

Long-term gain is always the preferred target in all faith traditions that teach believers to wait for their reward till after the day of judgment. Short-term objectives may appear as a result of preexisting need, and may be facilitated by the availability of resources and the immediacy of choices. Yet again a balance is needed in drawing up priorities in the face of limited resources. Economic and environmental needs may at times clash, and immediate economic returns take precedence over environmental concerns. However, Islam prohibits the exploitation or irretrievable depletion of the environment for the purpose of deriving any immediate economic benefit. Economic needs may be rationally assessed and met through the exercise of moderation in consumption, effective planning, and proper distribution. Any activity that ignores environmental interests and concerns will bring long-term difficulties, even in economic terms.

The concept of sovereignty in Islam is subject to the basic principle that all sovereignty belongs to God. All positions of authority derive their mandate from the legitimacy of their position and should be allowed the legitimate exercise of power as long as they carry out the covenant. The hierarchy of authority in the social context operates on the principle of justice and reciprocity as well as accountability. As in the domains of public versus private interest and individual versus common good, which are not mutually exclusive and are often interrelated, each higher level of sovereignty should not deny the legitimacy and authority of lower levels, even though it may supersede them on the principle of the common good being larger than the individual good; it should still restrain itself from denying or exploiting the lower level for fear of the highest authority, which in all matters belongs to Allah alone, to Whom all are accountable.

Religious Resources for Global Governance

The suggestion to use schools, research institutions, media, publications, community-based networks, and professional associations as "religious resources for global governance" is based on the premise of the separation of religion from these social structures. In the Islamic system, these social institutions will have built-in religious content. Therefore, instead of being consciously used as a religious resource, they will be recognized in their own right as the bearers and conveyers of the religious message. This message is based on the concepts of the sovereignty of God the Creator, the equality of his creation, and the principle of balance and justice to govern all human affairs.

Collaborating with the United Nations
and Its Specialized Agencies

Perhaps one major difficulty in working with the present setup at the UN is that it is not very hospitable to the global perspective. The UN is an organization of states, not of nations, and to the extent that it operates within the clearly defined principles of state sovereignty, it remains restricted in its ability to support and sustain issues that are not neatly confined to state boundaries. Environmental issues, for example, and those relating to health matters such as outbreaks of disease, are not always contained by the border guards within national boundaries. Similarly, cultural, faith, and religious traditions are not neatly confined, though some states may even claim religion as their *raison d'être*. Often, peoples of one faith sharing a common ethnic origin, language, and cultural tradition are separated by artificial state boundaries.

Furthermore, the state has acquired an authority and superiority to which all matters are subordinated. Moral principles, human lives, bilateral and multilateral relations are sacrificed to satisfy the interests of the state as perceived by its current leadership. The principle of state sovereignty has done much to contribute to the present-day global crises, where problems and solutions are complicated by rigid and often artificial divisions and become insurmountable due to national pride or considerations of "national security."

To operate on a global scale, we need to come up with parallel networks where nongovernmental organizations will come together and operate more or less free of the United Nations, which is bound by its own charter that recognizes the principle of state sovereignty and accepts the legitimacy of national self-interest. To ensure the kind of moral and spiritual transformation that is needed to bring long-lasting peace and security to the world community, we need newer instruments that will operate on a global scale and address issues raised above the mundane affairs of national governments. What is perhaps needed now is a massive interfaith effort to bring the people of the world together to devise plans and strategies that will enable us to enter the next millennium with the attitudes and motivations necessary to ensure the establishment of a just, moral, and peaceful world order.

We have seen, recently and repeatedly, the difficulties faced by the United Nations in resolving international conflict, and its inability to take effective moral positions on numerous current international issues.

We have also seen the failure of nation-states to provide peace to their regions and prosperity to their citizens. Economic hardships have intensified; war and conflict are rampant on the world scene; health is a major concern in all parts of the globe. Even the education system has failed to reach all segments in most societies, and has proved sorely incapable of providing even minimum skills, let alone the kind of preparation that will enable the individual and the community to face the rising challenges of the coming age.

Thus, it is now the turn of religion to shake off the inertia that set in after its engagement in centuries of interreligious conflict, which dictated economics and politics on the world scene. Today we need the moral authority, the spiritual strength that religion can impart, to launch an effort to "save the world" with vigor and confidence. Transcending state boundaries, religion and spirituality could penetrate to the very grassroots from where all wider movements draw strength. Thus, to supplement the United Nations' Herculean efforts to bring the states together and pool their resources, I would suggest the establishment of a parallel global organization to bring together representatives of different religious traditions, who would deliberate on matters of policy and planning and make recommendations for implementation by national governments on the basis of the moral and ethical standards upheld by the various faith traditions.

Conclusion

What is needed today is the moral authority of religion. The nation-states have shown their moral bankruptcy, though there are stirrings of concern among some "secular" national leaders. Unless religion and state come together and work hand in hand, the world will continue to see the accelerating deterioration of the world order, and while in our generation we still may anticipate the coming of the millennium with enthusiasm, our children may not be in such a positive frame of mind in welcoming the next century, unless we undertake some serious correctional measures here and now.

I suggest the establishment of a permanent world body comprising the leadership of the various faith traditions, which may be called (for lack of a more original name) the Parliament of World Religions. This Parliament will have a formal organizational structure through which it will perform an advisory function for national governments; but it will

also have an active executive board engaged in deliberating issues of policy, formulating and evaluating platforms for action, and coordinating the
activities of organizations such as those engaged in welfare, relief, and
charity work, which are traditionally related to religious institutions.

The mandate of this Parliament should be truly global. The Vatican
and other Christian churches, for example, have an excellent track record
in the promotion of welfare and charity work around the world. Though
generally a part of their evangelical mission, this kind of network of activity can be focused mainly on the betterment of the human condition,
irrespective of conversion rates. If all religions come to accept one another as legitimate systems of belief, recognizing that each person is entitled to hold his or her own beliefs according to individual convictions and
understanding, these efforts will be less aggressive and the world will be
more peaceful. If religions downsized their focus on winning converts and
upgraded their programs for welfare and the betterment of humanity, the
world would not only be more peaceful, but also more just and moral.

The world today needs a system of checks and balances. Democratic
governments have recognized this principle from their inception, but they
uphold it within the confines of their states and apply it to their national
constitutions, where these exist. In interstate matters there is a degree of
arrogance and self-centeredness, usually justified on the principle of national sovereignty, which would otherwise be unacceptable on the individual level and condemned as improper, immoral, unjust, or even
criminal. Nation-states are literally getting away with murder, and the
larger the numbers involved, the greater their impunity.[16]

It is becoming increasingly clear that nation-states cannot monitor
themselves, and certainly, in this post-bipolar world, cannot police each
other. On the global level there is a power vacuum that can only be filled
by a different type of authority, a higher order, represented by religion,
which can introduce an element of moral and spiritual concerns into
matters that secular organizational structures such as sovereign states and
their instruments have increasingly failed to address.

The issues in the twenty-first century will be qualitative in nature

---

[16] Francis Boyle quotes former Bosnian Prime Minister Haris Silajdzic, "If you kill one
person you are prosecuted; if you kill ten people you are a celebrity; if you kill a quarter-
of-a-million people you are invited to a peace conference." See Boyle, "Is Bosnia the End
of the Road for the United Nations?" in *Journal of Muslim Minority Affairs*, Vol. 17:2,
Oct. 1997.

and not quantitative. It is no longer a matter of how much change but what kind of change—for major change there will be. Policy decisions in the future will increasingly be moral decisions, in terms of their prioritization as well as their applications and consequences. Global governance will then be not just an ideal, but a necessity that will ensure our survival even in the foreseeable future. Indeed, religion and spirituality have an increasingly important role to play in stabilizing the world in the twenty-first century, and the sooner this is realized, the sooner the world can be on its way to achieving prosperity, justice, and peace.

Islamic Revivalism: A Global Perspective

Abdul Aziz Said and Nathan C. Funk

A t the dawn of the twenty-first century, we find ourselves in the midst of a global tectonic shift. The old order of industrial capitalism and monolithic nation-states is undergoing a transformation, and we do not yet know if the emergent post-industrial order will be a boon or a burden for humanity. We witness a continuing tendency toward market-driven transmutation of culture, in which a free-market economy is perceived to be the only road to democratic society and human flourishing, even as ethnic conflict and various forms of communalism reassert themselves throughout the world.

Economic globalization is showing itself to be an unbalanced process. A "global growing gap" defines relations between the North and the Global South. Cultural institutions and traditional structures of meaning are eroding in non-Western as well as Western contexts. While the affluent resort to the opiate of consumerism, ordinary people throughout the world are responding to experiences of insecurity by seeking to restore collapsed boundaries, to shore up or revive stable communal identities and systems of values. Through broad-based yet diverse social movements, they are seeking to meet the future on their own terms, and to avoid the prospect of remaining second-class participants in systems run according to the values and beliefs of others.

Islamic revival is such a defensive social and political movement, a broad-based reaction to Westernization, foreign manipulation, and internal malaise. Although its manifestations are remarkably widespread, Islamic revival is not a monolithic movement, nor is it reducible to the militant fundamentalism that captures the attention of the media.[1] Among the world's historical powers, only the Muslims, as a people, have not reversed the decline in their global status. The Japanese, the Chinese, and the Europeans have all regained their world influence. The Islamic people are trying to preserve their culture and identity, and Islamic revival is a way of defining who they are.

The issues that motivate the Islamic revival are similar to those which provide impetus to revival in other religious and communal contexts. In fact, the tension between nationalism and religion in the Islamic world bears a similarity to a split in Israel. Everywhere there is a latent dissatisfaction with what materialist, consumer-oriented society offers, and with the failures of national governments to offer their peoples more than a medley of technological "fixes" which amount to tinkering with inefficient political, social, and economic institutions. To derive adequate and creative responses to this dissatisfaction, we will have to suspend certain habits of thought and perception, empathize with the historical and cultural experiences of Muslims and other peoples, and envision more equitable and life-enhancing forms of intercultural cooperation.

Recognizing Revivalism

Two Faces of Fundamentalism. The inadequacies of economic globalization and dominant Western conceptions of progress are increasingly recognized by advocates of interreligious solidarity and cooperation. Nonetheless, communalist reactions to the dislocations associated with modernization and development are usually viewed through culturally tinted lenses. If the language used by policymakers, policy analysts, and journalists is accepted as an indicator, "fundamentalism" seems to be filling a gap in the post–cold war vocabulary for security threats.[2] The

---

[1] See Edward Azar and A. Chung-in Moon, "The Many Faces of Islamic Revivalism," in Richard L. Rubenstein, ed., *Spirit Matters: The Worldwide Impact of Religion on Contemporary Politics* (New York: Paragon House, 1987). For an exploration of the idea of "Islamic renaissance," see Anwar Ibrahim, "Islamic Renaissance and the Reconstruction of Civilization," *Islamic Horizons*, Vol. 25, No. 5 (September/October 1996), pp. 14–15.

[2] Laura Drake argues that "extremism" has become the "new 'ism'" by means of which US policymakers identify threats. She warns that this term is "relational" and "lacks the stability of a self-definition." Comparable caveats apply to the word "fundamentalism" as it is used to characterize the other as an inverted, mirror image of the self (Laura Drake, "Hegemony and Its Discontents: United States Policy Toward Iraq, Iran, Hamas, the Hezbollah and Their Responses," United Association for Studies and Research, Occa-

cold war has passed, but new cold wars are still thinkable.

Indeed, the term "fundamentalism," derived from the Western experience, has been applied to entire spectra of cultural, political, and religious activity. While the standards of academic research into fundamentalism have increased with the recent Fundamentalism Project of the American Academy of Arts and Sciences, the term nonetheless remains limited by cultural and intellectual baggage. As the director of the project, Martin E. Marty, has himself suggested, "the study of fundamentalisms holds up a mirror to scholars in the West."[3] To understand particularistic religious movements, we need to reflect more deeply on the outlooks and experiences of people who perceive themselves as revivers of religion. More often than not, what is called religious fundamentalism manifests under conditions of cultural, social, economic, and political marginalization. The defensive postures of certain religious and communal groups need to be understood in relation to that which provokes reaction. Concern about religious fundamentalism in the Islamic world and other locales should be tempered with reflection on an assertive type of political fundamentalism in the dominant Western culture, with its emphasis on materialistic science.

Insofar as we use the term "fundamentalism" in our Western discourse, we should use it evenhandedly and self-consciously. Fundamentalism can be defined as a kind of pathology of culture that arises when a group takes a subset of the basic tenets of a tradition, and either under the pressure of insecurity (in the case of Muslims, for example), or in the pursuit of hegemony (in the case of the West), uses them either to seek security by sealing off others, or to maintain dominance. In all conflict situations, people under stress react by reducing their own beliefs to a small, workable subset in order to fight and protect themselves. Fundamentalism, in this sense, implies a narrowing of the consciousness, and a closing off of the ability to hear and communicate. Yet, as we would like to underscore, a return to the larger frame of the culture and its humane values, always present if sought for, can open up the space for understanding, cooperation, or at the very least, deeper respect.

In the West, fundamentalism takes the form of cultural triumphalism. Cultural triumphalism is rooted in the prevailing Western vision of

---

sional Paper #12, September 1997).

[3] Martin E. Marty, "Explaining the Rise of Fundamentalism," *The Chronicle of Higher Education*, Vol. 39, No. 10 (October 28, 1992), p. A56.

linear progress in which the institutions and cultural realities of the West become the model future for all of humanity, or at least the best possible future which could be expected. This attitude, expressed with varying degrees of subtlety, implies a fusion of Hellenic rationalism with Hebraic messianism, as well as a conflation of the West's deepest spiritual and humanistic values with scientific materialism and existing forms of political, economic, and social life. The cultural triumphalist traces in his or her own cultural heritage a "great ascent" from backwardness, obscurantism, and tribalism, qualities which are in turn associated with those non-Western cultures which encounter difficulties while attempting to modernize. When assessing such cultures, the cultural triumphalist concludes that there is nothing to learn from them; modernization is prescribed as a way of adjusting to already-defined realities of state, nation, and economy. Valorization of cultural authenticity is associated with a risk of dangerous atavism, as the resources for betterment are believed to reside in the Western tradition. Democracy is reduced to minimum institutional requirements for effective participation in a global free-market economy; conflict resolution is understood as an engineering, isolating, mechanical process of adaptation and adjustment.

The view that Western culture is triumphant assumes that there are high and low culture forms—specifically that high culture is derived from Western Europe's Renaissance and Enlightenment and is automatically superior to others. Literate cultures, focused on abstraction and analysis, are superior to those based on anecdotal, folk, and oral traditions. Ethical and religious superiority are also identified with the dominant culture.

While the West has certainly made important contributions to global cultural resources—among them the notion that religious and political institutions need not be fused—the present overconfidence of the West manifests a reluctance to come to terms with, and trust in, cultural diversity. In recent years, much attention has been drawn to Samuel Huntington's "clash of civilizations" thesis. The notion of a "clash of civilizations" posits a contradiction between the epistemological and praxeological styles of the West and of the rest of the world. The West has little to learn and much to fear from the non-Western world; cultural diversity appears as a security threat.

At the present historical moment, the idea that the West has nothing substantive to learn from other civilizations is unhelpful, because it rules out partnership with other cultures. This makes it difficult for weaker, undervalued participants in the global cultural exchange—in the present case the Muslims—to perceive that they can do something besides merely "reflect or reject" the West. Hence, we would argue that just as the more intolerant and militant Muslim movements are unlikely to promote human flourishing, Western cultural triumphalism is also spiritually and humanistically unsound. Furthermore, the latter plays a role in producing the former, as Benjamin R. Barber maintains in his more balanced work, *Jihad vs. McWorld,*[4] arguing that uncompromising commercialism and communalist rejectionism are but two faces of one process.

Distinguishing Between Revivalism and Fundamentalism. The essence of what is called fundamentalism, in its religious as well as secular manifestations, is an equation of substance with particular limited forms, a virtual absolutization of that which is finite and partial. On the one hand, religious fundamentalism searches for existential security by strengthening in-group/out-group boundaries and assuming a defensive or combative posture in relation to out-groups. Political fundamentalism, on the other hand, celebrates particular institutions and denigrates others, claiming that particular modes of human organization exclusively embody such essential values as democracy, freedom, and truth. Both modalities reduce idealized ends to idealized means, forbidding alternative approaches. Each proclaims that one road to truth is the only road to truth.

Islamic fundamentalism, as a vigorous, exclusivist reaction to a perceived external threat, must be differentiated from Islamic revivalism, a movement to renew the community from within. Islamic revivalism implies efforts to satisfy human needs for identity and community, for participation in development and politics, and for sacred meaning. Under conditions of cultural, economic, and political marginalization, large numbers of people are returning to deeply embedded religious discourses as they search for authentic values and alternative means of responding to their problems. There is a sense among many that traditions have not been vital for hundreds of years, and that Western ideologies have not worked. Muslims are struggling to move beyond the notion that they must either reflect or reject the West; they are not satisfied merely with a choice between Ataturk and Khomeini. Islamic revival spans the political and ideological spectrum, influenced as much by local sociopolitical con-

---

[4] Benjamin R. Barber, *Jihad vs. McWorld* (New York: Times Books, 1995).

ditions as by religious faith.[5]

To grasp what is transpiring today in the Islamic world, a more nuanced appreciation of the Western experience is necessary. Although there are many writers who discuss the stamp of Calvinism on American and northern European cultures,[6] the stamp of Islam on the Islamic culture area is not always appreciated with the same subtlety. Just as there have been fundamentalist and revivalist movements in the West throughout the modern era, there have been fundamentalist and revivalist movements in the Islamic culture area as well.

We have to accept the continued role of Islam in Islamic countries on its own terms, and not merely as the vehicle of "irrational," antimodern extremism. Modernization theory, in this respect, is misleading, as it implies an artificial bifurcation between secularism and religiosity, in which the cutting edge of history renders religious movements and spiritual values insignificant, irrelevant, or illegitimate. Ironically, some ("orientalist") refutations of the relevance of conventional modernization theory in the Middle East maintain the same evaluation of the relative merits of secularly versus religiously defined culture, while simply appending a cruel exceptionalism for Muslim countries, which are "not ready for democracy" because they cannot implement the Western model. This analysis denies the dynamism of cultural and religious traditions and the possibility of democratic forms evolving organically out of a context of meaning familiar to people at the grassroots. Secular values of economic growth, individual choice, and technological progress are equated with modern, humane values, and Islamic values are associated with stasis and stagnation.

Contemporary thinking exhibits an understanding of the role of political and economic institutions in democracy, but a less sophisticated understanding of the role of social institutions. In the Middle Eastern context, we know that the institutions of democracy are not well grounded and that economic maldistribution is pervasive, but we have not devoted enough attention to social organization at the local level. Although local social institutions are imperfect, they do allow for the dis-

---

[5] For a useful introduction to the literature on Islamic revivalism, see Yvonne Yazbeck Haddad, John Obert Voll, and John L. Esposito, eds., *The Contemporary Islamic Revival: A Critical Survey and Bibliography* (New York: Greenwood Press, 1991).

[6] See, for example, Michael Walzer, *The Revolution of the Saints: A Study in the Origins of Radical Politics* (Cambridge, Massachusetts: Harvard University Press, 1965).

cussion of issues affecting people's lives. It is at this level that the language and values of Islam are most significant and authentic, and at which the gap between the formal institutions of state and the networks and realities of everyday life is most evident. Islamic social institutions are more dynamic and variegated than is generally recognized.

In addition to its social functions, religion serves an important, practical role in politics by offering recourse to a transcendental order—an order to which the Pharaoh can be held accountable. The oppressed can defend their rights by appealing to religious standards, to the divine will as it is understood. When the ruling regime persists in corruption and repression, Islam offers a vocabulary of resistance.

Islamic revivalism is not the enemy of the West. It is not even an entirely religious movement, nor is it, as some fear, monolithic and expansive. Islamic revivalists are seeking to restore an old civilization, not to create a new empire. As Michael E. Salla has suggested, it is worthwhile to consider Islamic revivalism in comparative perspective, as a "regional variation of a global religious revivalism that promulgates a normative perspective that critiques liberal democratic norms."[7] The different regional and local variations of revivalism no doubt exhibit somewhat different tendencies and perspectives, and all are worthy of further investigation.[8] The present case of Islamic revival sheds light on issues facing humanity as a whole. We are being challenged to resolve intercultural conflicts by respecting demands for cultural authenticity and human dignity within our emerging global civilization.

The Islamic Revival

The Roots of Rivalry and Revival. Beginning with the Treaty of Karlofca in 1699 and later the treaty of Kuchuk Kaynarca in 1774, the Ottomans retreated from Europe and Muslims were reduced to passivity in world politics. They were excluded from history. Their destinies were determined by the West. The rules and practices of current international relations reflect nineteenth-century Western experience and interests. Thus, the common bonding of the world today is the product of the con-

---

[7] Michael E. Salla, "Political Islam and the West: A New Cold War or Convergence?" *Third World Quarterly*, Vol. 18, No. 4 (1997), p. 740.

[8] David Westerlund, ed., *Questioning the Secular State: The Worldwide Resurgence of Religion in Politics* (New York: St. Martin's Press, 1996).

quest and acculturation into Western civilization of Islamic and other non-Western elites that occurred as the result of the West's political and economic expansion. The common language of the world has become largely Western in both form and content.

Cultural contact in this context of unequal political and cultural relations has blemished the exchange between Islam and the West. It has left the latter arrogant and insensitive and the former defensive and in-.secure. The sense of triumphant culture has become a profound source of conflict between the West and Islam. By asserting that what is right, true, and real is the same for everyone in the past, present, and future, cultural triumphalism favors and reinforces Western cultural values and styles and produces a displacement of Islamic culture. The continued triumph of Western civilization is sustained through mass media and educational systems, as well as by control of the symbols of legitimacy and status.

When independent Islamic states emerged following World War I and later World War II, the West expected that they would become its imitations; so did the Muslims. The first modern Islamic state, Ataturk's Turkey, embarked on a relentless campaign after World War I to sever that country's Islamic roots. After World War II, Ali Jinnah's Pakistan became the first country to declare itself Islamic, but it was so in name only. In reality, Pakistan was an adaptation of the Western nation-state system, moving in its postwar history from Jinnah through Ayub Khan to Bhutto and then to Zia's zealotry. In the same postwar period, Iran's history moved from the Shah through Bazargan and Bani Sadr to the Ayatollah Khomeini.

The establishment of modern Turkey and other nation-states in the Islamic world accompanied and accelerated intellectual and political discontinuity with basic values of Islam. Traditional Islamic institutions lost their effectiveness as organizing principles and as safeguards for social justice and political participation. The *shariah* (religious law) that served as a protective code for individual Muslims since the seventh century has suffered either from total neglect or from political opportunism. The universalism of Islam has not found expression in the new nation-states.

In fact, it is possible that Islamic rule has never been realized since the Prophet Muhammad's death. Two and possibly three of the Prophet's successors, the *khalifah* (caliphs), were assassinated, and this history leaves no unanimity among the faithful about the nature of Islamic rule.

Politics was marked by power struggles according to the rules of the profane world. Islam has been used by those in power to maintain themselves and by those aspiring to power to legitimize themselves, and here lies the present danger: that resorting to such religious justification for secular ends runs the risk of absolutism. There is always the risk that those in power could claim to be wielding dominion on behalf of God and could therefore assume absolute power over their political opponents. In the Islamic world, politics has always been confounded with religion in this way.

During the last quarter of the twentieth century, internal conflicts in the West and the assimilation and diffusion of Western technology within the Islamic world redressed the balance between these two cultures. Among other adjustments, there was a somewhat slow growth in the tide of self-confidence, as Islamic peoples rediscovered the inherent worth of their own cultures. Probably the most dramatic example is the awakening still underway in the multifaceted revival that is called Islamic fundamentalism by Westerners. This revival combines a rediscovery of the vitality of the Islamic experience with a determination not to submit any longer to the cultural humiliation of judging oneself by Western standards.

Today is a period of rapid social change in the world of Islam. The present experience of Muslims with Western cultural supremacy complicates the task of transition, because Western attitudes reinforce an alien system of values and thus accelerate the displacement of Islamic cultural norms that are already weakened. New symbols of legitimacy and status—wealth and nation-state—are introduced while many Muslims lose faith in their cultural heritage. Islam now faces the greatest challenge in its existence.

The Present Islamic Awakening. Contemporary Islamic revival is based on a long history of responses to the challenges encountered by Islam. Traditionally, Islam has provided two channels of response to challenges: *tajdid* (renewal) and *islah* (reform). Among the most famous historical proponents of renewal are Muhammad al-Ghazzali, Ahmad Ibn Taymiyyah, and Ahmad Sirhindi. During the late eleventh and early twelfth centuries, al-Ghazzali reconciled mysticism with mainline Islam. Two centuries later, Ibn Taymiyyah dealt with the challenge of idolatry and social upheaval brought on by the Mongolian invasion. During the sixteenth century, Mughal emperor Akbar sought to respond to the pluralism of Indian society by promoting a vision which emphasized the Islamic spirit of universalism at the expense of established religious forms, but Sirhindi opposed this and sought to defend boundaries between Hinduism and Islam.

In the nineteenth and twentieth centuries, the Islamic world had to respond to Western institutions and culture. Beginning in the late nineteenth century, Islamic reformers such as Muhammad Abduh and Jamal al-Din al-Afghani, impressed by European scientific and social advances, began an agonizing appraisal of the declining conditions in the Islamic world. A new school of thought, *salafiyah* (Islamic reformist), developed. Its aim was the reconciliation of Islamic precepts and Western social organization. In the early twentieth century, Hasan al-Banna moved Islamic revival from the realm of individual reforms to a popular movement by introducing the concept of mass organization. Sayyid Qutub, successor of al-Banna, built upon the latter's contribution by using the tool of ideology in an amalgam of Fascist and Marxist organizational principles. Islamic revival was transformed into a political movement exemplified in the emergence of the Green Shirts and the Muslim Brotherhood in Egypt and in the array of Islamic groups that continue to develop through today's Islamic world, including the Islamic Salvation Front in Algeria, the Islamic Group in Egypt, and al-Nahdah in Tunisia.

Islamic revival is a powerful and multifaceted movement that touches upon every aspect of life for Muslims. There is great diversity within and among the various Islamic groups, reflecting local, national, cultural, and economic realities.

Unfortunately, there is a growing tendency in the West to lump all Islamic movements together, thus narrowing Western understanding of the full range of Islamic forces at work. When Americans attack fundamentalism or Islamically oriented governments, they are assaulting, among others, allies of the United States such as Saudi Arabia and Pakistan. Iraq and Syria, two countries usually perceived as among America's most dangerous adversaries, are the most secular of the Arab states. Like the media, American policymakers have often proved to be surprisingly myopic, tending to view the Islamic world and various groups within it solely through the prism of extremism and terrorism. While this may be understandable in light of events in Algeria and in the occupied territories of Palestine and Lebanon, it fails to do justice to the complex reality of Islamic revival and undermines American interests in the Middle East and the Islamic world.

Common to advocates of Islamic revival, or Islamicists, is the affirmation of an Islamic ideological alternative to secular nationalism, Western capitalism, and socialism. In the Middle East, the failures of pan-Turanism (unity of the Turks), pan-Arabism (Arab unity), Arab nationalism and socialism, and Iranian nationalism have left an ideological vacuum. Far from a monolithic reality, Islamic revival is as diverse as the countries in which it is occurring. It spans the political and ideological spectrum, influenced as much by local sociopolitical conditions as by religious faith. For example, women serve in the security system of Muammar Qadhafi's populist Libya, yet women cannot drive vehicles in Saudi Arabia. Women enjoy voting rights in Pakistan and Iran but are disenfranchised in Sudan.

Despite vast disparities in attitudes, Islamicists hold in common a set of ideological beliefs. They view Islam as total way of life, for personal conduct and for the conduct of state and society. Westernization is regarded as the primary cause of the political, economic, and social ills of Muslim societies. Finally, followers of the Islamic revival movement believe that the introduction of the *shariah* will produce a moral, just, and self-reliant society.

Islamicists in the Islamic Group, al-Jihad, Hezbollah, the Armed Islamic Group, militant factions of Hamas, and an array of small radical organizations go beyond the above principles to see Islam and the West as involved in a historical power struggle of considerable duration, beginning with the Crusades and continuing under European colonialism, Zionism, and American imperialism. The West, especially the United States, is blamed for its support of unjust regimes in Tunisia, Morocco, Egypt, and the Arab states of the Gulf; for its unconditional support for Israel; and for its backing of the military usurpation of civilian government in Algeria. These radical groups, therefore, consider violent struggle against unjust rulers and those governments that support them as a justifiable strategy.

Islamic ideology and movements, or Islamism, have become an integral part of Islamic society and will inform future Islamic domestic and international politics. Islamists are found among the Western-educated as well as the untraveled, among literates and illiterates, transcending all classes, professions, and gender and age groups. The power of Islamic revival is manifested in many ways. Candidates running as Islamists have successfully entered elections in Kuwait, Algeria, Jordan, Lebanon, Sudan, and Tunisia. The revival has produced a new class of modern and educated Islamist elites who are no less visible than their secular counterparts and in every way as competent.

Islamic revival has developed into a broadly based social movement, functioning today in virtually every Islamic state and in communities around the world. The goal of this revival is to transform society through the transformation of individuals. Organizations known as *Da'wah* (Islamic call) exist at all levels of education, in all forms of communication, in banks and investment houses, in every type of social services, and in the police and military. Student associations are present in every Islamic country and elsewhere. Indeed, Islamic revival has produced a new generation of Islamists in every profession at every level in the Islamic world.

Beyond Confrontation, Toward Complementarity

The Need for Dialogue. The present relationship between the West and Islam resembles a fruitless debate. In this relationship, the inability of each party to hear the other only reinforces stridency and incomprehension. There continues to be a need to move beyond facile, stereotypical language and judgments. Stereotyping distracts the West and Islam from the search for a common ground. The West and Islam need to break the twin cycles of arrogance, which breeds contempt, and defensiveness, which fosters paranoia. The West should take the initiative because it is secure enough to do so. On the other hand, the Muslims should not be so insecure as to believe that they can only reflect or reject the West. The enduring strength and creative genius of authentic Islam can absorb the shocks of Western intrusions. Muslims can accept those creations of the West that are sure to complement the inevitable revitalization of Islam.

The Muslim image of the West is colored simultaneously by envy and admiration, fear and suspicion. Among most Muslims, Western civilization is seen as an example to be copied. Western technological, economic, and political achievements are appealing, while cultural penetration and the assertion of Western military, political, and economic power underscore Muslim fears. When Muslims look at Western materialism, they see cultural decadence.

The United States, the industrial nations of Europe, and Japan can participate in a potentially positive dialogue with Islam. In an effort to facilitate the articulation of social and political goals, the industrial nations could support Muslim efforts to develop democratic forms that are appropriate to their needs, to rediscover the life-affirming side of Islamic precepts, and to develop structures that promise a cultural future for the people and not merely a technological future that negates their values. By setting this as the agenda, the industrialized nations could participate in the reconstruction of an Islamic world that is nonviolent, stable, and productive.

Rethinking Democracy and Development. It is particularly self-defeating to exclude Islamicists if they are willing to participate in democratic politics. The central issue raised by the Islamic movements—the future of development in the Muslim world—is legitimate. By repressing Islamic voices, existing elites force the Islamic impulse into narrower channels characterized by violence and extremism. The United States should encourage Muslim governments to enter into dialogue with Islamicists. The exclusion of the people of the Muslim world from active participation in political life undermines global stability.

The reconciliation between Islam and democracy is a crucial first step toward peace and stable progress. Democracy, Western or Islamic, is not practiced anywhere in today's Arab world. Does it follow that Islam and democracy are not compatible? The answer is no. The practice of democracy is always less tidy than its definition, but its practice is more dynamic than its formal description and prescription. There are democratic precepts in Islam just as there are in other religions. There are also Islamic traditions, as in other religions, which in practice result in transgressions against democratic ideals. The claim of incompatibility between Islam and democracy equates Western (liberal) institutional forms of democracy with the substance of democracy. The *substance* of democracy is a human society that has a sense of common goals, a sense of community, wide participation in making decisions, and protective safeguards for dissenters. The *form* of democracy, on the other hand, is cast in the mold of the culture of a people.

There is nothing in Islam that precludes common goals, community participation, and protective safeguards. It is true that Western liberal forms of democracy, with their provisions for political parties, interest groups, and an electoral system, are alien to Islamic tradition. But democracy is not built upon institutions; it is built upon participation. The absence of democracy in Islamic countries is more the result of lack of preparation for it than of lack of religious and cultural foundations.

Democratic traditions in Islam, however, have been more commonly abused than used.

Currently, the door is open for a new thinking and reconceptualization regarding democracy. We should factor into this new thinking consideration of the roles of the community, the tribe, the individual, the state, and religion, so that we can go beyond the Western-based concepts of democracy.

"Developed"—modern and democratic—can also mean "Muslim." Currently, there is no available model for "modern, democratic, and Muslim" advanced by modernized Muslim thinkers. At the close of the nineteenth century in Egypt, liberal thinkers began to accept the Western democratic norm as reality. In so doing, they began to hang Islamic garb on Western concepts. It did not work then, and it is doubtful that it will work now. Muslims need to reexamine and reconstruct an Islamic idea of what is modern and Islamic.

The process of change has blurred the distinctions between modernization and development in the Islamic world. The developmental process is the way in which society and its members seek to reach their potential—a process with a goal, even if the goal is perceived as an ever-receding one. True, there is always a utopia by which this process is measured, one extracted from the experience of people and generalized into a vision of the desired society. However, since experience is constantly enlarged, it is natural that the utopian ideal changes. How we manage the tension between theory and practice, between reflection and experience—our praxeological style—determines how well we keep the dream alive. If we fail, the dream becomes a nightmare.

Modernization is the adoption of modern technologies for the uses of society. It attempts to make society more rational, efficient, and predictable, especially through the use of comprehensive planning, rational administration, and scientific evolution. Modernization also carries the connotation of a more productive society, at least in economic terms. Like development, modernization is always at least a partially conscious effort by some who have a vision of what modern society would look like. In the Islamic world, societal values are excluded from emerging patterns of development.

Modernization is not a substitute for development, but in much of the Islamic world, development is simply identified with modernization imposed from above without the construction of a popular base of support. Social justice and political participation in the Islamic world are sacrificed for modernization. The vitality of the vision of development can be derived only from the cultural reality of Islamic experiences. It cannot grow from either Western liberalism or some variety of socialism. Regardless of time and place, individuals and cultures must sweat out their own development to insure the greater expansion of their identity and dignity.

There is a tremendous amount of thinking to be done about development and Islam, precisely because Muslims are forced by today's conditions to make the connection between two worlds. The Islamic economic doctrine of the *shariah* is compromised by traditionalist-capitalist and secularist-socialist states alike. Present-day Islamic countries do not practice Islamic precepts patterned after the *shariah*. The socialists and secularists deny that religious law has strategic utility in modern materialism. The capitalists and traditionalists have the *shariah* out of its original shape. This perceived irrelevance of Islamic precepts to present conditions, whether implicit or explicit, has not been accompanied by indigenous intellectual development. The Islamic idea of development cannot be reduced to any of the existing models that prevail in the West today, where ultimately economic reasoning guides development policy, where it is appropriate to resolve social issues by economic rationality, and where consumerism is equated with happiness. Especially today, when many people in the West are trying to rethink the meaning of development to accommodate ecological and social criteria, Muslims need to reexamine and reconstruct an Islamic idea of development as well.

Islam and development can be reconciled when we free development from the linear, rational idea of progress canonized by the Western mind. The European Enlightenment postulated progress as the person's domain in nature established by reason and science. "Progress" was abandoned when the concept became a little too hollow to use—a trifle too obviously laden with Western superiority—and the concept of "development" was substituted in its place.

In the Islamic world, three possibilities for development must be examined: (1) a retaking of the road of "Westernizing," assuming the contradictions in the Western camp between liberals, Judeo-Christians, and Marxist-socialists can be resolved; (2) an acceptance of the hegemony of one of the Western groups or of a non-Western worldview; or (3) participation in the construction of truly eclectic, humanistic world culture. Only the third possibility will provide space for the growth of a truly Islamic model of development.

The inexorable dynamics of modern history rule out any pretensions by any group of establishing a world hegemony. Furthermore, it is obvious that such a view of a triumphant power is really alien to the genius of the three Western subcultures. The Judeo-Christian tradition insists that believers must always be open to new revelations of truth; liberals hold that reason and science march hand in hand toward a world brotherhood and sisterhood in which all will participate; and the Marxist-socialists believe in a scientific method that, if truly open-ended and able to move forward dialectically, will abandon dogmas outflanked by the advance of knowledge and the extension of human community.

The incompatibility of Islam with present economic requirements has resulted in frustration and cynicism. Amidst economic uncertainty, there has been lip service to Islam, capitalism, and socialism, combined with the failure to conform to the precepts of any of the three. Within this context, contemporary Islamic politics is thwarted and diverted by the personal interests of ruling elites.

The picture that emerges of government practices in the Islamic world bears little resemblance to Islamic precepts of social justice and political participation. Nor does it bear a likeness to Western liberal or socialist preferences. The tension between precept and practice has resulted as much from slow adaptation to rapidly changing conditions within Middle Eastern societies as from the impact of powerful ideas and forces from the West. Contradictions within Muslim societies have stifled creativity; indigenous intellectual developments have been few and frequently suppressed by governments. Khomeini's Shiite fundamentalism and the assortment of Sunni revival movements in the Arab world are the creation of these contradictions.

Neither the zealous nor the imitative responses of Muslims to the challenge of the West represent genuine revivals of Islamic civilization; rather, they evince negativism and identification with the "enemy." What is required is an Islamic alternative that is neither a superficial compromise nor a schizophrenic reaction—a response based on Islamic values that reflects the historical development of Islam while also responding to the challenges of contemporary life.

In the long run, it is better for the Islamic world to develop through its own Islamic traditions. Otherwise, Muslims will always be torn between traditionalism and secularism, between fundamentalism and Westernism. A change through continuity is more viable than a change through discontinuity. The challenge for Muslims is to develop the Islamic world through its own traditions, not through Western secular ideologies. The former are rooted in the heart of the people as mass culture, while the latter are uprooted from mass culture and can easily be seen as external penetration.

Islamic Contributions to World Order. Because Islamic traditions provide a set of powerful political precepts and practices with universal implications, Islam can also make important contributions to an integrated world order—one that affirms the unique value of all cultural traditions. In particular, Islam prescribes a strong sense of community and solidarity of people; it postulates a collaborative concept of freedom; and it demystifies the Western myth of triumphant material progress.

Islam sees the individual as the trustee of God's bounty. Individuals are required to lead a good life and to promote good deeds in the community, or *ummah*. Promotion of the community is an act of faith (*iman*) advocated in the Qur'an (the holy book of Islam) and Sunnah (practices of prophet Muhammad). The principle of social fraternity (*ikha ijtima'i*) defines the way Muslims organize themselves.

Islam views the community as a group of people cooperating for the sake of the common good, relying on the use of shared resources to achieve viability and creativity. A community is based on production to satisfy its needs; production requires regulations, and regulations lead to the establishment of a political system. The Islamic political system is the form of authority designed to regulate, direct policy, create just laws applied equally to all persons, and secure peace. The purpose of peace is the creation of harmony.

The Western liberal emphasis on personal freedom from restraint is alien to Islam. While in the liberal tradition personal freedom signifies the ability to act and is held in highest esteem, in Islam it is the ability to be or to exist that is foremost. Personal freedom in the latter view lies in surrendering to the divine will and is sought within oneself. It cannot be realized through liberation from external sources of restraint. Individual freedom ends where the freedom of the community begins.

From an Islamic perspective, being free means belonging to the community and participating with others in cultural creation. Freedom of thought, communication, and expression are all seen as absolutely necessary to achieve the highest level of self-renewing creativity, as is social, economic, and political equality of opportunity and dignity. Western liberalism posits freedom in order to avoid a despotic system, whereas Islam emphasizes virtue to perpetuate the traditions of society, which Islam often values as collective good. To some, such an approach denies the essential characteristics of freedom, for belonging to a community consciously demands some discipline and sacrifice. Yet the cultural anarchy of individualistic liberalism in the West is inconsistent with social balance. Furthermore, it has been oversold as a creative seedbed of culture and does not take into account the potential for creativity of noncoercive communities.

Societies have so often been repressive that a strong Western tradition has emerged that sees the elimination of repression and want as the chief goal of society. A false dichotomy has thus developed, with society seen as serving the individual. Too often—indeed, almost entirely—the cultural community in which most human realization must take place has been ignored. It is true that cultural systems, like political, economic, and social ones, have usually contained much to impede human development: forces such as prejudice, chauvinism, competitiveness, racism, sexism, and so on. This does not change the fact that the cultural community must be served by political, economic, and social systems, rather than the reverse.

There are many roads to humanistic cultural pluralism, many potential systems of communitarian, free, creative life, and many potential languages, arts, musics, dramas, and literatures that are compatible with humanistic ethics. No doubt, every community needs some "cultural revolution" to remove those things that dehumanize society or inhibit human development. But creativity and cooperation will only have a chance to replace conformity and competition as it becomes clear that the cultural community is the principal source of human realization. The enhancement of cultural communities at all levels of human organization, therefore, is necessary for moving beyond mutually negating fundamentalisms and toward coexistence.

In the Western pluralistic tradition, diversity is seen in terms of the coexistence of political systems but not of cultures. Cultural pluralism is rooted in an Islamic tradition of ethnic diversity that fosters a universalist tendency toward cultural broadness and flexibility. This heritage has allowed autonomous non-Muslim cultures to flourish within Islam to this day, while the West has succumbed to the destruction of native cultures and to sporadic, but virulent, anti-Semitism.

There is here a real opportunity for leadership. Today's challenge for Muslims is no more than the expansion of the original ideas of Islam. As Muslims seek to harmonize the Islamic spirit of communalism with the changing conditions of their own societies, they contribute to the betterment of our world.

The afflictions of triumphalism, cultural imperialism, and communal reaction undermine the viability of development—nationally, regionally, and globally. A retreat to a cultural ghetto by any group, be it Muslim, Christian, Jewish, Buddhist, or Hindu, is not only a denial of the rich diversity of the modern cultural experience, but also a rejection of responsibility for future generations. The inexorable dynamics of modern history rule out pretensions by any one group or cultural tradition of establishing a world hegemony. We have moved from a humanity that experienced its collective life as fragments of the whole to a humanity experiencing itself as whole.

First, second, and third worlds must become one world. Oppressors and oppressed must be seen as people; reason and intuition become faces of truth; planning and spontaneity become reality; civilization and barbarism become culture; propositional knowledge and anecdotal knowledge become the root of knowledge. World order becomes a historical process whereby human beings choose and create their future within the context of their environment to achieve a humanist and creative society. World order becomes a creative community.

Learning Cooperation Through Consensus

The only workable instrument for the conciliation between the West and Islam and, for that matter, for the ratification of interstate decisions in the emerging world order, will be a broad consensus of peoples and governments. The first truly global political community has begun to emerge around us. What we in the international-relations field called the interpenetration of states in recent decades has probably evolved so far as to be irreversible. In fact, it is ultimately inaccurate to speak of the West as distinct from Islam, or of Islam as opposed to the West. These clumsy distinctions are more appropriate as generalizations of popular mythology than as descriptions of actual international politics. The recent manifestations of neoconservatism in the West and religious revivalism in many parts of the world are masking the scale of global transformation now underway. Political rhetoric is essentially backward-looking: it translates contemporary issues into political distinctions of the past. This reactionary bias of political rhetoric is not the monopoly of practitioners of world politics. Media pundits and professional analysts are as much—if not more—the victims of rhetorical anachronisms.

Consensus, the distinctive political tool in relations among equals, has already gone far to replace armed force as the preferred instrument of national policy. "Realists" may object to the naïveté, the instability, or the shortsightedness of some manifestations of consensus, but it would be sheer folly to challenge either its existence or its power. The process of consensus is such a new method of reaching binding international decisions that mistakes and contradictions in its application are inevitable. Trial and error—seasoned by patience—will teach Westerners and Muslims the elements of an operational code to govern the new process, and consensus will become a more efficient and predictable instrument.

Consensus does not demand a radical transformation of the global system. Most of the old ways of thinking and acting in world politics will be useful in the future. Negotiation, persuasion, accommodation, and even certain forms of coercion will remain as standard features of interstate life. The loss of the ability to force a verdict by war will do little more than impose one more limitation on the practice of statecraft—a more fundamental inhibition than any the system has accepted up to this point, it is true, but nevertheless one that will leave room for vigor, imagination, and skill in framing and executing national policy.

The process of consensus does, however, underscore the obsolescence of the competitive model which has long dominated the practice of international relations. The competitive model is predicated upon the assumption that competition among nations, all pursuing their own self-interest, will, through Adam Smith's "invisible hand," miraculously lead to the increasing betterment of everyone. Consensus introduces a cooperative model of world politics which focuses on the benefits of international stability in the global system. No one country can impose it by itself. In fact, everyone has to make sacrifices. The cooperative model departs from the zero-sum, competitive power-politics model where one nation gains and the other loses, and moves toward common action resulting in mutual benefits.

In economics, the competitive model has functioned well to explain the provision and distribution of private goods. It served the very important function of guiding the stimulation of economic expansion and development. The problem is that the model simply failed to explain voluntary cooperation to provide public goods, as opposed to private goods. Public goods are those that are shared and enjoyed by a large number of people. Public goods cover a wide area of Western-Islamic relations including international management of energy resources, common security and the avoidance of Armageddon, and morality. Morality, which consists of ethical rules to guide our conduct, is something that everyone benefits from and that no individual can provide alone. It requires continued cooperation by everyone holding the ethical system in order to maintain it. Yet, in general, everyone has a temptation to let everyone else behave ethically and to exploit that behavior by taking advantage of the other people.

Voluntary cooperation to provide public goods, it seems, cannot be explained by simple self-interested behavior. It requires some minimal ethical assumption. Ethics can be seen as motivated not by pure altruism, but by a more enlightened self-interest, based upon a more inclusive conception of the self or of the community, in an increasingly interdependent and interconnected world. An ethical assumption to begin with is the existence of a norm of fairness, a norm that requires an individual to bear a share of the cost that is borne by those who are also cooperating in an action, rather than simply taking a free ride, as self-interest would dictate.

What are some of the characteristics of cooperation based on fairness that would be relevant to intercultural and interreligious cooperative relations? In the first place, such cooperation requires the identification and acceptance of shared objectives that can be reached only through cooperative efforts. Second, all of the potential cooperators have to have an expectation of personal benefit from this cooperative effort: they are not obligated by fairness to contribute to an enterprise from which they expect to get nothing back. A third important aspect of voluntary cooperation based on fairness is that there must be a fair distribution of the benefits and costs of cooperation. Questions of international social justice cannot be avoided. For example, we simply cannot expect Muslims—who see themselves in a position of weakness relative to the West and feel they are being repressed—to be willing to make any significant sacrifice of their own self-interest to benefit Western nations.

Let us emphasize that fairness is an ethical norm, which at times requires that we set aside simple self-interest in order to adhere to it. The norm of fairness, however, does not require unilateral self-sacrifice. It is not a norm of pure altruism. Fair individuals are obligated to contribute to a cooperative effort only if they can expect to receive benefits from the like contributions of others. This is a key characteristic of the underlying concept of reciprocity—the obligation to return a favor, or not to take advantage of someone who has done you a favor. In the case of Islam and the West, both Westerners and Muslims have to have an expectation of receiving benefits from the cooperation of others.

Because of the mutual expectation of benefits, cooperation based on fairness requires mutual trust. Since no one party can force any of the others to cooperate, and since each one has a selfish temptation not to cooperate, each must trust the others not to take advantage of both the opportunity and the temptation to cheat. Cooperation, then, requires mutual expectation of a willingness to sacrifice short-term self-interest for the common good.

Cooperation based on fairness involves some risk because there is a need to rely on mutual trust. The more confidence one has in the trustworthiness of the other cooperators, the less this risk will be. The role of fairness in the game is to obligate participating groups not to take advantage of each other in a risky situation. It is sometimes necessary to build a basis for trust by starting with relatively low-loss, low-risk cooperative ventures and working up to bigger, higher-payoff, but higher-risk enterprises.

A related problem is the double standard of morality often used. People often have one standard of ethics with regard to their in-group, however that is defined, and a different standard of ethics with regard to their perceived out-group. This may be one of the greatest challenges in building Western-Islamic and global cooperation, because people tend to draw their in-group lines, at the farthest extent, at their own national or cultural borders.

Though having shared objectives that benefit everyone is a necessary precondition for cooperation, it is not sufficient. There is a crucial role for leadership in converting shared objectives and a shared norm of fairness into effective cooperation. Leadership is needed to establish the mechanisms for cooperation and to ensure that efforts will be coordinated and that they will succeed. Leadership also has an important part in the formulation of common objectives in the first place. Mechanisms for cooperation must be established that determine the fair allocation of benefits and burdens, and identify the roles and responsibilities of the cooperative enterprise. Another role of leadership is to promote the development of solidarity. Solidarity is necessary for the underlying norm of fair reciprocity to be effective. Finally, leadership has the role of setting an example of sacrifice of immediate self-interest in furtherance of common goals.

The building of cooperation on the basis of consensus, fairness, and trust is important not only for generating utilitarian responses to pressing global problems, but also for renewing the world's cultural, religious, and spiritual traditions from within. Through investigating the challenge of revivalism, we arrive at an issue of even broader significance: the need for cultural disarmament[9] and nonpartisan spiritual values. To move beyond fear and distrust and provide scope for both universality and cultural authenticity, we will ultimately need to draw on the essential wisdom that is the common heritage of all humankind, which Aldous Huxley and others have referred to as the "perennial philosophy."[10] While, exoterically, the religions of the world are many, esoterically they are one: they arise from and return to a common source, and possess within themselves the resources for an extended epistemology by means of which the unity of existence may be discovered and the human personality transformed. It is by means of this unifying, perennial philosophy—which underscores the mystical, or spiritual dimension of religion—that we may come not only to cognize, but also to feel and experience, that the whole world needs the whole world. To evoke the vision of Ibn 'Arabi, a thirteenth-century Muslim philosopher, the whole of existence is reflected in the parts, and from the parts we gain the information to reconstruct an ever-greater whole. It is from such spiritual visions, present at the core of all the world's living traditions, that we may derive the faith to become architects of a new order of cooperation.

---

[9] Raimundo Panikkar, *Cultural Disarmament: The Way to Peace* (Louisville, Kentucky: Westminster John Knox Press, 1995).

[10] Aldous Huxley, *The Perennial Philosophy* (New York: Harper & Row, 1945).

BAHÁ'Í FAITH

Humanity's Coming of Age: The Bahá'í Faith and World Order

John Woodall

The purpose of religion…is to establish unity and concord amongst the peoples of the world. (Bahá'u'lláh)

It is a particular pleasure to participate in the efforts of Global Education Associates and its Religion and World Order Program, since the
goal it envisions—to "move toward a shared ethic" in the affairs of
humanity—can be seen as an expression of an explicit tenet of Bahá'í
belief. In the early years of this century, Abdu'l-Bahá, one of the Three
Central Figures[1] in the Bahá'í Faith, stated that developing such shared
views is an essential task in promoting a united global order. In an epis-
tle[2] describing "Seven Candles of Unity," He poetically elucidated those

---

[1] The Three Central Figures of the Bahá'í Faith are: (1) The Bab, Whose title means
"The Gate." In 1844, He was the Founder of an independent religion and the forerunner
of Bahá'u'lláh; (2) Bahá'u'lláh, Whose title means "The Glory of God," the Founder of
the Bahá'í Faith; (3) His eldest son, Abdu'l-Bahá, Whose title means "Servant of
Bahá'u'lláh," appointed by Bahá'u'lláh as His successor and the authoritative interpreter
of His Teachings.

[2] The "candles of unity" cited by Abdu'l-Bahá are: unity in the political realm, unity of
thought in world undertakings, unity in freedom, unity in religion, unity of nations, unity
of races, and unity of language. Abdu'l-Bahá states that "Each and every one of these
will inevitably come to pass, inasmuch as the power of the Kingdom of God will aid and
assist in their realization." For the full text, see *Selections from the Writings of Abdu'l-
Bahá*, The Universal House of Justice (Chatham, UK: W.&J. MacKay Limited, 1978),
pp. 29–34.

essential requirements to achieve the unity of the planet. Among these "Candles" He included the necessity to achieve "unity of thought in world undertakings." Efforts to promote such unity of thought are, therefore, dear to the heart of every Bahá'í.

From a Bahá'í viewpoint, the discussion of the role of religion in world order is central to understanding the very purpose of God in creating humanity and critical to its fortunes at this turning point in history. Seen from the perspective laid out by Bahá'u'lláh, we live in the age that God has ordained as the time of the ingathering of the peoples of the world, the time when humanity will come to see the blessings of peace both within the reality of the soul and in the world of human affairs. "The time foreordained unto the peoples and kindreds of the world has now come," Bahá'u'lláh proclaims. For God, in this Age, and in His boundless mercy, has infused the realm of human potential with new capacity and readiness to achieve the goal of establishing His Kingdom here on earth as it is in heaven.

The goal of world unity embodies the very spirit of the age in which we live and is the animating purpose that underlies the teachings of Bahá'u'lláh. To Bahá'í thinking, efforts that promote this principle move in accordance with the will of God and are destined to prevail. Those efforts that are based on lesser loyalties, being out of step with the spirit and needs of the times, continue to cause humanity's suffering. Since the spirit of the age is embodied in the principle of the oneness of humanity as children of one Almighty and All-Loving God, our prosperity and happiness are dependent upon our recognition of this truth and the conformity of our lives to its implications. This reality requires from us not only our spiritual allegiance, but that our lives be dedicated to the fulfillment of a common human destiny. Writing in His seminal 1875 work on the principles of world unity, *The Secrets of Divine Civilization*,[3] Abdu'l-Bahá adjured all humanity that:

> We must now highly resolve to arise and lay hold of all those instrumentalities that promote the peace and well-being and happiness, the knowledge, culture and industry, the dignity, value and station, of the entire human race.

Each of the world's religious traditions provides humanity with the means whereby these goals might be achieved. To Bahá'í thinking, it is

---

[3] Abdu'l-Bahá, *The Secrets of Divine Civilization* (Wilmette, Illinois: The Bahá'í Publishing Trust, 1970), p. 4.

because humanity has matured sufficiently in its collective life that it can now more fully understand and implement on a global scale the eternal truths of all religions. It is this movement into humanity's collective maturity that defines for this age such immense challenge and opportunity. To safeguard the transition to its collective maturity, the Bahá'í Writings focus primarily on those themes which elucidate the reality of the essential oneness of humanity and then develop the methods and institutions whereby this reality can be expressed in world governance and the flowering of a peaceful global culture.

It is important to understand from the outset that the Principle of the Oneness of Humanity is the chief and distinguishing feature of all Bahá'í teachings and that these teachings find their expression in the exposition of a pattern of world governance equal to the task of embodying that unity. Bahá'ís believe that the transformative spiritual power, the social principles, and the institutions necessary to move humanity toward its long-awaited destiny of world unity are not derivative teachings or extrapolations of the Writings of its Founder, but are expressly revealed and the primary purpose of the Writings of Bahá'u'lláh and the World Order He envisioned. These Writings, comprising the equivalent of over 100 texts, were revealed by Bahá'u'lláh in the nineteenth century during the course of the nearly 40 years of imprisonment and exile that He endured.

Since the inception of the Bahá'í Revelation in 1844, each of its Central Figures and the Bahá'í World Community that followed Them has, in innumerable Epistles, Proclamations, addresses, and statements, called on the rulers and peoples of the world to recognize its unity and unite under the care of a single global order defined by a system of global governance. Among the most notable of these efforts are the proclamations to the kings and rulers of the world revealed by Bahá'u'lláh from His place of exile during a time when the cruelties inflicted upon Him had reached their height. These summons reached their zenith in the revelation of Bahá'u'lláh's "Most Holy Book," a Text that embodies the Laws that will govern the pattern of world order into humanity's distant future and inspire and train individual souls and communities to achieve this end. During the life of Abdu'l-Bahá, this process of providing guidance for world order continued with "The Tablets of the Divine Plan," which define the process by which the spiritual regeneration of the planet will unfold. Unparalleled in religious history, the Testaments of Bahá'u'lláh and subsequently of Abdu'l-Bahá protect the Bahá'í Teachings from schism so that the power of unity they contain can evolve in coherent fashion in the global community.

The dramatic travels of Abdu'l-Bahá throughout Europe and America and the innumerable talks He gave on the eve of the First World War clearly laid out the reality of our spiritual lives, our unity as a human family, and the necessary principles required to unite humanity and avert the impending catastrophe He foresaw, a cataclysm that awaited humanity as a natural consequence of its failure to heed the spirit of the age. Next, the invitation He received to address the conference at the Hague which drew up the charter for the creation of the League of Nations testifies to the central place global governance has in Bahá'í belief. These stand out as the preeminent Texts on World Unity arising from a wealth of subsidiary Writings that together define the Bahá'í corpus. But far more compelling are the living examples of these Great Beings in sacrificing their all and enduring lifetimes of cruelties to breathe a new life into the world and give living substance to the spirit of the age.

Since that time, the entire Bahá'í World Community has had but one goal, to promulgate the spirit of unity throughout the world and to lay the foundation for the creation of those global institutions that can best preserve this unity and safeguard the interests of all the diverse peoples of the world. In each locality where Bahá'ís reside around the world, efforts are exerted to proclaim the oneness of humanity and to attempt to exemplify those virtues which will bind the hearts of all the peoples of the world into a single human family. At the global level, the Bahá'í International Community has offered its perspective on how the historic evolution of the international institutions embodied in the United Nations might continue to promote the interests and safeguard the unity of all of humanity's diverse peoples. Chief among the written expressions of these efforts are "The Promise of World Peace," published by the Universal House of Justice in 1986, and "The Turning Point for All Nations," published in 1995 on the occasion of the fiftieth anniversary of the signing of the United Nations Charter.

With the understanding that world order issues are at the heart of the entire Bahá'í experience, and given the vastness of the primary Bahá'í Texts that speak specifically to the questions asked by the Religion and World Order Program, it is impossible to provide more than the briefest of summaries of the principles that derive from these Writings and bear upon the intent of this exercise. Having stated this, we can now proceed with the outline questions.

Working Toward a Shared Global Ethic
Peace and Security

> Humanity, through suffering and turmoil, is swiftly moving on towards its destiny.

Perhaps nowhere but in the depths of human suffering do we see the greatest potential for good or evil in the human spirit. The twentieth century was marked as the bloodiest in human history; through this carnage we can see that the necessary relationships that form the core of civilized life have all been under assault. The meaning of these great sufferings in the lives of individuals, and now to an unprecedented scale in the collective life of the peoples of the world, is a question worth our considered attention. At heart, these travails have the power to inflame further conflict and aggression within our nature, or to awaken us to the reality of our oneness. Throughout history, war, genocide, and oppression have been justified as the necessary price to right some previous suffering. Yet, if we are alert to the deepest and noblest voice of our inner life, we are able to see the experience of suffering as the beginning of our sense of compassion for others. To choose compassion over hatred is the essential moral challenge our suffering presents to us. Now on such a wrenching scale across the globe, the suffering of the world compels us to choose to align our hearts to a conviction of the oneness of the human family. The choice before us is between global compassion, and frantic bitter hatred. To choose compassion consistently requires a largesse that is unsustainable to the individual heart. The move to global compassion requires a power that transcends the inertial pull of our limited personal identity. We require a power that will allow us to choose compassion against hatred and recrimination when our pain seems to allow us no other choice.

At the core of our being is a yearning for transcendence. Ultimately, this natural flight of the soul is that part of us that seeks its Maker. It is the pursuit of the Source of our being that pulls us from our self-centeredness and compels us toward the universal. It is a maxim of life that we take on the qualities of that which our heart seeks. Pursuit of the worldly elicits the worldly part of our nature; pursuit of the transcendent reveals those elements of human nature which are most linked with the divine. These qualities constitute a sacred trust with which each soul has been endowed by an All-Loving Creator. The purpose of religion, and of life itself, is to reveal this sacred trust in the life of an individual and in the world at large. At this turning point in history, this trust within each soul can only find its true expression in the service of the commonality of all humanity. Bearing witness to this reality of our soul's yearning is the beginning of an inner sense of peace and certitude in the wonder and grace of life that makes peace in the world possible.

If we remain strangers to this certitude and poise that comes from bearing witness to our being created from the Will of an All-Loving God, the compass to guide our individual and collective life is lost. The intrinsic pain that accompanies all life in this temporal world is then further magnified by our inability to bring meaning to our own struggle. Without an abiding sense of the grace of God, our life's struggles become embittered and lonely. They poison our relations with others and the world around us and undermine our sense of the value of all life. The results are seen everywhere. The decay of the relations between women and men in marriage and the subsequent failure to adequately nurture children are cardinal symptoms of this lack of spiritual direction. These most fundamental of social disruptions extend to the ensuing violence that marks ever-widening circles of society.

Separated from our spiritual nature, we still continue to seek some form of transcendence. We take shelter in outworn and parochial allegiances such as excessive nationalism, rigid ethnocentrism, or blind adherence to political ideology. Protecting these allegiances is then the justification for conflict. The foundations of justice are undermined as we seek dominance over others. Unaided by the spirit of abiding faith in the majesty of God which lifts up the heart and mind, this urge for sedition, contention, and conflict dominates our motivation. To Bahá'í thinking, these forces are the primary factors that promote evil in the world.[4] The quest for peace must, therefore, be grounded in an abiding sense of the grace of the All-Merciful pervading all creation. For there is no other power that can unfailingly free us from the inertia, selfish absorption, and inevitable conflict with others that the pain in life would otherwise provoke.

---

[4] "...the widespread differences that exist among mankind and the prevalence of sedition, contention, conflict, and the like are the primary factors that lead to the appearance of the satanic spirit." *Tablets of Bahá'u'lláh*, Universal House of Justice (Chatham, UK: W.&J. MacKay Limited, 1978), p. 177.

Humanity torn with dissension and burning with hatred, is crying at this hour for a fuller measure of that love which is born of God, that love which in the last resort will prove the one solvent of its incalculable difficulties and problems.[5]

The core of the challenge resides, then, in the heart of the individual. To be able to testify with the fullness of one's being to the abiding grace of God is to be free of the compulsion for contention for survival and dominance. It allows for the willing acceptance of the operation of God's will in one's life. In the life of communities and societies, it means that the desire to dominate others is abrogated. In the collective life of the world, to adopt such an attitude as the collective center from which society organizes itself means that the law for the struggle for existence itself is abrogated and a new and higher law of unity comes into play.[6] We live in a time when the law of love is meant to come into its fruition on a global scale.

This love for God, unequivocally directed toward His entire creation, is the clear premise for the world's true security. This is the age in which love must find its mature expression on a global scale. This theme is the very spirit of the age.

The Great Being saith: Blessed and happy is he that ariseth to promote the best interests of the peoples and kindreds of the earth.... It is not for him to pride himself who loveth his country, but rather for him who loveth the whole world. The earth is but one country and mankind its citizens.... The well-being of mankind, its peace and security, are unattainable unless and until its unity is first established.[7]

And it is to promoting this global unity that all the forces of the Bahá'í Writings are directed.

Economic and Social Justice

Building on the central role of the recognition of our common humanity

---

[5] Shoghi Effendi, *Bahá'í Administration* (Wilmette, Illinois: The Bahá'í Publishing Trust, 1968), p. 62.

[6] "But the Collective Center of the Kingdom...organizes the world of humanity, and destroys the foundation of differences.... antagonistic aims are brushed aside, the law of the struggle for existence is abrogated, and the canopy of the oneness of the world of humanity is raised...casting its shade over all races." Abdu'l-Bahá, *Tablets of the Divine Plan* (Bahá'í Publishing Trust, 1959), p. 24.

[7] Bahá'u'lláh, *Tablets of Bahá'u'lláh*, p. 167.

as children of a loving God, we then come to the question of the social application of these principles. Although there are explicit structural recommendations in the Bahá'í teachings regarding economic matters, the main contribution from the Bahá'í Writings is in the form of perspective and principle. These perspectives and principles are intended to be applied in an evolving manner as capacity and needs change in a progressively more united world.

Briefly, economies are derived from the natural interchanges within and between communities. Communities are defined by collective values and ethics. Economies, then, have their basis in certain ethical assumptions about the value and meaning of life. The importance of religion in economic questions lies in establishing these values. The most inclusive collective values are defined by the universal elements in the world's religions. Given the Bahá'í premise of the oneness of humanity, economic questions can be evaluated by the way they serve or detract from the support of the body of the entire human family. In this context, economic development is not simply the acquisition of material objects or benefits. We are not merely economic beings. Rather, economies ought to be considered the means by which resources and talents are used to promote the well-being of the body of humanity by supporting the flowering of the trust of God through the development of human potential.

The implications of this principle are vast and imply the eventual restructuring of the economic life of the planet. At the core is the idea of social justice. In the Bahá'í Writings, justice is accorded a preeminent position among the virtues that each individual is called upon to acquire.

On the individual level, justice implies the capacity to evaluate each situation in life on its own terms and to be free from preconceived ideas regarding solutions, so that one may "know of thine own knowledge." On an institutional level, justice implies coordination of the affairs of the resources of the planet in a unified way so as to meet the minimum needs of the entire body of humanity. Justice is in turn the foundation upon which true unity is established and maintained. The principle of the oneness of humanity sets the scale by which economic and social justice can be weighed. Justice must be defined as that which services the needs, spiritual and material, of the life of the entirety of humanity.

In economic terms, the degree to which these two aspects of justice, individual and institutional, are in balance will determine the success of a process of social and economic development. A global economy based on an appreciation of the oneness of humanity and the spiritual trust that each human life represents forms the premise for economic development. The Sacred Texts of the Bahá'í Faith offer many contributions to the development of economic and social justice, including coordination between local, secondary,[8] and global institutions; standardized currency, weight, and measures; profit-sharing; progressive income tax and negative income tax; control of monopoly; provision of a social safety net; wide distribution of wealth when passing between generations; encouragement of voluntary giving; the importance of individual effort to earn a livelihood; the elevation of work performed in the spirit of service to the station of worship.

Two critical elements in the creation of wealth and the stability of the global body politic include the reality of the equality between men and women in the sight of God and the essential need for universal education. In the Bahá'í Teachings, the education of women, the primary trainers of the next generation, even takes precedence over that of men if resources are scarce. Two standards by which community development should be measured are the degree to which women are educated and the degree to which the oneness of humanity is taught to children.

Bahá'u'lláh has ordained in His Writings that in each community where Bahá'ís reside, a constellation of devotional and social service institutions should develop. Schools, universities, hospitals, and homes for the aged, orphans, and travelers should be erected, centered around a house of worship. The intention of these institutions is to provide a living embodiment of the principle that the devotional life must be carried into the community as service. These centers will no doubt come to be the engines of a variety of economic development as Bahá'í communities grow in number and resources.

Human Rights

Another of the "Seven Candles of Unity" referred to above and elucidated by Abdu'l-Bahá is the "unity in freedom." Given the inherent real-

---

[8] Secondary institutions are defined as those that coordinate local efforts but are subsidiary to global structures. Primary structures would include local and global institutions, in that local institutions are the site of all direct economic and social activity, and global institutions protect the interests of the body of humanity. Some secondary institutions would include nation-states, regional governmental organizations, multinational corporations, nongovernmental bodies, and political entities that are not nation-states.

ity of human nature as a sacred trust placed in each soul by the Creator, society has the obligation to protect this trust. Each soul must have the freedom to develop this God-given trust. Human rights ultimately rest on a recognition of this divine trust within creation that places sacred importance on each life. Conversely, each individual not only has the responsibility to develop the qualities of God latent within them, but also has the duty to honor the mystery of creation in all souls whom they encounter. This balance between rights and responsibilities is essential to avoid the evils inherent in over-centralization of authority, to which institutions are prone, and in the rampant individualism that destroys the reciprocal bonds of society.

Rights derive from the essential purpose of creation. This purpose is expressed in a number of ways in the Bahá'í Writings: humanity was created to know and love God, humanity was created "to carry forward an ever-advancing civilization," so that humanity may "be regarded as one soul," "that everyone may become aware of the trust of God latent in the reality of every soul," and that "the light of Divine bounty, of grace, and mercy may envelop all mankind." These are a few examples of how this purpose is variously expressed. All that serves these ends are rights of the individual. All that one must perform to fulfill these ends are duties of the individual. Protecting this mission of every soul and nurturing the process of its fulfillment are the duties of institutions.

"Freedom," in a Bahá'í perspective, is not simply the right to do whatever one wants, regardless of the consequences to one's dignity or the rights of others. The Bahá'í Writings constantly elaborate on the verities of the mercy of God that pervades creation. Each event in the workings of Providence has concealed within it the potential to bring out those gems of the soul which God has entrusted to all people. Freedom speaks to the reality of choice that each human being faces in the decisions of daily life—to either choose to seek out the will of God in each moment of life, or not. At the most fundamental level, this choice resides solely with the individual. No institution or ideology can perform this task for the individual; hence the value Bahá'u'lláh places on the necessity for the individual to exercise justice, which stands out as "the best beloved of all things" in the sight of God. To develop the capacity to see with one's own eyes and know of one's own knowledge is a right no institutional or ideological power can prohibit. Each soul has the unfettered right to seek out this meaning in life without interference. To protect this capacity is another way of expressing the fundamental role of institutions that administer justice in society. It is the administration of justice that ultimately allows for the expression of the trust of God in the world.

Inherent in the notion of human rights is the necessity for institutional capacity to protect these rights. We saw in the past century the slow evolution of the idea of international institutions that can minister to a global community. Essential to this task is the creation of institutions that have the authority and jurisdiction to administer justice on a global scale. To Bahá'í thinking, global development and the creation of a peaceful world are impossible without such institutions. Simply defining the particular human rights and reciprocal duties accorded to individuals is, in the long run, a fruitless task unless those rights and duties are protected, enforced, and further elaborated by a world tribunal adequate to the task. This principle has been elaborated in many ways in the Sacred Texts of the Bahá'í Faith since its inception over 150 years ago.

Ecological Sustainability

In this time of transition to a global community, the world is paying a terrible price for the rigid adherence humanity gives to the dogmas of material consumerism and excessive individualism, on the one hand, and the right of the state over all considerations of human and natural value, on the other. Bahá'u'lláh enjoins His followers to develop a sense of world citizenship and a commitment to stewardship of the earth. His writings are imbued with a deep respect for the natural world and for the interconnectedness of all things.

Among the principles guiding the Bahá'í approach to conservation and sustainable development, the following are of particular importance:

- Nature reflects the qualities and attributes of God and should, therefore, be greatly respected and cherished. Nature is an emanation of God's will.

- All things are interconnected according to the law of reciprocity. This principle underlies both the operations of the universe and the responsibilities of humanity.

- We cannot separate the qualities of the human heart from the world in which we live.

- The oneness of humanity is the fundamental spiritual and social truth of the age.

To achieve successful interventions to address the rapid deterioration of the biosphere, and further, to steward its resources effectively for the indefinite future, will require far more than the *ad hoc* process by which environmental treaties and agreements are currently enacted. The various proposals to create the international machinery upon which adequate safeguards could be made miss the complexities inherent in such stewardship. It will clearly require a level of commitment to solving major problems not exclusively associated with the environment. These problems include militarization, the inordinate disparity of wealth between nations, racism, the lack of access to education, unrestrained nationalism, unbridled consumerism, and the inequalities between men and women. Long-term solutions will require a new and comprehensive vision of a global society supported by new values.[9,10,11]

Cultural Identity and Integrity

The preceding discussion outlined a number of principles which bear upon the reciprocity inherent in the principle of unity. Unity, as opposed to monolithic uniformity, implies reciprocal relations between diverse components in dynamic interplay. Unity is vibrant and dynamic. Uniformity is sterile and static. To speak of the oneness of humanity is to intend the unity of the species in all its diverse components.

The character of the Bahá'í community is decidedly global. The *Encyclopedia Britannica* states that, after Christianity, the Bahá'í Faith is the most disseminated religion in the world. This is quite an achievement considering the relative youth of this newest of the world's religions. What is also true is that the world community of Bahá'ís is united in its spiritual aspiration, free from the conflict and sapping of spiritual strength that results from schism. This unity of purpose provides the protective context truly to foster the richness of its diversity. Within the Bahá'í community a microcosm of a united world exists. United in the belief of the oneness of God, the oneness of purpose and inspiration of the world religions, and the oneness of humanity, the Bahá'í Faith creates the con-

---

[9] *International Legislation for Environment and Development*, Office of the Environment, The Bahá'í International Community.

[10] *Earth Charter*, Office of the Environment, The Bahá'í International Community.

[11] See also "The Bahá'í Faith and the Summit on the Alliance Between Religions and Conservation," Office of the Environment, The Bahá'í International Community, 1987.

text within which a real appreciation of diversity can flourish. Far more than mere tolerance for differences, the poise and assurance granted by a shared belief in the oneness of humanity provides the freedom to express cultural diversity for its intended purpose, as an expression of a component perfection of the whole of God's creation. The Bahá'í community reflects the unity it espouses. This is perhaps its most exciting contribution to the development of a united world.

Working Toward Global Governance

We stand on the threshold of an age whose convulsions proclaim alike the death-pangs of the old order and the birth-pangs of the new.[12]

Each age proclaims itself to be unique. But it is from the Sacred Texts of their Faith that Bahá'ís make this statement about this age. For these state that we live in a truly unprecedented historic moment. This transition period in the world can be likened to the tumultuous period in the life of an individual moving from the passionate but limited allegiances of adolescence into the reciprocity and maturity that characterize adulthood. The history of the world has been written in contexts that describe the evolution and flowering of culture at the tribal, city-state, and national levels. Individual cultures too have been the focus of history. Never before has it been possible to write history from the vantage point of a united global society. This is the goal toward which the inexorable forces of history compel humanity. To Bahá'ís, this process marks the coming of age of humanity and has been ordained by the Lord of History as His intention since time immemorial.

Bahá'u'lláh speaks of the special capacity that has been infused into the creation in this age, a capacity that is intended to lead to the unification of the planet and the edification of the souls of humanity.

The whole earth is now in a state of pregnancy. The day is approaching when it will have yielded its noblest fruit.... The onrushing winds of the grace of God have passed over all things. Every creature hath been endowed with all the potentialities it can carry. And yet the peoples of the world have denied this grace![13]

What the peoples of the world have thus far denied is the reality of

---

[12] Shoghi Effendi, *The World Order of Bahá'u'lláh* (Wilmette, Illinois: Bahá'í Publishing Trust, 1955), p. 169.
[13] Bahá'u'lláh quoted in Shoghi Effendi, *The World Order of Bahá'u'lláh*, p. 169.

the oneness and wholeness of humanity as the children of one loving Creator. This failure has been the underlying cause of the conflicts that defined the past century. The Bahá'í writings speak of the consequences of this denial. While it has always been true that humanity is the common creation of one God, scientific and technological discoveries have made this reality abundantly clear for the first time only in the past 150 years. Yet, the realization that the world is a common marketplace and the dissemination of communications technologies themselves do not make for a united world. For the first time in recorded history, the consequences of our failure to recognize our unity has reached global proportions as a result of these same technological advancements. The dogmas of a former age, represented by excessive nationalism, racism, and the materialistic philosophy represented by communism and extreme capitalism, have all proved incapable of providing humanity with the promise of peace and security these technological advancements espoused.

> Every system, short of the unification of the human race, has been tried, repeatedly tried, and found wanting.[14]

Two forces are moving across the world following the close of that tumultuous century. One is essentially destructive and is sweeping away the institutions of an order founded on parochial dogmas. The other is constructive in nature and springs from the reality of the oneness of humanity as it gathers the momentum of history to form new relationships and institutions that can support a unified global order. It is the process by which historic forces are compelling humanity closer to its God-given destiny of unity.

Global Civic Society

> The earth is but one country and mankind its citizens.[15]

Since the beginning of Bahá'u'lláh's revelation, the idea that all human beings are citizens of one world has been the central tenet of belief. All peoples of the earth are citizens of the world. Their citizenship is assured by birth. The criteria that will define a global civic society, however, must be achieved through united action. These criteria have been elucidated in innumerable ways in the Bahá'í writings; their common

---

[14] Shoghi Effendi, *The World Order of Bahá'u'lláh*, p. 190.
[15] Bahá'u'lláh, *Tablets of Bahá'u'lláh*, p. 167.

foundation is the capacity of individuals to manifest the virtues of trust, forbearance, forgiveness, equity, and loving kindness. These cannot be legislated. The role of religious communities in promoting these virtues is the bedrock upon which any success for a peaceful world must rest.

The sacred Texts of the Bahá'í Faith speak at length about these themes. Of note is the perspective that global unity will unfold in stages. In general, there are two processes. The first is the realignment of political forces and the creation of global institutions that can prevent war and regulate the sustainable development of the global community. This process, referred to in the Bahá'í Writings as "The Lesser Peace,"[16] has been building momentum since the League of Nations was created. Bahá'ís anticipate that this question will acquire more and more urgent attention. Failure on the part of the world's political powers to allow this process to move ahead is seen as one of the greatest causes of the continuing suffering of the great majority of the world's population.

A consequence of the political failure to stabilize the institutional framework for a new global order is the spiritual damage done to the morale of the generality of humanity. As a result, a false conviction has developed that humanity is essentially aggressive and selfish. This half-truth has resulted in a type of paralysis of the will. A sense of apathy and hopeless fatalism in inevitable conflict has poisoned the atmosphere and prevented a serious discussion of those measures which might best promote the establishment of a united world authority.

A core task for the development of a global civic society is the rehabilitation of the spirit of hope in the gifts an All-Loving God has placed within the inmost reality of each human life. Without this spiritual medicine, the long-term hope for a sustainable global system is bleak. In large part, such a spirit can and has been generated by the convening of global leaders for the purpose of addressing universally recognized problems. But to sustain such a spirit, more is required. There is need to mobilize the highest and noblest instincts of human nature. This is the province of religion. And it is upon each religious community that this effort rests.

For beyond the progressive stages which will mark the unfoldment of a new global order lies the superhuman task of welding the hearts of the peoples of the world into a conviction of their common divine heritage.

---

[16] Some translations of the original Persian refer to "The Great Peace," which is distinguished from "The Most Great Peace."

> Permanent peace among nations is an essential stage, but not, Bahá'u'lláh asserts, the ultimate goal of the social development of humanity. Beyond the initial armistice forced upon the world by the fear of nuclear holocaust, beyond the political peace reluctantly entered into by suspicious rival nations, beyond pragmatic arrangements for security and coexistence, beyond even the many experiments on cooperation which these steps make possible lies the crowning goal: the unification of all peoples of the world in one universal family.[17]

This process, a task extending into the next several centuries, is an inevitability in Bahá'í thought, and a destiny ordained by God. It is the second phase that complements and supersedes the "Lesser Peace," and is referred to as "The Most Great Peace."

Global Structures and Systems

Recent events in Cambodia, the Balkans, and Rwanda underscore the lack of global political will and the weakness of international institutions to prevent or abate war and its hideous accompaniment: genocide. Political will and adequate international institutions are required to create a stable world order. Without sufficient political will, already weak institutional mechanisms of collective security are undermined and rendered even more ineffective. This institutional ineffectiveness then reinforces and magnifies the decline in political will. These reciprocally reinforce each other in a downwardly spiraling cascade. The global anarchy and terror of the day are the result. A global culture of violence is being nurtured by the failure to create the political will and institutional framework that can support a unified global order.

Incremental efforts to stem the tide of chaos and promote the rule of law are welcome but woefully inadequate. While the great powers debate the extent of their commitment to these crises, a truly global response is put on hold. Over 100 years ago, Bahá'u'lláh called upon the leaders of the world to convene for the purpose of establishing a binding and permanent system of collective security. His call still excites the imagination and offers a clear blueprint by which "The Lesser Peace" can be established. These prescriptions for world governance were summarized by the Universal House of Justice:[18]

---

[17] *The Promise of World Peace*, p. 12.
[18] *Ibid.*, pp. 10–12.

World order can be founded only on an unshakable consciousness of the one-ness of mankind....

Elaborating the implications of this pivotal principle, Shoghi Effendi, the Guardian of the Bahá'í Faith, commented in 1931 that: "Far from aiming at the subversion of the existing foundations of society, it (the Bahá'í Faith) seeks to broaden its basis, to remold its institutions in a manner consonant with the needs of an ever-changing world. It can conflict with no legitimate allegiances, nor can it undermine essential loyalties. Its purpose is neither to stifle the flame of a sane and intelligent patriotism in men's hearts, nor to abolish the system of national autonomy so essential if the evils of excessive centralization are to be avoided. It does not ignore, nor does it attempt to suppress, the diversity of eth-nic origins, of climate, of history, of language and tradition, of thought and habit, that differentiate the peoples and nations of the world. It calls for a wider loyalty, for a larger aspiration than any that has animated the human race. It in-sists upon a subordination of national impulses and interests to the imperative claims of a unified world. It repudiates excessive centralization on one hand, and disclaims all attempts at uniformity on the other. Its watchword is unity in diversity....

"Some form of world super-state must needs be evolved, in whose favor all nations will have willingly ceded every claim to make war, certain rights to im-pose taxation, and all rights to maintain armaments, except for the purposes of maintaining internal order within their respective domains. Such a state will have to include within its orbit an International Executive adequate to enforce supreme and unchangeable authority on every recalcitrant member of the commonwealth; a World Parliament whose members shall be elected by the people in their respective countries and whose election shall be confirmed by their representative governments; and a Supreme Tribunal whose judgment will have a binding effect even in such cases where the parties did not voluntarily agree to submit their case to its consideration.

"A world community in which all economic barriers will have been perma-nently demolished and the interdependence of capital and labor definitely rec-ognized; in which the clamor of religious fanaticism and strife will have been forever stilled, in which the flame of racial animosity will have been finally ex-tinguished; in which a single code of international law—the product of the con-sidered judgment of the world's federated representatives—shall have as its sanction the instant and coercive intervention of the combined forces of the federated units; and finally a world community in which the fury of a capricious and militant nationalism will have been transmuted into an abiding conscious-ness of world citizenship—such indeed, appears, in its broadest outline, the Or-der anticipated by Bahá'u'lláh, an Order that shall come to be regarded as the fairest fruit of a slowly maturing age."

To Bahá'í understanding, the five issues raised earlier—peace and security, economic and social justice, human rights, ecological sustain-ability, and cultural identity and integrity—are impossible to maintain without this essential institutional framework of collective security.

Local Initiatives

Promoting the principle of the oneness of humanity is an essential foundation for peace. This needs to be accomplished at all levels of society. The Bahá'í community has been promoting this principle since its inception. In over 235 countries, territories, and islands where they reside, and in over 121,000 localities, Bahá'ís are promoting the principle of world citizenship. Following the principles referred to above, these efforts are coordinated globally by the Universal House of Justice through its various organs. Since 1983 the Bahá'í community has fostered social and economic development projects throughout the world which give high priority to literacy, cultural preservation, the training of women, and vocational skills, and operate on the principle of the oneness of humanity. Furthermore, these efforts operate on principles that collective action must benefit the community both spiritually and materially, and that projects must spring from the local consultative process and be supported primarily at the grass roots. These projects are intended to serve not only the Bahá'í communities which create them, but the larger community. They are also designed to become self-supporting as much as possible.

The Bahá'í community itself is an invaluable global asset. With its rapidly expanding network of communities, all motivated toward the same end of promoting world unity, all doing so using the unique qualities of their culture of origin, this global community represents a microcosm of the enlarging unity the world hopes to achieve. Our collective experience can offer hope and motivation to those who would question that such a vision might be possible.

Balancing Tensions
Individual Good and Common Good

The careful reader of Bahá'í Texts will find that principles of balance and moderation are repeatedly reinforced. Life, in its complexity, rarely offers clear-cut opportunities to implement one single principle. Oftentimes, one must seek a balance between opposing principles as consultation and the situation require. In this sense, the Bahá'í Teachings do not offer prescriptions, but principles and process. The rest is left to the individual and the community in consultation—to develop progressively the skills these principles will evoke when prayerfully applied in a united spirit. Moderation, then, means finding the skillful balance between virtues in a particular situation. Shoghi Effendi made this point in a letter to the Bahá'ís in America when he said:

> ...Nothing short of the spirit of a true Bahá'í can hope to reconcile the principles of mercy and justice, of freedom and submission, of the sanctity of the right of the individual and of self-surrender, of vigilance, discretion, and prudence on the one hand, and fellowship, candor, and courage on the other.[19]

The idea of balance, then, is familiar to the Bahá'í. It is important to recall that the Bahá'í teachings put great emphasis on creating and maintaining the spirit of loving unity; no decision or crisis should ever detract from this important prerequisite for creating enduring solutions to personal and community problems. This point is enacted in each Bahá'í community in the process of consultation. Having no clergy, the welfare of the community depends on each individual's active involvement in the deliberations determining the community's course of action.

The Bahá'ís are told in their authoritative texts that this unity can best be preserved if each individual speaks his or her views with perfect candor. Yet these opinions must be expressed with courtesy and tact, without intending to inflame or contend. Ideas are meant to clash, not individuals. The Bahá'í in consultation adopts an attitude of searching out the truth. Once his opinions are honestly and completely expressed, ownership of them is relinquished. One cares less for who said what, than for how dispassionate consultation reveals truths no single person may have imagined. Solutions larger than any individual are the result. This process is far superior to the act of compromise between contending views. For in such contention, larger truths are seldom revealed. Consultation welcomes the clash of opinions. Freeing oneself of the ownership of an idea allows the ideas to take flight in ways unimagined. As Abdu'l-Bahá poetically stated:

> The shining spark of truth cometh forth only after the clash of differing opinions.[20]

Once all views have been aired, a decision is carried by consensus if possible, or a majority vote. Once arrived at, a Bahá'í then adopts an at-

---

[19] Shoghi Effendi, *Bahá'í Administration*, pp. 63–64 (Wilmette, Illinois: Bahá'í Publishing Trust, 1974).
[20] Quoted by Shoghi Effendi, *ibid.*, p. 21.

titude of submission to the opinion of the majority. A "loyal opposition" does not exist. Rather, it is felt that by all parties working to implement the consultative decision it will more clearly be revealed if the decision was flawed and needs alteration. Also, in this way good decisions will not be undermined. Through consultation, the individual Bahá'í has reinforced in day-to-day life the value of unified action. This balanced discipline of the consultative process has a transformative and maturing effect on the character of the individual and the community as a whole.

Rights and Responsibilities

Implicit in the above is the notion of the right of the individual to express his or her views freely and completely. This is balanced with the responsibility of the individual to protect the spirit of unity within the community, and ultimately to abide by the decisions of the whole. Further elaboration of rights and responsibilities was mentioned above in "Working Toward a Shared Global Ethic: Human Rights."

Private Sector and Public Sector

Bahá'u'lláh placed responsibility for the provision of care of the needy primarily on the "House of Justice."[21] He was intending a time when Bahá'í local communities will play a major role in the administration of community affairs. In some parts of the world this is the case, where an entire village is Bahá'í. In such settings the public institution of the Local Spiritual Assembly would be considered responsible for ensuring the welfare of all needy. It is also true that Bahá'u'lláh called on those of means to give of their wealth voluntarily for the betterment of the poor. Before they were outlawed by the post-revolutionary government, private foundations did just this in Iran. From these statements in Bahá'í texts, it is apparent that Bahá'u'lláh left room for the creative application of public and private resources for the development of community life.

---

[21] The elected component of the Bahá'í administrative order calls for the creation of institutions at local, national, and international levels. Due to the formative nature of these institutions, they are not yet called by the name Bahá'u'lláh intended for them once they evolve into their full power and capacity. Currently, institutions of Bahá'í administration at the local and national levels are called "Spiritual Assemblies." Internationally, the governing body of the Bahá'í World Community is called the Universal House of Justice. It is anticipated that one day spiritual assemblies will be termed local and national Houses of Justice.

Long-Term and Short-Term Objectives

All the principles listed above in "Working Toward Global Governance: Global Civic Society" constitute what the Bahá'í community feels are matters requiring urgent attention by the peoples of the world, since they are the factors most essential for the creation of global citizenship and the establishment of an international institutional order to preserve it. Creating long- and short-term objectives **will** depend on what level of society is deliberating. Establishing priorities and timelines from among these items will require the consultative process to evaluate the need, resources, and possible course of action available.

Economic and Environmental Needs

This very important topic requires a reexamination of the idea of wealth, global community, and the relationship of humanity with the world of nature. Essentially, the Bahá'í Writings anticipate that the ordered life of the planet must be fundamentally realigned for sustainable growth to occur. The materialistic notion of wealth that currently captures the imagination of the world has led to a consumerism that is widely known to be unsustainable and that, through the depletion of soil, water, and air, is ultimately robbing vast numbers of people of the wealth that might otherwise be theirs. This topic was covered in more detail in "Working Toward a Shared Global Ethic: Ecological Sustainability."

Local, National, and Global Sovereignties

This point has been elaborated throughout the preceding discussion.

Religious Resources for Global Governance

The entire Bahá'í community represents a resource dedicated solely to the promotion of the oneness of humanity through a system of global governance. All of its local institutions and their educational resources, social and economic programs, media and publication abilities, and professional associations are directed toward this goal. Of note in the United States is the Bahá'í Chair for World Peace at the University of Maryland. A total listing of the international resources of the Bahá'í community is far beyond the scope of this paper and could be obtained by area of interest from the Bahá'í International Community Office.[22]

Collaborating with the United Nations and Its Specialized Agencies

Since the inception of the United Nations, the Bahá'í community has been committed to efforts to strengthen its effectiveness. During the first-decade review of the United Nations system, the Bahá'í International Community offered its "Proposals to the United Nations for Charter Revision" on May 23, 1955. These recommendations, which are based on the Writings of Bahá'u'lláh 100 years earlier, continue to form the basis of Bahá'í thought on United Nations reform. These recommendations were expanded upon at the fiftieth anniversary of the United Nations system with the document, "The Turning Point for All Nations."[23]

To quote that document, the Bahá'í perspective on UN reform is based on three initial propositions:

> First, discussions about the future of the United Nations need to take place within the broader context of the evolution of the international order and its direction. The United Nations has co-evolved with other great institutions of the late twentieth century. It is in the aggregate that these institutions will define—and themselves be shaped by—the evolution of the international order. Therefore, the mission, role, operating principles, and even the activities of the United Nations should be examined only in the light of how they fit within the broader objective of the international order.
>
> Second, since the body of humanity is one and indivisible, each member of the human race is born into the world as a trust of the whole. This relationship between the individual and the collective constitutes the moral foundation of most of the human rights which the instruments of the United Nations are attempting to define. It also serves to define an overriding purpose for the international order in establishing and preserving the rights of the individual.
>
> Third, the discussions about the future of the international order must evolve and excite the generality of humankind. This discussion is so important that it cannot be confined to leaders—be they in government, business, the academic community, religion, or organizations of civil society. On the contrary, this conversation must engage women and men at the grassroots level.

---

[22] Bahá'í International Community, 866 United Nations Plaza, Suite 120, New York, NY 10017 USA, Tel. (212) 803-2500, Fax (212) 803-2566.

[23] "The Turning Point for All Nations, A Statement of the Bahá'í International Community on the Occasion of the 50th Anniversary of the United Nations." Bahá'í International Community United Nations Office, New York, October 1995.

Broad participation will make the process self-reinforcing by raising awareness of world citizenship and increase support for an expanded international order.[24]

With these provisos, the convening of the world's leaders to define the parameters of the international order and fix the institutional structures that can best support it should be pursued with all vigor.[25]

To suggest modifications of the UN system first requires an understanding of the context of these suggestions in the evolving global order. The way in which the world order has been constructed since the end of the Second World War largely defines the successes and limitations of the UN system. A world in which two major political and economic ideologies struggled for the allegiance of the world's peoples and resources froze the UN's instruments and prevented their evolving into the forces they might have been for the promotion of a peaceful global order. In effectiveness, the UN cannot be compared to other institutions because it has never been more than what its component members have allowed it to be. To indict the UN, then, is essentially to indict the prevailing global order and the limitations of unfettered national sovereignty.

It is most helpful to view the effectiveness of the UN as an indicator of the cohesiveness of global identity. By and large, when the world is united in purpose, the UN is an effective instrument; when it isn't, neither is the UN. This point underscores the idea that UN reform must be considered in the context of envisioning the necessities of the evolving global order as a whole.

Taken as such, viewing the UN with an eye toward its evolution as an institution provides a sense of opportunity.

Studying the United Nations from this perspective unveils significant opportunities to strengthen the current system without the wholesale restructuring of its principles or the intensive re-engineering of its core processes. In fact, we submit that no proposal for UN reform can produce high impact unless its recommendations are internally consistent and direct the UN along a projected path toward a distinctive and relevant role within the future international order.[26]

Having made these points, the Bahá'í International Community in "The Turning Point for All Nations" calls for a series of efforts, both to

---

[24] "Turning Point," pp. 3–4.
[25] The details of this proposal were mentioned above in "Working Toward Global Governance: Global Structures and Systems."
[26] *Ibid.*, p. 7.

restructure the United Nations and to provide for the global framework that can support a stable world order. Regarding the United Nations, that document offers the following:

> First, the rule of law, and not arbitrary power, must become the guiding princi-
> ple for the new world order. In this regard, a representative and democratic
> body must serve as a legislature to enact the law. At present, however, the un-
> due weight placed on national sovereignty inhibits the natural development of
> regional and international institutions. This "undue weight" results in "a curi-
> ous mix of anarchy and conservatism" in the international order. The anarchy
> is seen in the unchecked lawlessness manifesting in militarism, organized crime,
> terrorism, and violence in the world, while the conservative forces are essen-
> tially marshaled to protect the rights of states. The scale on which these inter-
> national crises exist exceeds the reach of nation-states. An impartial and
> balanced reappraisal of the limits of state sovereignty is a critical component of
> UN reform. A system must evolve that guarantees state sovereignty where ap-
> propriate and delegates all other authorities to the appropriate level of govern-
> ance, be it local or international.

In this regard, in a reformed United Nations "the legislative branch and its voting structure will need to represent more accurately the people of the world as well as nation-states."[27]

Second, for the General Assembly's deliberations and enactments to have more than symbolic meaning, they must gradually come to possess the force of law with provisions for both enforcement and sanctions.

General Assembly: Five practical measures are put forth in "The Turn-ing Point for All Nations" that can be applied in the short term to strengthen the General Assembly, enhance its reputation, and align it with its long-term role within an evolving world order. These include raising the minimum requirements for membership; appointing a commis-sion to study borders and frontiers; searching for new financial arrange-ments; making a commitment to a universal auxiliary language and common script; investigating the possibility of a single international cur-rency.

Developing the capacity of the executive function is also essential for an effective United Nations. The primary function of the executive must be the enforcement of collective security arrangements. The shared ex-ecutive functions between the Security Council and Secretariat will re-quire reconsideration. Four measures are suggested in "The Turning

---

[27] *Ibid.*, p. 8.

Point for All Nations" in this regard: limiting the exercise of the veto power; institutionalizing *ad hoc* military arrangements; applying the notion of collective security to other problems of the global common; retaining successful UN institutions with independent executive functions.

Regarding the International Court of Justice (the World Court), several points are timely in considering ways to make its judgments more effective. At present, the court has authority only in cases where both parties agree in advance to abide by its ruling. Having no real jurisdiction, the court is essentially powerless. The Bahá'í International Community envisions that in time, the decisions of the World Court will be binding on all states. In the short term, extending the Court's jurisdiction and coordinating the thematic courts are preliminary steps toward that end.

Strengthening the role of individuals in global governance: along with the revisions to the structure of the UN system, such initiatives are essential. Releasing the potential of individuals is one of the primary roles of governance. Global governance must meet this challenge on an unprecedented scale to ensure its ultimate success. As mentioned earlier, promoting the principle of global citizenship, economic development, protecting human rights, advancing the status of women, promoting and emphasizing moral development are priorities tied closely to the advancement of civilization. Considering the primary role these play, they should be given special emphasis in the agenda of the United Nations.

Economic development: Launching a determined effort to secure the success of *Agenda 21* (the document produced by the UN Conference on Environment and Development in 1992) would go a long way to restarting meaningful efforts at sustainable global economic development.

Human rights: Three immediate actions are proposed: strengthening the UN machinery for monitoring implementation and follow-up; encouraging universal ratification of international human rights conventions; assuring respect for UN monitoring organs involved in human rights.

Status of women: "The Turning Point for All Nations" recommends increasing the participation of women in member-state delegations; encouraging universal ratification of international conventions that protect women's rights and improve their status; planning ahead for implementation of the Beijing Platform of Action.

The Bahá'í International Community, through its offices in New

York and Geneva, has been an active participant in UN affairs in its role as a recognized nongovernmental organization.[28] Bahá'í communities throughout the world are engaged in social, economic, and humanitarian activities that promote the goals elaborated in the Preamble of the UN Charter. The Bahá'í International Community United Nations Office is the voice of these activities to the world community.

Close working relationships or consultative status exists between the Bahá'í International Community and the UN Economic and Social Council (ECOSOC), the United Nations Children's Fund (UNICEF), the World Health Organization (WHO), the United Nations Environment Program (UNEP), the UN Center for Human Rights, the United Nations Development Program (UNDP), and the United Nations Development Fund for Women (UNIFEM). The Bahá'í International Community regularly participates in sessions of such UN bodies as the Commission on Human Rights, the Commission on the Status of Women, and the Commission on Sustainable Development. Between 1989 and 1993, it offered over 70 statements on a wide range of issues, as reflected in the most recent quadrennial report of ECOSOC.

But the greatest asset the Bahá'í International Community possesses in support of the United Nations is the community itself. A worldwide community of over 5 million highly dedicated women, men, children, and youth whose one goal is to promote the reality of the oneness of humanity presents to the world a great asset. Committed to nonpartisan involvement in the development of global culture and the preservation of the rich diversity of the peoples and resources of the world, the Bahá'í community is a microcosm of the world envisioned by seers and saints from time immemorial.

Developing Multireligious Initiatives

Bahá'u'lláh exhorted all humanity to "consort with the followers of all religions with friendliness and kindness." It is a central tenet of Bahá'í belief that all Founders of the great religions are inspired by the same God. Each provides the quickening impulse to human nature that is the very root of civilization. Each religion speaks to the deepest heart of the

---

[28] Coordination of Bahá'í involvement with international institutions of collective security began in 1926, with the establishment of the International Bahá'í Bureau at the League of Nations Headquarters in Geneva.

human soul, and there causes the trust of God to develop through faith and assurance. Each provides guidance toward the ethical life.[29] In speaking of the Founders of the great religions, Bahá'u'lláh explained:

> Their unity is absolute. God, the Creator, saith: There is no distinction whatsoever among the Bearers of My Message. They all have but one purpose; their secret is the same secret. To prefer one in honor to another, to exalt certain ones above the rest, is in no wise to be permitted. Every true Prophet hath regarded His Message as fundamentally the same as the Revelation of every other Prophet gone before Him.[30]

Appreciating the unity of the Messengers of God confirms us in our sense of humility before all great outpourings of the spirit. Understanding the Divine Purpose in sending these Founders of the great religions assures us of the importance and ultimate success of the endeavor to pursue religious collaboration in building effective systems of global governance. Again, in the Words of Bahá'u'lláh:

> God's purpose in sending His Prophets unto men is twofold. The first is to liberate the children of men from the darkness of ignorance, and guide them to the light of true understanding. The second is to ensure the peace and tranquility of mankind, and to provide the means by which they can be established.[31]

It is for the promotion of these aims that Bahá'ís direct all the energies of their lives. Despite these motives, in the land where their Faith was born, Bahá'ís still suffer harsh repression and persecution. By their example of steadfast hope, they bear witness to the truth that, by the grace of God, what is noble in human nature is what ultimately unites us all as one family. And amidst ceaseless persecution, it is to their faith in

---

[29] The Golden Rule is an ethic variously repeated in all great religions. *Buddhism:* "Hurt not others in ways that you yourself would find hurtful" (*Udana-Varqa*, 5:18). *Hinduism:* "This is the sum of all true righteousness: deal with others as thou wouldst thyself be dealt. Do nothing to thy neighbor which thou wouldst not have him do to thee after." *Judaism:* "What is hateful to you, do not to your fellow men. That is the entire Law, all the rest is commentary." *Zoroastrianism:* "That nature is only good when it shall not do unto another whatever is not good for its own self." *Christianity:* "As ye would that men should do unto you, do ye also to them likewise." *Islam:* "No one of you is a believer until he desires for his brother that which he desires for himself." *Bahá'í Faith:* "He should not wish for others that which he doth not wish for himself, nor promise that which he doth not fulfill."
[30] Bahá'u'lláh, *Gleanings from the Writings of Bahá'u'lláh* (Wilmette, Illinois: Bahá'í Publishing Trust, 1971), p. 79.
[31] *Ibid.*, p. 80.

the oneness of the human spirit under God's protection that we draw confidence in the emphatic promise of Bahá'u'lláh that:

> These fruitless strifes, these ruinous wars shall pass away, and the Most Great Peace shall come.

African Traditions

African Religion and World Order
by John S. Mbiti

Toward a Shared Global Ethic:
The Contribution of African Culture
by Mary J. Mwingira

African Religion and World Order

John S. Mbiti

The term "African Religion," as used here, refers to the traditional religious system of African peoples, which evolved through the centuries as they experienced life and reflected upon its realities and mysteries. African Religion had no founder, and we cannot give a date for its origin, but it seems to go back thousands of years and to have been woven into the total history of African peoples. This religious heritage is integrated into their whole worldview, with both local differences from place to place and certain commonalities that are widely spread throughout the continent. Many of the features of African Religion have parallels in other religions of the world. This gives African Religion considerable relevance for human society at large.

This paper will examine a number of elements of the African religious heritage that seem to have applicability to world order questions. These select elements have a positive value in the African setting; we would not wish to forget that in any system there are also unpleasant aspects, a host of demons. African Religion is not a religious paradise, nor is it going to solve problems which have bedeviled humankind from time immemorial. It is only a voice among many other voices, but perhaps a voice which has not been heard sufficiently in the global community. Furthermore, we should keep in mind that these elements make most sense within the contexts in which they developed, contexts that are a complex combination of cultural, historical, economic, and social factors. When taken out of their contexts, these elements lose something of their authenticity, genuineness, and naturalness; they may even get distorted and neutralized. In sum, they are basically particularistic in place and time.

Religion and Community

Writing over 50 years ago, Jomo Kenyatta, later to become the first president of the Republic of Kenya, observed among his people, the Gikuyu, that "There is no one man's religion." What he said about one part of Africa can be applied to many other African peoples. Religion is for the whole community, and the whole community is held together by its religion. In African Religion people or humanity are regarded as a composition of corporate individuals and interrelationships. One individual over against the community cannot stand up and claim a meaningful religion which does not relate to the rest of the community. To be is to be in community, in relation with others. This corporateness carries with it both privileges and responsibilities.

The African religious worldview on the community is perhaps best summed up in the statement: "I am because we are, and since we are, therefore I am." This philosophy can be illustrated by a variety of examples and considerations. Let us take a few of these. Throughout Africa we find traditional myths and stories that tell about the origin of humankind. In these, humans appear on the scene as either a couple or two couples (allowing for the wish to avoid incest among the first children). Whatever the origin of the human species, African Religion has the basic view that humankind is a unity from the very beginning.

This primeval unity has not been destroyed by time and history: it has simply been multiplied. Not only was humanity created in a nucleus community, but the method or substance of creation was one, according to African mythology. Thus, for example, it is told among the Bambuti Pygmies, the Fon, the Shilluk, and many others that God used clay to fashion the first human beings. The Yao, the Basuto, the Shonea and Zulu, among others, believe that the first people sprang from a hole in a rock; the Herero say that the first couple (husband and wife) came from a mythical "tree of life" situated in the underworld; the Chagga and the Azande hold that God burst out of a vessel or canoe and released the first people. A rather different myth from the Masai holds that one of four original gods came to the earth from the sky and became human; out of this sprang all human beings, starting with the Masai themselves. The Banyarwanda still have in their language the name of the first person:

Kazikamuntu ("Root-of-people").

Thus in African mythology, the roots of the peoples of the world spring from a primeval unity. African Religion has affirmed and tried to express this unity, even if it has been strongly opposed. We see the expressions of community in the social clusters of the family, the clan, the tribe, the nation, and humanity at large. There are obligations, responsibilities, and privileges for the individual and the community at all these points of reference. In African concepts, the family is a microcosm of human society as a whole; it is also the nerve center of the community. Within the walls of the family one learns to experience and practice the meaning of "I am because we are," for this is initially a biological and social awareness. One is in relationship with the biological ancestors without whom one cannot be. But that vertical line toward the original ancestry is matched also by a horizontal line, by which the individuals in a given traditional community are interrelated in such a way that each one has, literally, hundreds of social mothers and fathers, hundreds of brothers, sisters, uncles, and so on.

These social relations are not static, but living. When one member of the community suffers, the rest share the suffering and thus lighten the burden. When two members get married, in reality it is their respective families and communities who get married with them, and together hope for the procreation of children. African Religion affirms community also through the place and position given to children. Each young person is a carrier of seeds which should become the next generation. Marriage and procreation are a moral obligation imposed by the community on the individual, because they facilitate the renewal and perpetuation of the community.

Community within the traditional context includes both the living and the departed. According to African Religion, human life does not terminate with physical death. The person continues to exist in the spirit world, a world parallel to the world of the living. Therefore both the living and departed have intimate contacts. People claim to see the spirits of the departed, directly or through visions and dreams. The details about these links between the living and departed vary from place to place, but the main issue is that there is no clear separation between the physical and spiritual realms of human existence. The welfare of humans in this world has consequences for the welfare of humans in the spiritual world. People have an ongoing awareness of the world of the invisible and spiritual realities.

The ethical values that sustain the community are societal and relational. People are judged not only on the basis of what they are, but primarily on the basis of what they do. A person is "good" or "bad" in relational terms, the terms that relate him or her to the corporate community. The moral qualities that are valued most include kindness, showing of hospitality, truthfulness, respect for others (of older or higher rank), justice, protection (toward the younger and weaker), sharing, and so on.

Obviously this intimate corporate framework of society has its own problems. An African proverb summarizes the situation succinctly: "Axes carried in the same bag cannot avoid rattling with one another." So rattles and scratches are inflicted by individuals, and by the community and its members, upon one another. Nevertheless, the community element has withstood this rattling through many generations.

The Element of Celebration

The element of celebration is prominent in African Religion. To live is to celebrate. Celebration expresses praise, thanksgiving, and joy. In praise and thanksgiving toward God, the human soul acknowledges its dependence on God. People have many things for which to thank and praise God, including God's answer to their prayers, restoring them to good health, and giving them children, rain, and harvest.

Here is a traditional African song in which everything is summoned to offer praise to God. This prayer song is accompanied by movement of the body, dancing, clapping, and general rejoicing in the community.

> I shall sing a song of praise to God—
> Strike the chords upon the drum.
> God who gives us all good things—
> Strike the chords upon the drum—
> Wives and wealth and wisdom,
> Strike the chords upon the drum.

Celebration in African Religion is expressed through dances, festivals, and rituals. For the wider community, these festivals and rituals are related to the agricultural year and the keeping of livestock; within the smaller community the focus is on life span and concerns of the individual. Embodying what people believe and what they value most in life, rituals and festivals are religious ways of implementing these values and beliefs of society. They cement together the life of the individual with that of the community. Through them, the individual personalizes his or her part in the wider and corporate community. They provide continuity and unity among those who perform or attend them. The ritual world has a degree of sacredness and authority about it, and it links people with the divine realm.

Personal rituals highlight moments in the life of the individual for which there is cause to celebrate. Starting with pregnancy and continuing at birth, these personal milestones in some societies may mark naming, teething, puberty, circumcision and other forms of initiation, engagement, wedding, procreation, old age, death, and beyond. These rituals affirm the value of the individual; the individual matters and has a meaningful place in society. At the same time they integrate individuals more and more into the community of which they are members. The rituals provide occasions for community celebration. In personal rituals, the whole community is regenerated, and its rhythm of existence is reactivated and perpetuated.

Agricultural rituals and festivals have to do with both land and livestock. Farming rituals reaffirm the people's unity with soil, land, crops, and seasons of the year. There are, for example, individuals in many African societies who specialize in concerns of the weather, particularly rain. Rainmaking rituals, performed before the start of the rainy season, are religious acts of linking the sky with the earth, sanctifying life, renewing and reviving life both for human beings and other creatures. In this act, people play the role of the priest of nature, responsible toward nature, respecting nature and covenanting with nature. There are rituals performed when people clear forests or bushes to make a new field, which serve to remove danger and confer blessings upon the use of the new field. Rituals for sowing seeds, weeding the fields, tasting the first fruits, harvesting the crop, and even putting the harvest in store—these are occasions for celebrating, rejoicing, and blessing the seeds or harvest. Through them, people link themselves mystically with the world of plants and crops, soil and weather. They harmonize human life with the life of nature at large.

Stock-keeping rituals and festivals mark the killing, eating, milking, selling, and bloodletting of animals (cattle, sheep, and goats, in particular). Other rituals with animals relate to the drawing up or sealing of contracts. As with other agricultural rituals, human life is linked through ritual to that of animals in a mystical way.

There are also rituals that have to do with health, home, and family life. These are intended to prolong human life and make the life of the homestead and family run smoothly.

Festivals generally accompany many of these rituals. Thus, there are planting and harvest festivals, fishing and hunting festivals, coronation and accession festivals, and so on. In some societies, festivals are heightened by the use of masks, dancing, praying, benedictions, and general jubilation. Through festivals, the life of the community is renewed. People are entertained and their tensions are given an outlet. Festivals bring people together as a group and strengthen their unity and cohesion. Momentarily, the sorrows, fears, anxieties, and even loss through death in a given community are overcome by the power of festivals and celebration. Festivals renew the spiritual morale of the community. The rhythm of the rituals and festivals provides a therapeutic continuity of celebration of life, which gives people the courage and strength to smile even in the midst of adversities and hardships.

Healing, Health, and Wholeness

African peoples know only too well the ravages of diseases, natural calamities, famines, and suffering. In its own way, African Religion has tried to answer to this basic and common experience. Two thrusts have been developed: a search for the mystical causes of disease, and an approach to the question of health and healing from the perspectives of the whole community.

In the African worldview, disease, accident, and calamity are caused by mystical forces. It is not enough to explain that bad sanitation is responsible for a variety of intestinal infections. People want to find out *who*, and not just *what*, makes a particular person contract an intestinal infection. They want to know *who* and not *what* has caused someone to fall from a tree while picking fruit; *who*, not only *what*, has caused the young calves to die or the fields to produce poor crops.

The mystical causes must be identified and then dealt with accordingly. These are usually said to be magic, witchcraft, sorcery, broken taboos, the evil eye, a misfortune-causing "tongue" (word), and curses. Someone in the community is held responsible for provoking the mystical power, or for employing it secretly to victimize others or their property. In most of these cases, it is held that relationships between people among themselves, or between them and spiritual realities, have been broken, and consequently the offended party reverts to using mystical power to take revenge. But sometimes this is done out of jealousy and hatred among the people.

There exist, therefore, experts and specialists who handle this serious aspect of community life. These include the traditional doctors (not without reason, though wrongly, called "witch doctors" in popular missionary literature and propaganda), diviners, mediums, conductors of rituals, and priests who address themselves to this area. The professions of these men and women are highly respected in their communities. Those who serve in this capacity receive a "calling," followed by training (of up to ten years in some cases), a kind of "public" commissioning, and a sincere acceptance by their communities. As with any other profession, there are crooks who pose as experts but are only there to cheat and exploit the needy.

Traditionally, the process of solving such problems as illness, barrenness, or calamity starts with finding out who in the community has caused them through the use of mystical power. Then follows the use of medicaments and sometimes rituals of healing. The victim must be given the assurance that the mystical forces have been removed, and steps are taken to prevent their effectiveness if they should be employed against the victim again. By identifying the "who"-cause, the process of reconciliation and restoring good relations in the family or community is also set in motion. It is assumed that when good relations prevail in the community, there is no need for any member to do harm to another. The good health of one is the good health of all. The approach to health and wholeness is more sociological and pastoral than physical, even if people do not consciously draw such a distinction.

Exorcisms are commonly practiced in African societies. They point to the world of spiritual beings, especially the spirits of the departed. There are also spirits associated with natural objects. Both kinds of spirits are believed to "possess" people, and therefore to disturb the health of individuals and the community. Diviners identify which spirits have possessed someone, and exorcise them accordingly. Again the question of the community (of the living and the departed) is featured here, underlining the basic wish for a harmonious relationship between the world of human beings and the realm of spiritual realities.

Respect for Nature

Another basic element of African Religion concerns human relations with the world of nature. Humans are not masters over nature to exploit it without feeling or treat it without respect. Instead, people are one with nature, responsible toward nature, able to communicate with nature, and the chief priests of nature. Humans should stay in harmony with nature, caring for it so that nature may also care for them. If they misuse or abuse nature, nature will strike back and cause them to suffer.

This posture of the human person *vis-à-vis* nature is not "nature worship"—a term wrongly used by ignorant outside observers when they wrote about African religious life. Nature is potentially a friend with whom humans may communicate, whose cooperation they may solicit, and whose generosity is a benefit for them. These points are best illustrated by a prayer traditionally recited by the official keeper of the community woods and forests among the Didinga people in the Sudan. In this prayer, the earth, the woods, and the streams are personified in order to communicate with nature. The supplicant pleads with them, waits for their favor, and promises to thank them by offering the first fruits of the field and the blood of goats. These sentiments illustrate a wish to be in harmony with nature. It is assumed all along that God superintends human acts in relation to nature, since God is Creator and Keeper of both humans and nature. Here then is the prayer as it is recited by the "warden of the forest, master of the clan," in the presence of God, the departed, the living, and the earth (nature).

> O Earth, wherever it be my people dig, be kindly to them. Be fertile when they give the little seeds to your keeping. Let your generous warmth nourish them and your abundant moisture germinate them. Let them swell and sprout, drawing life from you, and burgeon under your fostering care: and soon we shall redden your bosom with the blood of goats slain in your honor, and offer to you the first fruits of your munificence, first fruits of millet and oil of sesame, of gourds and cucumbers and deep-mashed melons.
> O Trees of forest and glade, fall easily under the axe. Be gentle to my people. Let no harm come to them. Break no limb in your anger. Crush no one in your displeasure. Be obedient to the woodman's wishes and fall as he would have you fall, not perversely nor stubbornly, but as his axe directs. Submit yourselves freely to my people, as this tree has submitted itself to me. The axe rings, it bites into the tough wood. The tree totters and falls. The lightning flashes, its fire tears at the heart of the wood. The tree totters and falls. Before the lightning the tree falls headlong, precipitate, knowing neither direction nor guidance. But the Woodman guides the tree where he wills and lays it to rest gently

and with deliberation. Fall O trees of forest and glade, even as this tree has fallen, hurting no one, obedient, observant of my will.

O Rivers and Streams, where the Woodman has laid bare the earth, where he has hewn away the little bushes and torn out encumbering grass, there let your waters overflow. Bring down the leafy mold from the forest and the fertilizing silt from the mountains. When the rains swell your banks, spread out your waters and lay your rich treasures on our gardens.

Conspire together, O Earth and Rivers: conspire together, O Earth and Rivers and Forests. Be gentle and give us plenty from your teeming plenty. For it is I, Lomingamoi of the clan of Idots, who speaks, keeper of the clan lands, warden of the forest, master of the clan.

This prayer shows the considerable degree of human feelings toward nature and the personified feelings of nature toward people that are characteristic of African Religion. Nature is summoned to be "kind," to nourish the seeds, to give people out of its plenty and receive gratitude from them in return. Nature can show "anger" toward people, and "crush" them in its displeasure. Humans must, therefore, relate in a harmonious way to the woods, fields, ground, harvest, and animals.

African Religion is a total system that is fully integrated into the traditional life of the peoples of Africa. But what has been a fairly self-sufficient system for many generations is now being challenged by the demands of a changing world scene. The peoples of Africa have begun to become peoples of the world. There is a growing convergence with the rest of the world, a sharing of history, of destiny, of the fears and hopes of one world. The spreading of the Christian faith, the expansion of colonial Europe in the nineteenth and twentieth centuries, the miraculous fruits and promises of technology, these and many other factors have forced Africa to move out of isolation and provincialism, to a more global platform. This global orientation demands taking the future seriously.

But looking to the distant future has not been a strong element in African religious thought. It has entertained no concept of history moving either toward a particular goal or consummation, or toward an apocalyptic end of the world. African concepts of time emphasize the past and the present, plus only a brief projection into the future. African languages have difficulty expressing concepts of a distant future dimension of time. Whereas there are thousands of myths about the past, there are no myths of the distant future in African Religion.

African peoples have traditionally been deeply religious. Their worldview is a religious one, and it is out of that worldview that we have isolated some elements which could be added to the global world-order platform. These elements include emphasis on the basic unity of human-kind, on a community framework of life, on a posture of celebrating life, on a community approach to matters of health and wholeness, and on humankind's respect for nature. Africa brings these religious elements into the open in its interaction with the peoples of other continents and islands.

These elements have been of enduring value in the context of African traditional society. But can they be incorporated into the vision of world order? In what ways can the world realize the implications of the unity of humankind? Can we in the midst of today's injustices and strug-gles find and nourish a meaningful community life? Can we incorporate a spirit of celebration that respects the life of the individual as well as the life of the community? Is there still room and time for us to establish a relationship with nature that incorporates human respect for and respon-sibility toward nature?

Positive answers can be given to these questions, but they can only be answers in the process of struggling to make them come true. I am convinced that religion has a place and role to play in shaping this vision of the future of humankind and making it come true. Religion projects a certain order of life, carved out of people's experiences and reflections. Left to itself, religion might sacramentalize the whole of life. But obvi-ously life is more complex than that and other considerations exert their influence in shaping human life and history, such as politics, economics, ideologies, science, and technology. Nevertheless, we need a spiritual dimension to undergird the emerging development of human society. It is within religion that we can seek this spiritual undergirding. It is also within religion that we can best wrestle with the above questions and with the meaning, purpose, and ultimate destiny of human existence; and in this spiritual task, African Religion has a unique place and a special role to play.

Toward a Shared Global Ethic: The Contribution of African Culture

Mary J. Mwingira

Working Toward a Shared Global Ethic
Peace and Security

Harmony, peaceful coexistence, cooperation, and the sharing of tasks are among the greatest values of African societies. In the traditional setting, life is considered to be the most precious gift from God which is to be protected by all. There is a saying which stresses that any child, born or unborn, belongs to the clan and the community; no single person, including the mother who carries the baby in her womb, has the right to destroy or eliminate life. According to African tradition, therefore, the protection of life and nature is a common and joint responsibility of the entire community. The right to live is considered one of the most fundamental human rights of the African people.

Through the traditional extended-family system, children are always assured of protection and full parental care because a child has more than just one pair of parents. The brothers and male relatives of one's father, as well as the sisters and female relatives of one's mother, are all responsible as co-fathers and co-mothers, with full parental responsibilities to their brothers, sisters, and children. Sociologically, therefore, African children are not supposed to be orphaned or abandoned. In the current situation of great interdependence even among nations, this African principle of being each other's sisters and brothers, sons and daughters, can contribute to peace, security, and unconditional love for all.

Peace and security are moreover guaranteed by the principles of dialogue and participation of all concerned with an issue. In an effort to describe African democracy, Mwalimu Julius Kambarage Nyerere, the first president of Tanzania, said the following:

> The African people had their own way of ensuring democracy. In reaching decisions on an issue or how to solve a problem, the elders would sit under a tree or at the chief's homestead and talk, and talk, and talk, and talk...until they agreed.

A life of harmony was, and is still, a very important value among the people of Tanzania. Surrounded by countries of conflict, ethnic clashes, and unending wars on all borders, a special love for peace and security has for many years enabled Tanzania to be a peaceful home for refugees and avoid conflicts of war and fights within the country.

In the traditional system of chiefdoms, or councils of elders, and traditionally respected professions—goldsmiths, healers, fortune-tellers, rainmakers, birth attendants, and potmakers—there is a clearly defined relationship of power and authority. However, in most cases, power is exercised not violently but through the making of wise and acceptable decisions, and the ability to convince leaders or clients. Power is drawn from the people themselves, to be exercised for their own well-being and not their abuse or torture.

Special occasions like births, initiation ceremonies, weddings, and funerals are also opportunities to resolve conflicts within the family and at the clan level. Reconciliation and a peaceful atmosphere are prerequisites for blessed and fruitful family celebrations. At such occasions in southern Tanzania, for example, reconciliation among conflicting relatives is facilitated by clan elders. The people in conflict are required to chew special herbs and spit in each other's faces, then utter words of forgiveness. The elders, too, utter words of reconciliation and demand the shaking of hands. This is followed by sharing food from the same plate to mark the end of the conflict. This special ritual is done differently among other African tribes, but the basic principle is common. Peace of mind and heart is a precondition for effective and blessed community undertakings.

African teachings and traditions emphasize the significance of peace for development, appreciating the fact that only when peace prevails can sustainable development be achieved. The current world challenges, including violence and threats to global peace manifested by conflicting parties' unwillingness to reconcile, compel us to refer to our histories and cultures. There is a need to reawaken people's consciences and reintroduce positive values like the craving for peace of mind and heart and a life of harmony and absence of hypocrisy. Otherwise the world may find itself destroying the very persons it tries to protect and respect.

Economic and Social Justice

Where socioeconomic justice is concerned, the principle of collective responsibility for caring is crucial. Most African social systems have opted for what can be called "African socialism," denying the extremes of capitalism and Marxism. There is a rejection of individualism—that is, thinking of self and profit only—and also a rejection of class structures. The first president of Kenya, Jomo Kenyatta, had this to say regarding the economic and social systems of Africa, and Kenya in particular:

> We demand that our country would develop on the basis of the concept and philosophy of Democratic African Socialism. We reject both Western capitalism and Eastern communism and choose for ourselves positive non-alignment.

The main aim of Kenyatta was to build an economy which would ensure individual participation while respecting equal and equitable access to and control of resources and decisions, and collective responsibility. In the words of Kenneth Kaunda, the first president of Zambia:

> Let the West have its technology and the East its mysticism. Africa's gift to the world culture must be in the realm of human relationships.... Man is growing in self-knowledge and will one day fully realize his capabilities. He is painfully thrusting his way forward and will in the process evolve economic institutions to which he can be adjusted and within which his vices will be neutralized and his virtues strengthened.

The concern of Dr. Kaunda is that the world, learning from African humanism, should evolve a human-centered society as opposed to a materialistic and power-centered society. What is inherent in African economic systems is the guarantee of an adequate and secure livelihood to all members of the society. Economic justice and equitable distribution of goods and services are in a way ensured.

Another important principle worth mentioning here is the "communalism" of Dr. Kwame Nkrumah, first president of Ghana. He stressed that African societies are "cooperative-communalistic." He called upon the larger society, in this case the nations, to learn from village life and find ways of living as brothers and sisters, sharing resources. This is a challenge at all levels, even to the largest—the world. How can we find ways of crushing rising inequalities and mentalities of domination and bring about equality and respect of the weaker cultures, as well as a spirit of sharing? Solidarity has to be the basis of global economic development.

This brings me to highlight the policy of *Ujamaa*, or "familihood," advocated by Mwalimu Julius Kambarage Nyerere of Tanzania. The basic characteristics of Nyerere's and Tanzania's *Ujamaa* are as follows:

- Contribution and work by every member of society
- Respect for what one is and not for what one has
- Absence of exploitation
- Equality and equity
- Democracy: participation of all concerned in decisions and actions

Human Rights

The familihood system also guarantees respect for individual as well as collective human rights. It sees a great relationship, however, between individual and community rights and the importance of respecting the rights of others.

In 1981, the African heads of state who were members of the Organization of African Unity (OAU) adopted the *African Charter on Human and Peoples' Rights* at the OAU's 18th Conference. The Charter recognizes the rights and freedoms of individuals, but within the context of respect for others. It states strongly that each person is entitled to life and the respect and protection of that life. Under Article 18, the Charter recognizes the place and importance of the African family as a natural unit and the basis of society, and commits states to protect the family.

In the Charter, the role of the family is seen as the custodian of moral values, which are human-centered. Harmony and respect within the family unit are stressed by insisting on the elimination of all forms of discrimination against women and the importance of protecting the rights of children. The Charter therefore practically ensures that member states work on the promotion of human rights, especially the rights of women, youth, and children—in most cases the vulnerable groups.

Global society can draw a number of lessons from the African Charter. It is an instrument which can remind global citizens of the importance of placing people and humanity first, not only as individuals, but also as members of families and communities. It places great value on individual freedom in relation to the freedom of others and the need to be people-centered. The global economy must recognize and take into account equity and maintenance of human-centered development. This also refers to policies on industrialization and investments.

Working Toward Global Governance
Criteria for Global Civil Society

Some of the most important factors emphasized by *Ujamaa*, or familihood based on African traditions and faith, are solidarity and participation by all concerned. Even today, with great steps in civilization and technological advancement, nation-states are becoming less and less capable of controlling trends of behavior and meeting people's needs. Many resolutions and agreements passed at UN and regional meetings are becoming paper documents only, which are either domesticated into national laws and policies, or not implemented or followed up.

This is a clear indication that more than governments and good political will are required to manage life and ensure peace, security, economic and social justice, ecological sustainability, and cultural integrity. From the perspective of African values and beliefs, some of the criteria for global governance are as follows:

1. respect and recognition of each nation and each culture as a potential contributor to the new world order;

2. placing great value on nature and the integrity of creation;

3. participation by all, according to ability and experience;

4. work by all in society (all those with ability and capacity to work should work and be gainfully employed);

5. cooperation and solidarity;

6. tolerance and respect of the views and ideas of each person in the society, and maintenance of peace;

7. sharing of information, knowledge, technology, and techniques as well as material things, for the purpose of improving the quality of life for all in society;

8. respect for authority which is human and people-centered; and

9. fear of God, respect for life and the image of God in each person, and

respect of the work of God in creation and the works of human persons.

Although the above criteria are drawn from African faith values and traditions, it is also clear that they express the God- and humanity-centeredness of Christian life. Oswald Hirmer, one of the writers in the "Christian Leadership in Africa" series, writes in his book *The Gospel and Social Systems in Africa* about Christ's Manifesto. He mentions the Sermon on the Mount, the eight Beatitudes, and the Nazareth Proclamation (Luke 4:16–20) as the manifesto and guiding principles for Christian life. A deep reflection on the criteria mentioned above shows great similarities between Oswald Hirmer's Christ's Manifesto and the preconditions for global governance.

In the context of African life and communities, the spirit of solidarity, concern for one another, and communal responsibility is concretized through social action programs developed and implemented by various actors within civil society and nongovernmental organizations. The churches and other religious institutions play a leading role in providing education and health services to community members, as well as promoting higher economic living standards in rural and urban areas.

In order to allow for a new world order which will not be governed and dominated by the acquisitive and power-seeking culture, civil society has to apply pressure for a freedom of renewal. Governments must create space to build and renew relationships among people of different cultures and nations and reduce restrictions which exclude people on account of their economic, religious, or racial status. At the same time, it is important for those in power to recognize human limitations and vulnerability in relationship to God. Today, the tendency is to believe that we can build a world which is God- and values-free: this tendency leads to our own doom.

Global Structures and Systems
Local Initiatives

At the moment, most global structures and systems promote the concepts of the dominant cultures and survival of the fittest. The tendency is to create structures favoring liberalism and the promotion of individual human rights, and tending to ignore the rights of the weak and vulnerable. Even structures like the United Nations, and regional and/or continental unions of member states like the Organization of African Unity, seem to be governed by the wishes of the economically powerful, even if their charters and conventions talk about the common good. At global meetings the tendency is to end up with "consensus" documents which suffer from lack of concrete implementation and which are in most cases not binding at the local level unless they are domesticated.

We need policies which address the less privileged and encourage actors to assess the needs of the poor and oppressed ideologically, economically, socially, and culturally. We need policies which will not perpetuate the creditor-versus-debtor relationships of the North and South nations. We need to restructure the global companies which are working according to the principle of maximization of profits and marginalization of the human effort in production of goods and services.

However, global concerns of promoting world peace and environmental sustainability are very much consistent with our African values, especially that of respect for nature and the importance of a continuous quality of life. It is also important to recognize that the system of dialogue, with less rigidity and more open-mindedness, is a welcome idea. It is urged that the space created through meetings of commissions, councils, and various groups be better utilized to discuss and genuinely resolve conflicts—for example, reallocating resources for human development—rather than to express positions alone.

It is further observed that the significance of solidarity is more and more appreciated today as single nations recognize their limitations in coming to terms with global challenges and disasters. More regional groupings are being formed or strengthened. The European Union (EU), the Association of South East Asian Nations (ASEAN), the Southern African Development Community (SADC), and the East African Community are just a few examples.

At the same time there are local initiatives of solidarity and networking in Africa, including cooperative unions, farmers' unions, workers' guilds, and innumerable women's, youth, environmental, and professional nongovernmental organizations which help generate ideas and play an advisory role to higher levels. The world can draw lessons also from such initiatives, which share experience with higher national levels and from there to regional and international levels. It is only through respecting and taking seriously the ideas and practices of local people at local levels that the global system will be able to sustain global systems and structures. Feedback to local levels is also very important.

In Africa, as in other parts of the world, the Catholic Church has tried to put in place structures of dialogue and enrichment for both the hierarchy and the laity. For example, we have the African Conference of Bishops, known as SECAM; subregional structures for West Africa, Southern Africa, Eastern and Central Africa, the African Islands, and North Africa; and national-level Conferences and Councils of the Laity. The Councils of the Laity have structures down to the Small Christian Community level which give advice and ideas to higher levels and make decisions on the basis of Christian principles on questions of integral human development, peace and justice, and the promotion of ethics and moral values. Such local initiatives contribute to the formation of policies which are God-fearing and human-centered.

Balancing Tensions
Individual Good and Common Good

The African continent is still celebrating the African Synod of Bishops which took place in Rome in 1994. Currently the African churches are in the process of implementing the deliberations and findings of the Synod Fathers. One of the major steps, and indeed the central concern and preoccupation of these times, is the inculturation of Christ in the life of the African and the African family.

In dealing with the aspect of balancing tensions, I wish to stress that it is not easy to separate my Africanness from my Christianity. Indeed, African tradition and religion was Christocentric even before knowing about Christ Himself. Regarding the tension between individual good and common good, African and Catholic traditions both emphasize the love of self and neighbor in the same measure. The emphasis on community and family in the African way of life, which still prevails, helps to remind the individual not to ignore the interests and welfare of community members. It is therefore not easy to be orphaned or to suffer loneliness or starvation in the true African traditional setting. Individualism is considered to be selfishness; emphasis on the common good, but also the respect of each individual life, helps to balance any tension.

Rights and Responsibilities

The duty of each able-bodied and mentally sound person to earn a living through hard work is another positive value of the African tradition as

well as the Catholic religion. In most African traditions, rights are actually built into responsibilities and duties, with the exception of the right
to life. Even in this case, the responsibility to respect life is on all the
community members. Many African proverbs emphasize the fact that
there is no right without responsibility, or without conditions: one always
has a right, on condition that in the process of protecting or defending
one's right one does not deprive others of their rights. Rights are therefore relative and not absolute. This helps to balance the two.

The teachings of the Catholic Church, especially about life, strongly
emphasize the importance of balancing rights and responsibilities. According to Catholic teachings, the church is sent to all people without
exception. Deep concern has been expressed by the church about "the
widespread loss of the transcendent sense of human life, confusion in the
ethical sphere, even about the fundamental values of respect for life and
the family." The church calls upon people to examine themselves regarding their responsibility for defending life and also cautions about being carried away by the climate of secularism.

Private Sector and Public Sector

African tradition and Christianity both emphasize the necessity to encourage private initiatives without, however, allowing exploitation of labor, brain, or culture. Hence it is also stipulated in the traditional
teaching that all basic resources required by the public should be jointly
owned and/or controlled.

Resources like land, for example, belong to the public—the clan or,
in the case of Tanzania, the state. Land allocation can be done either by
village or community leadership or the state, but only after proper consultation and consideration of community or national priorities. Although the current trend is toward encouraging the private sector more,
there are checks and balances which ensure public control.

Economic and Environmental Needs

In the African context, the balance between economic and environmental needs is guaranteed. The life of the majority in the rural areas is
very close to nature. However, the introduction of cash-cropping, industrialization, and the use of agricultural chemicals for the purpose of
meeting economic needs have tended to destroy nature and the envi-

ronment. The churches in Africa are deeply engaged in encouraging and facilitating the protection and reinstatement of ecological balance through a number of programs.

Local, National, and Global Sovereignties

In our tradition, sovereignties are defined in a manner which avoids con-flicts and tension. The position of religious leaders is considered to be that of critical observers and authoritative, supportive counselors to gov-ernmental leaders. Sovereign leaders take leadership oaths by swearing according to their religious faith. Religious leaders are also the mediators when it comes to conflict resolution between different levels of authority. The tradition encourages and teaches people to respect authority, but also reminds authority that it is not self-imposed but God-given. There is a need to respect all levels of authority, also relating higher-level deci-sions to the bottom-up approach.

Religious Resources for Global Governance

One of the strongest heritages of the African people in general is the deep religiosity by which the lives of many are governed. The sociopoliti-cal organization of life and economic activities and interactions draw much of their mandate from religious principles and teachings. For more effective participation in the building of a humane and just world order, the reconciliatory and humanity-centered aspects of religious communi-ties can be utilized to motivate the actors—even if in some cases, intro-duced religions like Christianity, Islam, Hinduism, and currently the New Pentecostal churches have been criticized as "the opiate of the people."

Religions are indeed among the few institutions which bring together people of different cultural and racial backgrounds to work for a common vision. International religious bodies like the World Council of Churches, the World Lutheran Federation, and the Episcopates of the Catholic Church, as well as religious congregations which recruit people from dif-ferent cultures, are spaces for networking and the exchange of values. They help to break cultural barriers by encouraging the spirit of solidarity and brotherly/sisterly love.

In Tanzania, for example, instructions which could be used to create a just world order have either been nationalized or not established at all. There are also very few religious institutions of higher learning which could provide space for debate and reflection on a just world order. All the same, many secular institutions have chaplaincies and religious associations which try to reflect on issues of ethics, vision, and a moral base, as well as the need for guidance and counseling for youth and people depressed at all levels.

The churches and other religious organizations have communications facilities and networks which deal with issues such as participatory democracy, corruption, good governance, social ethics, moral and ethical issues (especially birth control), limitation of freedom, human rights, justice and peace, and the importance of reconciliation and conflict resolution. The church also plays a leading role in emphasizing the centrality of the family as the basic unit for transmission of culture and human values, and cautions the people about the negative consequences of global decisions, policies, and programs which disfavor human development.

Professional associations including national chapters of Pax Romana ICMICA, the Catholic Women's Organization, and associations of Catholic doctors, nurses, lawyers, and journalists play a leading role in provoking reflections on the quality of life, the integrity of creation, moral and ethical values, and the promotion of positive human relationships—respect for the other who is the complement of oneself.

The Pastoral Research Institute is engaged in research about the values, practices, and traditions of different tribes and communities. The findings are used to improve on the practices of the people and their religious life. For example, during 1997's efforts to live the spirit of the African Synod, the entire Catholic Church of Tanzania was involved in deep discussions and reflections on the way of life in traditional settings.

The guideline questions prepared by the Pastoral Department of the Bishops' Conference require communities to share their experience on what happens from the time of birth, to the upbringing of children, during courtship, before and during marriage, during sickness, and at death. The main purpose of the exercise is to get at the reality and the reasons behind such practices, in order to find out what can be uplifted in the process of inculturation—that is, of inbuilding Christian values and way of life in our culture in order to make Christianity truly Christian, but at the same time truly African. The experience thus drawn can also be utilized to build a more just world order—one which will learn to respect the different cultures without, however, undermining the importance of universality and the sharing of a common life and a common destiny.

Institutions of higher education also do a lot to promote reflections on issues of global justice, North-South relations, and the importance of a participatory approach. Nongovernmental organizations and community-based networks also act as pressure groups to demand justice and maintain awareness of these issues; solidarity groups could be formed between and among such groups to ensure the building of a better world for all.

Collaboration with the United Nations and Its Specialized Agencies

The increase in UN member states, together with apparent UN concern for human rights, women's and children's rights, sustainable development, ecological balance, and popular participation, are strengths of the UN. The United Nations could provide the expected and desired services for a just world order. The weakness of its organizations and agencies, however, is that their decisions are not completely binding. These decisions do not override national constitutions and laws, and require not only signature but also domestication and internalization into local laws. Hence, the conventions, treaties, and agreements are merely consensus documents which do not have great impact. Limitation of resources, lack of commitment, control by the economically powerful, and veto power also make the democratization processes superficial. There is a lot of lip service to conventions like that on the Elimination of All Forms of Discrimination Against Women and those detailing the economic, social, and political rights of the people.

This powerlessness of the United Nations is manifested by failure to bring about lasting peace in states experiencing conflicts and wars, like Zaire, Burundi, and Rwanda in Africa, and states in the Middle East and parts of Eastern Europe; as well as its failure to stem human rights violations in parts of Asia. The UN system is also weak in enforcing the domestication and implementation of ratified conventions, treaties, and charters. There is a growing and uncontrolled practice of substance abuse and illicit drug trafficking, in which poor and oppressed youth experience economic exploitation and risk their lives. Institutionalized corruption is another seemingly uncontrollable area which continues to make global structures the domain and mouthpiece of the wealthy and powerful.

On the one hand, values of peace, tolerance, respect, solidarity, human rights, and the rights of women, children, and the disadvantaged are advocated; but on the other hand, violence, intolerance, violations of rights, and environmental abuse through pollution are also increasing. UN programs seem to be overpowered by negative forces; they are also forced to sing the tune of the piper—the wealthy and powerful.

At the national level, the Tanzania Association of Non-Governmental Organizations and the Christian Professionals of Tanzania have been taking part in UN-convened meetings and conferences. We also collaborate in the programs of the United Nations Development Program on human rights, women's rights, and support to grassroots groups. We have a special program on Education for Participatory Democracy, and various committees are formed to implement, and monitor the implementation of, programs resulting from UN conferences like the Population and Development Conference in Cairo, the Beijing Conference on Women, Habitat II, and the World Food Summit, among others.

At the international level, Pax Romana ICMICA has consultative status with the UN Economic and Social Council and UNESCO. We are very active at the Human Rights Center in Geneva, the United Nations Centers in New York and Vienna, and the regional centers. In this work our main preoccupations are peace, culture, and ethics, as well as the contributions of Catholic and Christian intellectuals to these structures. We aim at ensuring a Christian presence in these structures as well as the promotion of religious and cultural values as the foundation for the building of the new world order. We also think it is important to develop alternative models for development which take into account the contributions of grassroots groups and people and their positive values in order to bring about change. Hence we expect UN projects and programs to concentrate more on the reduction of the gap between rich and poor, powerful and weak, and so-called "strong" and "weaker" cultures. Concrete steps must be taken to address the debtor-creditor relationship mentioned earlier, and to make sure that women and men will be valued for what they are and not for what they have.

Developing Multireligious Initiatives

It is important to develop and organize more interreligious conferences and dialogues to reflect on common values and concerns. As the issue of democracy and democratization becomes more and more a global concern, religious leaders and their followers should also seriously consider reflecting on democratization within their own structures and systems. It is encouraging to note that church initiatives have been taken to form councils for culture and interreligious dialogue, and to work for common ethical bases. At a time when secularism is increasing, in African cities as elsewhere, religions are challenged to testify for the role of religion in modern society. Contributions to world peace and the improvement of the quality of life must go hand in hand with the task of encouraging a deeper spirituality for the people. Religions still have the role and opportunity to help people find a deeper meaning in life and enable them to be more collaborative with, and responsible for, each other.

I believe religions are well placed to be defenders of justice and speakers for the voiceless in society. This can be done through special messages, sermons, or documents; and through programs of development aid or social services, religions can also, by example, practice democracy and justice, and must encourage the promotion of ecological balance.

Conclusion

This paper has attempted to share the African experience, with special reference to Tanzania. It is important for me to stress that the issues raised in the Guideline Paper are strategic issues, but within the African reality, the majority of the people are still preoccupied with addressing practical needs. It is difficult for them to conceptualize deep tensions at global levels. It is also very difficult for the majority to identify linkages between local, national, and global systems and how they impact and relate with each other.

As one famous African woman, Mrs. Gertrude Mongela, Secretary-General of the 4th World Conference on Women (Beijing 1995), said, "The problem is that there is a big difference between the women in the North and those in the South when it comes to claiming rights. While our friends in the North are looking for dishwashers, the women in the South (Africa) are looking for water to wash the dishes." With this quotation I invite all of us to pray for the gift of being better able to balance between theories and practice.

APPENDICES

APPENDIX A
Global Education Associates
Religion and World Order Project
Guideline Questions

APPENDIX B
Global Education Associates
Religion and World Order Project
Contributing Scholars

APPENDIX C
Global Education Associates
Religion and World Order Project
Revised Symposium Statement

APPENDIX D:
OTHER INTERRELIGIOUS STATEMENTS

Toward a Global Ethic (An Initial Declaration)

Declaration on the Role of Religion in the Promotion
of a Culture of Peace

Declaration of Principles on Tolerance

APPENDIX E
The Earth Covenant: A Citizens' Treaty
for Common Ecological Security

Global Education Associates Religion and World Order Project Guideline Questions

Most of the papers comprising this book were written in response to the following questions.

Working Toward a Shared Global Ethic

The creation of a peaceful, equitable, and sustainable future is, at its heart, as much an ethical and spiritual matter as it is a matter for economic and social policy and legal systems. In today's interdependent world, there is a need for strong ethical foundations for policies and systems at global as well as local and national levels. The new global-scale challenges that are accompanying the rapid growth of global economic and ecological interdependence require that we now move toward a shared ethic that, while respecting national, cultural, and religious differences, provides a common framework for responding to global challenges.

What values and principles can your sacred texts, ethical systems, teachings, traditions, history, and lived experience contribute to the development of such a shared global ethic? Specifically, how can these values and principles address the following issues?

Peace and Security
Economic and Social Justice
Human Rights
Ecological Sustainability
Cultural Identity and Integrity

Working Toward Global Governance

The question before the human community is not whether there will be a new world order. Rather, it is what kind of world order? On what values will it be based? Who will be its designers and decision-makers? Will it be a fragmented order of economic, ethnic, religious, and armed conflict? Will it be controlled by the economically and militarily powerful? Or will it be a genuinely participatory order, governed by effective international law and based on equity and economic and ecological sustainability?

Global governance is not world government. As articulated in the report of the Commission on Global Governance, *Our Global Neighborhood*, it is "the sum of ways in which individuals and institutions, public and private, manage their common affairs." The concept of global governance is based on three factors:

a) Government structures have limited capacities to meet the multiple needs of citizens and communities;

b) Many transboundary problems and opportunities surpass the competencies of national institutions and policymakers;

c) An emerging civil society of nongovernmental and citizens' organizations, professional and trade associations, economic enterprises, mass media, and educational and religion networks provide essential services and leadership at local, national, and global levels.

Governments will remain primary actors in global governance. United Nations agencies will play a pivotal role. But the aforementioned components of civil society are becoming important actors in managing our common affairs. Religious networks of schools, universities, alumni, research institutes, health and medical institutions, and community-based social and economic programs have unique potential for becoming effective partners in the task of global governance.

Building upon the values and principles of your religious and faith tradition, what recommendations would you make in the following areas:

Global Civic Society. Without a core set of values that respect individual human dignity and cultural diversity and participatory decision-making process, local communities and ecological systems become expendable. From the perspective of your values, what should be the criteria for a global civic society? For global citizenship?

Global Structures and Systems. It is necessary to develop global policies and systems to manage our common affairs. What global policies, systems, and instruments would be consistent with your values and principles? Specifically, how could the policies, systems, and instruments of your preferred world order address the above five issues?

Local Initiatives. The local and global are deeply interrelated. What "bottom-up" initiatives can be combined with transnational initiatives to create policies and systems capable of fulfilling your desired world order and forms of global governance?

Balancing Tensions. The achievement of a more peaceful, equitable, and sustainable future depends upon values and systems of governance that can balance the following tensions. What insights can your religious tradition give on balance in these areas of tension?

- individual good and common good
- rights and responsibilities
- private sector and public sector
- long-term and short-term objectives
- economic and environmental needs
- local, national, and global sovereignties

Religious Resources for Global Governance. What particular expertise, institutions, networks, and other resources can your religious community utilize to participate in the building of a just world order? Think laterally, considering your affiliates, such as:

- schools and institutions of higher education
- research institutions
- media and communication networks
- publications and media materials
- community-based networks and programs
- professional associations

Collaboration with the United Nations and Its Specialized Agencies

What do you judge to be the strengths and weaknesses of the current UN system in relationship to your ethical concern for a just world order? What are your recommendations to make the UN and its specialized agencies more effective instruments for a just world order? (Specify program areas and agencies.)

In what ways have members and organizations of your religious community been cooperating with United Nations organizations and programs? In what additional ways could your religious community collaborate with the UN and its agencies to make them more effective instruments for a just world order?

What materials, services, and processes might empower your religious community and its programs and institutions to become more active partners with the UN in concrete initiatives and projects at local, national, and international levels?

Developing Multireligious Initiatives

What kind of multireligious initiatives do you recommend for advancing systems of global governance that hear and respect the diversity that religions represent?

In what ways can your religious community incorporate world systems thinking into its educational programs?

What kind of multireligious initiatives do you recommend for advancing effective systems of governance that are more just, humane, and ecologically sustainable?

Global Education Associates Religion and World Order Project Contributing Scholars

The following individuals were contributing scholars to the Religion and World Order Symposium, May 3–7, 1997, sponsored by Global Education Associates and co-sponsored by the Fordham University Institute on Religion and Culture and the Center for Mission Research and Study at Maryknoll.

Dr. Saleha Mahmood-Abedin, *Institute of Muslim Minority Affairs, Saudi Arabia*

Dr. Ahmed Sidqi Al-Dajani, *Arab Organization for Human Rights, Egypt*

Dr. Taha Alalwani, *School of Islamic and Social Sciences, Virginia*

Dr. Mona Abul-Fadl, *School of Islamic and Social Sciences, Virginia*

Dr. M. Aram, *World Conference on Religion and Peace, India*

Rabbi Philip J. Bentley, *Temple Sholom, New York*

Dr. Beverlee Bruce, *Women's Commission for Refugee Women and Children, New York*

Rev. Dr. Joan Brown Campbell, *National Council of Churches, New York*

Sister Janet Carroll, MM, *Maryknoll Sisters Community, New York*

Dr. Julia Ching, *University of Toronto, Canada*

Dr. John B. Cobb, Jr., *Claremont Graduate School, California*

Rev. Richard Deats, *Fellowship of Reconciliation, New York*

Fr. Luis M. Dolan, CP, *Consultant, Interreligious Programs, New York*

Dr. Richard Falk, *Princeton University, New Jersey*

Mr. Nathan C. Funk, *The American University, Washington, DC*

Dr. Aklilu Habte, *former Director of Education Division UNICEF/World Bank, Maryland*

Mr. Gerry Hall, *Soka Gakkai International, California*

Dr. John Healey, *Fordham University, New York*

Mr. Jeffery Huffines, *National Spiritual Assembly of the Bahá'ís of the US, New York*

Mr. P.N. (Bawa) Jain, *Temple of Understanding, International Mahavir Jain Mission, New York*

Dr. Uner Kirdar, *Senior Advisor to the Administrator of UNDP, New York*

Ven. Chung Ok Lee, *UN Representative: Won Buddhism, New York*

Rev. Dr. Eileen W. Lindner, *National Council of Churches, New York*

Dr. Felix Marti, *Centre UNESCO de Catalunya, Spain*

Rev. Thomas Marti, *Maryknoll Mission Development House, Washington, DC*

Dr. Patricia M. Mische, *Global Education Associates, New York*

Mrs. Mary J. Mwingira, *Pax Romana, Tanzania*

Dr. Kusumita P. Pedersen, *St. Francis College, New York*

Dr. Joseph Prabhu, *United Religions Initiative, California*

Rev. John A. Radano, *Pontifical Council for the Promotion of Christian Unity, Rome*

Dr. Anne Reissner, *Center for Mission Research and Study at Maryknoll, New York*

Mr. Douglas Roche, OC, *Adviser to the Holy See Mission to the UN, Alberta, Canada*

Dr. Steven C. Rockefeller, *Middlebury College, Vermont*

Rev. Peter L. Ruggere, MM, *Maryknoll Peace and Justice Office, Washington, DC*

Dr. Abdul Aziz Said, *The American University, Washington, DC*

Dr. Harris Schoenberg, *Coordinating Board of Jewish Organizations, New York*

Dr. Pataraporn Sirikanchana, *The World Fellowship of Buddhists, Thailand*

Dr. Sulak Sivaraksa, *The International Network of Engaged Buddhists, Siam*

Prof. K.R. Sundararajan, *St. Bonaventure University, New York*

Dr. Robert Traer, *International Association for Religious Freedom, England*

Dr. Mary Evelyn Tucker, *Bucknell University, Pennsylvania*

Dr. William Vendley, *World Conference on Religion and Peace, New York*

Dr. Tu Weiming, *Harvard University, Massachusetts*

Dr. John Woodall, *International Bahá'í Community, Massachusetts*

Rabbi Dr. Bernard M. Zlotowitz, *Union of American Hebrew Congregations, New Jersey*

Global Education Associates Religion and World Order Project Revised Symposium Statement

Following is the revised statement resulting from the Religion and World Order Symposium, May 3–7, 1997, sponsored by Global Education Associates and co-sponsored by the Fordham University Institute on Religion and Culture and the Center for Mission Research and Study at Maryknoll.

1. We, the participants in the Religion and World Order Symposium at Maryknoll, New York, have come together as thinkers, scholars, believers, and practitioners to speak from our diverse religious traditions and out of a shared concern for a just, peaceful, and sustainable world order.

2. We have shared with each other our religious traditions in their own terms and languages. We have discovered that we have far more in common than we have differences. We celebrate this commonality and we respect our differences.

3. We are unanimously agreed that we live in a moment of extraordinary transformations in history. There is no question that there will be a new world order—only a question of who will participate in its making and on whose and what values it will be based.

4. We are also convinced that this is a crucial moment for the world's religious leaders and institutions, and that we must, as far as possible, speak with one voice on behalf of our traditions for the sake of a just and sustainable world order.

5. We recognize the long tradition of positive good religion has made in

world history. But we also recognize that religious leaders and religious institutions have not always been a positive force in that history. We know that religious differences have contributed to wars and have been used to justify wars and divisions. We regret these failures of the past and any present failures to speak out against the distortion of our spiritual traditions.

6.   We believe that the first step toward establishing a more humane world will be the recognition of existing wrongs and inequalities, and the recognition of those who are suffering: suffering poverty as the gap be-tween rich and poor increases dramatically; suffering torture and rape as refugee women and children; suffering from the loss of real freedom, even in democratic societies in which people have less and less control over their lives.

7.   We will not be silent in the face of this suffering. We will together challenge the myths and paradigms with which a reckless world order is justified. Drawing on our spiritual traditions, we will make common cause with all those working to alleviate human suffering.

8.   We are further agreed that the criteria for a global civilization are peace and security; a culture of nonviolence; economic and social justice; human rights; ecological security; cultural identity and integrity; and full participation and opportunity for women and men in society.

9.   We recognize that the crisis in the world's environment is beyond anything yet known in history and has reached a point where the very survival of the human species and other living species is now threatened. We must therefore emphasize strongly the interrelatedness of all things and the sacredness of all creation.

10. Moreover, despite the end of the cold war, disarmament has not been achieved. In fact, many nations are still resisting full disarmament and others are vigorously pursuing arms buildup and the development of more sophisticated systems of mass destruction. This, together with environ-mental degradation, now poses a threat to all life and civilization.

11. While calling for greater attention to global order and systems of governance, we recognize that all spirituality must be embodied and rooted in our families and local communities. We will continue to work for the protection of local communities, indigenous peoples, and the world's diverse local cultures.

12. Having shared in this consensus, we see the need for continuing multireligious initiatives. Our religious institutions continue to have as resources the trust and fidelity of their members, an infrastructure of institutions which have maintained teaching and practice, and a special moral authority in their communities. We see the need therefore for ever-stronger commitment to the worldwide interfaith movement and continuing meetings at all levels—local, regional, and global—to foster dialogue among the religious traditions on these moral and ethical issues.

13. Finally, we reaffirm our commitment to strengthen the United Nations as vitally important to peace and security and to the achievement of humane global governance, and we support this organization's continuing effort to reform its workings and procedures.

14. We urge our religious leaders, as well as governments and the United Nations, to give full support to the nongovernmental organizations (NGOs) which have contributed so much to maintaining the place of religion at the United Nations, and we look for an even more active role for the NGOs in the future.

15. These propositions reflect our hopes and our aspirations, and their expression and communication constitute our obligation—for "Who shall speak if we don't?" At the close of a tumultuous era, while facing the challenge of a new millennium, all these issues must be addressed—for "If not now, when?" and "If not us, who?"

(Signed)

Symposium Conveners:

Dr. Patricia M. Mische
President, Global Education Associates

Dr. John Healey
Director, Fordham University Institute on Religion and Culture

Dr. Anne Reissner
Director of Study, Center of Mission Research and Study at Maryknoll

Toward a Global Ethic (An Initial Declaration)

This interfaith declaration is the result of a two-year consultation among approximately 200 scholars and theologians from many of the world's communities of faith. On September 2–4, 1993, the document was discussed by an assembly of religious and spiritual leaders meeting as part of the 1993 Parliament of the World's Religions in Chicago. Respected leaders from all the world's major faiths signed the Declaration, agreeing that it represents an initial effort—a point of beginning for a world sorely in need of ethical consensus. The Council for a Parliament of the World's Religions and those who have endorsed this text offer it to the world as an initial statement of the rules for living on which the world's religions can agree.

The Declaration of a Global Ethic

The world is in agony. The agony is so pervasive and urgent that we are compelled to name its manifestations so that the depth of this pain may be made clear.

Peace eludes us...the planet is being destroyed...neighbors live in fear...women and men are estranged from each other...children die!

This is abhorrent!

We condemn the abuses of Earth's ecosystems.

We condemn the poverty that stifles life's potential; the hunger that weakens the human body; the economic disparities that threaten so many families with ruin.

We condemn the social disarray of the nations; the disregard for justice which pushes citizens to the margin; the anarchy overtaking our communities; and the insane death of children from violence. In particular we condemn aggression and hatred in the name of religion.

But this agony need not be.

It need not be because the basis for an ethic already exists. This ethic offers the possibility of a better individual and global order, and leads individuals away from despair and societies away from chaos.

We are women and men who have embraced the precepts and practices of the world's religions:

We affirm that a common set of core values is found in the teachings of the religions, and that these form the basis of a global ethic.

We affirm that this truth is already known, but yet to be lived in heart and action.

We affirm that there is an irrevocable, unconditional norm for all areas of life, for families and communities, for races, nations, and religions. There already exist ancient guidelines for human behavior which are found in the teachings of the religions of the world and which are the condition for a sustainable world order.

We Declare:

We are interdependent. Each of us depends on the well-being of the whole, and so we have respect for the community of living beings, for people, animals, and plants, and for the preservation of Earth, the air, water, and soil.

We take individual responsibility for all we do. All our decisions, actions, and failures to act have consequences.

We must treat others as we wish others to treat us. We make a commitment to respect life and dignity, individuality and diversity, so that every person is treated humanely, without exception. We must have patience and acceptance. We must be able to forgive, learning from the past but never allowing ourselves to be enslaved by memories of hate. Opening our hearts to one another, we must sink our narrow differences for the cause of the world community, practicing a culture of solidarity and relatedness.

We consider humankind our family. We must strive to be kind and generous. We must not live for ourselves alone, but should also serve others, never forgetting the children, the aged, the poor, the suffering, the disabled, the refugees, and the lonely. No person should ever be considered or treated as a second-class citizen, or be exploited in any way whatsoever. There should be equal partnership between men and women. We must not commit any kind of sexual immorality. We must put behind us all forms of domination or abuse.

We commit ourselves to a culture of nonviolence, respect, justice, and peace. We shall not oppress, injure, torture, or kill other human beings, forsaking violence as a means of settling differences.

We must strive for a just social and economic order, in which everyone has an equal chance to reach full potential as a human being. We must speak and act truthfully and with compassion, dealing fairly with all, and avoiding prejudice and hatred. We must not steal. We must move beyond the dominance of greed for power, prestige, money, and consumption to make a just and peaceful world.

Earth cannot be changed for the better unless the consciousness of individuals is changed first. We pledge to increase our awareness by disciplining our minds, by meditation, by prayer, or by positive thinking. Without risk and a readiness to sacrifice there can be no fundamental change in our situations. Therefore we commit ourselves to this global ethic, to understanding one another, and to socially beneficial, peace-fostering, and nature-friendly ways of life.

> We invite all people,
> whether religious or not,
> to do the same.

The Principles of a Global Ethic

Our world is experiencing a fundamental crisis: a crisis in global economy, global ecology, and global politics. The lack of a grand vision, the tangle of unresolved problems, political paralysis, mediocre political leadership with little insight or foresight, and in general too little sense for the commonweal, are seen everywhere: too many old answers to new challenges.

Hundreds of millions of human beings on our planet increasingly suffer from unemployment, poverty, hunger, and the destruction of their families. Hope for a lasting peace among nations slips away from us. There are tensions between the sexes and generations. Children die, kill, and are killed. More and more countries are shaken by corruption in politics and business. It is increasingly difficult to live together peacefully in our cities because of social, racial, and ethnic conflicts, the abuse of drugs, organized crime, and even anarchy. Even neighbors often live in fear of one another. Our planet continues to be ruthlessly plundered. A collapse of the ecosystem threatens us.

Time and again we see leaders and members of religions incite aggression, fanaticism, hate, and xenophobia—even inspire and legitimize violent and bloody conflicts. Religion often is misused for purely power-political goals, including war. We are filled with disgust.

We condemn these blights and declare that they need not be. An ethic already exists within the religious teachings of the world which can counter the global distress. Of course this ethic provides no direct solution for all the immense problems of the world, but it does supply the moral foundation for a better individual and global order: a vision which can lead women and men away from despair, and society away from chaos.

We are persons who have committed ourselves to the precepts and practices of the world's religions. We confirm that there is already a consensus among the religions which can be the basis for a global ethic—a minimal *fundamental consensus* concerning binding *values,* irrevocable *standards,* and fundamental *moral attitudes.*

I. No new global order without a new global ethic!

We women and men of various religions and regions of Earth therefore address all people, religious and non-religious. We wish to express the following convictions which we hold in common:

- We all have a responsibility for a better global order.
- Our involvement for the sake of human rights, freedom, justice, peace, and the preservation of Earth is absolutely necessary.
- Our different religious and cultural traditions must not prevent our common involvement in opposing all forms of inhumanity and working for greater humaneness.
- The principles expressed in this global ethic can be affirmed by all persons with ethical convictions, whether religiously grounded or not.
- As religious and spiritual persons we base our lives on an Ultimate Reality, and draw spiritual power and hope therefrom, in trust, in prayer or meditation, in word or silence. We have a special responsibility for the welfare of all humanity and care for the planet Earth. We do not consider ourselves better than other women and men, but we trust that the ancient wisdom of our religions can point the way for the future.

After two world wars and the end of the cold war, the collapse of fascism and nazism, the shaking to the foundations of communism and colonialism, humanity has entered a new phase of its history. Today we possess sufficient economic, cultural, and spiritual resources to introduce a better global order. But old and new ethnic, national, social, economic, and religious tensions threaten the peaceful building of a better world. We have experienced greater technological progress than ever before, yet we see that worldwide poverty, hunger, death of children, unemployment, misery, and the destruction of nature have not diminished but rather have increased. Many peoples are threatened with economic ruin, social disarray, political marginalization, ecological catastrophe, and national collapse.

In such a dramatic global situation humanity needs a vision of peoples living peacefully together, of ethnic and ethical groupings and of religions sharing responsibility for the care of Earth. A vision rests on hopes, goals, ideals, standards. But all over the world these have slipped from our hands. Yet we are convinced that, despite their frequent abuses and failures, it is the communities of faith who bear a responsibility to demonstrate that such hopes, ideals, and standards can be guarded, grounded, and lived. This is especially true in the modern state. Guarantees of freedom of conscience and religion are necessary but they do not substitute for binding values, convictions, and norms which are valid for all humans regardless of their social origin, sex, skin color, language, or religion.

We are convinced of the fundamental unity of the human family on Earth. We recall the 1948 Universal Declaration of Human Rights of the United Nations. What it formally proclaimed on the level of rights we wish to confirm and deepen here from the perspective of an ethic: the full realization of the intrinsic dignity of the human person, the inalienable freedom and equality in principle of all humans, and the necessary solidarity and interdependence of all humans with each other.

On the basis of personal experiences and the burdensome history of our planet we have learned

•   that a better global order cannot be created or enforced by laws, prescriptions, and conventions alone;

•   that the realization of peace, justice, and the protection of Earth depends on the insight and readiness of men and women to act justly;

•   that action in favor of rights and freedoms presumes a consciousness of responsibility and duty, and that therefore both the minds and hearts of women and men must be addressed;

•   that rights without morality cannot long endure, and that *there will be no better global order without a global ethic.*

By a global ethic we do not mean a global ideology or a single unified religion beyond all existing religions, and certainly not the domination of one religion over all others. By a global ethic we mean a fundamental consensus on binding values, irrevocable standards, and personal attitudes. Without such a fundamental consensus on an ethic, sooner or later every community will be threatened by chaos or dictatorship, and individuals will despair.

II. A fundamental demand:
Every human being must be treated humanely.

We all are fallible, imperfect men and women with limitations and defects. We know the reality of evil. Precisely because of this, we feel compelled for the sake of global welfare to express what the fundamental elements of a global ethic should be—for individuals as well as for communities and organizations, for states as well as for the religions themselves. We trust that our often millennia-old religious and ethical traditions provide an ethic which is convincing and practicable for all women and men of good will, religious and non-religious.

At the same time we know that our various religious and ethical traditions often offer very different bases for what is helpful and what is unhelpful for men and women, what is right and what is wrong, what is good and what is evil. We do not wish to gloss over or ignore the serious differences among the individual religions. However, they should not hinder us from proclaiming publicly those things which we already hold in common and which we jointly affirm, each on the basis of our own religious or ethical grounds.

We know that religions cannot solve the environmental, economic, political, and social problems of Earth. However, they can provide what obviously cannot be attained by economic plans, political programs, or legal regulations alone: a change in the inner orientation, the whole mentality, the "hearts" of people, and a conversion from a false path to a new orientation for life. Humankind urgently needs social and ecological reforms, but it needs spiritual renewal just as urgently. As religious or spiritual persons we commit ourselves to this task. The spiritual powers of the religions can offer a fundamental sense of trust, a ground of meaning, ultimate standards, and a spiritual home. Of course religions are credible only when they eliminate those conflicts which spring from the religions themselves, dismantling mutual arrogance, mistrust, prejudice, and even hostile images, and thus demonstrating respect for the traditions, holy places, feasts, and rituals of people who believe differently.

Now as before, women and men are treated inhumanely all over the world. They are robbed of their opportunities and their freedom; their human rights are trampled underfoot; their dignity is disregarded. But might does not make right! In the face of all inhumanity our religious and ethical convictions demand that *every human being must be treated humanely!*

This means that every human being without distinction of age, sex, race, skin color, physical or mental ability, language, religion, political view, or national or social origin, possesses an inalienable and untouchable dignity, and everyone, the individual as well as the state, is therefore obliged to honor this dignity and protect it. Humans must always be the subjects of rights, must be ends, never mere means, never objects of commercialization and industrialization in economics, politics and media, in research institutes, and industrial corporations. No one stands "above good and evil"—no human being, no social class, no influential interest group, no cartel, no police apparatus, no army, and no state. On the contrary: possessed of reason and conscience, every human is obliged to behave in a genuinely human fashion, to do good and avoid evil!

It is the intention of this global ethic to clarify what this means. In it we wish to recall irrevocable, unconditional ethical norms. These should not be bonds and chains, but helps and supports for people to find and realize once again their lives' direction, values, orientations, and meaning. There is a principle which is found and has persisted in many religions and ethical traditions of humankind for thousands of years: *What you do not wish done to yourself, do not to others.* Or in positive terms: *What you wish done to yourself, do to others!* This should be the irrevocable, unconditional norm for all areas of life, for families and communities, for races, nations, and religions.

Every form of egoism should be rejected: all selfishness, whether individual or collective, whether in the form of class thinking, racism, nationalism, or sexism. We condemn these because they prevent humans from being authentically human. Self-determination and self-realization are thoroughly legitimate so long as they are not separated from human self-responsibility and global responsibility, that is, from responsibility for fellow humans and for the planet Earth.

This principle implies very concrete standards to which we humans should hold firm. From it arise four broad, ancient guidelines for human behavior which are found in most of the religions of the world.

III. Irrevocable directives.

1. Commitment to a culture of nonviolence and respect for life. Numberless women and men of all regions and religions strive to lead lives not determined by egoism but by commitment to their fellow humans and to the world around them. Nevertheless, all over the world we find endless hatred, envy, jealousy, and violence, not only between individuals but also between social and ethnic groups, between classes, races, nations, and religions. The use of violence, drug trafficking and organized crime, often equipped with new technical possibilities, has reached global proportions. Many places still are ruled by terror "from above"; dictators oppress their own people, and institutional violence is widespread. Even in some countries where laws exist to protect individual freedoms, prisoners are tortured, men and women are mutilated, hostages are killed.

a) In the great ancient religions and ethical traditions of humankind we find the directive: *You shall not kill!* Or in positive terms: *Have respect for life!* Let us reflect anew on the consequences of this ancient directive: all people have a right to life, safety, and the free development of personality insofar as they do not injure the rights of others. No one has the right physically or psychically to torture, injure, much less kill, any other human being. And no people, no state, no race, no religion has the right to hate, to discriminate, to "cleanse," to exile, much less to liquidate a "foreign" minority which is different in behavior or holds different beliefs.

b) Of course, wherever there are humans there will be conflicts. Such conflicts, however, should be resolved without violence within a framework of justice. This is true for states as well as for individuals. Persons who hold political power must work within the framework of a just order and commit themselves to the most nonviolent, peaceful solutions possible. And they should work for this within an international order of peace which itself has need of protection and defense against perpetrators of violence. Armament is a mistaken path; disarmament is the commandment of the times. Let no one be deceived: there is no survival for humanity without global peace!

c) Young people must learn at home and in school that violence may not be a means of settling differences with others. Only thus can a culture of nonviolence be created.

d)   A human person is infinitely precious and must be unconditionally protected. But likewise the lives of animals and plants which inhabit this planet with us deserve protection, preservation, and care. Limitless exploitation of the natural foundations of life, ruthless destruction of the biosphere, and militarization of the cosmos are all outrages. As human beings we have a special responsibility—especially with a view to future generations—for Earth and the cosmos, for the air, water, and soil. We are all intertwined together in this cosmos and we are all dependent on each other. Each one of us depends on the welfare of all. Therefore the dominance of humanity over nature and the cosmos must not be encouraged. Instead we must cultivate living in harmony with nature and the cosmos.

e)   To be authentically human in the spirit of our great religious and ethical traditions means that in public as well as in private life we must be concerned for others and ready to help. We must never be ruthless and brutal. Every people, every race, every religion must show tolerance and respect—indeed high appreciation—for every other. Minorities need protection and support, whether they be racial, ethnic, or religious.

2.   Commitment to a culture of solidarity and a just economic order. Numberless men and women of all regions and religions strive to live their lives in solidarity with one another and to work for authentic fulfillment of their vocations. Nevertheless, all over the world we find endless hunger, deficiency, and need. Not only individuals, but especially unjust institutions and structures are responsible for these tragedies. Millions of people are without work; millions are exploited by poor wages, forced to the edges of society, with their possibilities for the future destroyed. In many lands the gap between the poor and the rich, between the powerful and the powerless, is immense. We live in a world in which totalitarian state socialism as well as unbridled capitalism have hollowed out and destroyed many ethical and spiritual values. A materialistic mentality breeds greed for unlimited profit and a grasping for endless plunder. These demands claim more and more of the community's resources without obliging the individual to contribute more. The cancerous social evil of corruption thrives in the developing countries and in the developed countries alike.

a)   In the great ancient religious and ethical traditions of humankind we find the directive: *You shall not steal!* Or in positive terms: *Deal honestly and fairly!* Let us reflect anew on the consequences of this ancient directive: no one has the right to rob or dispossess in any way whatsoever any other person or the commonweal. Further, no one has the right to use her or his possessions without concern for the needs of society and the Earth.

b) Where extreme poverty reigns, helplessness and despair spread, and theft occurs again and again for the sake of survival. Where power and wealth are accumulated ruthlessly, feelings of envy, resentment, and deadly hatred and rebellion inevitably well up in the disadvantaged and marginalized. This leads to a vicious circle of violence and counter-violence. Let no one be deceived: there is no global peace without global justice!

c) Young people must learn at home and in school that property, limited though it may be, carries with it an obligation, and that its uses should at the same time serve the common good. Only thus can a just economic order be built up.

d) If the plight of the poorest billions of humans on this planet, particularly women and children, is to be improved, the world economy must be structured more justly. Individual good deeds, and assistance projects, indispensable though they be, are insufficient. The participation of all states and the authority of international organizations are needed to build just economic institutions.

A solution which can be supported by all sides must be sought for the debt crisis and the poverty of the dissolving Second World, and even more the Third World. Of course conflicts of interest are unavoidable. In the developed countries, a distinction must be made between necessary and limitless consumption, between socially beneficial and non-beneficial uses of property, between justified and unjustified uses of natural resources, and between a profit-only and a socially beneficial and ecologically oriented market economy. Even the developing nations must search their national consciences.

Wherever those ruling threaten to repress those ruled, wherever institutions threaten persons, and wherever might oppresses right, we are obligated to resist—whenever possible nonviolently.

e) To be authentically human in the spirit of our great religious and ethical traditions means the following:

• We must utilize economic and political power for service to humanity instead of misusing it in ruthless battles for domination. We must develop a spirit of compassion with those who suffer, with special care for the children, the aged, the poor, the disabled, the refugees, and the lonely.

• We must cultivate mutual respect and consideration, so as to reach a reasonable balance of interests, instead of thinking only of unlimited power and unavoidable competitive struggles.

• We must value a sense of moderation and modesty instead of an unquenchable greed for money, prestige, and consumption. In greed humans lose their "souls," their freedom, their composure, their inner peace, and thus that which makes them human.

3. Commitment to a culture of tolerance and a life of truthfulness. Numberless women and men of all regions and religions strive to lead lives of honesty and truthfulness. Nevertheless, all over the world we find endless lies and deceit, swindling and hypocrisy, ideology and demagoguery:

• Politicians and businesspeople who use lies as a means to success;

• Mass media which spread ideological propaganda instead of accurate reporting, misinformation instead of information, cynical commercial interest instead of loyalty to the truth;

• Scientists and researchers who give themselves over to morally questionable ideological or political programs or to economic interest groups, or who justify research which violates fundamental ethical values;

• Representatives of religions who dismiss other religions as of little value and who preach fanaticism and intolerance instead of respect and understanding.

a) In the great ancient religious and ethical traditions of humankind we find the directive: *You shall not lie!* Or in positive terms: *Speak and act truthfully!* Let us reflect anew on the consequences of this ancient directive: no woman or man, no institution, no state or church or religious community has the right to speak lies to other humans.

b) This is especially true:

• for those who work in the mass media, to whom we entrust the freedom to report for the sake of truth and to whom we thus grant the office of guardian—they do not stand above morality but have the obligation to respect human dignity, human rights, and fundamental values; they are duty-bound to objectivity, fairness, and the preservation of human dignity; they have no right to intrude into individuals' private spheres, to manipulate public opinion, or to distort reality;

• for artists, writers, and scientists, to whom we entrust artistic and academic freedom; they are not exempt from general ethical standards and must serve the truth;

• for the leaders of countries, politicians, and political parties, to whom we entrust our own freedoms—when they lie in the faces of their people, when they manipulate the truth, or when they are guilty of venality or ruthlessness in domestic or foreign affairs, they forsake their credibility and deserve to lose their offices and their voters; conversely, public opinion should support those politicians who dare to speak the truth to the people at all times;

• finally, for representatives of religion—when they stir up prejudice, hatred, and enmity towards those of different belief, or even incite or legitimize religious wars, they deserve the condemnation of humankind and the loss of their adherents.

Let no one be deceived: there is no global justice without truthfulness and humaneness!

c) Young people must learn at home and in school to think, speak, and act truthfully. They have a right to information and education to be able to make the decisions that will form their lives. Without an ethical formation they will hardly be able to distinguish the important from the unimportant. In the daily flood of information, ethical standards will help them discern when opinions are portrayed as facts, interests veiled, tendencies exaggerated, and facts twisted.

d) To be authentically human in the spirit of our great religious and ethical traditions means the following:

• We must not confuse freedom with arbitrariness or pluralism with indifference to truth.

• We must cultivate truthfulness in all our relationships instead of dishonesty, dissembling, and opportunism.

• We must constantly seek truth and incorruptible sincerity instead of spreading ideological or partisan half-truths.

• We must courageously serve the truth and we must remain constant and trustworthy, instead of yielding to opportunistic accommodation to life.

4. Commitment to a culture of equal rights and partnership between

men and women. Numberless men and women of all regions and religions strive to live their lives in a spirit of partnership and responsible action in the areas of love, sexuality, and family. Nevertheless, all over the world there are condemnable forms of patriarchy, domination of one sex over the other, exploitation of women, sexual misuse of children, and forced prostitution. Too frequently, social inequities force women and even children into prostitution as a means of survival, particularly in less developed countries.

a)   In the great ancient religious and ethical traditions of humankind we find the directive: *You shall not commit sexual immorality!* Or in positive terms: *Respect and love one another!* Let us reflect anew on the consequences of this ancient directive: no one has the right to degrade others to mere sex objects, to lead them into or hold them in sexual dependency.

b)   We condemn sexual exploitation and sexual discrimination as one of the worst forms of human degradation. We have the duty to resist wherever the domination of one sex over the other is preached—even in the name of religious conviction; wherever sexual exploitation is tolerated, wherever prostitution is fostered or children are misused. Let no one be deceived: There is no authentic humaneness without a living together in partnership!

c)   Young people must learn at home and in school that sexuality is not a negative, destructive, or exploitative force, but creative and affirmative. Sexuality as a life-affirming shaper of community can only be effective when partners accept the responsibilities of caring for one another's happiness.

d)   The relationship between women and men should be characterized not by patronizing behavior or exploitation, but by love, partnership, and trustworthiness. Human fulfillment is not identical with sexual pleasure. Sexuality should express and reinforce a loving relationship lived by equal partners.

Some religious traditions know the ideal of a voluntary renunciation of the full use of sexuality. Voluntary renunciation also can be an expression of identity and meaningful fulfillment.

e)   The social institution of marriage, despite all its cultural and religious variety, is characterized by love, loyalty, and permanence. It aims at and should guarantee security and mutual support to husband, wife, and child. It should secure the rights of all family members.

All lands and cultures should develop economic and social relationships which will enable marriage and family life worthy of human beings, especially for older people. Children have a right of access to education. Parents should not exploit children, nor children parents. Their relationships should reflect mutual respect, appreciation, and concern.

f) To be authentically human in the spirit of our great religious and ethical traditions means the following:
• We need mutual respect, partnership, and understanding, instead of patriarchal domination and degradation, which are expressions of violence and engender counter-violence.
• We need mutual concern, tolerance, readiness for reconciliation, and love, instead of any form of possessive lust or sexual misuse.

Only what has already been experienced in personal and familial relationships can be practiced on the level of nations and religions.

IV. A transformation of consciousness!

Historical experience demonstrates the following: Earth cannot be changed for the better unless we achieve a transformation in the consciousness of individuals and in public life. The possibilities for transformation have already been glimpsed in areas such as war and peace, economy, and ecology, where in recent decades fundamental changes have taken place. This transformation must also be achieved in the area of ethics and values!

Every individual has intrinsic dignity and inalienable rights, and each also has an inescapable responsibility for what she or he does and does not do. All our decisions and deeds, even our omissions and failures, have consequences.

Keeping this sense of responsibility alive, deepening it and passing it on to future generations, is the special task of religions.

We are realistic about what we have achieved in this consensus, and so we urge that the following be observed:

1. A universal consensus on many disputed ethical questions (from bio- and sexual ethics through mass media and scientific ethics to economic and political ethics) will be difficult to attain. Nevertheless, even for many controversial questions, suitable solutions should be attainable in the spirit of the fundamental principles we have jointly developed here.

2. In many areas of life a new consciousness of ethical responsibility has already arisen. Therefore we would be pleased if as many professions as possible, such as those of physicians, scientists, businesspeople, journalists, and politicians, would develop up-to-date codes of ethics which would provide specific guidelines for the vexing questions of these particular professions.

3. Above all, we urge the various communities of faith to formulate their very specific ethics: what does each faith tradition have to say, for example, about the meaning of life and death, the enduring of suffering and the forgiveness of guilt, about selfless sacrifice and the necessity of renunciation, about compassion and joy? These will deepen, and make more specific, the already discernible global ethic.

In conclusion, we appeal to all the inhabitants of this planet. Earth cannot be changed for the better unless the consciousness of individuals is changed. We pledge to work for such transformation in individual and collective consciousness, for the awakening of our spiritual powers through reflection, meditation, prayer, or positive thinking, for a conversion of the heart. Together we can move mountains! Without a willingness to take risks and a readiness to sacrifice there can be no fundamental change in our situation! Therefore we commit ourselves to a common global ethic, to better mutual understanding, as well as to socially beneficial, peace-fostering, and Earth-friendly ways of life.

We invite all men and women,
whether religious or not,
to do the same.

Declaration on the Role of Religion in the Promotion of a Culture of Peace

We, the participants in the meeting, "The Contribution by Religions to the Culture of Peace," organized by UNESCO and the Centre UNESCO de Catalunya in Barcelona from 12 to 18 December, 1994,

Deeply concerned with the present situation of the world, such as increasing armed conflicts and violence, poverty, social injustice, and structures of oppression;

Recognizing that religion is important in human life;

Declare:

Our World

1. We live in a world in which isolation is no longer possible. We live in a time of unprecedented mobility of peoples and intermingling of cultures. We are all interdependent and share an inescapable responsibility for the well-being of the entire world.

2. We face a crisis which could bring about the suicide of the human species or bring us a new awakening and a new hope. We believe that peace is possible. We know that religion is not the sole remedy for all the ills of humanity, but it has an indispensable role to play in this most critical time.

3. We are aware of the world's cultural and religious diversity. Each culture represents a universe in itself and yet it is not closed. Cultures give religions their language, and religions offer ultimate meaning to each culture. Unless we recognize pluralism and respect diversity, no peace is possible. We strive for the harmony which is at the very core of peace.

4. We understand that culture is a way of seeing the world and living in it. It also means the cultivation of those values and forms of life which

reflect the worldviews of each culture. Therefore neither the meaning of peace nor of religion can be reduced to a single and rigid concept, just as the range of human experience cannot be conveyed by a single language.

5.   For some cultures, religion is a way of life, permeating every human activity. For others it represents the highest aspirations of human existence. In still others, religions are institutions that claim to carry a message of salvation.

6.   Religions have contributed to the peace of the world, but they have also led to division, hatred, and war. Religious people have too often betrayed the high ideals they themselves have preached. We feel obliged to call for sincere acts of repentance and mutual forgiveness, both personally and collectively, to one another, to humanity in general, and to Earth and all living beings.

Peace

7.   Peace implies that love, compassion, human dignity, and justice are fully preserved.

8.   Peace entails that we understand that we are all interdependent and related to one another. We are all individually and collectively responsible for the common good, including the well-being of future generations.

9.   Peace demands that we respect Earth and all forms of life, especially human life. Our ethical awareness requires setting limits to technology. We should direct our efforts toward eliminating consumerism and improving the quality of life.

10. Peace is a journey—a never-ending process.

Commitment

11. We must be at peace with ourselves; we strive to achieve inner peace through personal reflection and spiritual growth, and to cultivate a spirituality which manifests itself in action.

12. We commit ourselves to support and strengthen the home and family as the nursery of peace.

In homes and families, communities, nations, and the world:

13. We commit ourselves to resolve or transform conflicts without using

violence, and to prevent them through education and the pursuit of justice.

14. We commit ourselves to work toward a reduction in the scandalous economic differences between human groups and other forms of violence and threats to peace, such as waste of resources, extreme poverty, racism, all types of terrorism, lack of caring, corruption, and crime.

15. We commit ourselves to overcome all forms of discrimination, colonialism, exploitation, and domination and to promote institutions based on shared responsibility and participation. Human rights, including religious freedom and the rights of minorities, must be respected.

16. We commit ourselves to assure a truly humane education for all. We emphasize education for peace, freedom, and human rights, and religious education to promote openness and tolerance.

17. We commit ourselves to a civil society which respects environmental and social justice. This process begins locally and continues to national and transnational levels.

18. We commit ourselves to work toward a world without weapons and to dismantle the industry of war.

Religious Responsibility

19. Our communities of faith have a responsibility to encourage conduct imbued with wisdom, compassion, sharing, charity, solidarity, and love, inspiring one and all to choose the path of freedom and responsibility. Religions must be a source of helpful energy.

20. We will remain mindful that our religions must not identify themselves with political, economic, or social powers, so as to remain free to work for justice and peace. We will not forget that confessional political regimes may do serious harm to religious values as well as to society. We should distinguish fanaticism from religious zeal.

21. We will favor peace by countering the tendencies of individuals and communities to assume or even to teach that they are inherently superior to others. We recognize and praise the nonviolent peacemakers. We disown killing in the name of religion.

22. We will promote dialogue and harmony between and within reli-

gions, recognizing and respecting the search for truth and wisdom that is outside our religion. We will establish dialogue with all, striving for a sincere fellowship on our earthly pilgrimage.

Appeal

23. Grounded in our faith, we will build a culture of peace based on non-violence, tolerance, dialogue, mutual understanding, and justice. We call upon the institutions of our civil society, the United Nations system, governments, governmental and nongovernmental organizations, corporations and the mass media, to strengthen their commitments to peace and to listen to the cries of the victims and the dispossessed. We call upon the different religious and cultural traditions to join hands together in this effort, and to cooperate with us in spreading the message of peace.

Declaration of Principles on Tolerance

The member states of the United Nations Educational, Scientific, and Cultural Organization, meeting in Paris at the twenty-eighth session of the General Conference, from 25 October to 16 November 1995,

Preamble

Bearing in mind that the United Nations Charter states: "We, the peoples of the United Nations, determined to save succeeding generations from the scourge of war, ...to reaffirm faith in fundamental human rights, in the dignity and worth of the human person, ...and for these ends to practice tolerance and live together in peace with one another as good neighbors,"

Recalling that the Preamble to the Constitution of UNESCO, adopted on 16 November 1945, states that "peace, if it is not to fail, must be founded on the intellectual and moral solidarity of mankind,"

Recalling also that the Universal Declaration of Human Rights affirms that "Everyone has the right to freedom of thought, conscience, and religion" (Article 18), "of opinion and expression" (Article 19), and that education "should promote understanding, tolerance and friendship among all nations, racial or religious groups" (Article 26),

Noting relevant international instruments including:

- the International Covenant on Civil and Political Rights,
- the International Covenant on Economic, Social, and Cultural Rights,
- the Convention on the Elimination of All Forms of Racial Discrimination,
- the Convention on the Prevention and Punishment of the Crime of Genocide,
- the Convention on the Rights of the Child,
- the 1951 Convention relating to the Status of Refugees and its 1967 Protocol and regional instruments,
- the Convention on the Elimination of All Forms of Discrimination against Women,
- the Convention against Torture and other Cruel, Inhuman, or De-

grading Treatment or Punishment,
• the Declaration on the Elimination of All Forms of Intolerance Based on Religion or Belief,
• the Declaration on the Rights of Persons Belonging to National or Ethnic, Religious, and Linguistic Minorities,
• the Declaration on Measures to Eliminate International Terrorism,
• the Vienna Declaration and Program of Action of the World Conference on Human Rights,
• the Copenhagen Declaration and Program of Action adopted by the World Summit for Social Development,
• the UNESCO Declaration on Race and Racial Prejudice,
• the UNESCO Convention and Recommendation against Discrimination in Education,

Bearing in mind the objectives of the Third Decade to Combat Racism and Racial Discrimination, the World Decade for Human Rights Education, and the International Decade of the World's Indigenous People,

Taking into consideration the recommendations of regional conferences organized in the framework of the United Nations Year for Tolerance in accordance with UNESCO General Conference 27C/Resolution 5.14, as well as the conclusions and recommendations of other conferences and meetings organized by member states within the program of the United Nations Year for Tolerance,

Alarmed by the current rise in acts of intolerance, violence, terrorism, xenophobia, aggressive nationalism, racism, anti-Semitism, exclusion, marginalization, and discrimination directed against national, ethnic, religious, and linguistic minorities, refugees, migrant workers, immigrants, and vulnerable groups within societies, as well as acts of violence and intimidation committed against individuals exercising their freedom of opinion and expression—all of which threaten the consolidation of peace and democracy, both nationally and internationally, and are obstacles to development,

Emphasizing the responsibilities of member states to develop and encourage respect for human rights and fundamental freedoms for all, without distinction as to race, gender, language, national origin, religion, or disability, and to combat intolerance,

Adopt and solemnly proclaim this

Declaration of Principles on Tolerance

Resolving to take all positive measures necessary to promote tolerance in our societies, because tolerance is not only a cherished principle, but also a necessity for peace and for the economic and social advancement of all peoples,

We declare the following:

Article 1. Meaning of Tolerance

1.1 Tolerance is respect, acceptance, and appreciation of the rich diversity of our world's cultures, our forms of expression and ways of being human. It is fostered by knowledge, openness, communication, and freedom of thought, conscience, and belief. Tolerance is harmony in difference. It is not only a moral duty, it is also a political and legal requirement. Tolerance, the virtue that makes peace possible, contributes to the replacement of the culture of war by a culture of peace.

1.2 Tolerance is not concession, condescension or indulgence. Tolerance is, above all, an active attitude prompted by recognition of the universal human rights and fundamental freedoms of others. In no circumstance can it be used to justify infringements of these fundamental values. Tolerance is to be exercised by individuals, groups, and states.

1.3 Tolerance is the responsibility that upholds human rights, pluralism (including cultural pluralism), democracy, and the rule of law. It involves the rejection of dogmatism and absolutism and affirms the standards set out in international human rights instruments.

1.4 Consistent with respect for human rights, the practice of tolerance does not mean toleration of social injustice or the abandonment or weakening of one's convictions. It means that one is free to adhere to one's own convictions and accepts that others adhere to theirs. It means accepting the fact that human beings, naturally diverse in their appearance, situation, speech, behavior, and values, have the right to live in peace and to be as they are. It also means that one's views are not to be imposed on others.

Article 2. State Level

2.1 Tolerance at the State level requires just and impartial legislation, law enforcement, and judicial and administrative process. It also requires that economic and social opportunities be made available to each person without any discrimination. Exclusion and marginalization can lead to frustration, hostility, and fanaticism.

2.2 In order to achieve a more tolerant society, states should ratify existing international human rights conventions, and draft new legislation where necessary to ensure equality of treatment and of opportunity for all groups and individuals in society.

2.3 It is essential for international harmony that individuals, communities, and nations accept and respect the multicultural character of the human family. Without tolerance there can be no peace, and without peace there can be no development or democracy.

2.4 Intolerance may take the form of marginalization of vulnerable groups and their exclusion from social and political participation, as well as violence and discrimination against them. As confirmed in the Declaration on Race and Racial Prejudice, "All individuals and groups have the right to be different" (Article 1.2).

Article 3.   Social Dimensions

3.1 In the modern world, tolerance is more essential than ever before. It is an age marked by the globalization of the economy and by rapidly increasing mobility, communication, integration and interdependence, large-scale migrations and displacement of populations, urbanization, and changing social patterns. Since every part of the world is characterized by diversity, escalating intolerance and strife potentially menaces every region. It is not confined to any country, but is a global threat.

3.2 Tolerance is necessary between individuals and at the family and community levels. Tolerance promotion and the shaping of attitudes of openness, mutual listening, and solidarity should take place in schools and universities and through non-formal education, at home, and in the workplace. The communication media are in a position to play a constructive role in facilitating free and open dialogue and discussion, disseminating the values of tolerance, and highlighting the dangers of indifference toward the rise in intolerant groups and ideologies.

3.3 As affirmed by the UNESCO Declaration on Race and Racial Prejudice, measures must be taken to ensure equality in dignity and rights for individuals and groups wherever necessary. In this respect, particular attention should be paid to vulnerable groups which are socially or economically disadvantaged so as to afford them the protection of the laws and social measures in force, in particular with regard to housing, employment, and health, to respect the authenticity of their culture and values, and to facilitate their social and occupational advancement and integration, especially through education.

3.4 Appropriate scientific studies and networking should be undertaken to coordinate the international community's response to this global challenge, including analysis by the social sciences of root causes and effective countermeasures, as well as research and monitoring in support of policy-making and standard-setting action by member states.

Article 4.   Education

4.1 Education is the most effective means of preventing intolerance. The first step in tolerance education is to teach people what their shared rights and freedoms are, so that they may be respected, and to promote the will to protect those of others.

4.2 Education for tolerance should be considered an urgent imperative; that is why it is necessary to promote systematic and rational tolerance teaching methods that will address the cultural, social, economic, political, and religious sources of intolerance—major roots of violence and exclusion. Education policies and programs should contribute to development of understanding, solidarity, and tolerance among individuals as well as among ethnic, social, cultural, religious, and linguistic groups and nations.

4.3 Education for tolerance should aim at countering influences that lead to fear and exclusion of others, and should help young people to develop capacities for independent judgment, critical thinking, and ethical reasoning.

4.4 We pledge to support and implement programs of social science research and education for tolerance, human rights, and nonviolence. This means devoting special attention to improving teacher training, curricula, the content of textbooks and lessons, and other educational materials including new educational technologies, with a view to educating caring and responsible citizens open to other cultures, able to appreciate the value of freedom, respectful of human dignity and differences, and able to prevent conflicts or resolve them by nonviolent means.

Article 5. Commitment to Action

We commit ourselves to promoting tolerance and nonviolence through programs and institutions in the fields of education, science, culture, and communication.

Article 6. International Day for Tolerance

In order to generate public awareness, emphasize the dangers of intolerance, and react with renewed commitment and action in support of tolerance promotion and education, we solemnly proclaim 16 November the annual International Day for Tolerance.

The Earth Covenant:
A Citizens' Treaty
for Common Ecological Security

In 1988, Global Education Associates initiated a two-part strategy in a citizen-led drive for an Earth Charter to complement the UN Charter: (1) a citizens' treaty through which peoples around the world define and make a commitment to live by principles of ecological security, and (2) a citizen movement to pressure governments to agree to the same principles.

In 1989, GEA coordinated an international process of citizen input leading to The Earth Covenant: A Citizens' Treaty for Common Ecological Security. The document was drafted with input from people in 40 countries; circulating worldwide in over 20 languages, it has since been ratified by over 2 million people in more than 100 countries. The Earth Covenant represents a more mature stage in global democratization, in which citizens lay the normative foundations on which to build international law and global public policy.

As GEA President Emerita Patricia M. Mische wrote in 1989, "By signing the Earth Covenant, people around the world, from all walks of life, enter into a covenant with one another to care for the Earth and our common future. The Earth Covenant is not a petition to governments, nor is it anti-government. Governments alone have not caused the ecological crisis and cannot turn it around; much of the problem originates in the private sector, in the decisions we each make. We need to enter into partnership with governments to create a more ecologically sound future. We do not need to wait for government legislation to force us to be more environmentally responsible.

"We can establish laws in our own hearts and minds, and in relationship with one another, in which we bind ourselves to be more responsible for the state of our neighborhoods and the state of the Earth. In so doing, we help to create customary law and a global culture of ecological responsibility. We also help to create the political space which enables (and requires) governments to be more responsive and effective in protecting the Earth."

Preamble

We, the peoples of the Earth, rejoice in the beauty and wonder of the lands, skies, waters, and life in all its diversity. Earth is our home. We share it with all other living beings.

Yet we are rendering the Earth uninhabitable for the human community and for many species of life. Lands are becoming barren, skies fouled, waters poisoned. The cry of people whose land, livelihood, and health are being destroyed is heard around the world. The Earth itself is calling us to awaken.

We and all living beings depend upon the Earth and upon one another for our common existence, well-being, and development. Our common future depends upon a reexamination of our most basic assumptions about humankind's relationship to the Earth. We must develop common principles and systems to shape this future in harmony with the Earth.

Governments alone cannot secure the environment. As citizens of the world, we accept responsibility in our personal, occupational and community lives, to protect the integrity of the Earth.

Principles and Commitments

In covenant with each other and on behalf of the whole Earth community, we commit ourselves to the following principles and actions:

Relationship with the Earth: All life forms are sacred. Each human being is a unique and integral part of the Earth's community of life and has a special responsibility to care for life in all its diverse forms.

Therefore, we will act and live in a way that preserves the natural life processes of the Earth and respects all species and their habitats. We will work to prevent ecological degradation.

Relationship with Each Other: Each human being has the right to a healthful environment and to access to the fruits of the Earth. Each also has a continual duty to work for the realization of these rights for present and future generations.

Therefore—concerned that every person have food, shelter, pure air, potable water, education, employment, and all that is necessary to enjoy the full measure of human rights—we will work for more equitable access to the Earth's resources.

Relationship Between Economic and Ecological Security: Since human life is rooted in the natural processes of the Earth, economic development, to be sustainable, must preserve the life-support systems of the Earth.

Therefore, we will use environmentally protective technologies and promote their availability to people in all parts of the Earth. When doubtful about the consequences of economic goals and technologies on the environment, we will allow an extra margin of protection for nature.

Governance and Ecological Security: The protection and enhancement of life on Earth demand adequate legislative, administrative, and judicial systems at appropriate local, national, regional, and international levels. In order to be effective, these systems must be empowering, participatory, and based on openness of information.

Therefore, we will work for the enactment of laws that protect the environment and promote their observance through educational, political, and legal action. We shall advance policies of prevention rather than only reacting to ecological harm.

Declaring our partnership with one another and with our Earth, we seek to be faithful to the above commitments.

_____

(Signature)

I have signed the Earth Covenant, committing myself with others around the Earth to live an ecologically responsible life. Please enter my signature and address (below) in the Register of Signatories to the Earth Covenant.

_____

(Signature)

_____

(Print Full Name)

_____

(Street Address)

_____

(City, State/Country, Postal Code)

PLEASE RETURN TO: Earth Covenant, c/o Global Education Associates
475 Riverside Drive, Suite 1848, New York, NY 10115

About
Global Education Associates

Global Education Associates is a network of individuals and organizations in 90 countries working to help people understand and respond creatively to the crises and opportunities of today's interdependent world. Many issues today transcend borders and the competency of any single community or country to resolve them; effective and cooperative global systems are needed to address the causes of poverty, hunger, homelessness, environmental degradation, and violence and warfare. Our conferences, research, publications, and consulting services engage people from all cultures in mutual learning, analysis, and action for peace, human rights, social and economic well-being, ecological balance, and democratic participation. For more information contact Global Education Associates, 475 Riverside Drive, Suite 1848, New York, NY 10115 USA; phone (212) 870-3290; fax (212) 870-2729; globaleduc@earthlink.net; www.globaleduc.org.

Contributors

Saleha Mahmood-Abedin, Ph.D., is Director of the Institute of Muslim Minority Affairs in Jiddah, Saudi Arabia.

Dr. M. Aram (1927–1997) served as a president of the World Conference on Religion and Peace, a member of India's Upper House of Parliament, and a Vice-Chancellor of Gandhiram Rural University.

Philip J. Bentley is President of the Jewish Peace Fellowship and Rabbi of Temple Sholom in Floral Park, Queens, New York.

Julia Ching, Ph.D., is University Professor and R.C. and E.Y. Lee Chair Professor of Chinese Thought and Culture at the University of Toronto. Her most recent books are *Mysticism and Kingship in China* (Cambridge University Press, 1997) and *The Butterfly Healing* (Orbis Press, 1998).

Dr. John B. Cobb, Jr., is Professor Emeritus at Claremont School of Theology in Claremont, California.

Father Luis M. Dolan, C.P., is Emeritus UN Representative for the Temple of Understanding; Special Advisor to the Center for World Thanksgiving on 2000, International Year of Thanksgiving; and the United Religions Initiative coordinator for Latin America.

Dr. Richard Falk is Albert G. Milbank Professor of International Law and Practice at Princeton University, Princeton, New Jersey.

Nathan C. Funk is an adjunct faculty member and doctoral candidate in International Relations at the School of International Service at the American University in Washington, DC.

P.N. (Bawa) Jain is the UN Representative of the International Mahavir Jain Mission and the Temple of Understanding (The Interfaith Center of New York).

Rev. Dr. Eileen W. Lindner is Associate General Secretary for Christian Unity of the National Council of Churches of Christ of the United States.

John S. Mbiti, Kenyan by birth, is a Christian theologian who has taught at Makerere University in Uganda and several European and American universities. His books include, among others, *Concepts of God in Africa, African Religions and Philosophy,* and *New Testament Eschatology in an African Background.* The paper reprinted here is adapted from a presentation to the Lindisfarne Association and is copyrighted by the author.

Patricia M. Mische, Ed.D. is co-founder and President Emerita of Global Education Associates. Her works include *Toward a Human World Order: Beyond the National Security Straitjacket* (1977, with Gerald Mische) and *Ecological Security and the United Nations System: Past, Present and Future* (1998). She is currently Lloyd Professor of Peace Studies and World Law at Antioch College in Yellow Springs, Ohio.

Mary J. Mwingira is president of Pax Romana International Catholic Movement for Intellectual and Cultural Affairs in Dar-es-Salaam, Tanzania.

Dr. Abdul Aziz Said is Mohammed Said Farsi Professor of Islamic Peace at the School of International Service at the American University in Washington, DC.

Dr. Pataraporn Sirikanchana is an advisor to the World Fellowship of Buddhists and an Associate Professor in (and chairperson of) the Department of Philosophy, Faculty of Liberal Arts, Thammasat University in Bangkok.

Dr. Sulak Sivaraksa is the founder of the International Network of Engaged Buddhists in Bangkok, Siam.

Dr. K.R. Sundararajan is a professor of Theology at St. Bonaventure University in New York.

Dr. Robert Traer is General Secretary of the International Association for Religious Freedom and the author of *Quest for Truth: Critical Reflections on Interfaith Cooperation* and *Faith, Belief and Religion,* both published in 1999 by Dorset Press.

Dr. Mary Evelyn Tucker is Professor of Religion and East Asian Studies at Bucknell University in Lewisburg, Pennsylvania.

Dr. William Vendley is Secretary General of the World Conference on Religion and Peace.

Dr. John Woodall, a psychiatrist, is a Research Fellow at the Judge Baker

Children's Center at Harvard Medical School. He is a member of the Bahá'í International Community. This paper is adapted from the original text, which appears at www.globaleduc.org/woodall.htm, on the website of Global Education Associates.

Rabbi Dr. Bernard M. Zlotowitz is a Senior Scholar at the Union of American Hebrew Congregations in Fair Lawn, New Jersey.

About the Editors

Patricia M. Mische, Ed.D. is co-founder and President Emerita of Global Education Associates and the author of many works, including *Toward a Human World Order: Beyond the National Security Straitjacket* (1977, with Gerald Mische) and *Ecological Security and the United Nations System: Past, Present and Future* (1998). She has taught and lectured worldwide on issues of peace and security, human rights, environment and development, and alternative world futures, and is currently Lloyd Professor of Peace Studies and World Law at Antioch College in Yellow Springs, Ohio.

Melissa Merkling has edited various publications for Global Education Associates since 1985.